THE FRENCH REVOLUTION

"A lucid and lively introduction ... Students wishing to explore the frontiers of research in the subject can be reliably advised to start here."

William Doyle, *University of Bristol*

The French Revolution is a collection of key texts at the forefront of current research and interpretation, challenging orthodox assumptions concerning the origins, development, and long-term historical consequences of the Revolution. The volume includes a clear and thorough introduction by the editor which contextualises the historiographical controversies, especially those dating from 1989. The articles are woven into a sophisticated narrative, which covers areas including the inevitability of the Terror, subsequent issues for nineteenth-century French history, the intellectual connection, the later role of Napoleon, and the feminist dimension.

Gary Kates is Chair of the History Department at Trinity University, Texas. He is author of *Monsieur d'Eon is a Woman* (1995), *The Cercle Social, the Girondins and the French Revolution* (1985) and is an advisory editor for *Eighteen-century Studies*.

Rewriting Histories focuses on historical themes where standard conclusions are facing a major challenge. Each book presents 8 to 10 papers (edited and annotated where necessary) at the forefront of current research and interpretation, offering students an accessible way to engage with contemporary debates.

Series editor **Jack R. Censer** is Professor of History at George Mason University.

REWRITING HISTORIES
Series editor: Jack R. Censer

Already published

THE INDUSTRIAL REVOLUTION AND WORK IN
NINETEENTH-CENTURY EUROPE
Edited by Lenard R. Berlanstein

SOCIETY AND CULTURE IN THE SLAVE SOUTH
Edited by J. William Harris

ATLANTIC AMERICAN SOCIETIES
From Columbus through Abolition
Edited by J.R. McNeill and Alan Karras

GENDER AND AMERICAN HISTORY SINCE 1890
Edited by Barbara Melosh

DIVERSITY AND UNITY IN EARLY NORTH AMERICA
Edited by Philip D. Morgan

NAZISM AND GERMAN SOCIETY 1933–1945
Edited by David Crew

Forthcoming

HOLOCAUST: ORIGINS, IMPLEMENTATION AND
AFTERMATH
Edited by Omer Bartov

STALINISM
Edited by Sheila Fitzpatrick

ISRAEL/PALESTINE QUESTION
Edited by Ilan Pappe

REVOLUTIONS OF 1989
Edited by Vladimir Tismaneanu

THE FRENCH REVOLUTION

Recent debates and new controversies

Edited by Gary Kates

London and New York

First published 1998
by Routledge
11 New Fetter Lane, London EC4P 4EE

Simultaneously published in the USA and Canada
by Routledge
29 West 35th Street, New York, NY 10001

Selection and editorial matter © 1998 Gary Kates;
individual contributions © 1998 the individual contributors

Typeset in Palatino by RefineCatch Limited, Bungay, Suffolk

Printed and bound in Great Britain by
T.J. International Ltd, Padstow, Cornwall

British Library Cataloguing in Publication Data
A catalogue record for this book is available from the British Library

Library of Congress Cataloguing in Publication Data
The French Revolution: recent debates and new controversies/edited
by Gary Kates.
p.   cm. — (Rewriting histories)
Includes bibliographical reference and index.
1. France—History—Revolution, 1789–1799—Influence.   2. France-
-History—Revolution, 1789–1799—Historiography.   3. Historians—
Political and social views.   4. Civilization, Modern—French
influences.   I. Kates, Gary, 1952– .   II. Series.
DC148.F727   1997   97–12355
944.04—dc21

ISBN 0–415–14489–2 (hbk)
ISBN 0–415–14490–6 (pbk)

CONTENTS

CONTENTS

SERIES EDITOR'S PREFACE

Rewriting history, or revisionism, has always followed closely in the wake of history writing. In their efforts to re-evaluate the past, professional as well as amateur scholars have followed many approaches, most commonly as empiricists, uncovering new information to challenge earlier accounts. Historians have also revised previous versions by adopting new perspectives, usually fortified by new research, which overturn received views.

Even though rewriting is constantly taking place, historians' attitudes towards using new interpretations have been anything but settled. For most, the validity of revisionism lies in providing a stronger, more convincing account that better captures the objective truth of the matter. Although such historians might agree that we never finally arrive at the 'truth', they believe it exists and over time may be better approximated. At the other extreme stand scholars who believe that each generation or even each cultural group or subgroup necessarily regards the past differently, each creating for itself a more usable history. Although these latter scholars do not reject the possibility of demonstrating empirically that some contentions are better than others, they focus upon generating new views based upon different life experiences. Different truths exist for different groups. Surely such an understanding, by emphasizing subjectivity, further encourages rewriting history. Between these two groups are those historians who wish to borrow from both sides. This third group, while accepting that every congeries of individuals sees matters differently, still wishes somewhat contradictorily to fashion a broader history that incorporates both of these particular visions. Revisionists who stress empiricism fall into the first of the three camps, while others spread out across the board.

Today the rewriting of history seems to have accelerated to a blinding speed as a consequence of the evolution of revisionism. A variety of approaches has emerged. A major factor in this process has been the enormous increase in the number of researchers. This explosion has reinforced and enabled the re-testing of many assertions. Significant ideological shifts have also played a major part in the growth of revisionism. First, the crisis of Marxism, culminating in the events in Eastern Europe in 1989, has given rise to doubts about explicitly Marxist accounts. Such doubts have spilled over into the entire field of social history which has been a dominant subfield of the discipline for several decades. Focusing on society and its class divisions implied that these are the most important elements in historical analysis. Because Marxism was built on the same claim, the whole basis of social history has been questioned, despite the very many studies that directly had little to do with Marxism. Disillusionment with social history simultaneously opened the door to cultural and linguistic approaches largely developed in anthropology and literature. Multi-culturalism and feminism further generated revisionism. By claiming that scholars had, wittingly or not, operated from a white European/American male point of view, newer researchers argued that other approaches had been neg-lected or misunderstood. Not surprisingly, these last historians are the most likely to envision each subgroup rewriting its own usable history, while other scholars incline towards revisionism as part of the search for some stable truth.

Rewriting Histories will make these new approaches available to the student population. Often new scholarly debates take place in the scattered issues of journals which are sometimes difficult to find. Furthermore, in these first interactions, historians tend to address one another, leaving out the evidence that would make their arguments more accessible to the uninitiated. This series of books will collect in one place a strong group of the major articles in selected fields, adding notes and introductions conducive to improved understanding. Editors will select articles containing substantial historical data, so that students – at least those who approach the subject as an objective phenomenon – can advance not only their comprehension of debated points but also their grasp of substantive aspects of the subject.

Few historical topics have been subjected to more reconsider-ation than the French Revolution. Not so long ago a Marxist interpretation prevailed that employed an emphasis on class struggle to explain both the causes and consequences of the Revolution. Although one or another version of this view dominated for better than half a century, it was upstaged in the 1980s by a focus upon politics and ideas – the very factors that the revolutionaries themselves would have tended to emphasize. Many have embraced the new concepts. But this book identifies and defines a challenge to this recent opinion. This collection concentrates both upon feminist criticisms as well as a retort from a neo-Marxist view in which class interests still figure prominently. Whatever their differences – and they are large – they oppose the most recent view. Will one of these two views displace the others? For now, this book of essays suggests more, rather than a narrowing, debate.

Jack R. Censer

ACKNOWLEDGEMENTS

All extracts and articles published in this volume have already been published. We would like to thank the following copyright holders for permission to reproduce their work:

Chapter 1   Reprinted in an abridged format from Albert Soboul, *Understanding the French Revolution*, trans. April Ane Knutson (New York: International Publishers, 1988), pp. 274–99.

Chapter 2   Reprinted in an abridged format from *Past and Present* 60 (August 1973): 84–126.

Chapter 3   Reprinted from *Government and Opposition* 16:2 (Spring 1981): 200–18.

Chapter 4   Reprinted from *The French Idea of Freedom: The Old Regime and the Declaration of Rights of 1789*, ed. Dale Van Kley (Stanford: Stanford University Press, 1994), pp. 154–96, 388–92.

Chapter 5   Excerpted from William H. Sewell, Jr, *A Rhetoric of Bourgeois Revolution: The Abbé Sieyes* and What is the Third Estate? (Durham, NC: Duke University Press, 1994), pp. 29–40, 185–97.

Chapter 6   Reprinted in an abridged format from *The French Revolution and Social Change*, ed. Colin Lucas (Oxford: Oxford University Press, 1990), pp. 69–118.

Chapter 7   Reprinted from the *American Historical Review* 94 (April 1989): 271–301.

Chapter 8   Reprinted from the *American Historical Review* 100 (April 1995): 360–86.

Chapter 9   Reprinted from *Eroticism and the Body Politic*, ed. Lynn Hunt (Baltimore: Johns Hopkins University Press, 1991), pp. 108–30.

Chapter 10   Reprinted in an abridged format from Olwen Hufton, *Women and the Limits of Citizenship in the French Revolution* (Toronto: University of Toronto Press, 1992), pp. 89–130, 168–74.

Chapter 11   Reprinted by permission of the publisher from *A Critical Dictionary of the French Revolution*, ed. François Furet and Mona Ozouf, trans. Arthur Goldhammer (Cambridge MA: Harvard University Press, © 1989 by the President and Fellows of Harvard College), pp. 273–86.

ILLUSTRATIONS

FIGURES

TABLES

To the memory of François Furet (1927–1997)

INTRODUCTION

Gary Kates

"What? You have something *new* to say about the French Revolution?"

That was the reaction of one of my graduate school professors when he heard that I intended to write a doctoral dissertation on the French Revolution. Indeed, it is a sensible reaction. After all, whole forests have been cleared to make way for the historical literature on the French Revolution, as a trip to any decent college library will demonstrate. There, the casual stroller will discover stacks and stacks of books on every conceivable topic. Perhaps no other event in history has attracted so much attention.

Much of the problem with studying the French Revolution involves sorting through what others have said about it. Ever since Edmund Burke and Thomas Paine first argued about the Revolution's meaning, the debate on it has seemed almost as interesting as the event itself. That debate, of course, has spilled over into neighboring disciplines: political scientists, philosophers, sociologists, literary critics, and art historians have all given the French Revolution prominent weight in their fields. The French Revolution is perhaps the closest thing historians have developed to a litmus test: one's stance on the French Revolution inevitably reveals much about one's deepest ideological and political convictions.

This book deals only with a small, but significant, part of that debate: the quarrels that have captivated professional historians since the Revolution's 1989 bicentennial celebration. After all, since historians devote their entire careers to developing an expertise by way of its archives and bibliographies, they are

1

perhaps in the best position to comment on the Revolution's significance and meaning.

The study of the French Revolution by professional historians (as opposed to philosophers, writers, or journalists) is hardly a century old, barely half the temporal distance from the Revolution itself. It began with the Centennial celebration of 1889, when the Paris City Council awarded its first chair of the History of the French Revolution at the Sorbonne to Alphonse Aulard (1849–1928). Since then, the holder of this chair has been acknowledged as the dean of French Revolutionary studies.

Aulard's writings promoted democratic republicanism buttressing left-wing political parties of the Third Republic. Aulard had no sympathy for the monarchy. In his view, the despotic abuses of the Ancien Régime justified the violent uprising of 1789. Aulard admired the courage of the Constituent Assembly deputies, but in the end, he thought that they sheepishly balked from confronting a recalcitrant king and treasonous queen. The Constitution of 1791, a flawed document in Aulard's eyes that allowed the monarchy too much power, was weakened by the king's flight to Varennes in June 1791. The courage of Georges Danton and the other Paris militant activists pushed the Revolution beyond the halfway point. Aulard praised their efforts which culminated in the insurrection of 10 August 1792 and the declaration of France's first democratic republic based upon universal male suffrage. For Aulard, the establishment of a republic under the National Convention marked the zenith of the Revolution.[1]

After World War I, Aulard was challenged by his most gifted student, Albert Mathiez (1874–1932). Influenced both by the recent victory of Bolshevism in Russia, as well as by the awesome legacy of French socialist leader Jean Jaurès (himself an important historian of the Revolution), Mathiez rejected Aulard's beloved Danton as a corrupt bourgeois politician and, instead, defended wholeheartedly Robespierre's efforts to save France through the Terror. Mathiez's Marxism was pragmatic; but his defense of the Terror was nonetheless passionate and had great influence upon a generation of historians from Europe and the United States. In perhaps his most brilliant book, *La vie chère et le movement social sous la terreur* (The Cost of Living and Popular Movements During the Terror [1927]), Mathiez argued that the cost of living for ordinary Parisians improved more during the Terror than at any other time. In Mathiez's view, Robespierre was not a dictator hungry for arbitrary power, but a democratic politician responding to popular pressures from Parisian workers. Unfortunately, the gains of those sans-culottes were temporary; and, while the Revolution counted on their support, its bourgeois leaders turned against Robespierre and renounced sans-culottes participation and demands.[2]

Mathiez's influence was especially great because of the Société des Etudes Robespierristes (Society of Robespierrist Studies), the organization he founded that published documentary collections, books, and most importantly, the scholarly journal *Annales historiques de la révolution française*. By Mathiez's early death in 1932, the *Annales* had established itself as the premier journal of record for French Revolutionary historiography. Mathiez's successors closely followed the master: Georges Lefebvre (1874–1959), Albert Soboul (1914–82), and Michel Vovelle (b. 1933) all combined the Sorbonne's Chair of the History of the Revolution, and the editorship of the *Annales historiques*, with a commitment to Marxism usually demonstrated by membership in the French Communist Party. Consequently, in the century since the founding of Aulard's Sorbonne chair, the academy of French Revolutionary scholars has been dominated by left-wing socialists committed to a particular way of seeing the Revolution and to a special set of contemporary political values.

As it solidified into its own sort of orthodoxy, this Marxist interpretation could be summarized in the following manner: the French Revolution was not simply a political struggle from (evil) absolute monarchy to (good) democratic republicanism, but represented a deeper shift from feudalism to capitalism. The Revolution was led by an alliance between a bourgeois élite (owners of liquid capital), and popular classes (artisans and peasants), against the landowning nobility. The greatest success of such an alliance occurred in 1789, but after that it began to show signs of strains. By the summer of 1791, revolutionary events were marked by class conflict between the capitalist bourgeoisie and the popular classes. This struggle produced an urban political movement led by the sans-culottes, whose vision of a truly social revolution influenced nineteenth-century radicalism. The Terror represented the pinnacle of the sans-culottes movement in which the Jacobins established (albeit temporarily) the first modern democracy in a major European state. Thus the

French Revolution was essentially a class struggle in which one class was destroyed (the nobility), one class was awakened (the sans-culottes), and one class won control of the state (the bourgeoisie). In England and the United States, there was less of a commitment to Marxism among French Revolutionary scholars. Historians such as J.M. Thompson (1878–1956) or Louis Gottschalk (1899–1975) were not known for their political activism or party labels. Still, it is remarkable how easily a watered-down version of French Marxism spread throughout Anglo-American college texts between 1930 and 1970. Just as Gottschalk championed Mathiez's work in the 1930s, so R.R. Palmer (1909–) translated Lefebvre's most accessible book into English shortly after World War II.[3]

To be sure, there were some important differences between the Anglo-Americans and the French. During the 1930s, for example, Harvard historian Crane Brinton (1898–1968) adopted a skeptical position in his influential *Anatomy of Revolution*. In his view, the French Revolution was achieved by "moderates" who bravely fought the forces of the Ancien Régime, and busily tried to construct a regime based upon the noble virtues of liberty and equality. Such "moderates" were unable to halt the Revolution's surge toward war and anarchy, and the result was "the accession of the extremists," whereby freedom turned sour. Thrown off course by Danton, Robespierre, and the Jacobins, the Revolution toppled from liberty to tyranny.[4]

Outside of the historical academy there was a rich tradition stemming from Edmund Burke that viewed the Revolution itself as wholly unnecessary and, in fact, counterproductive for the establishment of liberty. Among scholars, their voices were isolated and ignored.

But no longer. During the past twenty-five years, there has been a transformation of enormous magnitude in the scholarship on the French Revolution. This change – one is tempted to call it a revolution – has been marked by the almost total collapse of the orthodox Marxist interpretation, and a range of sharp attacks on virtually all of its major points and approaches. The broad teachings of Mathiez, Lefebvre, and Soboul are today, even in France, discredited. Considering how monolithic orthodox Marxist interpretations of the Revolution had become since the 1920s, some sort of challenge within academia was inevitable – but if the attack was expected, the complete collapse of the Marxist paradigm was a surprise.

Alfred Cobban (1901–68), a distinguished professor at the University of London, deserves credit for breaking the first window (if not throwing the first stone) in the Marxist house. During a 1954 lecture, Cobban questioned whether the Revolution was led by a rising bourgeoisie. Analyzing those leaders of the Third Estate who opposed king and aristocracy in the Estates-General, Cobban noted that only 13 per cent were merchants, manufacturers, or financiers. This revolution was not, in fact, made by a capitalist bourgeoisie. Rather, Cobban argued that the greatest number of leaders came from the ranks of local, petty public officials – administrators, prosecutors, judges, and the like – hardly capitalists, and hardly people who had no connection to the Ancien Régime. Cobban agreed with the Marxists that the French Revolution was a social revolution; but it was one of "notables" not of capitalists.[5]

Beyond Cobban's graduate students, few colleagues paid much attention to his insights until his research was reworked into a book in 1964. By that time, his efforts were helped greatly by George Taylor of the University of North Carolina, whose important articles in mainstream journals added much empirical ammunition to the revisionist stockpile. Just as Cobban had robbed the Revolution of an angry revolutionary bourgeoisie, Taylor demonstrated how the investment patterns by bourgeois and noble families were remarkably similar.[6] By the 1970s, when Colin Lucas published his now-classic article reprinted in this volume, the Revisionist school had become an entrenched minority among French Revolutionary scholars.

No matter what is written about the French Revolution in England or the United States, it is really only France that counts. Revisionists would thus remain an iconoclastic minority until they could mount a beachhead in France. That occurred dramatically with the 1978 publication of François Furet's *Penser la Révolution française* (translated into English as *Interpreting the French Revolution*). Despite its turgid prose, the absence of new archival material, and an idiosyncratic structure, no other book has shaped the research agenda for French Revolutionary scholarship in the 1980s and 1990s more than this one.[7]

Furet (1927–1997) attacked the Marxist "catechisme," but he did much more than translate Cobbanite Revisionism for a French audience. Until Furet's book, most Revisionist attacks had come from social and economic historians who disputed the Marxist version of class struggle. Furet, on the other hand, hoped to restore "to the French Revolution its most obvious dimension, the political one, and of focusing attention ... in the ways of legitimating and representing historical action."[8] In Furet's hands, this meant a return to political theory and intellectual history. By studying more carefully the meaning of revolutionary rhetoric, historians could recapture the profound ideological change that occurred in how Frenchmen thought about politics. Furet ignited new interest in the cultural history of the Revolution, which had diminished into an isolated corner by the mid-1970s. Almost overnight that oldest of problems – the relationship of the Enlightenment to the French Revolution – was resurrected into a burning issue for debate and controversy.

Furet argued that advanced democratic ideas of certain Enlightened philosophers such as Jean-Jacques Rousseau became the heart and soul of the French Revolution. Democracy here did not mean governing by consent, or even respecting individual human rights. Rather, wrote Furet, the Revolution embraced a radical ideology of popular sovereignty so that any abuse of power could be excused so long as it was achieved in the name of *the people*. In short, democracy meant the power of a national state to defeat those who opposed its will. Consequently, Furet argued that the trajectory of the Revolution from its first day was toward the state using democratic ideology to rule in a despotic manner: that is, without regard for human rights. That process culminated, of course, in the Terror, which was the pinnacle of revolutionary democracy and dictatorship.

Just as Furet interpreted the early years of the Revolution as a kind of prologue to the Terror, so he viewed the Napoleonic Empire as its epilogue. Napoleon did not so much turn against the Revolution as consolidate its radical principles. Like the Jacobins of the Year II, Napoleon abused the rights of the people while acting in their name, and he continued the Revolution's bent towards administrative unity and political centralization. While he led the army to new glories, the campaigns he waged and the armies he championed had their roots in the war begun by the Jacobins in 1792 and 1793. For Furet, the Empire was but a late stage of the Revolution, with few fundamental differences.

Furet's attitude towards the revolutionary era is profoundly conservative. France becoming a democracy did not mean that its people became free: it meant that the collective French People was sovereign, and that each individual was subservient to it. Politicians who thought of themselves as democratic claimed to speak in the name of the whole people. Dissent was at best distrusted, since it could lead to factional strife that undermined unity. For Furet, the Terror was not an accidental phase of the Revolution but, rather, emblematic of the entire Revolution. Unlike Crane Brinton, who believed that circumstances had thrown the Revolution off course after a moderate phase filled with notable achievements, Furet argued that the Revolution was radical from the start, and its early achievements were only a mirage.

During the 1980s, as the bicentennial celebration approached, Furet followed up this suggestive essay with a series of more solid historical works. Many of them were joint projects from conferences and colloquiums, where he and his allies presented their approach to the Revolution in a more comprehensive but rarely systematic fashion. By 1989 Furet had become arguably the most important historian in the world of the French Revolution.[9]

Furet's ascendancy not only furthered the demise of Marxist historiography but also gave greater visibility in France to Anglo-American scholarship. Furet is perhaps the first major historian of the French Revolution to speak fluent English – and, given his unabashed admiration for the United States, he also enjoys speaking it at every opportunity. Furet is also perhaps the first to accept a permanent appointment at an American university – for much of the 1980s and early 1990s, he had a regular visiting appointment at the University of Chicago.

It is no wonder then that many of Furet's earliest and strongest supporters came from scholars working in the United States. Among them is Keith Baker, who introduced Furet to Chicago. In a series of brilliant articles, Baker has done much to revitalize the intellectual history of the Revolution by carefully tracing how certain Rousseauian strands of Enlightenment political ideology mutated into revolutionary Jacobinism. For him, as for Furet, the key conduit was the Constituent Assembly deputy, priest, and pamphleteer, Emmanuel-Joseph Sieyes, "the theorist who had done more than anyone to interject Rousseauian notions of national sovereignty into the assembly's debates."[10]

The influence of Rousseau upon the French Revolution has

been among the most heated debates in eighteenth-century studies, and no one has discussed this problem with more sensitivity and erudition than Baker. In 1762, Rousseau had set forth his theory of the general will in his small but difficult book, *The Social Contract*. In contrast to other Enlightenment thinkers such as John Locke, David Hume, or Thomas Jefferson, Rousseau believed that politics was largely the process of discovering the will of the nation. If a member of that nation was found in a small minority of citizens who were dissenting from the national will, Rousseau advised the citizen to drop such views and gladly yield to the majority of citizens. No citizen, argued Rousseau, had a right to go against what a nation wants for itself. Such a doctrine may be democratic (in the sense of being populist), but it clearly poses serious problems for protecting the civic rights of minority groups.

According to Baker, the Revolution's free-fall into Rousseauian democracy was not the product of 1792–3 when the nation was at war, but was the result of deliberate decisions made by the National Assembly as early as the summer of 1789. At the end of one well-known lecture delivered as part of a bicentennial commemoration in 1989, Baker argued that by accepting Rousseau's theory of the general will as the basis for rejecting an absolute royal veto in 1789, the Constituent Assembly "was opting for the Terror."[11]

Like Furet, Baker placed the Terror squarely at the center of the revolutionary process. The Terror was not some detour away from the Revolution's true goal: it was the outcome of the Constituent Assembly's repeated adoption of Rousseauian political principles. After reading Furet and Baker, it seemed impossible to condemn the Terror as a temporary deviation from some political norm. In Baker's view, the Terror occurred not only because of what happened in 1792 or 1793, but because of the way in which political power and violence had been reconceptualized in 1789.

Furet and his collaborators also differed from earlier Revisionists in one very significant manner: they undermined the very foundations of Liberal historiography. Since the early nineteenth century, most historical writing was done by those who championed the great event. Liberals, or Whigs, believed that the French Revolution, when taken as a whole, was necessary to move France and Europe from a pre-modern to a modern society. For Liberals, the Old Regime had become so ossified and paralyzed by its own internal contradictions that, by the late eighteenth century, only revolutionary change could resolve France's grave problems. By the mid-twentieth century, the notion of the Revolution as an agent of progress, despite its great faults, was shared by virtually all of the academic historical community, from Cobban to Soboul. If Anglo and American historians often accepted the views of French Marxists, it was because they shared fundamental attitudes about the nature of the Revolution as an agent of liberty.[12]

At the center of the Liberal approach to the Revolution is a periodization that separates a moderate and constructive early phase of the Revolution (1789–92) from the more radical and violent period that followed (1792–94). Liberal historians typically point to the great achievements of the early phase (passage of the *Declaration of the Rights of Man and Citizen*, abolition of feudalism, reorganization of the judiciary and administration, freedom for Protestants and Jews, etc.) as demonstrating the virtues of revolutionary change. Correspondingly, they typically explain away the excessive violence of the Terror by noting the grave circumstances that led to its establishment: war, economic dislocation, and counter-revolution.

To declare that the Terror was conceptualized or originated in 1789 is to say that the Revolution never went through a "moderate" phase: the entire political dynamic from the Tennis Court Oath through the death of Robespierre can be viewed as one great era in which the state wielded unprecedented authority in the name of the people, but usually not to their benefit. Indeed, in the hands of many recent Revisionists, the entire Revolution is viewed as one gigantic imposition forced on the backs of the peasants, who, of course, made up more than three-quarters of the population. "The violence was all rather senseless," remarks Canadian historian Donald Sutherland.[13] The French Revolution wasn't worth the trouble.

This conclusion would have surprised Alfred Cobban, the British historian who began revisionism forty years ago. For Cobban, the Ancien Régime was so beset with contradictions and structural problems that nothing short of revolution could reform the country; nor was the Revolution itself all senseless violence. The construction of a liberal political order, based upon respect for human rights and religious toleration would have been impossible without the clashes of 1789 and the achievements of the Constituent Assembly. For Cobban, the Third Republic was unthinkable without the first, even if the original model had its defects.[14]

The turning of recent French Revolutionary historiography against its Liberal foundations is startling. Certainly, the ascendancy of Neo-Conservative ideas in England and the United States have provided much fodder for recent Revisionism. Usually former Liberals themselves, Neo-Conservatives in the 1960s and 1970s turned against the whole idea of revolutionary change as itself illiberal. Associating the revolutionary process with fanaticism (read Bolshevism and later Iranian Islamic fundamentalism), Neo-Conservatives gave up their Rousseau for copies of Burke and de Tocqueville: progressive change occurs, they now argued, slowly and outside of institutions controlled by the state. Any efforts by the state to push through large-scale social or political programs were bound to lead to violations of property and civil liberties.[15]

Since the early 1950s, Neo-Conservative thinkers have had their own pet history of the French Revolution. In his 1952 classic, *The Origins of Totalitarian Democracy*, Jacob Talmon argued that the French state became a "totalitarian democracy" during the Terror in the sense that its social programs were designed to alter the course of every citizen's life, producing a secular version of a messianic age. In Talmon's view, such a state would become a harbinger for twentieth-century experiments on both the political right and left. Talmon traced the idea of totalitarian democracy back through Sieyes to certain key Enlightenment figures, Rousseau most prominent among them. While Talmon's history was attacked by Liberal historians – even his own PhD advisor Alfred Cobban dismissed his argument – the book succeeded in associating Rousseau with the Terror.[16]

Talmon's intellectual history has much in common with the newer approach of Furet. Both Talmon's and Furet's approach privilege political theory and the spread of ideas; both see a direct line from Rousseau through Sieyes to Robespierre; both associate Rousseauian democratic ideas with a collectivism that quickly turned oppressive; both, in short, see the Terror as the essence of the Revolution and view it as a harbinger of Bolshevism and Fascism. Talmon's methodology is primitive in comparison to that of Furet and Baker, whose perceptive investigations into discourse theory have significantly advanced the field. In contrast, Talmon's method tends to distort Enlightenment ideology by projecting twentieth-century meanings onto eighteenth-century ideas. Only the most extreme historians writing today, such as Raynauld Sécher, extend Talmon's view by arguing that the Terror culminated in a genocidal campaign in the Vendée resembling twentieth-century horrors.[17]

Whether in its older form from Talmon, or its more sophisticated version from Furet, Neo-Conservative Revisionism had clearly become the ascendant interpretation of the historical establishment in England, France, and the United States by the 1989 bicentennial celebration. In France, despite Michel Vovelle's semi-official position, it was Furet whom the media annointed "King of the Revolution," and who seemingly made an appearance at every academic conference and numerous French television shows.[18] In the United States, the best illustration of Revisionism's popularity was the enormous success of Simon Schama's mega-history of the Revolution, *Citizens*, which exaggerated Furet's arguments into slogans that at times echoed Margaret Thatcher if not Burke:

> the Revolution did indeed invent a new kind of politics, an institutional transference of Rousseau's sovereignty of the General Will that abolished private space and time, and created a form of patriotic militarism more all-embracing than anything that had yet been seen in Europe. For one year, it invented and practiced representative democracy; for two years, it imposed coercive egalitarianism.... But for two decades its enduring product was a new kind of militarized state.... The terror was merely 1789 with a higher body count.[19]

Since the bicentennial celebration, the most important developments in the historiography of the Revolution have been Neo-Liberal challenges to the position laid out by Furet and his colleagues. In this volume, we have selected four articles that seek to critique Furet's approach to the Revolution. While each of the authors approaches the Revolution differently, and while none would regard themselves in any kind of formal school with the other, we can nonetheless see the beginnings of a shared set of attitudes that may be classified as Neo-Liberal. First, unlike Revisionists, Neo-Liberal interpretations do not minimize the oppressive character of the eighteenth-century nobility. The aristocracy is seen as a distinct political group with interests separate and opposing those of commoners. Second, Neo-Liberal arguments insist that the period of the Constituent Assembly was substantively different (i.e., more moderate and more constructive) than the Jacobinism of the Terror. Third, Neo-Liberal interpretations claim that the collective violence of the Revolution's early years (such as that surrounding 14 July 1789, or even 10 August 1792) was often purposeful and necessary to the establishment of a liberal and free state.

These Neo-Liberal historians challenge the view that the Revolution was primarily a failure. A rising bourgeoisie may not have started the Revolution, but the revolutionaries successfully destroyed the Ancien Régime and refashioned a society that made a nineteenth-century liberal state possible. Some scholars, such as Colin Jones, are even willing to resurrect the notion that the Revolution did indeed involve a transition to capitalism. Still, the new approach to social cleavages seems different than Marxism, if only because Neo-Liberals define class more in terms of specific professions and occupations with varied social interests than in terms of a solid group with political interests. There is not much idealization among Neo-Liberals of either the sans-culottes or the Committee of Public Safety. In comparison with this burgeoning Neo-Liberalism, recent Neo-Marxist responses to Revisionism have not yet made much of an impact.[20]

Alongside the Neo-Liberal response to revisionism, the other significant recent trend in French Revolutionary scholarship has been the maturation of women's and gender history. Until the 1970s, few general histories or document collections on the Revolution included much information about women, feminism, or gender. This omission changed in the 1970s with the rise of a contemporary feminist movement; and it was clearly American feminists who set the pace toward a new history that took into account the fate of women and used gender as an analytical tool. One of the first articles in a major journal to deal with the topic was authored not by an established scholar, but by a female American graduate student obviously inspired by the women's movement.[21] When in 1979 three American feminist historians published a collection of primary documents devoted to French Revolutionary women, a new research agenda was established for the field.[22]

Unfortunately, that research did not filter down into college classrooms with any great speed, perhaps because of the traditional nature of much of the historical profession. Of course, the new research made us realize that women participated in every major event in the Revolution. We learned more about the movements of street women during the great events of the Revolution (such the October Days), as well as the influence of élite women in the clubs and presses of Paris. Unfortunately, however, that did not necessarily mean that this feminist-driven research changed the way that other specialists or college teachers approached the Revolution. Curiously, by classifying the new research as "women's history," it became possible for many historians to ignore or marginalize such research, and continue teaching their subject along the same old lines. Some professors muttered that knowing about women's participation was one thing; discovering how that participation changed the fundamental character of the Revolution was quite another. This kind of attitude seems to have been especially true in France, where Furet's recent general text as well as his and Mona Ozouf's *Critical Dictionary* ignore women, feminism, and gender.[23]

During the last decade or so, feminist-inspired historians have addressed this challenge by shifting research from studying women as such to exploring how gender might be used fruitfully as an analytical tool. Instead of identifying women as the primary subject, recent feminist historians have widened the scope to include revolutionary discourse, policies, events, culture – interpreted through the lens of gender. Benefiting from advances made in other fields, such as literary criticism and gay and women's studies, historians have become interested in how the Revolutionaries refashioned gender roles for both men and women and, correspondingly, how ideas regarding manhood and womanhood influenced the way revolutionary statesmen conceived of the new regime.

For example, historians have long known that women were formally excluded from organizing political clubs by the National Convention during the fall of 1793. But it has been too easy to see Jacobin attitudes as prejudicial, old-fashioned, and out of character with their more democratic political beliefs. Nonetheless, recent work shows that Jacobin ideas about women may not have been old-fashioned or prejudicial at all; when looked at from the perspective of gender, they may have been part of an effort to articulate a new and daring view of politics, in which both "men" and "women" are redefined in contrast to aristocratic gender roles: "Each sex is called to the kind of occupation which is fitting for it," the Jacobin deputy Amar declared on behalf of the Convention. "Man is strong, robust, born with great energy, audacity, and courage," while women are destined for "private functions." Historians who use gender as an analytical tool teach us that Amar is not making an old-fashioned statement about women, but rather, he is formulating a new (if dark) vision about how gender roles will function in modern republican politics.[24]

If we are to make sense of Amar's political program, we must learn how Jacobins like him used gender to differentiate one group of citizens from another. No one has pioneered this path more successfully than Lynn Hunt. In a study from the early 1980s, Hunt explored why the Jacobins replaced Marianne with Hercules as the anthropomorphic symbol of the French nation. What did it mean for the French nation to be represented by a man instead of a woman? In the article on Marie Antoinette reprinted in this volume, Hunt demonstrates how attitudes towards the French queen reveal much about the ways in which French revolutionary leaders hoped to shape sexual roles in the new republic.[25]

Of great importance in shifting the lines of research from "women" to "gender" is the recent work of an American feminist political scientist, Joan Landes. Grounding her research on the theories of German social theorist Jürgen Habermas, Landes argued that the crucial factor for women during the French Revolution was not their participation but rather their formal exclusion from political life altogether. Women were not simply forgotten or ignored by the Revolution's new leaders. Rather, "the collapse of the older patriarchy gave way to a more pervasive *gendering* of the public sphere." The lines between public men participating in civic life and domesticated women caring for family and children alone, argued Landes, were more purposively drawn by the Jacobins than ever before.[26]

Landes blames this development on Jean-Jacques Rousseau. His reformulation of political culture included a devastating critique of gender roles under the Old Regime. Elite women, Rousseau claimed, had overstepped their natural bounds and had attained entirely too much power and visibility, especially in Paris and Versailles. Indeed, in Rousseau's view, the feminization of the Old Regime nobility threatened to undermine any semblance of order and morality. The solution, Rousseau argued, would be to divide gender roles much more rigidly than had ever been the case for the French aristocracy. "The theorist of democratic liberty," Landes wrote of Rousseau, had "a profound mistrust of women such that he would deny them the most elementary political rights."[27]

Landes thus argued that the new "bourgeois political sphere"[28] was in many ways more regressive than what élite women had experienced under the Old Regime. Indeed, far from gaining political rights during the French Revolution, Landes claimed that the Old Regime showed far more toleration for public women than did its republican counterpart. From Landes historians learned, perhaps for the first time, that the omission of women from the *Declaration of the Rights of Man and Citizens* was not a prejudicial oversight, but rather, they were excluded because the Republic had been conceived as an exclusively masculine public space.

Landes sees her work as a contribution to left-wing feminism's critique of contemporary patriarchal limitations on female political power. Under the influence of Australian political theorist Carol Pateman, both Landes and Hunt hope to expose the patriarchal roots of liberal democracies, in order to prod them to initiate more radical change that would further empower women.[29] However, it is one of the great ironies of recent historical scholarship that this left-wing feminist scholarship has so far been more fruitfully deployed by Neo-Conservative Revisionist scholars than by anyone else.

Revisionists and the new feminist scholars share two essential attitudes about the Revolution: first, both groups believe that the Revolution marked a step backwards for women's rights. Second, both give credence to the ideas of Jean-Jacques Rousseau – it was his highly contentious ideas that gave rise to new notions of female domesticity.

The best example of the appropriation of feminist history for Neo-Conservative purposes is found in Simon Schama's *Citizens*, which arguably incorporated more recent scholarship on women than any other recent general history. Using Hunt's research on Marie Antoinette, Schama depicted the 1793 trial of the queen as merely one facet of "the stormiest phase of sexual politics in the Revolution." For Revisionists, the Jacobin attack upon Marie Antoinette and other public women such as Olympe de Gouges and Madame Roland, as well as the general closure of female

15

political clubs in 1793, are emblematic of a pervasive Rousseauian democratic despotism.[30]

In fact, this convergence of what might be labeled "feminist revisionism" is what makes possible the outlook of Olwen Hufton's piece in this volume, "In Search of Counter-Revolutionary Women." Hufton sees the Revolution primarily as an attempt by big-city folk to control the masses of poor rural peasants, who were not so much counter-revolutionaries in the ideological sense, but simply wanted to get out of the way of the political steamroller. When that became impossible, women had to fend for themselves, devising their own imaginative strategies for undermining Jacobinism in the countryside. "By looking at gender roles in the counter-revolution," Hufton hopes to "convey how it was possible for women to subvert the Revolution in the home and on the domestic front."[31]

The irony of a feminist revisionism shows just how much historical writing reflects greater trends operating in contemporary culture. After all, despite stereotypes that set up a mythic struggle between a Left that champions revolutionary struggle and a Right that seeks to prevent any major social change, today's college students and faculty across the political spectrum are generally highly skeptical about the efficacy of any revolutionary change, and at the same time, deeply committed to a civic culture that promotes equal opportunities for women and men. It is only natural and appropriate that their own political convictions influence how they perceive the French Revolution.

Sometimes new students of the Revolution – and veteran scholars as well – grow weary at the noisy debates over its meaning and place in history. Most historians choose their field not because of a fondness for theory or political polemics, but usually because of a love to study the documents themselves. Yet, the historiography of the French Revolution is so monumental that it often threatens to intimidate the young researcher. Is it really necessary to pay close attention to the polemics among historians and other partisans? Why isn't it possible to simply ignore the various schools of historical thinking, and to study the Revolution without becoming embroiled in its historiography?

Without historiography scholars would not know how to go about their business. We would be like travelers lost in the forest without a map – all the trees might look alike, and we would not know which path to travel. Instead of thousands of trees, we have primary source documents. And the first problem confronting the historian is deciding which document to investigate and what questions to ask about it. Without a rigorous historiography that compels us to think critically about our approaches, our political views, and our rhetorical strategies, we would have only our prejudices and our passions on which to rely. As in the nineteenth century, history without historiography might still be worth reading as literature, but it would rarely be considered part of the social sciences.

François Furet is right that "the French Revolution is over." We live in another age, and the problems of the late eighteenth century are no longer our own. Nevertheless, the legacy of the achievements and failings of that age are still with us. The French Revolutionaries dreamed of a world (like ours) dominated by democratic republics. They tried – and ultimately failed – to figure out what duties a democratic government had towards its citizens, and what responsibilities it had towards its neighbors. Our era may not be theirs but surely how we choose to write about their early efforts will help shape how our readers think about our own political problems.

NOTES

1 Paul Farmer, *France Reviews Its Revolutionary Origins: Social Politics and Historical opinion in the Third Republic* (New York, 1944), pp. 61–6; James L. Godrey, "Alphonse Aulard," *Some Historians of Modern Europe*, ed. Bernadotte E. Schmitt (Chicago, 1942), pp. 45–65.
2 James Friguglietti, *Albert Mathiez, historien révolutionnaire* (Paris, 1974).
3 Georges Lefebvre, *The Coming of the French Revolution*, trans. R.R. Palmer (Princeton, 1947). Because of his popular college text, *A History of the Modern World*, Palmer is probably the most influential American historian of the French Revolution. Palmer's highly sympathetic view of the Terror is presented in *Twelve Who Ruled: The Year of the Terror in the French Revolution* (Princeton, 1941).
4 Crane Brinton, *The Anatomy of Revolution* (New York, 1965 [originally published 1938]).
5 *The Social Interpretation of the French Revolution* (Cambridge, 1964). The 1954 lecture was reprinted in Cobban's *Aspects of the French Revolution* (New York, 1970), pp. 90–111.
6 George V. Taylor, "Types of Capitalism in Eighteenth-Century France," *English Historical Review* 79 (1964): 478–97; Noncapitalist Wealth and the Origins of the French Revolution," *American Historical Review* 72 (1967): 469–96.

7 François Furet, *Interpreting the French Revolution*, trans. Elborg Forster (Cambridge, 1981).

8 *Ibid.*, p. 27.

9 For his most concisely doctrinaire statement see the introduction to *Les Orateurs de la révolution française, tome 1: Les Constituents*, ed. François Furet and Ran Halevi (Paris 1989). See also *L'Héritage de la révolution française*, ed. François Furet (Paris, 1989); *Terminer la révolution: Mounier et Barnave dans la révolution*, ed. François Furet and Mona Ozouf (Grenoble, 1990); *La Gironde et les Girondins*, ed. François Furet and Mona Ozouf (Paris, 1991); *Le siècle de l'avènement républicain*, ed. François Furet and Mona Ozouf (Paris, 1993); *Dictionnaire critique de la révolution française*, ed. François Furet and Mona Ozouf (Paris, 1988; English trans. Arthur Goldhammer, Cambridge, MA., 1989); François Furet, *La Révolution* (Paris, 1988; trans. Antonia Nevill, Oxford, 1992 as *Revolutionary France 1770– 1880*). See also the series of conference proceedings organized by Keith Baker, Colin Lucas, and Furet, *The French Revolution and the Creation of Modern Political Culture*, 4 vols (Oxford 1987–93), which include several important articles by Furet and his colleagues.

10 Keith Michael Baker, *Inventing the French Revolution: Essays on French Political Culture in the Eighteenth Century* (Cambridge, 1990), p. 295.

11 *Ibid*, p. 305.

12 On the Liberal foundations of Marxist historiography, see George Comninel, *Rethinking the French Revolution: Marxism and the Revisionist Challenge* (London, 1987).

13 Donald Sutherland, "The Revolution in the Provinces: Class or Counterrevolution?," in *Essays on the French Revolution: Paris and the Provinces*, ed. Steven G. Reinhardt, *et al.* (College Station, TX, 1992), p. 116. see also his *France 1789–1815: Revolution and Counterrevolution* (New York, 1985).

14 For Cobban's more liberal views, see his *In Search of Humanity: The Role of the Enlightenment in Modern History* (New York, 1960), esp. Parts 4 and 5. For all his liberalism, however, Cobban was certainly no cheerleader for the Revolution and sometimes adopted a more critical posture. See, for example, "Local Government During the French Revolution," in *Aspects of the French Revolution* (New York, 1968), p. 130.

15 Irving Kristol, *Neo-Conservativism: Selected Essays 1949–1995* (New York, 1995).

16 J. L. Talmon, *The Origins of Totalitarian Democracy* (London, 1952). The book has been reprinted several times in paperback and has been translated into French, German, Hebrew, and Japanese. For Cobban's criticisms, see his *Rousseau and the Modern State*, 2nd ed. (London, 1964), pp. 29–31, and *In Search of Humanity*, pp. 182–5.

17 Raynauld Sécher, *La Génocide Franco-Français: La Vendée-Vengé* (Paris, 1986). See Hugh Gough, "Genocide and the Bicentenary: The French Revolution and the Revenge of the Vendée," *Historical Journal* 30 (1987): 977-88.

18 Steven Lawrence Kaplan, *The Historians' Feud* (Ithaca, 1994).

19 Simon Schama, *Citizens: A Chronicle of the French Revolution* (New York, 1989), pp. 184 and 447.

20 Neo-Marxist works include Comninel, *Rethinking the French Revolution*; E. J. Hobsbawm, *Echoes of the Marseillaise: Two Centuries Look Back on the French Revolution* (New Brunswick, 1989); and Morris Slavin, *The Left and the French Revolution* (Atlantic Highlands, NJ, 1995).

21 Jane Abray, "Feminism in the French Revolution," *American Historical Review* 80 (1975): 43–62.

22 *Women in Revolutionary Paris, 1789–1795*, ed. Darline Gay Levy, Harriet Branson Applewhite, and Mary Durham Johnson (Urbana, 1979).

23 Furet, *Revolutionary France; Critical Dictionary*, ed. Furet and Ozouf. For more general reflections on women's historiography see Joan Wallach Scott, *Gender and the Politics of History* (New York, 1988), pp. 15–50; and Karen Offen, "The New Sexual Politics of French Revolutionary Historiography," *French Historical Studies* 16 (1990): 909–22.

24 Amar's speech is reproduced in *Women in Revolutionary Politics*, pp. 213–17.

25 Lynn Hunt, "Hercules and the Radical Image in the French Revolution," *Representations* 1 (1983): 95–117, and included in her *Politics, Culture, and Class in the French Revolution* (Berkeley, 1984), pp. 87–119. Other recent examples of this approach to gender history include Madelyn Gutwirth, *The Twilight of the Goddesses: Women and Representation in the French Revolutionary Era* (New Brunswick, 1992); Geneviève Fraise, *Reason's Muse: Sexual Difference and the Birth of Democracy*, trans. Jane Marie Todd (Chicago, 1994); Christine Fauré *Democracy Without Women: Feminism and the Rise of Liberal Individualism in France*, trans. Claudia Goodman and John Berks (Bloomington, 1991); and Dorinda Outram, *The Body and the French Revolution: Sex, Class and Political Culture* (New Haven, 1989).

26 Joan B. Landes, *Women and the Public Sphere in the Age of the French Revolution* (Ithaca, 1988), p. 2. For criticisms of Landes's work see especially Dena Goodman, "Public Sphere and Private Life: Toward a Synthesis of Current Historiographical Approaches to the Old Regime", *History and Theory* 31(1992): 1–20; and Keith Michael Baker, "Defining the Public Sphere in Eighteenth-Century France: Variations on a Theme by Habermas," in *Habermas and the Public Sphere*, ed. Craig Calhoun (Cambridge, MA, 1992), pp. 181–211. Goodman and Baker tend to criticize Landes more for her understanding of Habermas than for her analysis of how gender roles changed during the Revolution.

27 p. 67.

28 p. 204.

29 Carole Pateman, *The Sexual Contract* (Stanford, 1988).

30 Schama, *Citizens*, p. 800. Along the same lines, see Patrice Higonnet "Cultural Upheaval and Class Formation During the French Revolution," in *The French Revolution and the Birth of Modernity*, ed.

Ferenc Fehér (Berkeley, 1990), pp. 69–102. For a Neo-Liberal response to this line of thinking, see Suzanne Desan, "'Constitutional Amazons': Jacobin Women's Clubs in the French Revolution," in *Recreating Authority in Revolutionary France*, ed. Bryant T. Ragan, Jr, and Elizabeth A. Williams (New Brunswick, 1992), pp. 11–35; and the introduction to *The French Revolution and Human Rights: A Brief Documentary History*, ed. Lynn Hunt (Boston, 1996).

31 Olwen H. Hufton, *Women and the Limits of Citizenship in the French Revolution* (Toronto, 1992), p. xxiv.

Part I

THE OVERTHROW OF THE MARXIST PARADIGM

Danton, Robespierre, Saint-Just, Napoleon, the heroes as
well as the parties and the masses of the old French
Revolution, performed the task of their time in Roman
costume and with Roman phrases, the task of unchaining
and setting up modern bourgeois society.

Karl Marx
The Eighteenth Brumaire of Louis Bonaparte

1

THE FRENCH REVOLUTION IN THE HISTORY OF THE CONTEMPORARY WORLD

Albert Soboul

Born in 1914 to small farmers, Soboul won scholarships to France's most prestigious schools and decided upon a career teaching history. In 1932 he joined the Communist Party, and after World War II he combined his innovative historical research with a commitment to Marxist politics. His most important book, Les sans-culottes parisiennes de l'an II *(1958), a study of Parisian workers during the Terror, established a new standard of scholarship for the social history of the Revolution. Along with British historians E.P. Thompson and George Rudé, Soboul was part of a group of social historians who hoped to reconstruct the lives of ordinary workers and activists during the revolutionary era. During the 1960's, their "history from below" approach influenced a younger generation of historians on both sides of the Atlantic. In 1967, Soboul was appointed to the Sorbonne's prestigious chair of the History of the Revolution. He died in 1975.*

The following article, originally published in 1969, is a digest of Soboul's Marxist approach to the Revolution. The first sentence encapsulates Soboul's entire perspective: the Revolution was much more than a political transformation; it was also essentially social and economic. Socially, it was a bourgeois revolution in the sense that political power moved from landed aristocrats to the bourgeoisie – that is, middle-class businessmen, professionals, and civil servants who claimed to represent the nation. Economically, it was a capitalist revolution in which this new bourgeois class transferred the source of wealth from land to more liquid forms of capital. The peasants and urban artisans (sans-culottes) began as the partners of the bourgeoisie against the nobility, but by 1792 had become its victims. The bourgeoisie consolidated victory between the Thermidorean Reaction that followed the Terror and the ascendancy of Napoleon Bonaparte. In this way, Soboul argues,

23

France did not actually become a democracy, because genuine political power was simply transferred from one élite group to another.

* * *

The Revolution of 1789–1794 marked the advent of modern society – bourgeois and capitalist – in the history of France. Its essential characteristic is to have effected the national unity of the country on the base of the destruction of the seigniorial regime and the privileged feudal orders; according to Tocqueville in *The Ancien Régime and the Revolution*, its "particular object was to abolish everywhere the remnants of the institutions of the Middle Ages."[1] Its historical significance is further clarified by the fact that the French Revolution in the end succeeded in establishing a liberal democracy. From this double point of view, and the perspective of world history which concerns us here, it deserves to be considered as a classical model of a bourgeois revolution.

The comparative study of the French Revolution thus poses two series of problems.

Problems of a general nature: those concerning the historical law of the transition from feudalism to modern capitalism. To take up again the question posed by Marx in book III of *Capital*, this transition is carried out in two ways: by the total destruction of the old economic and social system – that is, the "really revolutionary way" – or by the preservation of large sectors of the old mode of production in the heart of the new capitalist society – that is, the way of compromise.[2]

Problems of a special nature: those that bear on the specific structure of French society at the end of the Ancien Régime and that take into account the particular characteristics of the French Revolution in regard to the various types of bourgeois revolutions.[3]

From this double point of view, the history of the French Revolution cannot be isolated from that of Europe. In all the European countries, the formation of modern society is drafted in the very heart of the old economic and social system with its vestiges of feudalism, then forged at their expense. In all the European countries, this evolution was made with varying degrees to the advantage of the bourgeoisie. The French Revolution was not the first to benefit the bourgeoisie; before it, the revolution in Holland in the sixteenth century, the two revolutions of England in the seventeenth century, the American Revolution in the eighteenth century paved the way for this revolution. Once again it is a question of recognizing the specific traits of the French Revolution.

At the end of the eighteenth century, France and the major part of Europe were subject to what has been called the Ancien Régime.[4] This was characterized on the social plane by aristocratic privilege, on that of the State by monarchial absolutism of divine right.

The aristocracy, whose role had not ceased to diminish since the Middle Ages, nevertheless remained in the first ranks of the hierarchy.[5] The social structure of France was always essentially aristocratic; it conserved the character of its origin in the period when land constituted the only form of social wealth, and thus conferred on those who possessed it power over those who cultivated it. The Capetian monarchy had indeed, with great effort, stripped the feudal lords of their royal rights and the nobles and high clergy of all political influence. Having become subjects, the nobles and clerics had nonetheless remained the privileged; the feudal lords had kept their social and economic privileges, the seigniorial rights always underscoring the subjection of the peasants.

Socially privileged, but politically diminished, the aristocracy did not pardon the absolute monarch for having stripped it of all political authority; it denounced despotism and demanded liberty; it intended to have a share in the power. Its ideal of a *tempered* monarchy fitted into the framework of the theory of historic right. It had been expressed from the end of the reign of Louis XIV, particularly by Fénelon, whose political ideas were not only conveyed in the allegories of the *Adventures of Télémaque* (1699), but were more explicitly clarified in *The Projects of Government . . . to be proposed to the Duke of Burgundy*, published in 1711 under the title *Tables of Chaulnes*.[6] This anti-absolute aristocratic reaction was diversified, from the first half of the century on, in two currents: one of feudal reaction corresponding to the interests of the nobility of the sword, whose principal representative was the count of Boulainvilliers;[7] the other of parlementary reaction corresponding to the nobility of the robe, declaring itself by the publication in 1732 of the *Judicium Francorum*.[8] The theories of the parlementary and feudal reaction were taken up again in the middle of the century, no longer by obscure pamphleteers, but by Montesquieu, with the publication in 1748 of *The Spirit of the Laws*.[9] This aristocratic demand for liberty, in the face of monarchial absolutism, was only, as Georges Lefebvre remarked, a "relic of the past."

However, the rebirth of commerce and the development of craft production since the tenth and eleventh centuries had created a new form of wealth, personal and moveable, and thus given birth to a new class, the bourgeoisie, whose importance was established by admission to the Estates General in the fourteenth century. In the framework of the feudal society, the bourgeoisie had continued to expand to the very rhythm of the development of capitalism, stimulated by the great discoveries of the fifteenth and sixteenth centuries and the exploitation of the colonial worlds, as well as the financial dealings of a monarchy always short of money. In the eighteenth century, the bourgeoisie were leaders in finance, commerce, and industry; they provided the monarchy with administrative cadres as well as the resources necessary to operate the State. Thus, even while the aristocracy was becoming ossified in its caste, the bourgeoisie was expanding in number, in economic power, in culture and in consciousness. The progress of the Enlightenment had undermined the ideological foundations of the established order, at the same time that it was expressing the class consciousness of the bourgeoisie, and its good conscience. As a rising class, believing in progress, it was convinced that it was representing the general interest and assuming responsibility for the nation; as a progressive class, it offered a decisive attraction for the popular masses as well as for dissident sectors of the aristocracy. But bourgeois ambition, prompted by the social and economic reality, collided with the aristocratic order of laws and institutions.[10]

The bourgeoisie, like the aristocracy, hoped to have a share of the power and demanded liberty from the monarch. But rather than justifying this demand by historic right, as the aristocracy did, the bourgeoisie proclaimed natural right: society is founded on the free contract between its members; government, on the free contract between that one who governs and those who are governed, such that power is conceived only to benefit the community and to guarantee the rights of the citizens.[11] In 1724 the French translation of Locke's *Treatise on Civil Government*

(1690) appeared, a work that inspired the whole century. Theoretician of the English Revolution of 1688–9, Locke expressed the ideal of the bourgeoisie, transforming (one might say) "an historical accident into an event dictated by human reason." His political ideal – and this explains his profound influence – coincided with that of a bourgeoisie in full expansion, presenting a complex mixture of empiricism and rationalism: defend the established social order and property, but appeal to morality; concern with effective power, but necessity of consent; individualism, but recognition of majority rule.

Political freedom was certainly important, but even more so was economic freedom, that of enterprise and profit. Capitalism required freedom because freedom was necessary to assure its development, freedom in all its forms: freedom of the person, a condition for hiring labor; freedom of property, a condition for its mobility; freedom of thought, a condition for research and scientific and technical discoveries.

Unlike the aristocracy, the bourgeoisie did not demand only power and freedom; it meant to suppress privilege and acquire equal rights. In the second half of the eighteenth century, the bourgeoisie in effect found itself battling against the aristocracy. For centuries, the bourgeoisie had dreamed of becoming noble; the venality of offices had provided the means to this end. From the sixteenth century on, the French monarchy had put bourgeois wealth to good use by putting some public offices up for sale along with the added attraction of accompanying privileges and personal or hereditary nobility. Thus, while many bourgeois families were directly infiltrating the nobility, a nobility of the robe was being established, which, although sustaining ever closer relations with the aristocracy, nevertheless remained bourgeois, especially in the administration of its wealth. But in the eighteenth century, the nobility of the robe was tending to close its ranks, even while the bourgeoisie remained too numerous to be able to hope to be admitted.[12] "In one way or another," Sieyes wrote in his brochure *What is the Third Estate?* "all the branches of executive power have fallen to the caste that supplies the Church, the robe and the sword. A sort of spirit of co-fraternity makes the nobility prefer themselves to the rest of the nation. The usurpation is complete; they truly reign."[13] The bourgeoisie demanded the suppression of privilege, and equal rights.

In France, therefore, in the second half of the eighteenth century, the development of the capitalist economy, on the base of which the power of the bourgeoisie was erected, was checked by the feudal framework of society, by the traditional and regulated organization of property, production and trade. "It was necessary to break these chains," the authors of the *Communist Manifesto* wrote – "they were broken." In this way the problem is posed of the passage from feudalism to capitalism. It did not escape the most perceptive men of the period. Far from being inspired by an abstract individualism, as Taine would have it, the revolutionary bourgeoisie had a clear understanding of the economic reality that produced its strength and determined its victory. Barnave was the first to formulate, more than half a century before Marx, the theory of the bourgeois revolution. In his *Introduction to the French Revolution*, written in 1792, Barnave set down the principle that property *influences* institutions. "The reign of the aristocracy lasts so long as the farm population continues to ignore or neglect the arts, and landed property continues to be the only wealth. . . . Once the arts and commerce succeed in penetrating the people and create a new means to wealth to aid the laboring class, all is ready for a revolution in political laws: a new distribution of wealth produces a new distribution of power. Just as the possession of land elevates the aristocracy, industrial property elevates the power of the people; they obtain their freedom." When Barnave writes "people," he means the bourgeoisie.[14]

The Dutch and English revolutions had already shown that the deep causes of the bourgeois revolution are to be sought in the feudal vestiges and contradictions of the old society. But this aspect does not explain all the characteristics of the French Revolution. The reasons why it constituted, by its very violence, the most resounding episode in the class struggles that carried the bourgeoisie to power must be sought in certain specific traits of the French society of the Ancien Régime.

Without a doubt, the bourgeoisie would have been content with a compromise that would have given it a share of the power, similar to the English oligarchy of the eighteenth century. The aristocracy stubbornly refused, since all compromise stumbled against feudalism. The peasant masses could not tolerate the preservation of this system; the nobility as a whole could not envisage its suppression, which would mean their decline. On the basis of the economic and social compromise represented by the repurchase of feudal rights decreed in principle on the night of 4 August (1789) and systematized by the law of 15 March 1790, the Constituent bourgeoisie for a long time tried desperately to reach a political compromise with the aristocracy.[15] The obstinate resistance of the bulk of the small nobility that lived for the most part from landed income, the stubborn and aggressive will of the peasants to end all vestiges of feudalism, were reason enough for this policy of compromise and conciliation. In order to triumph, the bourgeoisie had to resolve to form an alliance with the popular masses.

The popular masses bore all the weight of the Ancien Régime: they could no longer tolerate it.

The popular urban masses, artisans and shopkeepers, journeymen and apprentices, service workers, to a lesser degree manufacturing workers, were pushed to revolt by the worsening of their living conditions. These have been exposed by the works of C.-E. Labrousse.[16] From 1726–41 to 1785–9, the long-term rise in prices brought about a 62 per cent increase in the cost of living. On the average, bread accounted for about half of the popular budget; the seasonal variations in the price of grain raised the price of bread by 88 per cent in 1789. This price increase forced the wealthy categories to economize; it overwhelmed the poor. The nominal increase in wages, 22 per cent on the average, did not come close to compensating the increase in prices. As usual, wages followed prices, but without catching up; more precisely, real wages were lowered by about 25 per cent. This worsening of living conditions of the popular masses did not escape the better observers of the period: as early as 1766, Turgot first formulated the "iron law" of wages, in his *Reflections on the Formation and Distribution of Wealth*. More than to the demands for liberty, the popular urban masses were sensitive to the demand for daily bread; they placed up front the question of subsistence. They countered the demand for economic freedom with the right of survival, very specifically price controls and regulation. They countered the equal rights that the bourgeoisie claimed from the aristocracy with "equal enjoyment."[17]

The popular urban masses, soon to be designated by the term sans-culotterie, properly speaking, lacked class consciousness. Scattered in numerous workshops, neither specialized – as a result of limited technological development – nor concentrated in large enterprises or industrial districts, often poorly differentiated from the peasantry, the wage-earners were no more capable than the peasants of conceiving effective solutions to their misery; the weakness of the guilds vouched for that. Hatred of the aristocracy and unmitigated opposition to the "fat" and the rich provided the ferment of unity for the laboring masses. When the poor harvests and the resulting economic crisis set them in motion, they lined up, not as a distinct class, but as part of the craft industry, behind the bourgeoisie. In this way, the most effective blows were struck against the old society. But this victory of the popular masses could be only a "bourgeois victory"; the bourgeoisie accepted the popular alliance against the aristocracy only because the masses remained subordinate. In the opposite case, the bourgeoisie would have renounced, as in Germany in the nineteenth century and to a lesser degree in Italy, the support of allies deemed too dangerous.

The peasant masses constituted the bulk of the French population, doubtless 22 to 23 million out of about 28 million.[18] In 1789, the great majority of the peasants had been free for a long time, serfdom surviving in only a few regions, Nivernais and Franche-Comté in particular. The feudal relations of production nonetheless dominated the countryside, as is evidenced by the seigniorial fees and ecclesiastical tithes. Certain historians tend to minimize the weight of feudalism at the end of the Ancien Régime. Tocqueville had already answered them in a chapter of *The Ancien Régime and the Revolution*: "Why feudal rights had become more odious to the people in France than anywhere else." If the French peasant had not possessed the land, he would have been less sensitive to the burdens that the feudal system placed on landed property.[19] It would even be appropriate, in order to better define the problem, to specify quantitatively the feudal imposition; for the three subdivisions of Aurillac, Mauriac and Saint-Flour, according to fiscal documents, it would be about 10 per cent of the taxed product (that is, the average net product), not taking into account the *lods et ventes* (fees received by the lord on the price of sold inherited property), the *banalités* (exclusive rights of lord to maintain a mill, an oven or a winepress) and the *dîme* (ecclesiastical tithe).[20] Yet it is the total weight that tenure supported in relation to production that we would have to determine in order to have an idea of the relative burden imposed by the whole of the *feudal complex*. In these same subdivisions of

Haute-Auvergne, a third of the revenues of the seigniory, in round numbers, came from feudal rights. This percentage would in a large measure account for the resistance of the Auvergne nobility to the abolition of feudalism, for their refusal of all compromise, and in the last analysis for the agrarian troubles as counter-revolutionary endeavors from 1789 to 1792 and 1793. "Imagine," writes Tocqueville regarding the French peasant of the eighteenth century, "the condition, the needs, the character, the passions of this man, and calculate, if you can, the store of hate and desire amassed in his heart."[21]

To the hatred of feudalism, let us add the hunger for land that tormented the peasant, made still sharper by the demographic upsurge that characterized the eighteenth century. While about 130,000 members of the clergy shared 10 per cent of the land among themselves, very unequally moreover, the nobility (about 350,000 persons) held about 20 per cent; while the bourgeoisie held for themselves about 30 per cent, the portion for the 22 to 23 million peasants was only 35 per cent.[22] We cannot stress enough the importance of the peasant question in the heart of the bourgeois revolution. For Gramsci, Jacobinism, the very essence of the French Revolution, is characterized by the alliance of the revolutionary bourgeoisie and the peasant masses.

The popular masses, peasant or urban, had a social ideal corresponding to the economic conditions of the times: conception of a limited right to property, protest actions against concentration of farming and industrial concerns. In order to freely dispose of their persons and their labor, peasants and artisans first had to break their enforced allegiance, whether attached to the land or prisoners of the corporation. These conditions explain their hatred of the aristocracy and the Ancien Régime and the fact that the popular classes were the driving force of the bourgeois revolution. But, whether they were immediate producers or dreaming of attaining that state, peasants and artisans understood property to be based on individual work and dreamed of a society of small independent producers; in a confused way, they intended to prevent the establishment of a monopoly of wealth along with a dependent proletariat.[23] These profound aspirations account for the social and political struggles during the Revolution, of their turns and progression. From 1789 to 1793, we saw a deepening of the struggle of the bourgeoisie against the aristocracy, marked by the

31

growing role of the middle layers and the popular masses, not by a change in the nature of the social struggles. In this sense, it is possible to speak of a "change in the front" of the bourgeoisie after the fall of Robespierre: before and after 9 Thermidor, since that aristocracy had not been disarmed, they remained the basic enemy. This was proved by the law of 29 November 1797, inspired by Sieyes, that reduced the former nobles to the state of foreigners. The French Revolution is indeed "a bloc": antifeudal and bourgeois throughout its various ups and downs.

This rooting of the Revolution in French society, this continuity and unity, were underscored by Tocqueville with his customary lucidity, while noting their necessity. "What the Revolution was least of all was an accidental event. It is true that it took the world by surprise, and yet it was only the complement of a much longer work, the sudden and violent termination of an undertaking on which ten generations of men had worked.[24]

If the French Revolution was the most dazzling of the bourgeois revolutions, eclipsing by the dramatic character of its class struggles the revolutions that preceded it, this was due to the obstinacy of the aristocracy rooted in its feudal privileges, refusing all concessions, and to the opposing determination of the popular masses. The bourgeoisie had not sought the ruin of the aristocracy, but the refusal of compromise and the counter-revolution obliged them to pursue the destruction of the old order. But they only achieved that by forming an alliance with the rural and urban masses, to whom they were forced to give satisfaction: the popular revolution and the Terror made a clean sweep; feudalism was irremediably destroyed and democracy established.

The French Revolution took the "truly revolutionary path" from feudalism to capitalism. By wiping the slate clean of all feudal vestiges, by liberating the peasants of seigniorial rights and ecclesiastical tithes, and to a certain degree from community constraints, by destroying the trade monopolies and unifying the national market, the French Revolution marked a decisive stage on the path to capitalism. Suppressing feudal landed property, it even freed small direct producers, making possible the differentiation of the peasant mass and its polarization between capital and wage labor. This led to entirely new relations of production; capital, once under feudal domination, was able to make the value of work mercenary. In this way, the autonomy of capitalist production was finally assured in the agricultural domain as well as the industrial sector. Two conditions appeared necessary in this passage to capitalist society, in the light of the French Revolution: the breaking up of feudal landed property and the emancipation of the peasants. The agrarian question indeed occupies "an axial position" in the bourgeois revolution.

The active element of this revolution was less the commercial bourgeoisie (to the extent that they remained solely commercial and intermediary, they accommodated themselves to the old society – from 1789 to 1793, from the "Monarchiens" to the "Feuillants," then the Girondists, they generally supported compromise) than the mass of small direct producers from whom the feudal aristocracy exacted overwork and overproduction with the support of the judicial apparatus and the means of constraint provided by the State of the Ancien Régime. The political instrument of change was the Jacobin dictatorship of the small and middle bourgeoisie, supported by the popular masses, social categories whose ideal was a democracy of small autonomous producers, independent peasants and artisans, freely working and trading. The peasant and popular revolution was at the heart of the bourgeois revolution and pushed it forward.[25]

The victory over feudalism and the Ancien Régime did not, however, mean the simultaneous appearance of new social relations. The passage to capitalism is not a simple process, by which the capitalist elements develop in the womb of the old society until the moment when they are strong enough to break through its framework. A long time would still be needed before capitalism would assert itself definitively in France; its progress was slow during the revolutionary period, the dimension of enterprises often remaining modest, with commercial capital dominating.[26] The ruin of feudal landed property, and the corporative, regulated system, by assuring the autonomy of the capitalist mode of production, also uncompromisingly paved the way for bourgeois relations of production and trade – revolutionary transformation par excellence.

Overturning economic and social structures, the French Revolution at the same time shattered the state apparatus of the Ancien Régime, sweeping away the vestiges of old autonomies, destroying local privileges and provincial particularisms. It thus made possible, from the Directory to the Empire, the establishment of a modern State responding to the interests and requirements of the new bourgeoisie.

The French Revolution holds a singular place in the history of the contemporary world.

As a revolution for liberty, it invoked natural right, as did the American Revolution, and conferred upon its work a universal character that the English Revolution had ignored. But who could deny that the Declaration of 1789 affirmed this universality with much more force than the American Declarations? Let us add that the French Declaration went much further on the road to freedom, affirming freedom of conscience and admitting Protestants and Jews into the "city"; but by creating the civil state, on 20 September 1792, it also recognized the right of the citizen to adhere to no religion. It liberated the white man but by the law of 4 February 1794, it also abolished "Negro slavery in all the colonies."

As a Revolution for equality, the French Revolution went far beyond the revolutions that preceded it. Neither in England nor in the United States was emphasis placed on equality, as the aristocracy and the bourgeoisie were partners in power. The resistance of the aristocracy, the counter-revolution and the war forced the French bourgeoisie to push the struggle for equal rights to the first rank. In this way it could rally the people and win. But what was drafted in 1793–4 was a regime of social democracy characterized by a compromise between bourgeois conceptions and popular aspirations. The popular masses realized what fate awaited them: that's why they demonstrated hostility to the economic freedom that opened the way to concentration and capitalism. At the end of the eighteenth century, the ideal of the people was that each peasant would be a landowner, each artisan independent and each wage earner protected against the all-powerful rich.

After 10 August 1792, when the throne was overturned, and the revolutionary bourgeoisie had instituted universal suffrage and sealed its alliance with the sans-culottes, it was indeed necessary to go beyond theoretical equality of rights and move toward that "equality of enjoyment" that the people demanded. This led to the management of the economy to set prices in harmony with wages and assure daily bread for all: price controls and regulation were instituted by the law of the "general maximum" on 29 September 1793, and war manufacturing and foreign commerce were nationalized. There was also the endeavor to establish public education accessible to all by the law of 19 December 1793. In addition, there were also the beginnings of social security with the law of national charity of 11 May 1794. This egalitarian republic filled the propertied bourgeoisie with indignation and dread; after 9 Thermidor, it was banned forever. But the conviction remained in the consciousness of the people that freedom without equality meant only privilege for some, that liberty and equality are inseparable, that political equality by itself can be only a façade when social inequality asserts itself. "Liberty is but a vain phantom when a class of men can starve others with impunity," the *enragé* Jacques Roux had declared to the gallery of the Convention on 21 June 1793. "Equality is but a vain phantom when the rich, through their monopolies, exercise the right of life and death on their fellow men."[27]

Finally, as a revolution for unity, the French Revolution made the nation one and indivisible.[28] Certainly the Capetian monarchy had established the territorial and administrative framework of the nation, but without completing this task; in 1789, national unity remained imperfect. The nation was still divided territorially by the incoherence of administrative divisions and the persistence of the "feudal parcelling"; the diversity of weights and measures and interior customs posed obstacles to the formation of a national market. Moreover, the nation was socially divided, for the Ancien Régime was organized into a hierarchy and partly into guilds. (As Georges Lefebvre remarked, whoever says "guild" implies "privileges.") Everywhere inequality reigned in a nation created by a unitary government, whose cohesion had been reinforced in the eighteenth century through the multiple bonds woven by material progress, the expansion of the French language, the development of culture and the brilliance of the Enlightenment.

Once the orders, states, and guilds were abolished, the French people were free and equal under the law, constituting a nation, one and indivisible. The rationalization of institutions by the Constituent Assembly, the return to centralization by the revolutionary government, the administrative exertions of the Directory, the reconstruction of the State by Napoleon – all completed the work of the monarchy of the Ancien Régime, destroying autonomies and particularisms, putting in place the institutional framework of a unified State. At the same time, the consciousness of a unified nation was awakened and strengthened by civil equality, the 1790 federations movement, the development of the network of Jacobin societies, and the antifederalism and the congresses or *central meetings* of the popular societies in 1793. The advances of the French language went in the same direction. New economic ties reinforced the national consciousness. Once the feudal parcelling was destroyed, and the tolls and interior customs abolished, the "withdrawal of barriers" to the political frontier tended to unify the national market, which was, moreover, protected from foreign competition by a protectionist tariff. The French Revolution gave a strength and effectiveness to the national sovereignty that up till then it had not had.

A new public international law was expressed. Seeking to define its principles, during the affair of the German princes who owned land in Alsace, Merlin de Douai in effect posited the nation conceived as a voluntary association against the dynastic State. Speaking on 28 October 1790, he said, "There is between you and your Alsacian brothers no other legitimate title of union than the social pact formed last year between all old and modern French people in this Assembly" – an allusion to the decision of the Third Estate on 17 June 1789 to proclaim itself a National Assembly, and to that of the Assembly on the following 9 July to declare itself a Constituent Assembly, and to the *federative pact* of 14 July, 1790. One sole question, "infinitely simple," remained: that of knowing "if it is to these diplomatic parchments that the Alsacian people owe the advantage of being French . . . What do these conventions matter to the people of Alsace or the people of France, when in the times of despotism, they had as their object to unite the first to the second? The Alsacian people joined the French people because they wanted to; it is their will alone, and not the treaty of Münster, that legitimized the union."[29] This will had been demonstrated by participation in the Federation of 14 July 1790. The international public law was revolutionized as the interior public law was – nations now had the right to self-determination.

After ten years of revolution, the French reality appeared to be radically transformed. The aristocracy of the Ancien Régime was ruined, its privileges and social domination stripped away with the abolition of feudalism. We should not stretch this point, however; many nobles did not emigrate and succeeded in safeguarding their landed patrimony; the Napoleonic consolidation restored their social prestige; the squire replaced the feudal lord. The fusion of this landed aristocracy and the upper bourgeoisie constituted the dominant class in the new society.

At the other extreme of the social scale, the popular urban classes had not drawn any positive advantage from the Revolution. In fact, by proclaiming economic freedom, and by prohibiting unions and strikes by the Le Chapelier law of 14 June 1791 – a truly constituent law of free-trade capitalism (the prohibition persisted until 1864 for the right to strike and until 1884 for the right to unionize), the bourgeois revolution left the popular urban classes defenseless in the new economy. Liberalism, founded on the ideal of an abstract social individualism, profited the most. Economic freedom accelerated the concentration of industrial enterprises, transforming the material conditions of social life, but at the same time altering the structure of traditional popular classes: how many artisans, working their way up in industry, were reduced by capitalist concentration to the rank of proletarians?

The peasantry were split up, in the end. The abolition of the ecclesiastical tithe and real feudal rights profited only the land-owning peasants; farmworkers and sharecroppers gained only from the abolition of serfdom and personal feudal rights. The national lands were sold in such a way that peasant property was increased to the advantage of those who already owned land: the *laboureurs*, or big farmers from the regions with large areas of cultivation. In the Nord department from 1789 to 1802, their share of the land rose from 30 to 42 per cent (that of the bourgeoisie rose from 16 to 28 per cent, while the percentage held by the nobility decreased from 22 per cent to 12 per cent, that of the clergy from 20 per cent to 0). From that time on, a powerful minority of proprietary peasants, attached to the new order, rallied around the bourgeoisie in its conservative proposals. In this way is the social work of the French Revolution measured in the countryside, an accomplishment further clarified by comparative study. While the French peasant increased his share of the land, the English peasant, freed from serfdom and feudal obligations from the beginning of modern times, was expropriated in the course of the vast movement of regrouping and enclosure of lands, and was reduced to the ranks of a wage-earning day laborer – free, certainly – but without land. In Central and Eastern Europe, serfdom persisted; the great landowning nobles exploited their lands by means of statute labor owed to them by the peasants. Serfdom was not abolished until 1807 in Prussia, 1848 in Bohemia and Hungary, and 1861 in Russia. And the liberated peasant did not receive any land; the aristocracy maintained its landed privilege until the revolutions of the twentieth century. By comparison, as far as the society resulting from the French Revolution goes, Jaurès was able to speak of "rural democracy."

Upon seizing power in November 1799, Bonaparte declared, "the Revolution is over." He thus assigned an end point to the task of demolishing the Ancien Régime. But it was not in the power of a single man, no matter how brilliant, to change the characteristics of the new society that had already been clearly sketched. The actions of the First Consul, then the Emperor, whatever his evolution may have been, essentially belonged to the line of the revolutionary heritage. The desire for order on the part of both old and new property owners facilitated the stabilization efforts of the Consulate. The social hierarchy was re-established, with the administration reorganized according to the wishes of the "notables"; but control of the government eluded them. In 1814, the Charter allowed them to believe that they would see themselves in power: the aristocratic reaction, once again, contested their claim. In this sense, the Restoration represents the epilogue of the drama. The Revolution in 1789 did not really end until 1830 when, having brought a king to power who accepted their principles, the bourgeoisie took definitive possession of France.[30]

The characteristics that we have just sketched account for the repercussions of the French Revolution and its value as an example in the evolution of the contemporary world. Without a doubt, the armies of the Republic and then of Napoleon knocked down the Ancien Régime in the European countries they occupied, more by force than by ideas. By abolishing serfdom, by freeing the peasants of seigniorial fees and ecclesiastical tithes, by putting in circulation the wealth of *mainmorte*, the French conquest cleared the path for the development of capitalism. If nothing remained of the continental empire that Napoleon had had the ambition to found, it nevertheless destroyed the Ancien Régime everywhere it had time to do so. In this sense, his reign prolonged the Revolution, and he was indeed its soldier, a fact for which the sovereigns of the Ancien Régime never ceased reproaching him.[31]

After Napoleon, the prestige of the Revolution did not vanish. With the passage of time, it appeared both as the daughter of reason and the daughter of enthusiasm. Its memory evoked a powerful emotion, the storming of the Bastille remaining the symbol of popular insurrection and *La Marseillaise* the battle song for liberty and independence. In this sense, the French Revolution indeed has mythical value, in the sense Georges Sorel intended: it seduced the imagination and the heart; announcer of better times, it incited people to action. Beyond this revolutionary romanticism, its ideological attraction was no less powerful; the French Revolution affirms itself as an immense effort to set society on a rational foundation.

The French Revolution is consequently situated in the very heart of the history of the contemporary world, at the crossroads of the diverse social and political currents that divided nations and still divides them. A classical bourgeois revolution, it represented – by the uncompromising abolition of feudalism and the seigniorial regime – the starting point for capitalist society and a liberal representative system in the history of France. A peasant and popular revolution, it tried twice to go beyond its bourgeois limits: in year II an attempt that, despite the inevitable failure, still served for a long time as a prophetic example; and, at the time of the Conspiracy for Equality, an episode that stands at the fertile origin of contemporary revolutionary thought and action. This explains these vain but dangerous efforts to deny the French Revolution its historic reality or its social and national specificity. But this also explains the shaking felt throughout the world and the way the French Revolution still stirs the consciousness of the people of our century.

Tocqueville, in *The Ancien Régime and the Revolution*, recalls the "two principal passions" of the French at the end of the eighteenth century: "one, deeper and coming from farther back, is the violent and inextinguishable hatred of inequality"; "the other, more recent and not so deeply rooted, led them to wish to live not only as equals, but free." That was 1789: "a time of inexperience, without a doubt, but also of generosity, enthusiasm, virility and grandeur, a time of immortal memory, which men will turn to regard with admiration and respect. . . . Thus the French were proud enough of their cause and themselves to believe they could be equal in liberty."

Equality in freedom: an ideal never attained, but always pursued, that never ceases to inflame men's hearts.

NOTES

Source Reprinted in an abridged format from Albert Soboul, *Understanding the French Revolution*, trans. April Ane Knutson (New York: International Publishers, 1988), pp. 274–99.

1 *L'Ancien Régime et la Révolution*, book II, chap. I, ed. 1952, with an introduction by G. Lefebvre, p. 99.

2 *Capital*. vol. III, chap. XX, "Historical view of merchant capital." On the problem of the transition from feudalism to capitalism, cf. *The Transition from Feudalism to Capitalism, A Symposium* by P.M. Sweezy, M. Dobb, H.K. Takahashi, R. Hilton, C. Hill, London, 1954. R. Hilton, "Y eut-il une crise générale de la féodalité?." *Annales, E.S.C.*, 1951. no. 1; G. Procacci. G. Lefebvre and A. Soboul, "Une discussion historique: du feudalisme au capitalisme." *La Pensée*, 1956, no. 65.

3 These are problems posed in particular by G. Lefebvre, "La Révolution française dans l'histoire du monde," *Annales, E.S.C.*, 1948, reprinted in *Etudes sur la Révolution française*, 1954, 2nd edition, 1963, p. 431.

4 The expression *Ancien Régime* appeared at the end of the year 1789; naturally it is charged with emotional content: there is almost a repudiation in this alliance of words (F. Brunot, *Histoire de la Langue française*, vol IX, *La Révolution et l'Empire*, p. 621). The expression, consecrated by its use, is historically valid; we understand poorly the obscure reasons why certain historians currently are tending to reject it.

5 On the problems of the French nobility in the eighteenth century, we will content ourselves with citing one old article: M. Bloch, "Sur le passé de la noblesse française: quelques jalons de recherche," *Annales d'histoire économique et sociale*, 1936, p. 336; and a recent article: A. Goodwin, "The Social Structure and Economic and Political Attitudes of the French Nobility in the Eighteenth Century;" International Committee of Historical Sciences, XII Congress, Vienna, 1965, *Rapports. I. Grands thèmes*, p. 356; by the same author, "General Problems and the Diversity of European Nobilities in the Modern Period," *ibid.*, p. 345. We refer to the critical bibliography of J. Meyer. *La Noblesse bretonne au XVIII*e *siècle*, Paris, 1966, vol. I, P. XXI.

6 See B. Mousnier, "Les Idées politiques de Fénelon," *XVII*e *siècle*, 1951–52.

7 Boulainvilliers (1658–1722), *Histoire de l'ancien gouvernement de la France, avec XIV lettres historiques sur les parlements ou Etats généraux* (1722), *Essai sur la noblesse de France contenant une dissertation sur son origine et son abaissement* (1732).

8 *Le Judicium Francorum* reprints an anti-absolutist pamphlet from the time of the Fronde, *Les vertiables maximes du gouvernement de la*

France justifiées par l'ordre des temps depuis l'établissement de la monarchie jusqu' aux temps présents (1652). See also, in the same line, a writing circulated in manuscript copies, *Essai historique concernant les droits et prérogatives de la Cour des pairs de France.*

9   See basically book XXX. Cf. L. Althusser, *Montesquieu. La politique et l'histoire*, 1959.

10 We can only refer here to general works: J. Aynard, *La bourgeoisie française*, 1934; B. Groethuysen, *Origines de l'esprit bourgeois en France*, vol. I: *L'Eglise et la Bourgeoisie*, 1927; F. Borkenau, *Der Uebergang vom feudalen zum burgerlichen Weltbild. Studien zur Geschichte der Philosophie der Manufakturperiode*, 1934; see the remarks of L. Febvre, "Fondations économiques. Superstructure philosophique: une synthèse," *Annales d'histoire économique et sociale*, 1934, p. 369. Of precise documentary interest are the studies relating to the bourgeoisie in *Assemblée générale de la Commission centrale . . .*, 1939. Commission d'histoire économique et sociale de la Révolution, 1942, vol. I. p. 33; P. Léon, "Recherches sur la bourgeoisie française de province au XVIIIe siecle," *L'Information historique*, 1958, no.3. p. 101. On the current orientation of research, E. Labrousse, "Voies nouvelles vers une histoire de la bourgeoisie occidentale aux XVIIIe et XIXe siècles," *X Congresso internazionale di scienze storiche . . . 1955. Relazionei*, Florence, 1955, vol. IV, p. 365.

11 On natural right, an ample bibliography will be found in R. Derathé, *Jean-Jacques Rousseau et la Science politique de son temps*. Paris, 1950. Natural right was developed in the seventeenth century by Protestant authors, principally jurists – Grotius, Althusius, Hobbes, Pufendorf – certain of whom were then translated and commented on by Barbeyrac et Burlamaqui. The authors of the seventeenth century were criticized by Rousseau who drew the logical consequences from natural right, by formulating the theory of inalienable and indivisible popular sovereignty.

12 See J. Egret. "L'Aristocratie parlementaire à la fin de l'Ancien Régime," *Revue historique*, July–September 1952, p. 1. Essential are the works of J.-Fr. Bluche, *L'Origine des magistrats du Parlement de Paris au XVIIIe siècle*, 1956, *Les magistrats du Parlement de Paris au XVIIIe siècle, 1715–1771*, 1960.

13 *Qu'est-ce que le Tiers Etat?* by Em. Sieyes, critical edition by Ed. Champion, Paris, 1888, p. 35.

14 *Oeuvres de Barnave*, published by M. Bérenger de la Drôme, 1843, vol. I, p. 12 and p. 13. The *Introduction à la Revolution française* has been republished by F. Rude, Paris, 1960. In fact, this important text is still awaiting a critical edition. Having forcefully affirmed the necessary connection between political institutions and the movement of the economy, Barnave attaches to it the educational movement, "To the degree that the arts, industry and commerce enrich the laboring class of people, impoverish the great landowners and bring the classes closer together by fortune, the progress in education brings them closer by custom and recalls, after a long oblivion, the primitive ideas of equality."

41

15 The important problem of repurchase of feudal rights and of their abolition has been definitively tackled by Ph. Sagnac, *La Législation civile de la Révolution française*, 1898; in a still valuable sketch, A. Aulard, *La Révolution française et le Régime féodal*, 1919; M. Garaud, *La Révolution et la Propriété foncière*, 1959. But only local or regional monographs would permit the drawing up of a true and complete picture of the partial survival, the vicissitudes and the final disappearance of the feudal regime during the Revolution: let us indicate two classical works, A. Ferradou, *Le Rachat des droits féodaux dans la Gironde. 1790– 1793*, 1928: J. Millot, *L'Abolition des droits seigneuriaux, dans le département du Doubs et la région comtoiśe*, 1941. Likewise, on the agrarian riots and the jacqueries which, from the Great Fear to the definitive abolition of feudal rights (1793 July 17), marked the revolutionary history of the peasantry, we have only fragmentary local studies at our disposal. This history remains to be written.

16 C.-E. Labrousse, *Esquisse du mouvement des prix et des revenus en France au XVIIIe siècle*, Paris, 1933, 2 vol.; *La Crise de l'économie française à la fin de l'Ancien Régime et au début de la Révolution*, Paris, 1944.

17 On the social aspirations of the popular masses, see A. Soboul, *Les sans-culottes parisiens en l'an II*, Paris, 1958, part II, chap. 2.

18 On the peasant question, the works of Georges Lefebvre are essential: *Les Paysans du Nord pendant la Révolution française*, 1924. *Questions agraires au temps de la Terreur*, 1932, *La Grande Peur de 1789*, 1932, and the articles appearing and regrouped in *Etudes sur la Révolution française*, 1954, 2nd edition, 1967; "Répartition de la propriété et de l'exploitation foncières à la fin de l'Ancien Régime," 1928, p. 279; "La Vente des biens nationaux," 1928, p. 307; "La Révolution française et les Paysans," 1932, p. 338.

19 *Op. Cit.*, p. 99, "The effect of the Revolution has not been to divide the soil but to liberate it for a moment. All the small landowners were, in effect, severely hampered in the exploitation of their lands and endured many constraints that they were not allowed to deliver themselves from." (p. 102) "If the peasant had not owned the soil, he would have been insensitive to several of the burdens that the feudal system laid on landed property. Of what importance was the tithe to one who was not a farmer? It was imposed on the product of cultivation" (p. 105).

20 M. Leymarie, "Les Redevances foncières seigneuriales en Haute-Auvergne," *Annales historiques de la Révolution française*, 1968, no. 3.

21 *L'Ancien Régime et la Révolution*, p. 106.

22 G. Lefebvre, "Répartition de la propriété et de l'exploitation foncières à la fin de l'Ancien Régime".

23 The petition of the Parisian section of Sans-Culottes of 2 September 1793 intended to not only limit "the profits of industry and commerce" by general price controls, and limit the extent of agricultural exploitations ("Let no one be able to hold more land to rent than what is needed for a determined quantity of plows"), but to also impose a maximum on wealth. What would it be? The petition does

not specify, but makes it clear that it would correspond to the small artisan and shopkeeper property: "Let no one have more than one workshop, or one shop." These radical measures, concludes the Sans-Culottes section, "would make the too great inequality of wealth disappear gradually and increase the number of property owners" (*Bibliothèque nationale*, Lb 40 2140, imp. in-8°, 6 p.).

24 *L'Ancien Régime et la Révolution*, p. 96.

25 On the theoretical aspects of these problems, see M. Dobb, *Studies in the Development of Capitalism*, London, 1946. H.K. Takahashi, *Shimin Kakumei-no kozó* [Structure of the bourgeois revolution], Tokyo, 1951, reviewed by Ch. Haguenauer, *Revue historique*, no. 434, 1955, p. 345.

26 We must however stress the progress of the economy in the course of the Napoleonic period which was tightly bound to the revolutionary period. See E. Labrousse, "Le Bilan du monde en 1815. Eléments d'un bilan economique la croissance dans la guerre." Comité international des sciences historiques, XIIth Congress, Vienna, 1965. *Rapports I Grands thèmes*, p. 473.

27 *Adresse présentée à la Convention nationale au nom de la section des Gravilliers*, by J. Roux (Archives nationales, W 20, d. 1073, imp in-8°, p. 12).

28 On this problem in its totality, see A. Soboul, "De l'Ancien Régime à l'empire problème nationale et réalités sociales." *L'Information historique*, 1960, pp. 59–64 and 96–104.

29 *Moniteur*, vol. VI, p. 239.

30 See above for the comparison that must be established between the French Revolution of 1830 and the "respectable" English Revolution of 1688. Both ended up replacing one king with another, without attacking the social structure in any way. In July, 1830, it was a matter of a sort of legal insurrection punishing the violation of the Charter. But the fundamental difference to which the Anglo-Saxons are especially sensitive, is that the Revolution of 1688 was "respectable" because it was provoked by the leaders of the social hierarchy and carried out without the intervention of the popular masses. In France, Charles X was expelled not by a William of Orange, but by the people of Paris, armed behind barricades. See in this line the review by G. Lefebvre, in the *Annales historiques de la Révolution française*, 1955, p. 176 of the book by L. Pinkham. *William III and the Respectable Revolution*. Cambridge, Mass., 1954.

31 *Lendemains*, no. 12, November, 1978.

2

NOBLES, BOURGEOIS, AND THE ORIGINS OF THE FRENCH REVOLUTION*

Colin Lucas

This 1973 article by a then relatively young Oxford professor quickly became one of the most important weapons in the Revisionist arsenal – and its author went on to become Master of Oxford's Balliol College. The reason for its success lies in its bold attack upon the Marxist view of the Revolution as characterized by a class struggle between an ascending bourgeoisie and ossified nobility. Using an array of empirical evidence, Lucas shows that by the end of the Ancien Régime, the bourgeoisie and the nobility were both part of a "homogenous" ruling élite. Lucas shows that by this time privileges that were once perhaps monopolized by the nobility had become shared between the two groups. Lucas finds many bourgeois commoners who were privileged from taxes, who acted as lay seigneurs on landed estates, and who added the particl2 "de" to their name. In short, he finds bourgeois everywhere whose authorities overlapped with noblemen, and whose lifestyle imitated noblemen – indeed, bourgeois who were even confused by contemporaries as noblemen.

But such an analysis, however novel and challenging, begs the question of why the Revolution occurred in the first place. If an embittered bourgeoisie did not cause the Revolution, who did? The last part of the article deals with this fundamental question, in which Lucas proposes what might be called a non-Marxist class analysis: the political crisis from 1786–88 convinced the sector of privileged bourgeois commoners that their social pathway to full landed noble status was now being barred, and that Ancien Régime social structure was about to become much more closed. The fear of being shut out, rather than any kind of revolutionary class consciousness or genuine class difference, is what in the end motivated them to revolt.

After almost twenty-five years, Lucas's remarkable article continues to stimulate much debate among historians because of its imaginative web of social and political analysis.

* * *

Once upon a time, the historians of the French Revolution labored fraternally in the vineyards of the past. They were united in simple yet satisfying beliefs. In the eighteenth century, the French bourgeoisie had become aware of the increasing disparity between its wealth and social usefulness, on the one hand, and its social prestige and opportunities, on the other. Its way was blocked and recognition of its worth denied by a decaying class of parasitic, hereditarily privileged, noble landowners. Its vitality was further jeopardized by a monarchy not only committed to antiquated aristocratic values, but also incapable of giving the country that firm yet benignly restrained direction under which the initiative of men of business might flourish. The conflict of these elements produced the French Revolution. It was, furthermore, a deeper conflict between the progressive capitalist-orientated classes and the retrograde aristocratic classes. The French Revolution was won by the bourgeoisie, despite some interference from below, thus establishing the framework for the emergence of the capitalist economy and a class society and – *eureka* – the modern world. This, in capsule form, was the interpretation of the revolutionary crisis of the late eighteenth century favoured by the great authorities of the first half of this century from Jaurès to Soboul, each one giving to it a more or less explicitly Marxist tone according to his personal convictions.[1] But Marxist or non-Marxist, we were all united in the belief that we could not escape this groundswell of history.

This interpretation has been the subject of increasing debate among Anglo-Saxon historians ever since the publication in 1964 of the attack launched upon it by the late Professor Cobban in his Wiles Lectures of 1962.[2] A parallel, though apparently unrelated, debate has also been developing in France, where Monsieur Furet and Monsieur Richet in particular have been attempting to elaborate a more theoretical schema than Cobban's yet on basically the same lines.[3] Cobban's essential contribution to the historiography of the French Revolution was to question the notion of the bourgeoisie as a capitalist or even proto-capitalist class. He thereby questioned the whole nature of the Revolution. Cobban was a brilliant polemicist and his book displays both the qualities and the defects of this type of writing. He had an unerring eye for the weaknesses in the arguments of others; but they tended to capture his attention to the exclusion of all other considerations. His book, therefore, remained a very piecemeal affair, concerned primarily with destroying what he took, rightly or wrongly, to be a number of commonly accepted fallacies with only a relatively loose thread connecting them. Cobban made no attempt to produce any systematic construction to replace the whole edifice of interpretation, which he was very conscious of having undermined.[4] At most, he carved a few stones for a new façade. Thus, for example, he proposed a new definition of the revolutionary bourgeoisie, which he saw as a declining class of venal officeholders, yet he did not attempt to work out the structure of social conflict implied in such a view. He presumably believed this group to be but one element of the Ancien Régime bourgeoisie and he also suggested that the nature of the bourgeoisie was altered during the Revolution, yet he did not try to examine what the bourgeoisie was before the Revolution nor what the relationship was between the various component parts that he perceived. Above all, Cobban does not seem to have questioned the notion that a noble-bourgeois class conflict was the fundamental element in the genesis of the Revolution. He merely sought to alter one part of that proposition. In this sense, therefore, he retained a class interpretation of the French Revolution which did not stray too far from the classic mould.

Nevertheless, Cobban's remarks on the nature of the revolutionary bourgeoisie, together with Professor Taylor's fundamental work on French capitalism in the eighteenth century, have in fact brought into question the whole schema of the Revolution as the product of a conflict between nobles and bourgeois, as Taylor himself has pointed out.[5] For such an interpretation is necessarily based on the premise that there existed in eighteenth-century France two distinct and antagonistic classes of bourgeois and nobles. If, however, in our attempt to define the eighteenth-century bourgeoisie we can discover no such clear division, then it becomes extremely difficult to define a class conflict. But, in that case, we have to decide why, in 1788–89, groups which can be identified as non-noble combatted and defeated groups which can be identified as noble, thereby laying the foundations of the political system of the nineteenth-century bourgeoisie; and why they attacked and destroyed privilege in 1789, thereby destroying the formal organization of eighteenth-century French society and preparing a structure within which the socio-economic developments of the nineteenth century might blossom.

The orthodox approach to the upper strata of eighteenth-century French society has always been to stress exclusively the elements of disparity and division within them and to split them into two clearly defined and clearly antagonistic classes of nobles and bourgeois. Such an approach ignores all the elements that conferred on these strata a degree of homogeneity in some important respects. We may understand this without difficulty if, instead of peering so closely at the top of society, we stand back and attempt to view it as a whole. Whatever the distinctions and whatever the striking differences in wealth levels inside these strata, they achieved a certain common identity as a minority with disproportionate wealth in relation to the mass of poor Frenchmen. The primary articulation in Ancien Régime society was not the distinction between the privileged and the Third Estate; rather, it was between those for whom manual labour provided their livelihood and those for whom it did not.[6] Clearly, this division, in common with all those in this society, was neither rigid nor absolute. It did not have the character of a boundary, but more that of a frontier with its attendant no-man's-land formed by transitional categories. The inhabitants of this zone were the artisans – the sans-culottes in Paris – the degree of whose penetration into the ranks of the lesser bourgeoisie can be determined by the extent to which trading activity had become preponderant in the combination of trade and manual production which characterized their state.[7] Moreover, some trades were more prestigious than others, either inherently so or because of local factors, and allowed those who exercised them to reconcile status with manual labour more easily than in the majority of cases.[8] For example, those engaged on luxury articles, such as the goldsmiths (*orfèvres*) or the wig-makers (*perruquiers*), derived status either from the value of their raw material or from the nature of their clientele.[9] This was a highly permeable frontier: the passport was basically the acquisition of a modest capital.[10]

There was, then, an important and real sense in which all levels of the bourgeoisie and nobility attained in very general terms a community of interest in face of the vulgar mechanic classes and of the vile and abject poor.[11] At the other end of the scale, the apparent simplicity of the distinction between privileged and unprivileged is misleading. In reality no such absolute, horizontal division existed. Certainly trade was definitely inferior; certainly the hereditary noble was evidently superior. But between the two the permutations, the nuances, the ambiguities were infinite. The pursuit of ennoblement remained a realistic enterprise for the bourgeoisie of the eighteenth century.[12] The king continued to concede Letters of Nobility to honorable, successful and well-connected men.[13] Venal offices which carried nobility – particularly the office of *secrétaire du roi*, certain judicial posts, and municipal office in nineteen towns – could be purchased throughout the century. Privilege, which, in its origin, was the most tangible expression of noble social superiority, had long since been infiltrated by non-nobles. Fiscal exemption, the commonest form of privilege, could be acquired without particular difficulty by men of substance and even, in a partial way, by men of very little substance.[14] On the other hand, the eighteenth-century noble always paid some taxes – more indeed than the wealthy bourgeois of certain towns favored by a history of bargains with the Crown – while, in practice, rich commoners benefited as much as nobles from the complaisance, deference or laxity of administrators and collectors of taxes.[15] Similarly, seigneurial rights were certainly not restricted to the nobility. They had become a merchandise possibly more readily obtainable than venal office. Fiefs and rights had been divided, subdivided, and shared out to such an extent that in some places it was impossible to know their origin. In 1781, 22 per cent of the lay seigneurs in the *Election* of Le Mans were non-nobles.[16] Just before the Revolution, the Duc de Chaulnes sold his seigneury and viscounty of Amiens to a certain Colmar, a Jew and therefore definitely not noble, while the Polignacs' alienation of their seigneuries in the Velay around the beginning of the century was a veritable godsend for the socially ambitious wealthy of that region.[17] In sum, between the privileged noble and the unprivileged commoner stood an important transitional category of indeterminate social mutants. They were neither nobles nor commoners. Indeed, almost everywhere except in Normandy, the appellation "noble" really meant a superior sort of non-noble; hence the birth certificate of the future Director

Larevellière-Lépeaux stated that he was the son of "nobleman Jean-Baptiste de la Revellière, bourgeois of the town of Angers".[18] How noble was a man whose office conferred on him personal nobility but who had not yet served the twenty years necessary to obtain the *lettres d'honneur* which declared that nobility now hereditary in the family?[19] Was a man privileged or not when he possessed a fief, where he paid no taxes and levied seigneurial dues, and also non-noble land, where he paid both taxes and dues? Of course, it had been stated as early as the Ordinance of Blois (1579) that possession of a fief in no way made a man noble. But, when taken with a certain lifestyle and other similar attributes, it was an important element in helping to make a man appear noble. And in social promotion in this period, appearances were the first step towards reality. In the 1780s an authority on jurisprudence complained that the usurpation of rank had got quite out of hand with men ennobled (*anoblis*) styling themselves in a manner reserved to lords of early fifteenth-century extraction, and commoners of good standing having themselves addressed as *marquis, comte, vicomte,* or *baron,* and even passing themselves off as such in legal documents.[20] More modest, but more commonplace, were the eighteenth-century families which had added the particle to their name,[21] and had acquired over a number of generations a surreptitious accumulation of partial recognitions of privileged status which allowed them to establish as a fact exemptions and privileges to which they had no real documented right. Provided that such a family was of some wealth, conformed to the standards of noble behavior, and married advantageously, it was sufficient for its members to claim indefatigably enough and for long enough a customary privileged position in order to obtain ultimately the Intendant's tacit acquiescence to their inclusion in some list of privileged persons, thus achieving irrefutable evidence of privileged status. A sustained effort of this kind by succeeding generations could finally be crowned either by the grant of Letters of Nobility or by an official decision ratifying explicitly or implicitly a claim to nobility.[22]

Jaurès sought to explain these anomalies as "a hybrid social force at the junction of the Ancien Régime and the new capitalism."[23] Obviously, such an interpretation alone was capable of safeguarding the concept of two distinct and antagonistic classes. In fact, however, it does not seem possible to discern a fundamental cleavage at this time between the bourgeoisie and the nobility. The middle class of the late Ancien Régime displayed no significant functional differences from the nobility, no significant difference in accepted values and above all no consciousness of belonging to a class whose economic and social characteristics were antithetical to those of the nobility.[24] The commercial middle class of France at this time was not capitalist in one vital respect. The business of making money was subordinated to a non-capitalist social ideal, and social classifications and values did not depend upon a notion of productive force. The middle class accepted really without debate aristocratic values and sought to gain social approval by adhering to these standards. Social promotion required the abandonment of trade as soon as was financially possible. The consistent pattern of the eighteenth century, as of the seventeenth, was that commercial families placed their capital in land, in government and private annuities (*rentes*), and in venal office, all of which gave returns on investment in the order of 2 to 4 per cent, instead of seeking the higher returns on commercial investment.[25] These men were dominated by the social motive, not by the capitalist profit motive. They accepted that trade was by definition ignoble and dishonorable. If the corn merchant speculated on the misery of the times or if the cloth merchant risked his all in the chance of large profits from army contracts, it was in order that their progeny might the more quickly retreat into the social respectability of professional status and that, hopefully, they might themselves retire to live the life of noble idleness on revenues from land, government stock, and private loans.[26] Thus, in economic terms, nobles and bourgeois resembled each other to the extent that both sought to secure the greater part of their fortune in non-capitalist forms; at the same time, nobles indulged quite as much as wealthy commoners in proto-capitalist industrial and financial activities.[27] It seems difficult to perceive here the representatives of significantly different stages "in a complex set of socio-economic relationships, the one feudal, the other capitalist".[28] Such fundamental divisions and their ensuing antagonisms did not properly begin to appear in France until the nineteenth century, possibly during the reign of Louis-Philippe, and even then the socio-economic pattern described in this paragraph remained predominant among the entrepreneurial group.[29]

Hence, in the upper reaches of French society the great articulation was not between noble and commoner which, as I have tried to show, is an almost impossible division to demonstrate. It was between those who traded and those who did not. Of course, this dividing line, like all the others in this society, was neither absolute nor drawn horizontally across society. Each family made its own calculation of the amount of fortune necessary before severing its connection with the generating source of wealth in trade.[30] In the few great cities and seaports, with their opportunities for massive accumulation of wealth, oligarchies of trading families appeared, of such great wealth that social respect and even noble status could not be denied them.[31] Clearly, such men may be adduced as evidence of a capitalist haute-bourgeoisie in the classic sense; but the extent to which their careers are typical of the middle class as a whole is highly debatable and we shall refer later in this essay to other senses in which their situation may have been significant in the structure of this society. Moreover, in most cases, despite having been able to rise so high socially while in trade, even they quickly sought to take root among the landed nobility and retreated behind the discretion of intermediaries if they continued their business interests.[32]

In general it would appear true to say that above this frontier of trade – and always provided the possession of a level of wealth sufficient not to live meanly – there stood an élite whose internal distinctions could not destroy a common identity between its component elements.[33] It was united, in the first place, by its control of landed property, both directly as the landowning class and indirectly through the exercise of seigneurial rights. In the second place, the tangible manifestations of social superiority – essentially fiscal and seigneurial privilege – were becoming increasingly accessible during the century to the majority of its members without regard to their nobility or lack of it. This is very clearly the message of the difficulties which one encounters in trying to distinguish between noble and rich commoner. The third major element of unity is that *in origin* the nobility of the late eighteenth century was no different from those members of the élite who had not yet achieved noble rank. Already in 1660 an observer estimated that hardly 5 per cent of noble families could trace their lineage back to the medieval feudal age.[34] The great majority of the nobility of France dated from the sixteenth, seventeenth, and eighteenth centuries.[35] They were the product of that very same patient acquisition of social pre-eminence upon which the non-noble élite of the later eighteenth century was so ardently engaged.[36] Most of the élite shared a common origin in that, in the first instance, it was some measure of wealth which had given them access to land and office.[37] From that base, there began the slow ascension through the devious channels of a careful accumulation and permutation of a succession of progressively prestigious offices, of advantageous marriage alliances, of inheritances, and so on.[38]

What I have said does not necessarily deny the existence of a "middle class" that was within the élite and that did not merely consist of the trading elements – these latter both stood outside the élite and played little direct part in the genesis of the Revolution. But until considerably more detailed research which does not postulate a "bourgeoisie" separate from and in contradiction with the élite has been accomplished, it is difficult to define it exactly. Above all, one may debate whether such a definition would be of major significance when there is little evidence that it possessed either a "class consciousness" or an alternative social structure. This argument does, however, deny the notion of two clearly defined and clearly antagonistic classes of nobles and bourgeois in eighteenth-century France and therefore denies the existence of a class conflict in the classic sense. It does not deny – and is not intended to deny – the existence of very real distinctions, divisions and antagonisms within this élite. Nor does it deny the existence of a social crisis, for, as H.R. Trevor-Roper remarked in quite a different context, "social crises are caused not by the clear-cut opposition of mutually exclusive interests but by the tug-of-war of opposite interests *within one body*".[39] It is quite wrong to consider that the upper reaches of late Ancien Régime society were static and decaying. Any analysis confined to only a few decades will inevitably project a static image unless that period be one of actual crisis or revolution. A wider context of a couple of centuries suggests that, on the contrary, this élite was the product of a process of evolution and that it was still evolving.

It is evident from the preceding pages that the nature of the nobility had been undergoing tremendous change since the end of the fifteenth century. Indeed, the historian of the later Valois would not find unfamiliar our description of the ambiguity of the frontier between nobles and commoners, with its references to the escape from trade, venal office, usurpation, the adoption of the particle, ennoblement, and the purchase of fiefs, of elements of privilege, and of nobility itself. Noble complaints about the debasement of their estate sound very much the same whether written in the 1780s or the 1580s. The combined action of three major factors seems to have been responsible for this development: first, the financial difficulties of the late medieval and Renaissance nobility; second, the attempts of the emergent absolute monarchs to secure their power upon a service nobility; third, the financial difficulties of these monarchs which prompted them to abandon ennobling offices into the possession of their incumbents and subsequently to resort to the downright sale of privileges and offices. The great period of the transformation of the élite was unquestionably the seventeenth century. It was in this period that the monarchy expanded its power and the business of its government enormously, and thus multiplied its officials and the machinery for the enforcement of its will; it was also the period when a great series of wars, undertaken on an unprecedented scale and in a time of economic instability, obliged the monarch to exploit office and privilege for revenue purposes.[40] This double process, reaching its apogee under Louis XIV, accelerated the infiltration of the nobility by wealthy commoners which had been taking place during the sixteenth century. More important perhaps, by encouraging its generalization, it finally rendered irrevocable the sixteenth-century encroachment on characteristically noble attributes by wealthy non-nobles.[41] Louis XIV in particular exploited every financial opportunity provided by office and privilege.[42] He even resorted several times to the direct sale of nobility, whereas neither of the eighteenth-century kings did more than sell the confirmation of nobility acquired in the normal ways. His extensive warfaring allowed commoners to enter the officer corps in relatively large numbers.[43] A man with wits enough to discover profit in the ruins of the economy and intelligence enough to further the extension of royal power could rise rapidly. In this sense, we may restore a dimension to Saint-Simon's much abused description of the Sun King's rule as the "reign of the vile bourgeoisie." Early in the seventeenth century, the famous jurist and political theorist Loyseau still based his work on the concept of a society divided into three separate estates. In the last decade of that same century the theorist Domat, whose writings influenced jurists for the next ninety years, was dividing society on a functional basis: the first rank, with honor, dignity, and authority, he accorded to the prelates, high magistrates, and military commanders; and in the second rank, endowed with honor but not dignity, he placed without differentiation – and this is significant in the context of this essay – the *avocats*, the doctors, the members of the liberal and scientific professions generally and also the "gentlemen" (*gentilhommes*).[44]

This, then, had been the heyday of social promotion and, as a result, not merely was the composition of the nobility altered but also its traditional attributes diffused and its traditional functions adulterated. The situation in the later eighteenth century was simply the development of conditions already apparent in the second half of the seventeenth.[45] By the end of the Ancien Régime, the distinction between the Robe nobility and the Sword nobility, which had appeared so vital during the preceding two centuries, had become largely meaningless. Similar lifestyles, intermarriage, the parallel pursuit of military, judicial and administrative careers by the different sons of the same Sword or Robe family had abolished the distinction.[46] Some old provincial nobles still attached a significance of prestige to the profession of arms, but found rich commoners among their brother officers for most of the century. After 1750 the most important distinction inside the nobility was that between the men of noble descent (*noblesse de race*) and those ennobled (*anoblis*). But since, as we have seen, the vast majority of noble families had originally been ennobled, noble "purity" was essentially a biological question of survival while successive generations of nobles left the family origins behind. With all other things being equal, the *anobli* family of the sixteenth century was, in 1780, more prestigious than that of the seventeenth century, which was in turn more prestigious than that of the eighteenth century.[47]

But all these distinctions, by whose shifting complexities Frenchmen sought to keep abreast of social evolution, mask from us as they did from contemporaries the fact that the fundamental effect of these changes was to alter nobility over a long period of time from being the expression of certain hereditary virtues to being the crude expression of great wealth and powerful connections.[48] At the end of the Ancien Régime this evolution was not complete, it was only implied. There existed a hybrid situation in which men sought to express complex social realities in symbols and language whose connotations referred to a qualitatively different structure.[49] The tension of the later eighteenth century was produced in no small measure by a problem of definition and perception. Frenchmen still accepted that nobility was the purest expression of social superiority. They accepted, as the medieval world had accepted, that it reflected virtue. Echoing three centuries of noble spokesmen, not to mention such figures as Boileau and La Bruyère, one obscure Poitevin count began his memoirs in the 1790s with the statement that "the titles of nobility contain no merit unless they reside upon virtue without which they can only be considered as useless baubles".[50] But ever since the sixteenth century they had debated what was this virtue, testifying by their debate to the presence of the evolutionary trend. [51] By the eighteenth century, the notion of virtue had clearly been extended to include both the chivalric concept of "without fear and without reproach" and also the notion of great political, administrative, diplomatic, and judicial talents such as render signal service to the honor and power of the monarch. Much of the debate continued to revolve, as it always had done, around the degree to which such forms of virtue were hereditary or due to environment and education, that is to say whether nobility was in the blood or in the mind.[52] Most writers sought some compromise to accommodate both. But, as the century wore on, a new notion of virtue came to challenge these and to change the nature of the debate, thus reflecting more accurately the increasing departure of the élite from its old standards and its old composition. This was a notion culled by the highly educated professional groups from their reading of the Latin authors such as Cicero, Livy, Sallust, and Tacitus, upon whom the eighteenth-century schools laid increasing emphasis.[53] It was the Roman Republican definition of virtue as civic virtue – the interest in, the care for, and the adeptness at the defence of the *res publica*. This radical notion implying that nobility belonged only to those capable of administering, and by extension ultimately of ruling, looked forward in a real sense to the Revolution. The Montagnard Laignelot was to exclaim in 1793: "Virtue is simply the love of the Republic: the Romans were great only because they were virtuous."[54]

[*In the next section, Lucas argues that while French society did not exhibit a classic class conflict between nobility and bourgeoisie, it did experience "stress zones" of genuine social conflict. Such zones included urban landowners, military officers, and administrative office holders. Here social mobility may have lessened during the 1780s, producing a social crisis that led to the Revolution.*]

Should one, therefore, agree with one recent historian in seeing the outbreak of revolution in France as essentially a political event?[55] In this context, the importance of the decision by the Parlement of Paris in September 1788 (largely endorsed by the second Assembly of Notables) that the Estates-General should meet in its form of 1614, has never been ignored.[56] But the nature of its significance has not perhaps always been exactly recognized. This decision polarized the component elements of the élite and crystalized their latent tensions by reintroducing from the early seventeenth century concepts of French society which, already obsolescent at that time, were by now totally erroneous.[57] The conditions demanded for entry into the noble electoral assemblies were far more rigorous than any that had been imposed for noble gatherings and lists during the preceding century.[58] The electoral procedure thus took on the aspect of a seventeenth-century type inquiry into nobility. The frontier between noble and non-noble, which had been of diminishing importance, was suddenly and artificially reimposed. The decision to separate the nobility from the Third Estate pushed the central and lower echelons of the élite down into the Third Estate. It rent asunder what was essentially by now a homogeneous social unit, and identified quite gratuitously a section of that unit as irremediably inferior and to be confused not merely with the trading classes but also with the manual laborers and the vile and abject poor. It is in this context that one must understand the apparent paradox of the fact that the leading voices at the national level against this decision in late 1788 were those of "liberal" nobles.[59] As far as those who were directly affected by these measures are concerned, it needs no temerity to suggest that the *anobli* Le Chapelier, for instance, discovered his revolutionary vocation when he was excluded, despite his bitter protests, from the electoral assembly of the Breton nobility.[60] But, in general, the position of the *anobli* was naturally somewhat ambivalent. It was men further down in the channels of promotion who reacted most categorically to the situation. At Rennes, to use examples from Brittany again, it was the *procureurs* of the *Présidial* who led the attack on the oligarchy of *anoblis* in the Municipality for refusing to endorse a demand for vote by head, and it was the *avocats* who organized the electoral campaign there, while at Saint-Malo and in most of the other Breton towns except Nantes the professional groups again took the initiative in the agitation.[61] This was the situation in most of France. In Provence, however, although the same direct effects of the decisions relating to the calling of the Estates-General are visible, the situation was somewhat different in that the polarization was already well under way by this time.[62] But, at root, a similar catalyst had operated, for the conflict took shape in the debate during the later months of 1787 over whether the provincial Estates of Provence should be re-established in the form of their last meeting in 1639, a debate which the Third Estate lost. Once again, the lawyers had taken a leading part and continued to do so in 1788.

It was their experience of problems in social promotion which rendered many of the people thus implicitly demoted by the Parlement's decision so sensitive to such distinctions.[63] This helps to explain why the traditional liberal professions provided so many of the leaders of the Third Estate movement at the local level during the winter of 1788–9. This decision was all the more critical because it seemed to arbitrate definitively between two contradictory trends in recent comparable situations: it was all the more of a shock because the Estates-General were supremely more important than any of those situations and because this decision ran counter to the conceptions which the government had apparently been favoring. In 1787, following an earlier experiment by Necker in the Berry and a plan submitted to the Assembly of Notables by Calonne, Loménie de Brienne had established a three-tier structure of municipal, intermediary, and provincial assemblies to handle some aspects of local government.[64] Although a proportion of seats in all these bodies was reserved to the privileged orders, the system called for elections to the lowest assembly among the men of property on a tax franchise and for each assembly to designate to the one above it. Above all, there was to be no distinction by Order, voting was to be by head, and the Third Estate had double representation. Moreover, the events at Vizille in the Dauphiné in July 1788 seemed to confirm this trend towards the unity of an élite of comfortable men of property. On the other hand, the decision of September 1788 echoed the most exclusive and antiquated formulas of representation which the government had conceded, by omission at least, to the renewed Estates of Provence. Together these two events, reinforced in December 1788 by the widely read and extremely reactionary *Mémoire des Princes présenté au roi*, could appear as the final implementation of a threat long expressed. We do not yet possess a close study of the disputes between nobles and commoners during the years preceding the Revolution. But it is possible to argue that they usually arose because the nobleman acted in such a way as to suggest not merely that the respectable commoner was inferior socially, which in relative terms within the élite he obviously was, but that he was on a par with the vulgar mass. The nobleman who insisted on his precedence in church would certainly mortify the pride of the well-to-do commoner; but the nobleman who thrashed the son of a bourgeois was treating him as he would treat a domestic servant or a street porter – it was even worse when he had the job done for him by his lackeys.[65] This is of course an extreme example. The propagandists of the Third Estate in Brittany still remembered the reception of the demand formulated ten years previously that the provincial Estates authorize commoners to be admitted to the charitable institution for poor gentlemen, which they indeed had helped to subsidize.[66] "What, do they not have the poorhouses (*hôpitaux*), the workhouses (*maisons de force*), and the prisons?" a nobleman had inquired, thereby implicitly excluding all commoners from the élite and consigning them without distinction to those institutions which catered not merely for the honest though humble poor, but also for the vagabonds and beggars who stood outside society altogether. Of course, all this was very tame when compared with noble behaviour during the previous two centuries.[67] It is significant of the changing situation of the commoner elements of the élite that their sensitivity to this kind of attitude should have been such as to make them often the aggressors in violent quarrels.

This, then, was what Mallet du Pan was expressing in his oft-quoted observation – "The nature of the debate has completely changed. King, despotism, and constitution are now very secondary questions; the war is between the Third Estate and the other two Orders."[68] In this sense, the doubling of the representation of the *Tiers* was a wholly irrelevant concession. The revolt of the Third Estate was a revolt against a loss of status by the central and lower sections of the élite with the approval of those elements of the trading groups which were on the threshold of the élite. It was this social group which became the "revolutionary bourgeoisie." The abbé Sieyes became such an influential personality because he expressed precisely their aspirations.[69] Under the rhetoric of his most celebrated pamphlet, *Qu'est-ce que le Tiers-état?* he was not in fact pressing the social and political claims of all those he defined as the Third Estate in the first chapter, but only those of the group which he called "the available classes of the Third Estate."[70] In all his political writings, Sieyes conceived of society as composed essentially of two peoples, the property owners and the "work machines," and demanded the union of the property owners in defence of property against the poor. He militated against the privileged orders because their existence prevented that union; from the beginning to the end of the Revolution he extolled the notables as a homogeneous social and political élite. In 1789, the system of elections served this revolt for, whereas the direct election procedure for the First and Second Estates produced a faithful reflection of the stress zones within them, the indirect elections of the Third Estate not only eliminated the non-élite groups (and therefore the stress zones that their relations with the élite constituted), but also brought in a solid and unified group of professional men, that is to say precisely those who were the most directly affected by the contraction of the traditional channels of promotion. Once the Third Estate had taken control in July 1789, the National Assembly abandoned the Ancien Régime structure of privilege with reluctance and considerable reservations in August. It was hardly the act of an assembly of bourgeois liberating themselves from the restricting fetters of feudalism. Indeed, the abbé Sieyes did all he could to reverse it.[71] These men became the champions of an attack on privilege in part by the force of the logic of revolutionary politics in the context of the popular revolt of 1789. But they also did so as a consequence of a number of confusions. Obliged to become the leaders of the Third Estate, they presented their own grievances as those of the whole of the Third Estate. Certainly, they expressed hostility to the nobility, but their grievance was one of political and social definition in the precise context of 1788–9. However, the mere fact that they did express this hostility encouraged the peasantry, initially at least, to identify privilege predominantly with the nobility rather than with the élite as a whole and to confuse the grievances of the "revolutionary bourgeoisie" with its own.[72] It was this which enabled the revolutionary behavior of the representatives of the Third Estate to find support among the protest movements of the vile and abject sections of the community, which were not their natural allies. Furthermore, in 1788–9 the circumstances and background which have been elaborated in this essay allowed the "revolutionary bourgeoisie" to identify, erroneously and in general terms, the Ancien Régime nobility as an exclusive group threatening its social position, while the political developments of the early days of the Estates-General incited it to confuse this conception of the nobility with the system of absolute monarchy, and to see the two as interdependent and as allies. But such a thought-process necessarily imposed the identification of the nobility as a distinct social group, which, as we have seen, was an unrealistic enterprise; the easiest solution to this paradox was to indulge in another confusion and to identify the nobility by the traditional system of privileges which had originally been specifically noble attributes. Thus, spokesmen of the Third Estate could quite happily refer to the first two Estates as the "privileged Orders", forgetting that they themselves were in many cases at least partially privileged. It was for this reason that the attachment of the "revolutionary bourgeoisie" to that system of privilege, in which they themselves participated, was weakened. In mid-1789 the combination of the counter-offensive of the Ancien Régime and anti-privilege pressure from below brought the revolutionary leaders to jettison privilege.

However, the true sense of the rejection of the Ancien Régime system of privilege by the "revolutionary bourgeoisie" was revealed by the Constitution of 1791. In this document, this assembly of men from the Ancien Régime élite redefined that same élite in such a way that it could never be divided again by artificial distinctions within it. The characteristic of élite status was recognized to be the control of landed property. The tangible attribute of élite status was defined as access to public office and the political control of the country. This is the sense of a Constitution which made every public position elective and largely confined eligibility to men of some substance expressed in property. The Thermidorians and the Directorials reasserted these same conceptions of politics and society far more explicitly and successfully, as the surviving Jacobins, not to mention Babeuf, clearly understood.[73] The Constitution of 1791 in no way implied a rejection of the Ancien Régime nobility, for it was comprised within this definition as much as were wealthy non-nobles.

It was merely because some noble elements chose rather vociferously not to participate that the Revolution was made to appear as a revolt against the nobility as a social class. In the same way, the technical detail of the ordering of the Estates-General, while crystalizing the tensions of the Ancien Régime, also forced them to be expressed in terms which can easily be taken as those of a conflict between nobles and bourgeois, a conflict which did not exist in any very meaningful sense in the eighteenth century. Nevertheless, the redefinition of the élite by the Revolution was indubitably of fundamental importance. Although nobility as an institution was only momentarily abolished and Napoleon was indeed to reinforce it in a certain sense, the revolutionary crisis did result in the emergence of an élite defined in terms of landholding and function, with the hereditary element confined to the simple passage of wealth and its advantages from one generation to another in a family. The Revolution did therefore provide a social framework within which the acquisition of nobility was to be increasingly irrelevant and which allowed élite status to develop into the attribute of men of wealth however acquired and however expressed. In this sense, we may say that the Revolution made the bourgeoisie even if it was not made by the bourgeoisie.

NOTES

Source Reprinted in an abridged format from *Past and Present*, 60 (August 1973): 84–126.

* *Acknowledgement* I would like to thank Dr John Roberts and my colleague Dr I. Prothero for their perceptive criticisms of this essay in its final stages.

1 Perhaps the clearest statement of this schema is to be found in A. Soboul, "Classes and Class Struggles during the French Revolution," *Science and Society*, xvii (1953), 238–57: e.g., "The essential cause of the Revolution was the power of a bourgeoisie arrived at its maturity and confronted by a decadent aristocracy holding tenaciously to its privileges."

2 A. Cobban, *The Social Interpretation of the French Revolution* (Cambridge, 1964).

3 D. Richet, "Autour des origines idéologiques lointaines de la Révolution française: élites et despotismes," *Annales: Economies; Sociétés, Civilizations* (hereafter *Annales E.S.C.*) xxiv (1969), 1–23; F. Furet, "Le catéchisme de la Révolution française," *Annales E.S.C.*, xxvi

(1971), 255–89; C. Mazauric, *Sur la Révolution française* (Paris, 1970), 21–113.

4 A. Cobban, "The French Revolution, Orthodox and Unorthodox," *History*, lii (1967), 149–59.

5 G. V. Taylor, "Types of Capitalism in Eighteenth-Century France," *English Historical Review*, lxxix (1964), 478–97, and "Non-Capitalist Wealth and the Origins of the French Revolution," *American Historical Review*, lxxii (1967), 469–96, esp. 490.

6 Cf. E.G. Barber, *The Bourgeoisie in Eighteenth-Century France* (Princeton, 1955), 15; M. Couturier, *Recherches sur les structures sociales de Châteaudun* (Paris, 1969), 221–2; A. Daumard and F. Furet, *Structures et relations sociales à Paris au milieu du XVIIIème siècle* (Paris, 1963), 68.

7 In this point resides the weakness of using professional categories as social categories. Not only can there be significant wealth differences between two carpenters or two stonemasons, but also significant functional differences. Cf. M. Thoumas-Schapira, "La bourgeoisie toulousaine à la fin du XVIIème siècle," *Annales du Midi*, lxvii (1955), 315, 318.

8 One can suggest that the inferiority of surgeons (*chirurgiens*) to doctors (*médecins*), although clearly connected with their barbering, may also be imputable in part to the predominantly manual nature of their profession.

9 Note how Chaumette, terrorist *agent national* of Paris, seems to have tried to substitute "jeweller" (*bijoutier*) for "shoemaker" (*cordonnier*) as his father's profession on his birth certificate: *Papiers de Chaumette*, ed. F. Braesch (Paris, 1908), 12.

10 A calculation of the fortunes of the joiners (*menuisiers*) of Toulouse reveals an average of 1,000 *livres* for the masters, 600 for those companions who subsequently became masters, and 470 for those who did not: J. Godechot, "L'histoire économique et sociale de Toulouse au XVIIIème siècle," *Annales du Midi*, lxxviii (1966), 371.

11 Richet, "Autour des origines idéologiques lointaines de la Révolution française."

12 E.g. H. Carré, *La noblesse de France et l'opinion publique au XVIIIème siècle* (Paris, 1920), 3, 12–14, and F.L. Ford, *Robe and Sword* (New York, 1965), 208–9. Cf. J.G.C. Blacker, "Social Ambitions of the Bourgeoisie in Eighteenth-Century France and their Relation to Family Limitation," *Population Studies*, xi (1957), 46–63, and P. Goubert, *L'Ancien Régime*, 2 vols (Paris, 1969), i, 145 ff.

13 E.g. J. Meyer, *La noblesse bretonne au XVIIIème siècle*, 2 vols (Paris, 1966), i, 321–442.

14 E.g., out of a total of 1,715 names on the tax rolls of Montargis in 1789, 852 were marked either as being exempt or privileged, or else as having a special status: B. Hyslop, "Les élections de la ville de Montargis en 1789," *Ann. hist. Rév. fr.*, xviii (1946), 125; cf. G. Bouchard, *La famille du conventionnel Basire* (Paris, 1952), 91–2.

15 C.B.A. Behrens "Nobles, Privileges, and Taxes in France at the end of the Ancien Régime," *Econ. Hist. Rev.*, 2nd ser., xv (1962–3), 451–75;

M Marion, *Histoire financière de la France depuis 1715*, 3 vols (Paris, 1914–28), i, 10–12.

16 P. Bois, *Les Paysans de l'Ouest* (Le Mans, 1960), 378. But the regional variations were great; around Dieppe there was only one non-noble for thirty-six noble fief holders: M. de Bouard (ed.), *Histoire de Normandie* (Toulouse, 1970), 339.

17 A. Young, *Travels in France*, (ed.) C. Maxwell (Cambridge, 1950), 8; G. Sabatier, "L'Emblavès au début du XVIIIème siècle", in P. Léon (ed.), *Structures économiques et problèmes sociaux du monde rural dans la France du Sud-Est* (Paris, 1966), 88–90. Cf. M. Bouloiseau (ed.) *Cahiers de doléances du Tiers-Etat du bailliage de Rouen* (Paris, 1957), i, xxix, on the dispersion of the seigneuries in the duchy of Longueville during the same period.

18 A. Brette, "La noblesse et ses privilèges pécuniaires en 1789," *La Révolution française*, xxvi (1906), 102.

19 Note, for example, how one inhabitant of Saint-Etienne, who at the beginning of the Revolution certainly considered himself, and was considered by others, to be a noble, was able to vote in the Year VI by arguing that his father had been a *secrétaire du roi* for only fourteen years and that therefore he himself could not possibly be noble: Archives Départmentales (hereafter A.D.), Loire, L. 276, proceedings of electoral assembly at Saint-Etienne, Year VI.

20 Quoted by Carré, *La noblesse de France*, 14.

21 160 signatures on the Tennis Court Oath had the particle: Brette, *op. cit.*, 104.

22 E.g. V.R. Gruder, *The Royal Provincial Intendants* (Ithaca, 1968), 130; F. Bluche, *Les Magistrats du Parlement de Paris au XVIIIème siècle* (Besançon, 1960), 95; G. Lefebvre, *Etudes Orléanaises*, 2 vols (Paris, 1962–3), i, 165–70.

23 J. Jaurès, *Histoire socialiste, 1789–1900*, 12 vols (Paris, 1900–8), i, p. 40.

24 Taylor, "Non-Capitalist Wealth and the Origins of the French Revolution," *passim*. Cf. Godechot, "L'histoire économique et sociale de Toulouse," 363–74; Barber, *The Bourgeoisie in Eighteenth-Century France*, 62–3; J. Sentou, *Fortunes et groupes sociaux à Toulouse sous la Révolution* (Toulouse, 1969), 79–322, esp. 182–3. P. Léon ("Recherches sur la bourgeoisie française de province au XVIIIème siècle," *L'Information historique*, xxi (1958), 101–5) believes that the division between the nobility and the bourgeoisie can be seen in the tax registers, provided that one recognizes a number of "enclaves" and operates a selection among the office-holders on the fringes of the Robe nobility. This sort of categorization (which is a fairly common approach to the problem) seems unrealistic in view of what we know about tax exemption; it is also extremely arbitrary, as indeed the author admits.

25 But there were variations: both F. Bluche (*Les Magistrats du Parlement de Paris au XVIIIème siècle* (Besançon, 1960), p. 170) and R. Forster (*The Nobility of Toulouse* (Baltimore, 1960), 104, find returns of 5 per cent for the Parlements they study, while the government annuities (*rentes*) paid 5 per cent at most, as did private ones under the law at least.

26 Cf. M. Vovelle and D. Roche, "Bourgeois, rentiers, propriétaires: éléments pour la définition d'une catégorie sociale à la fin du XVIIIème siècle," in *Actes du 84ème congrès national des sociétés savantes* (Paris, 1959), 419–52; also Sentou, *op cit.*, 191–2 and 253 on the connection between the *rentier* and professional groups.

27 Taylor, *op. cit.*; G. Richard, "Les corporations et la noblesse commerçante en France au XVIIIème siècle," *L'Information historique*, xx (1957), 185–9; Meyer, *La noblesse bretonne*, i, 151–8.

28 J. Kaplow, "On 'Who intervened in 1788?'", *American Historical Review*, lxxii (1967), 498.

29 D.S. Landes, "French Entrepreneurship and Industrial Growth in the Nineteenth Century," *Journal of Economic History*, ix (1949), 45–61.

30 There are of course countless individual examples, each with its own, different permutation of the elements contributing to such a promotion; Taylor (*op. cit.*) presents some, as does O. Hufton (*Bayeux in the Late Eighteenth Century* (Oxford, 1967), 61). A very clear example of a family in the act of transferring – marrying profitably, buying land and office, yet hesitating to abandon trade altogether – is provided by the future revolutionary Laurent LeCointre and his brother in the 1770s and 1780s: T. Lhuillier, "Laurent LeCointre (de Versailles)," *La Révolution française*, xv (1895), 234–56.

31 E.g. G. Richard, "A propos de la noblesse commerçante de Lyon au XVIIIème siècle," *L'Information historique*, xxii (1959), 156–61. A royal decree of 1767 accorded the wholesale merchants (*négociants en gros*) the reputation of "living nobly" and some privileges.

32 E.g. the complaint from Toulouse in 1773 that the moment a merchant obtained the ennobling office of *capitoul*, "he considers trading to be a thing very much beneath his dignity": M. Marion, *Dictionnaire des institutions de la France aux XVIIème et XVIIIème siècles* (Paris, 1968), *v.* "noblesse".

33 The notion of an élite was first examined in general terms by D. Richet, "Autour des origines idéologiques lointaines de la Révolution française". See also H. Luethy, *La banque protestante en France*, 2 vols (Paris, 1959–61), ii, 15–25, and Goubert, *L'Ancien Régime*, i, 235. Cf. the interesting comment on such a view in Mazauric, *Sur la Révolution française*, 107.

34 D. Bitton, *The French Nobility in Crisis* (Stanford, 1969), 98.

35 A Goodwin, "The Social Structure and Economic and Political Attitudes of the French Nobility in the Eighteenth Century," in *XIIème congrès international des sciences historiques*, 5 vols (Vienna, 1965), i, 356–65; Gruder, *The Royal Provincial Intendants*, 177–80. Cf. Bayeux in 1789, where five-sixths of the noble families could not claim nobility before 1500; the nobility of the majority of them was acquired during the seventeenth and early eighteenth centuries: Hufton, *Bayeux in the Late Eighteenth Century*, 41.

36 E.g. the interesting comparison established by R. Bouscayrol, "Les origines familiales et sociales de Romme et de Soubrany," in *Gilbert Romme et son Temps* (Publications de l'Institut d'Etudes du Massif Central, Paris, 1966), 23–42.

37 Cf. Lefebvre, *Etudes Orléanaises*, i, 171–3; Sentou, *Fortunes et groupes sociaux à Toulouse*, 253–4 M. Bloch, *Les caractères originaux de l'histoire rurale française*, 2 vols (Paris, 1961–4), i, 142–3.

38 E.g. Bosher, *French Finances*, 61–2, 69–71, 178, 278–84; Gruder, *op. cit.*, 136–9, 142–66; Meyer, *La noblesse bretonne*, i, 171–422, esp. 349–61; Lefebvre, *op. cit.*, i, 175–6. A few spectacular careers are detailed in Forster, *The Nobility of Toulouse*, 24–6. Cf. Couturier, *Recherches sur les structures sociales de Châteaudun*, 236 ff.

39 H. R. Trevor-Roper, "Trevor-Roper's 'General Crisis': Symposium," repr. in Trevor Aston (ed.), *Crisis in Europe*, 1560–1660 (London, 1965), 114.

40 Note how the concession of hereditary nobility to the members of the great law courts of Paris and the provinces coincided with moments of acute financial embarrassment – 1644–5, 1691 and 1704; there is a similar pattern in the sales of nobility: Marion, *Dictionnaire des institutions de la France, v.* "noblesse".

41 R. Mousnier, *La vénalité des offices sous Henri IV et Louis XIII* (Rouen, 1946), *passim*.

42 Ford, *Robe and Sword*, 12.

43 E.G. Léonard, "Le question sociale dans l'armée française au XVIIIème siècle", *Annales E.S.C.*, iii (1948), 139–40.

44 R. Mousnier, *La société française de 1770 à 1789*, 2 vols (Paris C.D.U., 1970), i, 11–15.

45 Cf. R.B. Grassby, "Social Status and Commercial Enterprise under Louis XIV", *Econ. Hist. Rev.*, 2nd ser., xiii (1960–1), 19–38.

46 Ford, *op. cit., passim*. Cf. Bluche, *op. cit.*, 116 and 303; Forster, *op. cit.*, 26 and 103; Carré, *La noblesse de France*, 34 ff.; Berthe, *op. cit.*, genealogy facing 56.

47 Bluche, *op. cit.*, 87–92; Meyer, *op. cit.*, i, 362.

48 Cf. Lefebvre, *op. cit.*, i, 171–3.

49 Possibly, we should ascribe the maintenance of old forms partly to the action, or inertia, of the socially conservative Sully and Richelieu at a time when the composition of the social èlite was undergoing radical change, partly to the consequences of their policies: cf. R. Mousnier, "Sully et le Conseil d'Etat des Finances," *Revue historique*, cxcii (1941), 68–86; O. Ranum, "Richelieu and the Great Nobility," *French Historical Studies*, iii (1963), 184–204; F.E. Sutcliffe, "Agriculture or Industry: a French dilemma at the period of Henry IV," *Bull John Rylands Library*, liv (1972), 434–48. I am grateful to Professor Sutcliffe for discussing several of these points with me.

50 P.A. Pichot and F. Masson (eds) *Un Vendéen sous la Terreur: mémoires inédits de Toussaint-Ambroise de la Cartrie* (Paris, 1910), p. 87; cf. Ford, *op. cit.*, 9, n. 9.

51 Bitton, *The French Nobility in Crisis*, pp. 77–91; Richet, "Autour des origines idéologiques lointaines de la Révolution française".

52 M. Reinhard, "Elite et noblesse dans la seconde moitié du XVIIIème siècle", *Rev. d'hist. mod. et contemp.*, iii (1956), 5–37. Cf. an anonymous pamphleteer at Orléans in 1789; "nobility does not reside in parchments . . . it is to be found in the heart, in the mind, in the way

of thinking of those of our Order": Lefebvre, *Etudes Orléanaises*, i, 187.

53 H.T. Parker, *The Cult of Antiquity and the French Revolutionaries* (Chicago, 1937), *passim*; F. Delbèke, *L'action politique et sociale des avocats au XVIIIème siècle* (Louvain, 1927), 9, 11, 19 and 23. The clearest expression of this is J-P. Brissot, *Un Indépendant à l'ordre des avocats, sur la décadence du Barreau en France* (Berlin, 1781).

54 C.L. Chassin, "La mission de Lequinio et Laignelot," *La Révolution française*, xv (1895), 133.

55 Taylor, "Non-Capitalist Wealth and the Origins of the French Revolution," 491.

56 E.g. Lefebvre, *Quatre-vingt-neuf* (Paris, 1939), 58.

57 Sée, "Le rôle de la bourgeoisie bretonne à la veille de la Révolution, *Annales de Bretagne*, xxxiv (1920)," 410: "The really active campaign of the Third Estate begins in October (1788)".

58 Brette, "La noblesse et ses privilèges pécuniares en 1789," 97 and 124.

59 Cf. Eisenstein, "Who intervened in 1788?" *American Historical Review*, xxi (1965), 77–103. Note also that only ten of the *General Cahiers* of the Third Estate thought that its representatives were sovereign and should ignore those of the privileged Orders: Hyslop, *French Nationalism in 1789* (New York, 1967), 69. The liberal noble Gouy d'Arcy wrote at the end of 1788, "What is an Order in an Empire? It is an essential portion of the governnent, it is a fundamental class of society, and in both of these respects, there are only two Orders in France, the patricians and the plebeians": quoted by A. Decouflé, "L'aristocratie française devant l'opinion publique à la veille de la Révolution", in R. Besnier (ed.), *Etudes d'histoire économique et sociale du XVIIIème siècle* (Paris, 1966), 37.

60 Meyer, *La noblesse bretonne*, i, 436–8; Cf. Egret, *La Pré-révolution française* (Paris, 1962), 353.

61 Sée, *op. cit.*

62 J. Egret, "La Pré-révolution en Provence", *Ann. hist. Rév. fr.*, xxvi (1954), 195–213.

63 See the instruction given by the electoral assembly of the Third Estate of the Forez to its deputies to refuse to admit any of the distinctions of nobility which might humiliate the Third Estate. Note also the great protests against the imposition of distinctively different costumes on the three Estates in April 1789; the Forezian deputies argued, significantly enough, that "the Third Estate's interest is that nothing should be *innovated*" (my italics). G. Lefebvre and A. Terroine (eds) *Receuil de documents relatifs aux séances des Etats-Généraux*, 2 vols (Paris, 1953–62), i, 69, 76–82.

64 P. Renouvin, *Les assemblées provinciales de 1787* (Paris, 1921), 79 ff.

65 Already in 1700 a wealthy merchant resented being described by any formula that might also be used of his tailor: Grassby, "Social Status and Commercial Enterprise," 27–8. Note also the agitation over the militia during the century and Barbier's comment that it put the son of the wholesale merchant on the same level as servants, workers and shopboys: E.J.F. Barbier, *Journal historique et anecdotique du règne de*

Louis XV, ed. A. de Villegille, 4 vols (Paris, 1857–75), ii, 353–4. Daniel Mornet, *Les origines intellectuelles de la Révolution Française* (Paris, 1933), p. 436, cites some cases of such quarrels, but they are very uninformative, although army officers (and I have referred to their stress zone situation) figure rather prominently in the examples he has chosen.

66 Meyer, *La noblesse bretonne*, ii, 1,114.
67 E.g. E. Fléchier, *Mémoires sur les Grands-Jours d'Auvergne*, ed. M. Chéruel (Paris, 1856), *passim*.
68 Lefebvre, *Quatre-vingt-neuf*, 58.
69 E. Sieyes, *Qu'est-ce que le Tiers-état?*, ed. R. Zapperi (Geneva, 1970), esp. 27–43.
70 *Ibid.*, 143: "les classes disponibles du Tiers-état".
71 *Ibid.*, 31–3.
72 Cf. Lefebvre, *Etudes Orléanaises*, i, 73: "The wealthy peasants (*laboureurs*) and the artisans only spoke out frankly against the seigneur.... The hostility towards traders and members of the liberal professions, and more generally towards all town dwellers, which indubitably existed, does not transpire ..."
73 Cf. I. Woloch, *Jacobin Legacy* (Princeton, 1970), especially pp. 155–6. But note the social assumptions expressed by the Jacobin Garnerin in the middle of Year II when he denounced speculation by the Jews; "There are some among them rich to the tune of fifteen or twenty millions' worth of assignats, and who do not have a sou's worth of landed property": Véron-Réville, *Histoire de la Révolution française dans le département du Haut-Rhin* (Paris, 1865), 194. R. Marx, *Recherches sur la vie politique de l'Alsace pré-révolutionnaire et révolutionnaire* (Strasbourg, 1966), *passim*, contains interesting illustrations of the practice of this situation at all levels throughout the Revolution. Cf. Cobban, *Social Interpretation of the French Revolution*, 81 ff.

Part II

THE REVISIONIST ORTHODOXY

I shall show how a government, both stronger and far more autocratic than the one which the Revolution had overthrown, centralized once more the entire administration, made itself all-powerful, suppressed our dearly bought liberties, and replaced them by a mere pretense of freedom; how the so-called "sovereignty of the people" came to be based on the votes of an electorate that was neither given adequate information nor an opportunity of getting together and deciding on one policy rather than another; and how the much vaunted "free vote" in matters of taxation came to signify no more than the meaningless assent of assemblies tamed to servility and silence.

Alexis de Tocqueville
foreword to *The Old Regime and the French Revolution*

3

THE FRENCH REVOLUTION REVISITED

François Furet

In this lecture, originally given at the London School of Economics in December 1980, François Furet distills in a lighter style many of the ideas that are elaborated in his monumental book, Interpreting the French Revolution. *Furet begins the talk by trying to come to terms with the fierce and partisan historiography that has dominated the study of the Revolution. His explanation is twofold. First, France's own nineteenth-century political history of revolving regimes and political instability meant that the legacy of the Revolution continued to live on in the fiery speeches and idealistic plans of French statesmen (some of whom were important historians). Second, the outbreak of the Bolshevik Revolution in 1917 made any interpretation of its French precursor a loaded political act. Not until the 1970s, when militant Bolshevism had decayed beyond repair, was it possible to look at the Revolution from a truly fresh perspective.*

This new viewpoint involves relating Tocqueville's idea regarding the growth of the centralized state with a sophisticated understanding about the birth of modern democracy. In his 1856 classic, The Old Regime and the French Revolution, *Alexis de Tocqueville argued that the French Revolution did not so much mark the overthrow of the Ancien Régime as its culmination. By abolishing feudalism, guilds, economic regulation, and noble privilege, the Revolution continued trends begun under the absolute monarchy. Once the noble privilege and institutions were gone, nothing stood between the individual citizen and the all-encompassing power of the centralized state.*

Furet's work is concerned with explaining how this transformation came about. He suggests that by undermining the traditional social order of the Ancien Régime, the monarchy created, in Furet's words, a kind of "empty space" that weakened the monarchy's sense of legitimacy. Rather suddenly, the idea of "the people" moved into this void,

*creating a 'mobilized society' that 'disarmed the state.' The Revolution,
then, is seen as 'the torrential birth of democratic politics and ideology'
in which the centralized state is refashioned with far more power and
authority than dreamed possible by the eighteenth-century monarchs.*

* * *

I should like to start with an extremely simple statement about
the French Revolution. This is that there are many historical
arguments among historians on many subjects, but that none of
these arguments is so intense and so heated as the one which
takes place in every generation about the French Revolution. It
is as though the historical interpretation of this particular subject and the arguments of specialists directly reflect the political
struggles and the gamble for power. It is true that we are all
aware today that there are no unbiased historical interpretations: the selection of facts which provide the raw material for
the historian's work is already the result of a choice, even
although that choice is not an explicit one. To some extent, history is always the result of a relationship between the present
and the past and more specifically between the characteristics of
an individual and the vast realm of his possible roots in the
past. But, nevertheless, even within this relative framework, not
all the themes of history are equally relevant to the present
interests of the historian and to the passions of his public. The
subject of Clovis, for example, and of the Frankish invasions,
was of burning interest in the eighteenth century, because historians of that era thought that the Frankish invasions were the
source of the division between the nobility and the common
people: the conquerors having evolved into the nobility and the
conquered having become the commoners. Today, the Germanic
invasions are no longer considered to contain or reveal any
secret about French society: they have become once again a subject for historiography, left to scholars and to the arguments of
specialists.

To be convinced that the French Revolution, in contrast, is not
like any other historical subject, one has only to look at the particular violence of the polemics engendered by its study: it is as
though the Revolution had prolonged the original conflict for two
hundred years and as if the main function of its history was to
renew and to maintain it.

This specific historiographic situation appeared with particular clarity in the nineteenth century, as it was linked at that time to the long survival of the revolutionary phenomenon. In fact, the French from 1815 to 1880 were perpetually enacting the same historical drama, the elements of which had been given once and for all between 1789 and 1799. First of all, they 'restored' their former kings, but not the former kingship, in order to re-enact against them in 1830 what they imagined to be an English 1688, that is, a successful 1789, with a new monarchy linked to a new political and social order. But the revolutionary process which they believed that they had exorcised *à l'anglaise* by the change of dynasty remained the symbol of their national destiny. The year 1848 saw a constituent assembly, a legislative assembly, a Bonaparte. The second Republic found actors for all the roles in the great revolutionary repertory, Lamartine as Brissot, Ledru-Rollin as Robespierre, the nephew Bonaparte as his uncle. The same combination of parliamentary impotence and Jacobin nostalgia which had led to 18 Brumaire brought a second Bonaparte to power under the aegis of memory. The Second Empire collapsed like the first because it was defeated in war, but only to open the way first to the new Jacobin resurrection, which was the Paris Commune, and afterwards to the final attempt to restore the former monarchy in the guise of the 'moral order.' Then began, almost one hundred years after the explosion which we call the French Revolution, the apparently terminal struggle which was to found the Third Republic on the victory of the principles of 1789.

[*Between 1815–1940, France experienced the following regimes: The Bourbon Restoration of Louis XVIII and Charles X (1815–30); The July Monarchy of Louis-Philippe (1830–48); The Second Republic (1848–52); The Second Empire of Napoleon III (1852–70); The Third Republic (1870–1940).*]

Thus, the French of the nineteenth century lived on a repertory of political forms which was rich and yet limited: rich because it allowed for a very rapid rhythm of change of regime; limited because all the characters in the repertory had been invented in the last decade of the eighteenth century, within the period which we call the French Revolution in the strict sense of the word. It is, therefore, not surprising that the Frenchmen of the nineteenth

century felt that they were living in a sort of indefinitely prolonged French Revolution: every episode in the political history
of the country offered them, through its duplicating character, all
the elements of identification with (or rejection of) the primordial
event. Chateaubriand, Tocqueville, Michelet, Quinet continued to
relive the Revolution through their own experiences.

This explains why the point of reference of the whole of
politics, of the thought and of the history of the nineteenth
century and particularly of romantic politics, thought, history,
was centered around the Revolution. The Revolution represents
the moment when the old world tipped over towards the new
and thus also the abolition of the former and the arrival of the
latter: it is the Revolution which holds the title-deeds of the
national legitimacy, recognizes the claimants, defines the political
families and their share in the legacy. The royalist Right detested
the Revolution, but all its thoughts were directed against it and
related to it. The liberal bourgeoisie endorsed the Revolution, in
part at least. The Bonapartists derive all their ancestors from
it. The Republican Left adopted it as its standard. But if the
Revolution offered to all of them the reasons for remembering
their origins (happy or unhappy), it was because it enveloped
them in the civilization which it had created and which made all
of them, friend or foe, its sons. The Revolution was thus written
only in its own words.

One could illustrate the intellectual constraints of this kind of
closed circuit with the example of the historiographical treatment
reserved for that particular episode in the Revolution, which is
the Terror, particularly in the form it took of a system of repression carried out by the state. The counter-revolutionary Right had
no difficulty in including the Terror in its general condemnation
of the Revolution and even in making it the very symbol of revolutionary perversion because of the highly spectacular violence
which it implied. But in doing so, it is led to attribute the Terror
either to the intentional villainy of the historic actors (the theory
of the plot) or to the exemplary design of Providence (as in Joseph
de Maistre). The link between the Revolution and the Terror is
only seen through the ineluctability of evil, under its psychological or theological form: but this is merely to beg the question.

For the Terror embarrasses even more deeply the supporters of
the French Revolution, regardless of which branch of the 'Left'
they belong to. The liberals, indissolubly linked to 1789, reject

1793. This was Guizot's problem and also that of his friend, Mignet. Even before the problem appeared in reality, in July 1830 (they were to solve it then by resorting to Louis Philippe), they had encountered it historically: 1793, they claimed, was not contained in 1789; it was, on the contrary, an unhappy deviation which must not be repeated. Everything of value in the French Revolution was already there in 1789.

Farther to the Left, and a generation later, Edgar Quinet rediscovered the same question: an intransigent republican, with an unbreakable attachment to the legacy of 1789, this exile from the Second Empire was forced to pick and choose from the revolutionary legacy. Just as Robespierre, so the Second Empire was strong, in his view, only because of Jacobin goodwill. He set his face therefore against everything in the Revolution which weakened liberty, the dictatorship, the Terror of 1793–4, the harbinger of the coup d'état of Brumaire. By the same token, the Terror, far from being consubstantial with the Revolution became, on the contrary, the emergence of its antithesis from within the Revolution, its anti-principle, the resurrection of the Ancien Régime within the new and the corruption of the new by the old. If Robespierre was to be blamed, it was not because he wanted to force the future: it was because he reincarnated Richelieu and absolutism.

The Jacobin Republicans of the same period, who polemicized against Quinet, accepted the Terror as part and parcel of the revolutionary legacy. But they excused it rather than explained it. What I am saying is that their interpretation of the terrorist dictatorship – in Louis Blanc, for example – was a circumstantial one. If the Revolution resorted to coercion and to the guillotine, it was because it was constrained to do so by its internal and external enemies. Within this line of argument – which resembles the plea of 'extenuating circumstances' in our courts – the Terror is no longer thought of as inseparable from the Revolution. It was one of its risks, not one of its component parts. And if 1793–4 was a particularly heroic period, it was because it was victorious rather than because of the means it used to achieve victory. In other words, the difference between Mignet, Quinet and Louis Blanc is not that one or the other tried to conceptualize the Terror as an intrinsic element in the mechanics of revolution: on the contrary, all three of them, distant though they might be from each other on the political chessboard, thought of the Terror as

75

external to the Revolution and independent of it. The first said of the Terror that it was a regrettable deviation in relation to 1789. The second that it was a resurgence of absolutism. The third that it was a necessity imposed by the enemies of the Revolution. These interpretations imply different and even contradictory value judgments on the revolutionary phenomenon – within a general agreement with 1789 – and a common dissociation, at the analytical level, of the pair Revolution–Terror. In other words, they defined themselves or rather they differentiated themselves by the way in which they identified themselves with the revolutionary heritage, rather than by the way in which they understood or analyzed it.

At this stage of the argument, it could be objected that this type of historiographical identification with the French Revolution should have died out with the final triumph of the Revolution: it should not have been able to survive for long the victory of the Third Republic. But it was the opposite that happened: the revolutionary historiography of the twentieth century is just as passionate, partisan, and exclusive as that of the nineteenth century, although the real political stakes linked with the French Revolution have gradually disappeared and no one any longer contests, at least since 1945, the values of 1789 and their legitimacy.

This is because something very simple has happened: the polemics about the conflict between Monarchy and Republic have been replaced by the intellectual and political polemics engendered by the socialist revolution. In fact, the socialists of the second half of the nineteenth century visualized their activity as something at once allied to and distinct from that of the democrats. Allied because democracy is in their eyes the essential condition of socialism; distinct from, because it is a historical stage of the social organization destined to be overtaken, and because 1789 is for them a stage in a historical process in which the socialist revolution does the overtaking. But in reality these two struggles for democracy and for socialism are two successive manifestations of a dynamic of egalitarianism which has its roots deep in the events of the French Revolution.

Thus a linear history of the progress of mankind was composed, of which the first stage was the flowering and the diffusion of the values of 1789 and the second stage was to fulfill all the promises of 1789 by means of the socialist revolution. It is basically a two-handled mechanism of which the pre-1917 great socialist authors had not yet, and rightly, set the second stage, since the second stage had not yet arrived. Jaurès, for example in his *Histoire socialiste de la Revolution française*, built the narration of the French Revolution around what was still only a hope and surrounded the Jacobin epic with a kind of great halo which proclaimed a more decisive liberation of mankind. The French Revolution was pregnant with hope which had a name but which had not yet a face.

Everything changed in 1917. The socialist revolution acquired a face; the French Revolution ceased to be a matrix of probabilities on which another liberating revolution could and should be modeled. It was no longer the field of possibilities, discovered and described by Jaurès; it had become the mother of a real event, dated, fixed, which had taken place and which was the Russian Revolution of October 1917. In 1920, in a little book, an academic historian of the French Revolution, Albert Mathiez, emphasized the kinship between the government of the Mountain and the Bolshevik dictatorship of the civil war period, that is, of the heroic period of the Russian Revolution. I quote:

> Jacobinism and Bolshevism are two dictatorships born of civil war and of war, two class dictatorships operating through the same means: terror, requisitioning and taxes; and having, in the last resort, the same goal: the transformation of society and not only of the Russian or French society, but of the universal society.

Moreover, as Mathiez underlined, the Russian Bolsheviks have always had in their minds the example of the French Revolution, especially of its Jacobin period. The Russian revolutionaries were obsessed by the presence in history of the French Revolution which had preceded them. This was one of the great differences between the two revolutions, since by definition the French men of 1789 had no model.

We know, for example, that after the seizure of power by the Bolsheviks, and especially after Lenin's death, all the Russian revolutionaries, from Trotsky to Zinovýev, including Bukharin, feared a Thermidor, since Thermidor was supposed to have brought the French Revolution to an end. Thus, Thermidor, with all its pejorative connotations, was a threat to the Russian Revolution. And again Thermidor was the harbinger of Bonaparte. In the imagination of the triumvirate Stalin–Zinov́yev–Kamenev, it was Trotsky who represented Bonaparte. The former head of the Red Army re-embodied, for a time, and this was to be fatal to him, the main risk that the Revolution would be liquidated. In other words, the example of the French Revolution was a source of permanent contamination of the Russian Revolution. This contamination played upon the minds of the actors in that revolution; but it also existed in the opposite sense in the minds of many historians of the French Revolution who sympathized instinctively with both revolutions.

The 'overtaking' of the French Revolution by the Russian Revolution has thus displaced the stress and interest in contemporary historiography from the period of 1789 to the period of 1793, from the founding period of the French Revolution to the Jacobin period; this has had some positive effects upon scholarship: to the extent that for thirty or forty years the stress has been laid on the role of the popular masses in the French Revolution, the subject has become one which is reasonably well studied.

But if this telescoping of the history of the two revolutions has had positive effects, it is nonetheless true that the projection of the vision of 1917 upon the narration of the events of 1789 has been the source, at the interpretative level, of grave inconveniences. In the first place a simplified and simplifying Marxism has taken the place of the sometimes contradictory but valuable analyses of the French Revolution left to us by Marx and Engels themselves. There is often in this history, as it has been written after the Bolshevik Revolution, a sort of linear perspective in which the bourgeois revolution, rallying behind it the peasantry and the urban popular masses, enables the transition from the feudal 'mode of production' to the capitalist 'mode of production' to be made. In this interpretation, the dictatorship of the Mountain is singled out as the most popular episode in the process, and is endowed at the same time with the most progressive significance, namely that of accomplishing through war and terror the tasks assigned previously to the bourgeois revolution as well as the task of announcing the liberations to come, notably the Russian Revolution. As a result, the French Revolution was pushed more and more out of kilter in relation to its own chronological reality, drawn from 1789 towards 1793, then suddenly interrupted at the moment of Robespierre's fall, without anyone realizing the inherent contradictions in calling a historical process a 'bourgeois revolution' and in bringing it to an end just when its non-bourgeois period had ceased and its bourgeois period had reached its culmination.

If these contradictions, to which I shall return, in a history which has become a sort of lay teleology dominated by two successive visions which overlap each other, if these contradictions are not more often perceived, this is surely because the history of the French Revolution is not merely something to be studied or an academic discipline: it has also social significance. What gives it its pre-eminent status among all the other subjects in French history is less the discussion of a Marxist schema – which is a kind of feedback from the Soviet revolution – than a far more powerful, political and emotional appeal which is nothing less than the interpretation of the French Revolution through itself, at once as the keystone of a great nation and as the liberator of universal society.

The history of a founding event is for every collectivity a ceremony, a commemoration of its origins as well as an understanding of its meaning and as everyone knows, the magic of commemorations is created more by the quarrels of the heirs over the legacy than by any critical discussion of the inheritance. There are royalist commemorations in which the misfortunes of the king, the loss of legitimacy are mourned. There are bourgeois commemorations in which, on the contrary, the new national contract of 1789 is celebrated. There are revolutionary commemorations which stress the dynamic of the founding event and the promises it brings with it of a more egalitarian future. But no matter what the nature of the commemoration, behind these quarrels over the legacy, the heirs share the same vision, the same reference back to the origins. In this sense, it is probably inevitable that every history of the Revolution should be up to a point a commemoration. But I would suggest that if it is not possible to reduce completely the Shamanistic part in every history of the Revolution, it has become absolutely necessary for the historian to preserve an acute awareness of it and to try to reduce or to control it, in making as clear as possible his own intellectual standpoint as well as the problems with which he is trying to deal, through this mass of events of every kind which is called the French Revolution.

In order to illustrate and to develop my argument, I shall start with the work of Tocqueville which I shall use to test one of the fundamental concepts which the French Revolution has given rise to and which in consequence dominates its whole history: this is the concept of the 'before' and the 'after,' separated by a radical break.

If the revolutionary conscience can be defined by an idea, it is indeed this one: the Revolution severed the web of history between an old and a new, a before and an after; this is what I have called the zero point. The men who made the Revolution felt that by their action something was irretrievably destroyed and that something new was set in its place or, as Goethe said at Valmy, a new era had begun. The revolutionary world was characterized in fact by an exceptional mobilization of the habitually inert social forces and by a highly developed ideological capital in politics. If I use the expression 'ideology' here, it is to express two ideas: first of all that all the intellectual, moral, and social problems of mankind had become politicized and that, therefore, there was no human misfortune that could not be blamed on politics. Second, that the revolutionary militants identified their lives with the defense of their ideas, and there was thus an essential intolerance in the revolutionary ideology similar to that of religious ideology in its heyday. In other words, politics has become for the revolutionary conscience the realm of good and evil of the old and the new. It is politics that draws the dividing line between the good and the bad, the patriots and the counter-revolutionaries, thus creating a historical universe which is entirely new compared with the 'normal' periods in history.

Now it is this awareness, this revolutionary ideology which, since 1789, had defined what the Revolution had brought to an end: the Ancien Régime has since become a central concept in our national historiography; it feeds our textbooks; it is the cornerstone of our chronological constructs. The Ancien Régime is the before, marked by the minus sign of what has been destroyed: the Revolution is the 'after,' the new, the point of the break, the take-off of a new history.

This spontaneous conception of the revolutionary ideology cannot, however, be that of the historian, since the craft of a historian consists in dominating the whole of temporal continuity; but it can influence him and cause him to overestimate the part played by the break and by the new in the revolutionary phenomenon. It is here that the work of Tocqueville remains very actual because it is characterized by a critique of the revolutionary phenomenon, by a critique of what can be called the illusion of the Revolution about itself. What Tocqueville said to his contemporaries was: 'The Revolution was not the beginning of a new history of France: it is the flowering of our past.' You know the argument. At the heart of this analysis there lies the problem of the formation of the centralized state and of the domination of the communities and the civil societies by that state. Taking this as his starting point, Tocqueville shows that the Revolution was the crowning point of the work of the kings of France and that Robespierre and even more Bonaparte were the true heirs of Louis XI and Louis XIV. The Revolution therefore did not represent a break but, on the contrary a continuity, contrary to its own idea of itself.

Tocqueville's interpretation could be extended to fields other than that of state, for example to the foreign policy of the Revolution which multiplied, magnified, dramatized, but which in the end espoused the great conflicts of the French kings. One can equally show without difficulty to what extent the Revolution was the heir of the Ancien Régime in the realm of thought: it preserved for example the superstitious belief in military values, in honor and glory, which are values typical of nobility, values which the Revolution democratized but without changing their significance. This appeared clearly under the Empire: the postrevolutionary army, formerly the monopoly of the nobility, became the arena for the promotion of commoners. But in both cases, the army remained *par excellence* the bearer of the highest social prestige. In other words, the Revolution changed everything but by preserving everything.

But I want to limit myself to the central point in Tocqueville's analysis in which he suggests that the main characteristic of the French Revolution was the strengthening of the domination of society by the administrative state. Tocqueville starts in fact from the premise of what I call the Revolution as process or the Revolution as balance-sheet (in contrast with the Revolution as event) and this process is one of continuity: the Revolution extends, consolidates and perfects the twinned pair which was in his eyes the administrative state and the egalitarian society of France and which had both been developed characteristically by the monarchy. Therefore, if one takes seriously, as one should, this historical judgment, there is a complete divorce between the objective history of the Revolution, its significance or its balance-sheet and the awareness which the actors in the Revolution had of their own action. They thought that they were breaking with the past, while in reality they were bringing it to fruition; in holding up to obloquy the despotism of Louis XIV, they were preparing the triumph of Bonaparte. In other words, how can one think simultaneously of the Revolution as a radical rupture and as an essential continuity? What kind of process of continuity is it which takes the road of revolution?

There is at least one aspect from which this apparent paradox is not difficult to understand. It is that of the objective process through which the Revolution, by destroying the traditional forms of the former society, creates the conditions for the omnipotence of the centralized state. In fact, the society of the Ancien Régime neglected the individual; it recognized only the *corps*, such as the orders, the corporations, the associations around the possession of a profession or an office, the communities of people, etc. This explains why what we call the Ancien Régime worked by means of a perpetual process of bargaining – especially fiscal bargaining – between the central state in the hands of bureaucracy at Versailles and society, organized into *corps* and communities, resisting the encroachment of the absolute monarchy in the name of its 'privileges,' that is, of its traditional liberties. Now the Revolution realized in practice the simplifying promise of the philosophy of the eighteenth century: it destroyed all the *corps* root and branch in order to leave only individuals confronting the state under the name of citizens, whose task it now was to renegotiate a new social contract, based on their rights. Hence the opportunity (which does not mean the necessity) for the state to extend its powers and its control over society. Already Mirabeau, in his secret letters to the court in 1790 and 1791, was advising Louis XVI to draw strength from the destruction created by the Revolution and to build up a stronger state than the former one, a state which he called the 'national monarchy.' What! said he to the king of the Ancien Régime, you no longer have any nobility, clergy, or Parliament, nor any of those *corps* which spent their time in defying your authority and yet you complain. You should, on the contrary, take advantage of these circumstances to realize the dream of your ancestors and establish at least a really strong royal authority, which would be the monarchy of the Revolution. As it happened, ten years later, Bonaparte was to follow his advice.

But if the process by which the Revolution created the conditions for the increased power of the administrative state is relatively easy to analyze, that process was nevertheless the embodiment of the exact opposite of what the revolutionaries had wanted to do and had believed that they had done: that is, to free the individual from despotism and to give him back his liberty with his rights. Now, Tocqueville says almost nothing about this second aspect of the revolutionary paradox. He was obsessed by the analysis of the causes and of the effects, and he never analyzed – or had time to analyze – what had actually taken place between the causes and the effects, between 1789 and 1799. This was quite simply the French Revolution as an event, as the event which, on the contrary, embodied the radical will to extirpate the past.

There are in the third volume of *L'Ancien Régime* some answers to these questions, such as the replacement of the politicians by the intellectuals in eighteenth-century France or the spread throughout all classes of society of a democratic state of mind: but the extraordinary dynamism of the egalitarian ideology in the years 1789–93 remains for Tocqueville a kind of sacrament of evil, a kind of inverted religion. Nowhere in his work is there any conceptual connexion between his theory of the French Revolution and revolutionary action, as it was experienced, in the way characteristic of the period – as, for example, the Jacobin phenomenon. Tocqueville makes us wonder if one can ever establish such a connexion; he forces us to disconnect, at least for a while, the two parts of this confused amalgam which makes up the 'history of the Revolution' and to cease juxtaposing the analysis of homogeneous discourse, the one following from the other.

This is not only because these 'events' which are of a political and ideological nature, could not be causally analyzed in terms of economic or social contradiction. It is because even if conducted on the level of the political system and its legitimacy, such an analysis could not take into account what was radically new in the speedy development of the Revolution. There is in the concept of revolution, taken in this sense, something which belongs only to its history as it was lived and which does not conform to the logical sequence of cause and effect: this is the appearance on the stage of history of a practical and ideological mode of action which differs entirely from everything which went before. A given type of political crisis renders this mode possible but not necessary and the revolt itself does not offer any precedent since it is by definition part and parcel of the old political and cultural system.

There is, thus, in the French Revolution a new type of historical praxis and conscience which are linked to a type of situation but are not defined by it. It is this ensemble which must be explained in detail if one wants to interpret rather than to proceed as though the revolutionary conscience, the normal product of legitimate discontent, was the most natural thing in human history. In fact, the Marxist popular interpretation of the history of the French Revolution turns the world upside down: it situates the revolutionary break on the economic and social level while nothing more resembles French society under Louis XVI than that same society under Louis-Philippe. And as that interpretation is at one with the revolutionary conscience and shares its illusions and values, it is unable to see what is most radically new and mysterious in the French Revolution and, on the contrary, perceives it as a normal product of circumstances and a natural chapter in the history of the oppressed. For neither capitalism nor the bourgeoisie had any need for revolutions in order to appear in and to dominate the history of the major European countries in the nineteenth century. But France is the country which, through the Revolution, invented democratic culture, and which revealed to the world one of the fundamental meanings of historical action.

Let us first look at the circumstances. What matters here is not the problem of poverty or of oppression, but the problem of the relation between freedom on the social plane and on the political plane. If the Revolution was invention, disequilibrium, if it set in motion so many unexpected forces that the traditional mechanisms of politics were transformed thereby, it was because the Revolution took over an empty space or rather that it proliferated in the hitherto forbidden and suddenly conquered sphere of power. In this dialogue between the societies and their states, which is one of the most profound threads of history, everything, because of the Revolution, tilts towards society and away from the state. For the Revolution mobilized society and disarmed the state: this is an exceptional situation which opens up for society a field of action which is nearly always barred to it. From 1787 the kingdom of France was a society without a state. Louis XVI continued to gather around his person the consensus of his subjects, but behind his façade of tradition, there was confusion within the gates; the royal authority, nominally respected, no longer extended its legitimacy over its agents. 'The King had bad Ministers, perfidious advisers, evil *intendants*.' It had not yet been realized that the meaning of this perennial refrain of the monarchy when times were hard was no longer to exalt the royal authority, but to institute the control of the citizens. It was a way of saying that civil society, in which the example is set by those above to those below, freed itself from the symbolic power of the state at the same time as from its rules.

The year 1789 arrived: for the highest nobleman as for the humblest peasant the 'revolution' was born at the coming together of several series of events, very different in kind, since an economic crisis (itself complex, being at once agricultural and 'industrial,' meteorological and social) emerged alongside the political crisis which had existed openly since 1787. It is in this coming together of a heterogeneous series of events which gave unpredictability to the situation, a situation which, viewed retrospectively in the light of the illusions of spring 1789, was to be transformed into a necessary consequence of the bad government of men and hence as the stake in the struggle between the patriots and the aristocrats. For the revolutionary situation is not characterized solely by this power vacuum into which the new forces swept and by the 'free' activity of the social body. The revolutionary situation is inseparable from a kind of hypertrophy of the historical conscience and from a system of symbols shared among the social actors. From 1789, the revolutionary conscience was the illusion of conquering a state which no longer existed in the name of a coalition of well-meaning people and forces which prefigured the future. From the beginning, the revolutionary conscience constantly outbid real history on behalf of an idea, as if its function was to reconstruct through the imagination the whole social edifice which had fallen to pieces. The outcry against repression began when that repression collapsed. The Revolution was the historical interlude which separated one power from another power and in which the concept of human action in history replaced what existed.

In this unforeseeable and accelerated drifting, this concept of human action borrows its aims from the reverse of the traditional principles of the social order. The Ancien Régime was in the hands of the king, the Revolution was the accomplishment of the people. The old France was a kingdom of subjects, the new France was a nation of citizens. The old society was one of privilege, the Revolution established equality. There developed an ideology of the radical break with the past, a formidable cultural dynamism of equality. Everything from then – economy, society, politics – bent to the impetus of ideology and of the militants who were its bearers; every line, every institution was merely provisional, faced with this unimpeded torrent.

The word ideology is used here to describe two things which I think form the bedrock of the revolutionary conscience. First of all, that all individual problems, all moral or intellectual problems have become political and there is no human misfortune which is not susceptible to a political solution. Then, to the extent that everything can be known and everything can be transformed, action depends on knowledge and ethics; the revolutionary militants therefore identified their private lives with their public life and with the defense of their ideas; this was a formidable logic which reconstituted in a secular form the psychological certainties of religious belief. If politics had become the realm of what was true and what was false, if it was politics that drew the line separating the good from the bad, then we are faced by a historical universe with an entirely new dynamic. As Marx saw clearly in his early works, the Revolution embodies the illusion of politics: it transforms that which has been experienced into that of which one is conscious. It ushered in a world in which every social change could be imputed to known living forces, with their parts to play; like mythical thought, it clothed the objective universe in subjective wills, in those who were either responsible agents or scapegoats according to the standpoint. Action no longer met with obstacles or restrictions, but only with adversaries, preferably traitors; by the frequency of these mental images one recognizes the moral universe which characterizes the revolutionary explosion.

Freed from the bonds of the state and from the constraint of the sovereign power which were masking its disintegration, society re-formed itself on the ideological plane. This world populated by wills, which recognized only the faithful or the enemy, possessed an incomparable capacity for integration. It opened up what has since been called 'politics,' namely a language at once common and contradictory of debates and action revolving around the issue of power. Not that, naturally, the French Revolution invented politics as an autonomous realm of knowledge: to take only Christian Europe, the theory of political action as such dates from Machiavelli, and learned discussion on the historical origins of social institutions was at its height in the seventeenth century.

But the example of the English Revolution shows that the spiritual background or collective mobilization and activity remained religious. What the French launched at the end of the eighteenth century was not politics as the secular and distinct field of critical reflection, but democratic politics as a national ideology. The secret, the message, the radiance of 1789 lies in this discovery which had no precedent and was to have such vast consequences. And if, out of all the traits which, although they are separated by a hundred years in time, are common to the English Revolution and the French Revolution, there is not one which could give the former the role of a universal model which the second has played since it first appeared on the stage of history, it is precisely because what was missing in Cromwell's Commonwealth, all wrapped as it was in religion and frozen in the return to before the Fall, was what transforms Robespierre's language into the prophecy of new times: democratic politics, which had become the arbiter of the destiny of men and of peoples.

The expression 'democratic politics' does not mean here the collection of rules or procedures destined to organize the working of the public authorities starting from the electoral consultation of the citizens. It describes a system of beliefs which constitutes the new legitimacy, born of the Revolution, and according to which 'the people,' in order to establish the liberty and the equality which are the aims of collective action, must break the resistance of its enemies. Politics, having become the supreme method by which these values are achieved and the inevitable test of wills, good or bad, has only one public actor, who incarnates these values and whose enemies are hidden, since their design cannot be avowed. The 'people' is defined by its goals, and is an amorphous mass of the well intentioned. It is through this oblique approach, which excludes representation, that the revolutionary conscience reconstructs an imaginary society in the name of and starting from, the individual will. This is also how it solves the great dilemma of the eighteenth century which was to think of the social in terms of the individual. If the individual is to be defined in terms of the aims of his political action, it is enough for these aims to be as simple as those of ethics, for the Revolution to be able to found both a language and a society, or rather to found a society through a language: what is called a nation. This was the Feast of the Federation.

This type of analysis has the double advantage of restoring to the French Revolution its most obvious dimension, which is of a political nature, and to place at the centre of our reflections the true solution of continuity by which it separates the before and the after, that of legitimation and the staging of historical action. The action of the sans-culottes of 1793 was not important because it was the action of a 'popular' social group (impossible by the way to define in socio-economic terms) but because it expressed in its chemically pure state that revolutionary staging of political action, the obsession with betrayal and plot, the rejection of representation, the will to punish, etc. And nothing enables us or will ever enable us to explain those dramatizations starting from a social situation, made up of contradictory interests. It seems to me that the first task of revolutionary historiography is to rediscover the analysis of the political as such. But the price to be paid is twofold: we must, on the one hand, stop seeing the revolutionary conscience as a quasi 'natural' product of oppression and discontent; and on the other hand we have also to conceptualize this strange 'child' – at least in a chronological sense – of philosophy.

Thus in order to write the page left blank by Tocqueville on the period which runs from 1789 to 1799, between the origins of the Revolution and its outcome, the period which was the Revolution itself, any historical reflection must inevitably embark on an analysis that Tocqueville himself never undertook, of what constituted the specificity of the revolutionary phenomenon and of its radical novelty in the history of the world, namely the torrential birth of democratic politics and ideology. The French Revolution is the period in which social and political legitimacy suddenly tilted away from the divine right of kings towards the sovereignty of the people and in which society as a whole was continually reformed by the permanent celebration of the democratic contract in the name of the will of the people.

If this system of beliefs excludes the normal functioning of a representative regime, it is because the French of that period experienced collectively the paradox of democracy explored by Rousseau: there can be no intermediate structure, in terms of the representation of the citizens, between the general will and the individual wills which go to make the former. Because a disposition of this kind, by transferring some wills to others by the mechanism of the delegation of sovereignty, would establish a screen of particular interests which would shatter the balance necessary between the liberty of the individual and his subordination to the law. In order to be free and to found a free people, each citizen should at all times take part in the formation of the general will.

The practical experience of this logical impasse of democracy is to be found in the conception that the French Revolution held of power, and more generally of politics: power, which had at all times to reflect the people and to absorb symbolically in this identification the whole of the social sphere. This explains, moreover, not only a phenomenon like the Terror, the role of which is symbolically to re-establish this identity of power and people by means of the punishment/expulsion of plotters, and the villains. But above all this experience of 'pure' democracy which absorbs power and society into the same abstract vision of the people, restores, without knowing it is doing so and by reversing it, the image of the old monarchical power, that of the 'absolute' king. In the old society, the seat of power was occupied by divine right by the king: it was never vacant except at the price of an act which was both heretical and criminal; the king was the owner of society, encompassing it completely and embodying the people. The Revolution exorcised the curse which surrounded this incarnate monarchy by means of an inverted consecration: it was no longer power which was the people – it was the people which was the power. Here is where we discover, at the level of imaginary symbolism, the secret of what Tocqueville had perceived at the level of objective processes: if the Revolution succeeded in establishing an administrative state infinitely stronger than the monarchy of Louis XIV, it was because it carried in it and with it an image of 'absolute' power: in other words, it absorbed society in the name of the people. This is the reverse side of the image of Ancien Régime – it places the people in the place of the king – which is what gives the whole dimension to the revolutionary break. But that image also subordinates the social to the symbolic representation of the state, which explains why 'pure democracy' was finally embodied in a king of democracy: Robespierre and then Bonaparte.

Pure democracy culminated in the government of the Terror. And if Bonaparte was able "to put an end" to the Revolution, it was because he himself is the plebiscitary version of the Revolution: that is to say, the form discovered, at last, by which society establishes a power which derives everything from itself and yet remains independent of it and above it, like the Terror, but which offers to a new king what it had looked for in vain since 1789, since it was a contradiction in terms: the possibility of a democratic administration. The Revolution had come to an end because France had rediscovered its history, or rather had reconciled its two histories.

To understand this, one has only to agree to consider the Revolution in its conceptual centre, and not to dilute it in a vague evolutionism designed to dignify even more the virtues of the actors. The originality of contemporary France is not that it passed from an absolute monarchy to a representative regime or from the world of the nobility to bourgeois society: Europe took the same path without revolution and without Jacobins – even though events in France were able here and there to accelerate the evolution and to provide the model for its imitators. But the French Revolution was not a transition – it was a beginning and an original vision. This is what is unique in the French Revolution and gives it its historical interest; and it is this uniqueness which has become universal: the first experience of democracy.

Source Reprinted from *Government and Opposition*, 16:2 (Spring 1981): 200–18. Given as the first *Government and Opposition* public lecture at the London School of Economics and Political Science on 4 December 1980.

4

THE IDEA OF A DECLARATION OF RIGHTS

Keith Michael Baker

= new

The passage of the Declaration of the Rights of Man and of the Citizen was one of the earliest and most enduring acts of the French Revolution, celebrated not only in modern France, but in all modern constitutional regimes. It was the bedrock upon which all other legislation flowed, and from which a new political culture emerged. Where the Ancien Régime had been defined by privilege, the new one was characterized by rights; where the Ancien Régime was composed of subjects loyal to a king, the new one was enshrined by the Declaration as citizens loyal to one another in the form of the French nation.

Every history of the Revolution mentions the passage of the Declaration, but it is rarely studied in any depth. Because it was so fundamental to the Revolution, most historians have viewed its passage as virtually inevitable and without much drama. After all, once the Constituent Assembly passed the Declaration, it was neither rescinded nor changed by any of the factions that subsequently held power.

Keith Baker's great accomplishment here is to show that the passage of the Declaration was no foregone conclusion; that the Declaration presented the Constituent Assembly deputies with an array of choices; and how they made those choices illuminates a great deal about the early months of the Revolution. Usually, historians have viewed the language of the Declaration as simply incorporating the ideas of the Enlightenment. Baker agrees but insists that the Enlightenment did not present the Revolution with a prefabricated ideology, but rather, the Enlightenment itself was full of competing "discourses" about politics. differing views *The Constituent Assembly may have insisted that every citizen had certain rights; but what deputies meant by the term citizen, and what they meant by the term right, was by no means clear.*

By the end of the article, Baker shows that Rousseau's political language had perhaps the most important influence on how the deputies

91

thought about the Declaration. The decision regarding which phrases to include or revise were not simply semantic arguments; they were choices between "competing definitions of sovereignty." The affirmation of Rousseauian language, therefore, meant that ideas first developed in Rousseau's Social Contract *would come to have a profound impact on the Revolution.*

* * *

The search for origins can be hazardous. In the case of the Declaration of the Rights of Man and of the Citizen, its pitfalls have long been evident in the classic exchange between Georg Jellinek and Emile Boutmy, now a century old. In 1895, Jellinek set out to demolish two prevailing opinions regarding the sources of the Declaration. The first traced the principal inspiration of the text to the philosophy of Rousseau. Jellinek had little difficulty in pointing out that the essential terms of the social contract, as Rousseau imagined it, involved the complete transference to the community of all the individual's rights. Nor did he fail to note Rousseau's insistence that, since the general will emanated from all and applied to all, individual citizens needed no guarantees against the sovereign they collectively constituted.[1] This being the case, Jellinek concluded, "the principles of the *Contrat Social* are accordingly at enmity with every declaration of rights."[2] The idea of a Declaration of Rights had to find its origin elsewhere.

In the opinion providing Jellinek's second target, this origin was assumed to lie in the American Declaration of Independence. Jellinek, however, deemed the opening paragraph of the latter document far too general to serve as the model for the French text, which he found instead in the bills of rights preceding many of the constitutions adopted by the American states between 1776 and 1783. The French may have packaged their declaration in a more metaphysical wrapping, flavoring it perhaps with a Gallic hint of Rousseauism. But Jellinek's comparison of articles and clauses left him convinced that the essential ingredients of the Parisian product were imported from Virginia, with embellishments from Massachusetts and Maryland, North Carolina and New Hampshire, Pennsylvania and Vermont. The French articles, he concluded, "brought out nothing new, or unknown to the American stipulations."[3]

The prevailing wisdom thus demolished, at least to his own

satisfaction, Jellinek went on to trace the American defense of rights to two earlier traditions. First came common law protection of the rights of Englishmen, rights these latter enjoyed not by their very nature as individuals but as members of a common people. Jellinek traced this tradition to the forests of Germany, primal source of that Teutonic conception of the state in which "prince and people form no integral unity, but stand opposed to each other as independent factors."[4] Second came the Reformation, its affirmation of religious individualism issuing in claims for the right to liberty of conscience that lay at the heart of the American experience. In this experience, Jellinek argued, the common rights of Englishmen were gradually infused with higher value as rights endowed upon all individuals by their Creator.

Not surprisingly, such an assertion of the Germanic, protestant sources of the Declaration of the Rights of Man elicited an irritated response from across the Rhine. It came from Emile Boutmy in 1902.[5] Boutmy found no contradiction in the claim that Rousseau's arguments had inspired many of the articles of the Declaration of Rights, whether or not their author had actually made a case for a declaration of this kind. Nor did he see anything to preclude a sovereign people from utilizing this form to promulgate an essentially Rousseauian understanding of the principles of equality and universality as the essence of freedom under the law. Neither the form nor the content of the French Declaration owed much in Boutmy's judgment to the American models. In his analysis, similarities between the American and French documents (when they were not the illusory effect of Jellinek's method of comparison) derived less from any direct influence than from a common matrix of eighteenth-century thought. The differences were in any case more fundamental. They were differences in style, between the crabbed juridical idiom of the American declarations and the vibrant, universalistic tones of the French. And they were differences in substance, between Anglo-Saxon insistence upon the limits upon power and an indisputably Gallic – and transparently Rousseauian – affirmation of freedom through the common exercise of sovereignty.

Not that Boutmy insisted on the influence of the *Social Contract* alone. Behind Rousseau, he descried Locke, Montesquieu, Voltaire, and other exponents of the theory of natural rights. In his view, indeed, the Declaration of the Rights of Man and of the Citizen gave quintessential expression to the thinking of an entire century. Where Jellinek traced the origins of this affirmation of individual rights back to the Reformation, Boutmy saw it as the essential offspring of Enlightenment. Liberty of conscience, he insisted, was not the fruit of the Reformation, which had to the contrary inflamed the sectarian intolerance of religious fervor. Toleration was the child of the Enlightenment, which finally dared in the name of reason to free humanity from the scourge of religious passions. The signature of the Declaration of the Rights of Man was that of "the whole eighteenth century, destroyer of all tradition, creator of natural right."[6]

Who was right, Jellinek or Boutmy? Perhaps both? Perhaps neither? Jellinek was surely justified in insisting upon the fundamental importance of the example the Americans offered in prefacing their state constitutions with explicit declarations of rights. It would now be difficult to deny, in the face of Franco Venturi's research, the passionate interest in these constitutions evoked in France (as elsewhere in Europe) in the years preceding the Revolution.[7] Nor, after the careful recent readings of the debates of the Constituent Assembly by such scholars as Marcel Gauchet and Stéphane Rials, could one dismiss the urgency with which the Constituents sought to define and distinguish, with an eye to the American models, their own views of the meaning of a declaration of rights and its proper relationship to the constitution they had sworn to create.[8] Define *and* distinguish: for it is abundantly clear that the French deputies kept the American example in mind for a variety of purposes, those on the right of the Assembly warning against its dangers no less vociferously than those on the left set out to surpass its limitations.

If Jellinek's insistence on the pertinence of the example of the American bills of rights to the composition of the French declaration seems to have been borne out by subsequent research, however, few scholars would now subscribe to his assertion that all the essential articles of that document came from across the Atlantic. Nor would many deny Boutmy's contention that the French deputies drew on Rousseauian formulations at absolutely crucial points in the composition of their document, in ways that went far beyond the application of Gallic style to Anglo-Saxon truths. Few, moreover, would even wish to dispute Boutmy's more general claim that the Declaration bears the marks not only of Rousseau but of Enlightenment thinking in many of its aspects.

Why, indeed, contest a claim that is so general as to be virtually meaningless?

For the fact of the matter is that the Declaration of the Rights of Man and of the Citizen is an immensely complex document. It was also drawn up with enormous difficulty and great urgency, at the cost of bitter argument, inevitable linguistic compromises, and dramatic theoretical tensions, by an assembly profoundly divided over the nature and purpose of the text it was struggling to construct. It seems remarkable, in retrospect, that neither Jellinek nor Boutmy appears to have been in the least interested in the process by which the Declaration of the Rights of Man was actually composed, or the purposes it was intended to serve. Whether there should be a declaration of rights; what it would mean if there were; whether it should be drafted or proclaimed before or after the redaction of a new French constitution; what articles it should contain; how its every clause might be worded: each of these issues was highly contested, within the National Assembly and outside it, in the summer of 1789. Each involved a struggle to define the nature and meaning of the revolutionary situation; each bore on the political choices of language from which the Declaration of the Rights of Man and of the Citizen eventually emerged. Arguments invoked and ideas espoused in the debates doubtless came from many sources; it is important to identify them as precisely as possible. But the study of origins and influences cannot capture the particular significations these arguments and ideas assumed in the context of the assembly's debates, nor can a historical pedigree alone fix the meaning of the text to which the debates ultimately gave rise.

Fortunately, it has been one of the salutary effects of recent scholarship to shift attention precisely from questions of origins and influences to questions of meaning and situation. Before it was a text, Marcel Gauchet has aptly remarked, the Declaration of the Rights of Man was an act.[9] It was a speech act, one might say, that derived its meanings – for they were as multiple as they were contested – less from the historical sources of its particular utterances than from the illocutionary force of these utterances in a particularly tense and complex situation. In what follows I shall first try to sketch the principal competing understandings, in pre-revolutionary discourse, of the act of promulgating a declaration of rights; then I shall turn to the process of deliberation which led the National Assembly finally to take such an act.

95

THE AMERICAN MODELS

An undated, fragmentary note among the papers of the abbé Emmanuel-Joseph Sieyes, the French Revolution's first constitutional theorist, offers a fascinating comment on the history of declarations of rights before 1789. Earlier documents of this kind were, in Sieyes's view, no more than chapters in the history of despotism. Assuming the form of treaties between masters and their rebellious subjects, he argued, they were no more than pacts between two contending powers who wished to demarcate the boundaries between their respective rights and prerogatives. Forced by circumstances to recognize the subjects' grievances, a despotic ruler would make concessions that "loosened some links in the chain of general servitude". But by accepting these concessions rebellious subjects in effect acknowledged their ruler's sovereignty. Declarations of rights were thus drawn up

> the way one reaches a settlement before a notary. The general and common character of all the declarations is always the *implicit recognition* of a seigneur, a suzerain, or a master to whom one is naturally obligated, and of some oppressions one wishes no longer to endure. Everything comes down to these words: "you promise not to renew this link in your chain."[10]

In Sieyes's analysis, the American Revolution was the first to break with this traditional pattern in that it overthrew the entire yoke of despotism rather than merely alleviating it. But the break was not complete. In drawing up their bills of rights, the Americans continued to regard the governments they were establishing in the same spirit of suspicion with which they had confronted the power they had overthrown: they wished, above all, to guard themselves against abusive authority. "They declared their own rights, it appearing that thus reassured one could go about one's business in peace. The memory of ills suffered, of those most resented, guides the pen of the authors of the *declarations of rights*."[11]

It was a profound mistake, Sieyes thought, for the Americans thus to persist in conceiving a declaration of rights in the traditional manner, as a direct response to immediate injuries. Declarations drawn up on this assumption could only be particular in their articles, as each people recalled its most bitter grievances.

But particularistic declarations of this kind, insisted the French theorist, must ever be the symptom of incomplete revolutions. A people regaining its complete sovereignty needs only the universal.

> It cannot say: man, the citizen, will not bear such and such a chain. It must break them all. All that was *different* in the declaration of rights of all the peoples of the earth cannot enter into its declaration.... There is only that which is common to all; that which belongs to man, to the citizen.

On this assumption, the entire character of a declaration of rights must change. "It ceases to be a settlement, a transaction, a condition of a treaty, a contract, etc., between one authority and another. There is *only one* power, *only one* authority."[12]

Was this characterization of traditional declarations accurate as a description of the bills of rights adopted in the American state constitutions? Alexander Hamilton, writing in *The Federalist*, certainly thought so. He argued:

> It has been several times truly remarked, that bills of rights are in their origin, stipulations between kings and their subjects, abridgements of prerogative in favor of privilege, reservations of rights not surrendered to the prince.... It is evident, therefore, that according to their primitive signification, they have no application to constitutions professedly founded upon the power of the people, and executed by their immediate representatives and servants.[13]

But that was in 1787. The bills of rights were much closer in their assumptions about government to a very different theory, which Hamilton himself espoused in 1775 when he argued the principle that "the origin of all civil government, justly established, must be a voluntary compact between the rulers and the ruled."[14] This principle of compact, it was insisted, required

> that certain great first principles be settled and established, determining and bounding the power and prerogative of the ruler, ascertaining and securing the rights and liberties of the subjects, as the foundation stamina of the government; which in all civil states is called the constitution, on the certainty and permanency of which, the rights of both the ruler and the subjects depend.[15]

Like the Declaration of Independence, the American bills of rights bolstered traditional collective claims with new appeals to the rights of individuals. But their essential concern was the defense of the common law freedoms of the ruled against their rulers. Born of rebellion against the despotism of Crown and Parliament, they extended the same mistrust of power to the magistrates and legislative bodies upon whom authority would be conferred by the new state constitutions. They were intended to ensure the continued exercise of those rights of the people which could never be divested by any compact. Hence the formulation of the "DECLARATION OF RIGHTS made by the Representatives of the good people of VIRGINIA . . . which rights do pertain to them and their posterity, as the basis and foundation of Government." Hence, too, the "Declaration of the Rights of the Inhabitants of the Commonwealth or State of Pennsylvania." These declarations, and others similarly entitled, defended the collective rights of the inhabitants of each state against their magistrates and representatives. The Massachusetts declaration, for example, burst with references to "the people of this Commonwealth" – "the people" whose rights it reserved in order "to prevent those, who are vested with authority, from becoming oppressors."[16] By contrast, the French Declaration of the Rights of Man and of the Citizen refers only once to "the French people," only once to "the nation," and several times, but only in an abstract generic sense, to "society" (or its members). The collectivity from which the document is ultimately held to derive is virtually effaced by the abstract form of its appeals to universality. Part of the task of understanding the Declaration of the Rights of Man and of the Citizen must be to explain this profound difference between the American models the French deputies invoked as they began to discuss their declaration of rights and the text of the document upon which they were finally able to reach agreement.

THE USES OF A DECLARATION OF RIGHTS

The first French declaration of rights bore all the characteristics of a traditional bill of rights. It was that "declaration of the rights of the nation" proclaimed on 3 May 1788 by the Parlement of Paris in its last-ditch resistance to monarchical policies. This defiant resolution of the king's magistrates against the encroaching despotism of his ministers was perhaps the purest expression of what

I have elsewhere called the "discourse of justice" in eighteenth-century French politics. The discourse of justice drew on the conceptual resources of a constitutional tradition with deep roots in French history: a tradition effaced by the growth of absolutism since the sixteenth century but dramatically revived and reworked in the constitutional conflicts of the late eighteenth. As these conflicts escalated, so did the vehemence with which parlementry theorists reasserted the existence of fundamental laws limiting royal sovereignty, falling back upon these laws as the indispensable ramparts of an historical constitution to which both king and nation were party.

Accordingly, the declaration of 3 May sought to avert the despotism of an unconstrained royal will by appealing to a compact between the people and its ruler – a compact the magistrates construed as perpetually renewed by "a general oath, that of the coronation, which unites all of France with its sovereign." It declared that France was a monarchy governed according to fundamental laws fixing the rights of the Crown, on the one hand, those of the nation on the other. These latter included the right of the nation to give its free consent to taxation through the organ of the Estates-General, "regularly convoked and constituted"; the irremovability of judicial magistrates and the rights of the courts to register the legal expression of the king's will in accordance with the constitutional laws of each province and the fundamental laws of the state; protection of each citizen from arbitrary arrest by the right to trial, without delay and only by "his natural judges."[17]

The rights of the nation, it was to turn out after 25 September 1788, were also held by many to include the constitutional separation of the Three Estates of the realm and their separate representation in the Estates-General. The political explosion over that claim transformed the pattern of French political contestation, opening up conflicts over the composition and form of the Estates-General that were only to be resolved by the revolutionary creation of the National Assembly on 17 June 1789. It also introduced a profound ambiguity into these conflicts. For after 25 September 1788, French political discourse revolved around two overlapping but quite distinct issues: the issue of liberty, or the need to limit power, specifically the power of the monarch and his administrative agents; the issue of equality, or the need to assert power – initially the power of the king; ultimately the power appropriated by the nation itself – to destroy aristocracy and institute civil equality. This ambiguity ran throughout the debates that occurred, before the Estates-General met and in its early weeks, over the existence or non-existence of a French constitution and the necessity to fix one. It ran, similarly, through the many demands or proposals for a declaration of rights that would characterize such a constitution.

In this context, a formal declaration could be seen as a means of reasserting traditional rights of the French people against abuses of power, but it could also be used to reinforce the defense against arbitrary rule (as in the American examples) by appeal to the doctrine of natural rights. This was the syncretic spirit in which *cahiers* could demand "a declaration of national rights," "a re-establishment of the French nation in all the rights of man and of the citizen," "a French charter which will assure for ever the rights of the king and of the nation," a proclamation of the rights that "belong as much to each citizen individually as to the entire nation," or a "fundamental declarative law, enunciating the natural, essential and imprescriptible rights of the nation."[18] In such formulations, historical rights frequently merged with natural rights, those of the nation intermingling with those of the individual. In such demands, too, a declaration of rights frequently seemed synonymous with a constitutional charter. Assuming the power of the monarch, they sought to contain it: they envisaged the limitation of an existing power rather than the institution of a new one.

The same may also be said of more liberal projects for a declaration of rights, written with the American example more explicitly in mind. The marquis de Lafayette's first draft for a declaration of rights in January 1789, for example, assumed that France was and would remain a monarchy in declaring that "Nature has made men equal, and the distinctions between them necessitated by the monarchy are based, and must be measured against, general utility."[19] It insisted that "all sovereignty resides essentially in the nation" (amended in subsequent drafts to read "the source of all sovereignty resides [imprescriptibly] in the nation");[20] but this proposition led directly to a statement of the principle of division of powers, in a grammar that subtly acknowledged the existing authority of the king. The legislative, Lafayette proposed, "*must be* principally exercised by a numerous representative assembly," while the judiciary "*must be* entrusted to courts whose sole function is to keep the repository of the laws," applying them strictly, independently, and impartially. But the executive, he wrote, "*belongs* solely to the king."[21]

In Lafayette's succeeding drafts for a declaration of rights, specific references to the monarch were gradually effaced. His final version of a declaration, presented to the National Assembly in July 1789, offered a far more abstract formulation of the principle of the balance of powers, now justified on the grounds that the common good "requires that the legislative, executive and judiciary powers be distinct and definite; and that their organization assure the free representation of citizens, the responsibility of [administrative] agents, and the impartiality of judges."[22] But Lafayette still explained the necessity of such a declaration as crucial "at the moment when the government takes a certain and determinate modification, such as the monarchy in France."[23]

It was in the same spirit of the modification of existing institutions that Jean-Joseph Mounier, famed for his pre-revolutionary leadership of the constitutionalist resistance in Grenoble, drew up his own draft declaration of the rights of man and of the citizen. In Mounier's analysis, presented to the National Assembly in a speech of 9 July on behalf of its first constitutional committee, the deputies had indeed been charged (in the language of the Tennis Court Oath) to "fix the constitution" of France. Yet they had not been charged to begin that task *de novo*. "The French are not a new people that has just left the forests to form an association," Mounier emphasized in a language that was to echo throughout the assembly's early debates, "but a vast society of twenty-four million persons that wishes to tighten the bonds uniting all its parts and to regenerate the realm, a society for whom the principles of true monarchy will always be sacred."[24] Mounier held it to be the deputies' task to build a complete constitutional order upon the basis of fragmentary historical foundations and rudimentary fundamental laws. In his thinking, the tradition of French constitutionalism, eroded by decades of ideological contestation, had indeed been reduced to its barest minimum: the enduring national choice of monarchical government, on the one hand; the principle of consent to taxation, on the other. But the deputies, he nevertheless insisted, had been assembled to regenerate their monarchy, not to inaugurate an entirely new social contract.

Accordingly, when Mounier came at the end of July to prepare a draft declaration of rights for discussion by the National Assembly's second constitutional committee, he offered a text by which the "representatives of the FRENCH NATION, convoked by the king, gathered in a NATIONAL ASSEMBLY," would "declare and establish by the authority of our constituents, as Constitution of the French Empire, the fundamental maxims and rules, and the form of government."[25] Like Lafayette's draft declaration, Mounier's began with the proposition that "nature has made men free and equal in rights. Social distinctions must thus be based on common utility." Like Lafayette's, it insisted that "the source of all sovereignty resides in the nation; no body, no individual can have authority that does not emanate expressly from it." Like Lafayette's, too, its provisions for limiting the monarchical power included a formula for the separation of powers. "To prevent despotism and assure the empire of the law," it proclaimed, "the legislative, executive and judiciary powers must be distinct and cannot be united." Similar formulations recurred in the draft declaration Mounier formally presented to the Assembly on 27 July, this time on behalf of its constitutional committee. But the committee found it particularly important to elaborate upon the case for the separation of powers. "To prevent despotism and assure the empire of the law, the legislative, executive and judiciary powers must be distinct," it now insisted. "Their union in the same hands would put those entrusted with them above all the laws, for which [those so entrusted] would be able to substitute their own wills."[26] For Mounier and his allies on the constitutional committee, this principle would eventually be translated into an argument for constitutional government dividing and balancing powers along the lines of the English model.

Within this constitutionalist discourse of justice, then, there was a close link between the idea of a declaration of rights and the notion of a separation of powers. Each was seen as a fundamental device for limiting an existing monarchical power: the first by establishing the incontrovertible rights of the individual and the nation, the second as an indispensable constitutional guarantee of the preservation of those rights. But there was no necessary logic linking the project of a declaration of rights to specific constitutionalist assumptions regarding the separation of powers. The two could, indeed, be conceived as strictly antithetical. This much is made entirely clear in the extended notes added to the French edition of John Stevens's *Observations on Government* published early in 1789.[27] Stevens's *Observations* had been written in 1787 to repudiate the conception of a balance of powers elaborated in Delolme's account of the English constitution and preferred to Americans as the model of political freedom in John Adams's *Defence of the Constitutions*. In 1789, the French translation of his work became the vehicle for a sustained attack, by the marquis de Condorcet and Pierre-Samuel Dupont de Nemours among others, on the essential assumptions of balanced government in the Anglo-American style.

For political rationalists like Condorcet and Dupont de Nemours, heirs to the physiocratic tradition, the idea of separating and balancing powers was the very epitome of incoherence. Tyranny would be destroyed not by an artificial and irrational balancing of potentially arbitrary wills, they argued, but by setting forth the first principles of social organization in a rational exposition of the rights of man. The American declarations had been neither systematic nor complete; but the Americans had had the genius to recognize the need to put these declarations first, before any merely constitutional provisions. It was only necessary to reason more systematically from this premise to arrive at a declaration of rights that would be universally applicable. "One can reach such a degree of perfection in this genre that there could not be two declarations in the entire universe that would differ from one another by a single word. Where would arbitrary governments be then?"[28]

In the logic of this physiocratic discourse of reason, the very act of declaring the rights of man was the fundamental antidote to despotism. Publicity itself was the essence of a declaration of rights; publicity itself was the force that would make such a declaration the measure of all governments and the touchstone of all laws. "Ignorance is the first attribute of savage and isolated man," François Quesnay had insisted in his *Droit naturel*; "in society it is the most fatal human infirmity, it is an enormous crime, for ignorance is the most general cause of the evils of the misfortunes of the human race."[29] If ignorance was the principal cause of human misfortunes, it followed that instruction was their principal remedy. Accordingly, Quesnay, the founder of the physiocratic school, had made it one of his fundamental maxims of government that *"the nation be instructed in the general laws of the natural order, which evidently constitute the most perfect government."*[30]

103

Public tranquility and prosperity were possible only to the degree that knowledge of these laws was made general, he insisted.

> The more a nation applies itself to this science, the more the natural order will dominate within it and the more its positive order will be regular. No one would propose an unreasonable law in such a nation, because the government and the citizens would immediately see its absurdity.[31]

In physiocratic theory, then, public knowledge of the rational principles of social order – which is to say, of the natural rights and duties of individuals in society – was the essential remedy for abuses of power. The very self-evidence of these principles, once communicated to an entire nation, would render despotism impossible because absurd – just as it would render constitutionalist notions of checks and balances obsolete because incoherent and dangerous. For decades, accordingly, physiocratic propagandists had argued against political mechanisms for dividing authorities and multiplying countervailing powers. For decades, they had proclaimed that authority should be unitary but rational, transformed from within by the logic of social reason, constrained from without only by the direct and immediate force of enlightened public judgment. Those seeking means to prevent the abuse of wealth and power had invented "a thousand different kinds, all totally useless," insisted another physiocratic propagandist, the abbé Nicolas Baudeau, in his *Introduction à la philosophie économique.* But the only truly efficacious means of achieving this end was public, general, and continual instruction in the (physiocratic) principles of the natural social order. "All the other means, such as republican forms, political counterforces, and the demand for human and positive laws, are insufficient remedies to halt abuses of the predominant force."[32]

Writing in 1771, at the height of the constitutional struggles over the Maupeou Revolution, Baudeau had been anxious above all to defend the principle of unitary authority in the service of enlightened reform. Not surprisingly, then, he had reserved his most emphatic scorn for those remedies against arbitrary power favored in the constitutionalist discourse mobilized in opposition to chancellor Maupeou's attack upon the parlements. In his vocabulary, "fundamental laws" could be reduced to vestiges of arbitrary human wills lacking any foundation in the principles of social order, and hence destructive of the true rights of mankind;

an "intermediary power," in its turn, was ultimately no more than a means of preventing what was beneficial to society and ensuring what was harmful to it. As for "countervailing forces," were they really more than "the shock of blind, exclusive, oppressive, usurping passions against other blind, exclusive, oppressive, usurping passions, as celebrated modern writers understand and formally explain?" Could they ever be more than a recipe for social disorder and political confusion? "This continual battle among repositories of authority ceaselessly struggling . . . is evidently a state of war; it is the antithesis of society – in its principle, in its action, in its effects."[33]

Never more baldly stated than by Baudeau, opposition to the constitutionalist program for separating and dividing powers remained a fundamental tenet in physiocratic thinking. Unitary political authority at once sustained and transformed by publicity into the exercise of social reason; ignorance, that most profound source of human ills, eliminated by general knowledge of the true principles of social order; arbitrary government rendered impossible by the immediacy of enlightened public judgment: these were the essential maxims of the physiocratic discourse of reason as it took form in the last decades of the Old Regime. These, too, were the convictions that gave the issue of a declaration of rights its supreme importance to Condorcet and Dupont de Nemours on the eve of the Revolution.

The rationalist case for a Declaration as the essential remedy against arbitrary power was passionately made in Condorcet's *Idées sur le despotisme, à l'usage de ceux qui prononcent ce mot sans l'entendre*. He argued:

> The sole means of preventing tyranny, which is to say the violation of the rights of men, is to bring all these rights together in a declaration, to set them forth there clearly and in great detail, to publish this declaration with solemnity, establishing there that the legislative power, under whatever form it is instituted, can ordain nothing contrary to any of these articles.

The more detailed and comprehensive this declaration, Condorcet insisted,

> the clearer and more precise it will be; the surer of being protected from any tyranny will be the nation that has rec-

105

ognized it and become attached to it by principle, by opinion. For any tyranny evidently attacking one of these rights would see general opposition arise against it.

Liberty would thus be secured at no cost to public tranquility or social progress. For an enlightened nation "armed with this shield would cease to be anxious about every innovation."[34]

Not that Condorcet and Dupont lacked anxiety themselves as they watched the Estates-General assemble. Whatever the long-term effects they expected from a declaration of rights in transforming the nature of French politics and society, their insistence on the importance of such a document was also motivated by a more immediate concern: fear of what the Estates-General might do once it seized legislative power. Preoccupied for decades by the need to transform royal authority from within rather than limiting it from without, and for that reason unenthusiastic about the convocation of the Estates-General, these advocates of enlightened administrative reform now found the risks of despotism augmented rather than diminished by the prospective assertion of popular will.[35] While Condorcet warned of the dangers in his *Idées sur le despotisme*, Dupont reiterated physiocratic doctrine concerning the definition of legislative power in another note added to the *Examen du gouvernement d'Angleterre*. There he insisted that legislative will can never be unlimited; even the people does not have the right to act unjustly. From this it followed necessarily that "legislation in its entirety is contained within a good declaration of rights." And not only legislation, of course, but legislators. This was the obscure wisdom Dupont found locked into the canny linguistic fact that at the origins of societies men had chosen *legislators*, not *legisfactors*: those who would bear the law from the repository of nature rather than making it of their own will. Necessary as a guide to the legislators, a declaration of natural rights would also provide the very touchstone by which their actions would be judged.

> Every citizen has the right to subject [them] to the test of this touchstone by a free discussion, communicated as broadly as possible to other citizens. This is why the invention of printing is infinitely helpful; this is why liberty of the press must be placed among the imprescriptible rights of all and of each.[36]

Palladium of rationality, the declaration would by its very presence transform political will into public reason.

For Condorcet and Dupont, therefore, a declaration of universal human rights would not only serve as an instrument of social and political transformation. No less important, it would become an immediate safeguard against the potential dangers of revolutionary political will. It is striking, however, that Sieyes, that other heir to physiocratic doctrine, placed quite a different inflection upon physiocratic language in this respect. To be transformed, in his judgment, power had first to be seized. Before it could become an instrument for the rationalization of society, a declaration of rights had to function as a justification for revolutionary legitimacy.

The revolutionary potential of a declaration of rights for such use was made quite explicit by Sieyes in writing, on behalf of the duc d'Orléans, the latter's instructions regarding the *cahiers* to be drawn up in the electoral assemblies of the baillages under his jurisdiction. The very first item appearing in these instructions under the rubric of "most pressing national needs" concerned a Declaration of Rights. Such a document would designate the purpose of the legislative body, Sieyes explained, while also propagating among the people the true principles of social existence. But no sooner had Sieyes enumerated these two general purposes of a declaration of rights than he slipped into a more urgent, unenumerated third, linking the need for a declaration precisely to the exigencies of a revolutionary moment.

"One sees how a declaration of rights is a constitutional need in our present position," the *Instructions* argued; "we are far from directing our conduct only according to the principles of the social order." It followed from this extraordinary situation that, in the forthcoming Estates-General, constituent power (in Sieyes's new political language) would necessarily be confused with constituted power, the will of the nation necessarily usurped by its representatives. "It will be necessary to allow this usurpation," Sieyes maintained, "as we would surely allow our friends the initiative to seize our possessions from the hands of a stranger, even without any special charge from us to do so." The essential point was that the deputies make good use of this usurpation.

> and that in arrogating to themselves the right to give us a
> constitution, they place therein a principle of reformation fit

to be developed, to follow constantly the progress of enlightenment, and to recall it to its true origin.[37]

Thus the revolution, Sieyes already announces in effect, will be a revolution of the deputies; entrusted with legislative power, they will seize constituent power on behalf of the nation even in the absence of any explicit charge to do so. In this revolutionary usurpation of power, the gap in legitimacy will be filled by "presenting the peoples with the table of their essential rights, under the title of *Declaration of Rights*."[38]

For Sieyes, then, the most immediate use of a declaration of rights would be to proclaim and legitimate the assertion of a revolutionary political will, breaking with all existing powers. In this manner, his project for a declaration of rights found its justification within a radical discourse of will invoking a language of national sovereignty. But it did not thereby lose its importance within a rationalist discourse of society. Here, as elsewhere in his political theory, Sieyes blended Rousseauian and physiocratic themes.[39] No sooner would the nation recover the exercise of its sovereignty, he anticipated, than it would use its power to institute a new order inaugurated in accordance with the necessary and universal principles governing the social art. Hence the two general purposes of a declaration of rights to which he had earlier adverted. In the first, a declaration

> designates for the legislative body the social *goal* for which it is created and organised; it leaves [the legislative body] all the power, all the force to arrive at this goal with a firm step, and at the same time it surrounds it with precautions, such that it possesses neither power nor force the moment it wishes to diverge from the road set out for it.[40]

Note the formulation: the declaration designates the goal to be followed by the legislative body, but it leaves this body all the power to reach that goal; at the same time, it functions in such a way that this power is lost immediately the legislative body diverges from the purpose set out for it. Power was not to be checked by countervailing power in Sieyes's imagination. It was to be either exercised or lost – turned on or off, as it were, by some kind of automatic switch governing its flow through the political grid. It would circulate through the political system with the same ease as wealth would circulate through the ideal, unimpeded economy.

What would govern the operation of this switch? Sieyes does not make his answer to this question explicit in this text. But a clue may be found in the second of the general purposes he has earlier attributed to a declaration of rights: to serve as an instrument of enlightenment, "penetrating the generality of the citizens with the principles essential to all legitimate, which is to say *free*, human association."[41] Put these two purposes of a declaration of rights together and the point seems clear. Sieyes's declaration will rationalize power by setting forth for everyone to see the principles underlying all social organization. On this basis, a representative body will be instituted to decide on behalf of the nation, but in accordance with invariable principles; the nation in its turn will be enlightened to such a degree that any act of the legislative body in contravention of its rationally established purposes will automatically and immediately become null and void. Under the aegis of a declaration of rights, power will be exercised rationally, or not at all.

The constitutionalist limitation of power as conceived within a discourse of justice, the revolutionary appropriation of power justified within a discourse of political will, the transmutation of power understood within a discourse of social reason: these were some of the hopes invested in a declaration of rights before the Estates-General met. They afforded many competing possibilities as regards the purpose, the form, and the content of a declaration. But transformed into a National Assembly after 17 June 1789, the deputies of the French nation had first to decide whether they wanted a declaration of rights at all.[42]

DECLARATORY DILEMMAS

On 27 June, Louis XVI, reluctantly acquiescing for the moment in the National Assembly's existence, ordered that it be joined by those clerical and noble deputies who had continued to meet in their separate assemblies. Bertrand de Barère, writing in *Le Point du jour*, celebrated this reunion of the nation's representatives as finally inaugurating the reign of reason. He declared:

Doubtless the assembly's first use of its time and enlightenment will then be given to the declaration of the rights of the nation and the constitution of the state on unshakeable foundations. The force of opinion will finally destroy the slavery of abuses; natural justice will bring to an end the tyranny of usages; the courageous and enlightened patriotism that animates all the national representatives will at last achieve the most beautiful revolution accomplished on earth.[43]

But this was the rhapsody of a man who thought that the constitution could be sketched out in the work of a day. He was soon to discover otherwise.

The assembly now called upon to establish a declaration of rights labored under immense difficulties. Its size was enormous: a body of some twelve hundred persons could not easily reach agreement regarding the draft of any document. The terms of its composition also remained profoundly ambiguous, consisting as it now did of the deputies of the Third Estate who had declared themselves a National Assembly on 17 June, the liberal members of the privileged orders who had voluntarily decided to join it before or after that date, and the more recalcitrant clerical and noble deputies who found themselves in this common assembly only on the king's orders. Moreover, it had no established organization and forms of procedure, and no accepted rules for deliberation and voting, all of which remained to be defined. Its conditions of existence remained uncertain: early discussion over a declaration of rights took place as the assembly found itself surrounded by royal troops threatening its dispersal; later debate was interrupted by the crisis of widespread unrest in the provinces. And it faced a constantly escalating series of issues as the deputies were obliged, in response to successive crises, to take on the functions of a legislative and executive body in addition to those of a constituent assembly.

All of these conditions merely served, however, to exacerbate the assembly's most profound problem: the radical uncertainty of its constitutional task. By the Tennis Court Oath, the National Assembly had sworn not to disperse until the constitution of the realm had been "established and strengthened . . . on solid foundations."[44] But what did it mean to "establish" or "strengthen" the constitution? Was there a constitution to be restored – an ancient constitution ravaged by despotism, whose remnants were to be recovered, reassembled on more secure foundations, and reinforced with new protections? Or was there, to the contrary, a constitution to be created – a constitution instituting a true political order where none had previously existed? The division over this matter to be found in the mandates the deputies had brought to Versailles was made clear to the National Assembly by the comte de Clermont-Tonnerre, reporting on behalf of its constitutional committee, on 27 July 1789. He affirmed:

> Our constituents want the regeneration of the state, but some have expected it from the simple reform of abuses and the reestablishment of a constitution that has existed for fourteen centuries. ... Others have regarded the present social order as so vitiated that they have demanded a new constitution, and (excepting monarchical government and its forms, which the hearts of all the French are disposed to cherish and respect) they have given you all the powers necessary to create a constitution.[45]

The question of a declaration of rights lay at the very heart of this dilemma. Indeed, as Clermont-Tonnerre acknowledged, the demand for such a declaration was "the sole difference existing between the *cahiers* desiring a new constitution and those demanding only the reestablishment of what they regard as an existing constitution."[46] Nor was Clermont-Tonnerre simply reporting on the language of the *cahiers* in this respect. He was also recapitulating a fact that had become abundantly clear in the assembly's earliest deliberations. To debate the question of a declaration of rights was necessarily to open up the most profound differences within the assembly regarding the nature of its constitutional task.

Reporting to the assembly on 9 July, on behalf of its first committee on the constitution, Mounier had done his best to efface these differences by defining a common ground upon which all could agree. In his analysis, it was more important to give French government a determinate form than it was to decide whether a new constitution was thereby being instituted or an old one restored or perfected. "Let us fix the constitution of France," he exhorted the deputies. "And when good citizens are satisfied with it, what will it matter that some say it is new and others say it is old, provided that by general consent it assumes a sacred character?"[47] The same spirit of compromise led Mounier to insist at once on the necessity for a declaration of rights and the means of containing its potential dangers. To be good, he reasoned, a constitution had to be founded upon, and clearly protect, the rights of men. This required that "the principles forming the basis of every kind of society" be reiterated in advance, so that each constitutional article might be understood as a consequence of one of these principles. Mounier deemed it essential, however, that the statement of principles take the form of a short, concise preamble to the constitution, rather than becoming a separate document. Otherwise, "arbitrary and philosophical ideas, if they were not accompanied by their consequences, would make it possible to imagine other consequences than those accepted by the Assembly."[48] The declaration of rights should accordingly be considered an integral part of the constitution, to be neither definitively adopted until the constitution itself was completed, nor published separately from it. Only in that way could the dangers of abstract principles be contained by positive constitutional provisions.

What dangers? Chosen to define a middle ground, Mounier's language remained oblique. But the concerns to which he was alluding were quickly made more explicit by the comte de Lally-Tollendal in response to the first actual draft of a declaration of rights presented to the Assembly: that proposed on 11 July, to enthusiastic applause, by Lafayette. Lally-Tollendal did not repudiate the idea of drawing up a declaration of rights as a necessary preliminary to the drafting of the constitution, but he expressed alarm at the possibility that such a document might take on a life of its own before the completion of the constitution. The French, he insisted, were not

> an infant people announcing its birth to the universe . . . a colonial people breaking the bonds of a distant government. [They were] an ancient and immense people, one of the world's first, which gave itself a form of government for the past fourteen centuries and obeyed the same dynasty for the past eight, which cherished this power when it was tempered by customs and will revere it when it is regulated by laws.[49]

Such a society, he feared, could be rapidly thrown into disorder by the spread of metaphysical principles and abstract notions of equality.

Isolated from precise constitutional provisions, Lally-Tollendal warned, a declaration of natural rights would open the Assembly to charges that it was subverting authority and throwing all social order into confusion. It would lead to the possibility that "disturbed imaginations, misunderstanding our principles ... [or] perverse minds wishing to misunderstand them, would give themselves over to disorders or willfully go to extremes." It would produce problems and delays at a time when "the people suffers and demands real help from us, far more than abstract *definitions*." Ascent to the metaphysical peaks of natural right principles had therefore to be followed by a rapid return to the plain of positive law:

> Let us certainly go back to natural law, for it is the source of all the others; but let us pass quickly down the chain of intermediary propositions; and let us hasten to descend again to the positive law which attaches us to monarchical government.[50]

The "incalculable dangers" of metaphysical abstractions in a complex traditional society, and the more compelling need for inmmediate, practical measures of political and social reform and social relief: these were to become the central themes in the arguments of the many deputies within the assembly who opposed a prior declaration of rights. Clearly sounded by Lally-Tollendal on 11 July, they received overwhelming support. At his suggestion, Lafayette's proposed Declaration of Rights was quickly referred to the thirty *bureaux* into which the assembly had divided itself for regular discussion in smaller groups, a measure that effectively precluded its immediate adoption by the assembly as a whole.

Three days later, on 14 July, surrounded as they were by the royal troops that threatened their very existence as a body, the deputies returned again to the issue raised by Lafayette's motion. "In what circumstances if not when they are violated must we recall the rights of men?" a deputy had demanded. "They would be the enemies of monarchy who said that a declaration of rights is contrary to it."[51] But some deputies wanted a declaration of rights to be placed at the beginning of the constitution, as its foundation; others would only accept a declaration that would appear at the end of the constitution, as its consequence. All that could be agreed, after lengthy debate, was that a declaration of rights should appear somewhere in the constitution. That decision, in its turn, simply raised the question of how the constitution itself would be drawn up. Eventually, the assembly decided upon the appointment of an eight-person constitutional committee drawn from the three orders in proportion to the numbers of their representatives. But even as the deputies debated, a popular uprising was underway in Paris. That evening they received the news of the storming of the Bastille. They were not to hear from their new committee until 27 July.

When it came, the anxiously awaited committee report was divided into three parts, presented respectively – with obvious symbolism – by a deputy from each of the Three Estates that had been so precisely balanced in the committee's composition. The first, offering a general outline of the committee's views, was brought to the assembly with the moral authority of the clergy by Jérôme-Marie Champion de Cicé, archbishop of Bordeaux. The second, the report on the *cahiers* prepared by the comte de Clermont-Tonnerre, carried the weight of tradition. Analyzing the content of the *cahiers*, it divided their constitutional demands into "acknowledged principles" (monarchical government, consent to taxation, the sanctity of property and liberty) and still open questions. But these latter included such issues as the balance of the three Estates within the Estates-General, as well as its constitutional relationship to the monarch. Clermont-Tonnerre's vocabulary offered a striking contrast to the language the National Assembly had been forging since 17 June – and with it a powerful reminder of the traditional social claims still to be fully confronted within an assembly where deputies drawn from the three Estates now so ambiguously coexisted. It underlined the fact that the difference Clermont-Tonnerre reported between those *cahiers* demanding the restoration of a traditional constitution and those demanding a new one – the difference he found symbolized in their positions regarding a declaration of rights – necessarily involved the constitution of society as well as of its government.

It was left to a deputy of the Third Estate, Mounier, to present the articles on which the committee had so far agreed. They consisted of a statement of the principles of French monarchical government, preceded by a Declaration of the Rights of Man and of the Citizen. For the constitutional committee had indeed accepted the arguments for a prior declaration of rights as an indispensable means of establishing the principles upon which a new constitution should be based – and judged by the nation as a whole. "This noble idea, conceived in another hemisphere, must preferably be transplanted first among us," proclaimed Champion de Cicé.[52] He was convinced that the deputies wanted the ineffaceable principles of the rights of man constantly before them. They wanted the nation

> to be able, at every moment, to relate and compare to [principles] each article of the constitution it has entrusted to us, to assure itself of our faithful conformity to them, and to recognize the obligation and duty that arise for it to submit to laws that inflexibly maintain its rights.

They wanted, in erecting "a continual guarantee for us against our own errors," to ensure that, should any future power seek to impose laws incompatible with the principles so declared, "this original and perpetual model would immediately denounce to all citizens the crime or the error."[53]

But if the National Assembly needed a declaration of rights to secure its own revolutionary legitimacy, it needed also to guard against the dangers of such a document. True to the logic of Lally-Tollendal's earlier warning, the constitutional committee had therefore hastened to move from abstract principles to positive law. Its proposed declaration was to be welded as tightly as possible to the forms of a monarchical constitution. Written by Mounier on the model of Lafayette's earlier draft and his own, the Declaration the committee presented on 27 July was "short, simple, and precise" – as Mounier had earlier insisted it should be. In opting for it, the committee had emphatically set aside the alternative model for a declaration of rights, that of the systematic exposition of the principles of political association presented to it by Sieyes.[54]

Champion de Cicé portrayed this choice as a strategic rather than a philosophical one. He allowed Sieyes's version the virtue of building a systematic and complete exposition upon the first principles of human nature, "following it without distraction in all its developments and in its social combinations." Indeed, he praised it as the work of a genius "as profound as it is rare." But this was only to ask whether there were not disadvantages "perhaps in its very perfection," since its philosophical qualities might place it beyond the comprehension of the universality of citizens. In Mounier's draft, to the contrary, Champion de Cicé found the same principles of human nature enunciated in "formulations that are complete, but detached one from another."[55] The educated, in reading them, could fill in the logical connections; the uneducated could retain them more easily as separate propositions, free from an intimidating philosophical apparatus.

This was a shrewd understatement of the implications of choosing Mounier's draft over Sieyes's. There was more involved than mere form. It was Sieyes's claim that only a systematic exposition of the rights of man could make clear that the deputies were acting not simply to limit an existing authority but to institute an entirely new order through the exercise of an originary constituent power.[56] Behind the choice between Mounier's telegraphic articles and Sieyes's extended, systematic exposition, as the deputies were soon to discover, there still lay the fundamental question of whether the French were reforming a traditional system of government or inaugurating a new society.

RIGHTS OR DUTIES?

Before the National Assembly could decide the issue of a Declaration of Rights, it had first to decide how to decide. It was not until 29 July that it reached agreement on its rules of procedure, including the fundamental one that decisions would be reached by simple majority vote (with no provision for graduated pluralities to protect the rights of privileged minorities). At the same time, it was decided that the deputies would continue to meet daily in the separate *bureaux* for more informal discussion, while assembling for deliberation in general session only twice weekly. This latter arrangement seems to have found little favor among the most fervent advocates of a declaration of rights, particularly those endorsing Sieyes's draft. They detected little prospect of early action as *bureaux* meetings, when not inconclusive, continued simply to reject the draft declarations submitted to them.[57] By the evening of 30 July, Charles-François Bouche was already proposing that the assembly meet daily in plenary session, rather than twice weekly.[58] Compromise with ancient prejudices was all that Bouche expected from intimate assemblies, like the *bureaux*, in which ideological differences were blunted by traditional habits of deference.[59] He looked instead for decisive action from large assemblies in which "spirits are fortified and electrified; names, ranks, and distinctions count for nothing; everyone ... will regard himself as a portion of the sovereign whose representative he is.[60] Bouche's motion was passed the following day, on 31 July. He was about to have his electrifying general debate.

Thus it was in the uncertain early days of August that the National Assembly, constantly inundated as it was with news of widespread popular disorder throughout the countryside, came finally to debate whether the constitution should actually begin with a declaration of rights. On 1 August, opponents of a prior declaration failed to turn the assembly's discussions immediately and exclusively to the business of the constitution, "such as it must be in a monarchical state, without there being any need for a declaration of rights."[61] No fewer than fifty-six deputies thereupon declared their intention to speak – and began doing so at such length that the first day's debate produced a call (from none other than the impatient Bouche) for a time limit on speeches![62] "The moment has finally arrived when a great revolution in ideas and things is going to transport us, so to say, from the mire of slavery to the land of liberty," rhapsodized the *Journal des Etats-Généraux*. "In the new hemisphere, the brave inhabitants of Philadelphia have given the example of a people seizing back its liberty; France will give it to the rest of the globe."[63] The *Point du jour* was more measured in its assessment. In Barère's judgment, the moment had come for the deputies of the French nation to decide whether the practice of the New World could indeed be naturalized in the Old; whether the examples of nascent republics might be followed in an ancient monarchy; whether there were now greater dangers to be feared from a declaration of the rights of man than from ignorance and contempt for them. "It was in the midst of these doubts and uncertainties," he reported, "that the debates began."[64]

The charge of those opposed to a prior declaration of rights in the current circumstances was led by Jean-Baptiste-Marie Champion de Cicé, bishop of Auxerre. Unlike his brother, the archbishop of Bordeaux, this noble prelate remained among those who mistrusted the transatlantic example of a country inhabited only by "propertyholders, farmers, equal citizens." He deemed it necessary for the French to establish laws to hold society together before announcing indiscriminately the ideal of equality.[65] This reasoning found substantial support. The principles of the rights of man were eternal, Antoine-François Delandine acknowledged; they had been clearly demonstrated by modern philosophers. But since they were easily misunderstood by the people, they were

117

more wisely reserved to legislators capable of recognizing in the postulate of equality "a philosophical fiction that disappears as soon as there is born, alongside a feeble infant, another stronger one whose intellectual faculties will be greater." An abstract declaration would be dangerous, Delandine insisted, precisely because "each individual, interpreting it at will, could give it a terrifying extension."[66]

Pierre-Victor Malouet expounded along similar lines. "They took man in the bosom of nature and presented him to the universe in his original sovereignty," he acknowledged of the Americans. But it was one thing to do this in a society untouched by the legacy of feudalism, among a people already prepared for democracy by its customs, manners, and geography. It was quite another to do so in the midst of a vast mass of propertyless persons long oppressed and ignorant, a multitude desperately seeking subsistence in the midst of luxury and opulence. In such a situation, the bonds of society had first to be tightened, the classes brought together, the roots of luxury attacked, the spirit of family restored, love of the *patrie* consecrated; only then would it be wise to "announce in an absolute manner to suffering men, deprived of knowledge and means, that they are equal in rights to the most powerful and most fortunate." The conclusion was clear. "An explicit declaration of general and absolute principles of liberty and natural equality can destroy necessary bonds. Only the constitution can preserve us from universal disruption."[67]

The most radical response to these arguments was an avowedly (if quirky) Rousseauian one. Jean-Baptiste Crenière, deputy of Vendôme, invoked the *Contrat social* in distinguishing the constitution of a people from the mere form of its government. "Since every association is voluntary," he argued, "only the will of the associates can determine their relations." A people's true constitution was the act of association by which an assemblage of individuals agreed to form a political society; only by virtue of that act did they acquire rights in their relations one to another. Thus a true declaration of rights, enunciating the terms of the contract by which the French constituted themselves as a people, was necessarily prior to the institution of any particular form of government.[68]

Beyond a passing correction from Mounier, Crenière's speech elicited little response from other deputies. None was prepared to follow him so boldly in a reading of Rousseau that reduced rights to the consequences of a political convention.[69] Those favoring a prior declaration of rights preferred instead to find justification for the assembly's actions in principles beyond human will. "The rights of man in society are eternal; no sanction is needed to recognize them," reasoned the young comte de Montmorency-Laval. It followed that a declaration of rights was the essential foundation of the constitutional edifice; it had to be laid before this edifice could be constructed.[70]

In this view, there was greater danger of disorder in preserving ignorance and prejudice than in declaring universal truths. "The truth cannot be dangerous," insisted Guy-Jean-Baptiste Target, author himself of a much-discussed draft declaration. Moreover, any attempt to conceal the truth would be both criminal and useless. "The people does not sleep for ever; it is gathering its forces to overthrow the yoke with which it is burdened; we must direct its efforts with wisdom and prudence."[71] It would be a profound mistake to stress the dangers of a declaration of rights, added the comte de Castellane, particularly in a moment of social unrest "when all the springs of government are broken, and the multitude abandons itself to excesses that inspire fear of even greater ones." To the contrary, the "true means of stopping licence" was "to lay the foundations of liberty."[72] "Philosophical and enlightened peoples are calm," Antoine-Pierre-Joseph-Marie Barnave reassured the assembly; "ignorant peoples act restlessly." It followed necessarily that the constitution be preceded by a simple declaration comprehensible to all, a declaration that would become an indispensable *catéchisme national*.[73]

But there were many more-experienced catechizers in the National Assembly than Barnave, and they were far from imagining his catechism of *rights*. In fact, members of the clergy were conspicuous in the debate during its third day as they insisted that any declaration of rights also comprise a declaration of *duties*. The development was a telling one: it meant that the debate was shifting from the issue of whether there should be a prior declaration to the question of what it should contain. The *Point du jour*, in its account of the assembly's deliberations, reported:

> One of the most interesting spectacles for a philosopher is to observe the rapid progress of truth and reason in the national assembly. The first day of the debates, it seemed doubtful whether even the idea of a declaration of rights

separate from the constitution would be adopted; the second day, the objections raised against all declarations (this
example to French liberty given by American liberty) evap-
orated; finally, the third day, the discussion was only about
whether the declaration of duties would be combined with
the declaration of rights.[74]

On this third day, over repeated appeals for an immediate vote on
the issue of a prior declaration, the assembly suddenly began to
hear demands that any exposition of principles preceding the
constitution include duties as well as rights. "This was one of the
most tumultuous of sessions," reported the *Journal des Etats
Généraux*, describing the "hurricane of ideas" that blew as successive speakers persisted in the face of cries *"Aux voix! Aux voix!"*[75]
The clash of opinions was fundamental, touching as it did upon
the deepest convictions regarding the nature of enduring social
bonds. "Let us first establish and fix the duties of man; for to
whom shall we give laws when the very natural spirit of
independence has excited all minds and broken the bonds that
maintain the social pact?" urged Pierre-Charles-François Dupont,
one of the deputies of the Third Estate of Bigorre.[76] "If a declaration is necessary," thundered the bishop of Chartres, "there is a
pitfall to avoid. There is a risk of awakening egoism and pride.
The flattering expression of *rights* must be accompanied by *duties*
as a *corrective*. . . . It is desirable that there be, at the head of this
work, some religious ideas nobly expressed."[77] The abbé Baptiste-
Henri Grégoire, future revolutionary bishop, was no less passionate in insisting that a declaration of the rights of man was
inseparable from a declaration of the duties necessarily parallel-
ing and limiting them. While some deputies countered with the
argument that duties were simply the corollary of rights – and
therefore needed no explicit exposition – others now struggled, in
refutation, to prove the converse. In the meantime, the Jansenist
canon lawyer Armand-Gaston Camus obstinately demanded a
formal vote on his amendment to the motion: "Will there, or will
there not, be a declaration of the rights and duties of man and of
the citizen?"[78] In the shouting match that followed, the clergy
demonstrated its passionate conviction of the dangers of any
attempt to found a society on purely individualistic principles.
The demand for a declaration of duties was strong enough
to dictate a roll-call vote but not to convince a majority of the

deputies: the motion was defeated by 570 to 433. Nevertheless, the issue had been a decisive one. In voting against a declaration of duties, the deputies had in effect opted for a declaration of rights.[79] Before closing the morning session of 4 August, the assembly decreed – "almost unanimously" – that the constitution would indeed be preceded by a Declaration of the Rights of Man and of the Citizen.

It is scarcely necessary to describe the events of the evening session of that same day. Acting on the celebrated Night of the Fourth of August to abolish every vestige of the "feudal regime," the National Assembly suddenly swept aside the bonds of a trad-itional social order opponents of a prior declaration of rights had been so anxious to defend. The writers of Mirabeau's *Courier de Provence* saw a direct – and surprising – connection between this "holocaust of privileges" and the preceding debate. They claimed the emotional abandonment of privileges was sparked by a des-perate final maneuver on the part of those still opposed to a prior declaration.[80] This is an unlikely interpretation: the plan to pro-pose an abandonment of privileges seems rather to have come from those favoring a declaration of rights than from those oppos-ing it.[81] Yet there is little doubt that the emotions that swept the National Assembly on the Night of the Fourth of August were charged as much by the frustrations and delays of the preceding debates over a declaration as by the need to restore social order. "A great question agitated us today; the declaration of the rights of man and of the citizen has been deemed necessary," acknow-ledged one deputy during that night of sacrifices. "The abuse the people makes of these same rights presses you to explain them, and to establish with skillful hand the limits it must not cross." The assembly, this deputy nevertheless insisted, "would have prevented the burning of chateaux" had it been quicker to declare its determination to annihilate "the terrible instruments" of oppression they contained.[82] The deputies had indeed left it very late. Now those who had pressed for a prior declaration of rights rushed to embrace the immediate concrete actions their opponents had long demanded as an alternative. Making dra-matic use of the sovereignty to which it had laid claim on behalf of the nation, redefining property rights in the act of upholding them, the National Assembly began to give substance to its notion of the rights of man and of the citizen.

"A DIFFICULT WORK"

It was to take the deputies a week to translate into legislative form the momentous decisions of the Night of the Fourth of August. Having done so, they returned immediately to the question of the Declaration of Rights – only to be confronted by the dozens of proposed declarations which had by then accumulated. Anxious for a text that would provide a basis for rapid deliberation, the assembly agreed on 12 August to form a Committee of Five to consolidate the various proposals into a working text.[83] Led by the comte de Mirabeau and Jean-Nicolas Démeunier, an authority on American politics and a strong advocate of a declaration of rights, the committee quickly set aside the existing proposals to produce a new version of its own.

This draft appears to have been composed largely in Mirabeau's "workshop" with the help of the Genevan exiles he had assembled to constitute his personal writing-stable and think-tank. Mirabeau "had the generosity, as usual, to take the work upon himself and give it to his friends," one of them, Etienne Dumont, later recalled.

> There we were, then, with Du Roveray, Clavière and himself, drafting, disputing, adding one word and eliminating four, exhausting ourselves in this ridiculous task, and finally producing our little piece of marquetry, our mosaic of supposedly eternal rights that had never existed.[84]

Indeed, Dumont claimed to remember that, feeling all the absurdity of a "puerile fiction" as dangerous as it was fallacious, he became so disenchanted with the entire project that even Mirabeau and the other Genevans were persuaded of its futility.

It is difficult to evaluate these recollections written much later by a man who was to end up editing that classic refutation of the Declaration of the Rights of Man and of the Citizen, Jeremy Bentham's *Anarchical Fallacies*. Etienne Clavière and Jacques-Antoine Du Roveray, after all, were political refugees, veterans of a revolutionary democratic movement that had claimed the inspiration of Rousseau, and almost certainly acquainted with the textbook account of natural rights theory propounded by their compatriot, Jean-Jacques Burlamaqui. Indeed, Du Roveray's *Thèses philosophiques sur la patrie*, published in Geneva in 1767, had ended in a political call strikingly similar to a famous phrase of the preamble they now prepared for the Declaration of the Rights of Man: "Our misfortunes must instruct us, we owe all our ills to forgetfulness of these eternal maxims."[85] It seems unlikely, then, that Mirabeau's Genevans were quite as disenchanted with their task as Dumont later suggested.

At the same time, it is undeniable that when Mirabeau offered his committee's work to the National Assembly on 17 August, he did so with striking reservations. The great orator began:

> The declaration of the rights of man in society is doubtless only an exposition of some general principles applicable to all forms of government. From that point of view, one would think a labor of this nature very simple and little susceptible of contestations and doubts.

But the committee had not found it so. Indeed, it had

> quickly realized that an exposition of this kind, when it is destined for an old and almost failing political body, is necessarily subordinate to many local circumstances and can only ever attain a relative perfection. From this perspective, a declaration of rights is a difficult task.

The assignment was all the more arduous, Mirabeau continued, insofar as it involved the composition of a document to serve as preamble to a constitution not yet decided, to be prepared in a few days (as the Assembly had charged) as a digest of many conflicting proposals, and to be cast in a manner appropriate for the use of a people "prepared for liberty by the force of facts and not by reasoning."[86]

The *Courier de Provence* (written for Mirabeau mostly by Dumont and Du Roveray) was even more direct about the difficulties of drawing up a declaration of rights in a revolutionary situation. It found its argument in Rousseau's observation that society is advantageous only insofar as all its members have something and none have too much. The journal explained:

> This profound truth contains the cause of the difficulties of making a *declaration of rights* for a people grown old in its prejudices. Truth commands that everything be said, and wisdom invites temporization; on the one hand, the force of justice propels beyond the timid considerations of prudence on the other, the fear of exciting a dangerous fermentation

alarms those who do not wish to buy posterity's good at the price of the present generation's misfortunes. Oh you, tyrants of the earth, you did not feel half the misgivings, in covering it with evils and ravages, that its benefactors experience in seeking to remedy them![87]

Whatever their views regarding the intrinsic logic of a declaration of rights, these veterans of revolution in Geneva were apparently convincing themselves, and Mirabeau, that a declaration might produce a general conflagration in a complex and corrupt society. They acknowledged that a philosopher writing for eternity without thought of addressing the multitude was obliged to be uncompromising in announcing the rights of humanity. But it now seemed that the political actor in an immediate situation had necessarily to be more cautious – especially in regard to the dangers of popular misunderstanding. The people could not be armed with ideological weapons unless it was also taught their use, "for fear that it might abandon itself to fury in a first transport of drunkenness, turn them against itself, then cast them aside with as much remorse as horror."[88]

The Committee of Five had nevertheless produced a draft. And in doing so, Mirabeau explained to the Assembly on 17 August, it had preferred a series of articles in the more direct American style to the "scientific abstraction" favored by Sieyes and his supporters. Like the Americans, it had sought to present "political truths . . . in a form that could easily become that of the people, to whom alone liberty matters, and who alone can maintain it." Like them, it had opted for the language of "everyday life and simple reasonings." Like them, it had aimed to evoke "the sensations that have served to kindle liberty . . . setting aside, as far as possible, all that presents itself under the apparatus of novelty." Nonetheless, Mirabeau acknowledged, the committee had encountered many problems in realizing this form. It had proven difficult to distinguish what was natural to humanity from what was specific to particular societies; to enunciate the principles of liberty without entering into details or drifting into the formulation of laws; to avoid carrying "resentment of the abuses of despotism to the point of composing less a declaration of the rights of man than a declaration of war against tyrants." In brief, the Committee of Five had fallen far short of the ideal declaration of rights that "would contain axioms so simple, evident and fertile in consequences that it would be impossible to diverge from them without being absurd and one would see all Constitutions emanate from them."[89]

A revealing remark this, for it suggests that while Mirabeau and his colleagues had rejected the philosophical style of exposition favored by Sieyes they were still far from abandoning the rationalist ideal to which it was linked. Nothing, indeed, revealed this ideal more clearly than the language of the preamble which Mirabeau now proposed:

> The representatives of the French people constituted as the National Assembly, considering that ignorance, forgetfulness, or contempt for the rights of man are the sole causes of public misfortunes and the corruption of government, have resolved to re-establish, in a solemn declaration, the natural, inalienable and sacred rights of man; in order that this declaration, constantly present to all members of the social body, may ceaselessly remind them of their rights and duties; in order that the acts of the legislative and the executive power, since it will be possible to compare them at each moment to the goal of every political institution, may be the more respected; in order that the demands of the citizens, henceforth founded on simple and incontestable principles, may always be directed towards the maintenance of the Constitution and to the happiness of all.
>
> In consequence, the National Assembly recognizes and declares the following articles.[90]

The language of this preamble is, of course, virtually identical to that ultimately adopted in the final version of the Declaration of the Rights of Man. But it appealed less to the popular experience Mirabeau had been invoking than to the physiocratic ideal of a rationality that would unerringly guide the individual choices driving the entire system of modern society. Nor is this surprising. Mirabeau, that often wayward son of a founding father of physiocracy, had certainly been willing in his earlier *Essai sur le despotisme* to reiterate physiocratic demands for instruction that would allow every act of legislation to be compared directly to the ineffaceable and imprescriptible natural laws establishing the rights of man.[91] And he acknowledged the same inspiration yet again in debating the fate of his committee's recommendations. "Everything is in this principle – so elevated, so liberal, so fertile –

that my father and his illustrious friend, M. Quesnay, consecrated thirty years ago, and M. Sieyes has perhaps demonstrated better than any other" he admitted; "and all the rights, all the duties of man derive from it."[92]

In this case, though, the physiocratic vision was rapidly conflated with the Rousseauian ideal of collective freedom achieved by the exercise of a common political will. For the articles that followed in the declaration of rights drafted by Mirabeau's committee were strikingly Rousseauian. Having declared that all men are born free and equal, the draft offered a definition of political association that came directly from the *Contrat social*:

> Every political body receives its existence from a social contract, express or tacit, by which each individual places his person and his faculties in common under the supreme direction of the general will, and the body simultaneously receives each individual as a part.

This formulation was followed, in turn, by an article defining a constitution as the explicit expression of the will of the nation, subject to change by that will at any moment.

> Since all the powers to which a nation submits itself emanate from the nation, no body, no individual can have authority that does not derive expressly from it. Every political association has the inalienable right to establish, to modify or to change the constitution, that is to say, the form of its government, the distribution and the limits of the different powers composing it.

And, in due course, there appeared the Rousseauian insistence that "the law, being the expression of the general will, must be general in its object, tending always to assure all citizens of their liberty, property, and civil equality."[93]

A draft of this kind, presented with such ambivalence, did little to lay the basis for consensus among the deputies. In fact, it invited a virtual reprise of the arguments of 1–4 August. The ensuing debate left the Assembly, on 18 August, in a state of utter indecision. In the absence of support for Mirabeau's draft, it was simply thrown back to where it had been a week earlier – which is to say, faced with dozens of competing drafts for a declaration of the rights of man. Its only hope now seemed to be to choose one of these drafts and discuss it article by article. But even as the deputies began to vote on this procedure, Mirabeau suddenly adopted a new tack. Abruptly, he proposed reiterating the decision to make a declaration of rights an integral and inseparable first chapter of the constitution, but postponing the composition of this declaration until other parts of the constitution had been determined.[94] This meant, in effect, that the Assembly would simply confess its inability to agree on any draft, quietly retreating from its earlier decision to begin its constitutional work with a declaration of rights. Applauded by some, Mirabeau's maneuver was bitterly attacked by others as the arrogance of an orator cynically convinced of his ability to manipulate the Assembly's decisions. In response, the report of the Committee of Five was simply referred to the *bureaux*. A day later, it was formally rejected as a basis for further discussion.

At an impasse, the deputies reverted to earlier disagreements over the procedural advantages of continuing the search for a text in a general assembly or referring it again to the *bureaux*. This time, it was Lally-Tollendal's turn to insist that they either decide upon the language of a declaration or abandon the attempt. The Assembly's inability to arrive at a draft seemed in his judgment simply to underline the dangers of such a project. "If the twelve hundred of us have such difficulty in agreeing upon the manner of understanding this declaration," he demanded, "can we believe that it will fix the reasoning of twenty-four million in a uniform manner?" In this view, the assembly should immediately adopt a short, clear declaration, hastening to draw true practical consequences from its principles before others drew false ones. If this was impossible, it should save its time and proceed directly to a constitution – as Mirabeau had suggested. Lally-Tollendal reminded the deputies:

> The people is waiting, wanting, suffering; it is not for its happiness that we leave it any longer prey to the torments of fear, the scourge of anarchy, the very passions devouring it, which it will one day blame on those who have inflamed them. Better that it recover earlier its liberty and tranquillity; let it sooner receive the effects and later know the causes.[95]

Faced with this call either to act or to abandon the entire effort of a declaration, a majority of the deputies decided, finally, to cut the Gordian knot. Agreeing to an immediate choice of a text that would serve as a basis for detailed discussion, the Assembly opted for one of the more laconic draft declarations earlier presented to it, that proposed by its Sixth Bureau.[96] With sudden energy flowing from desperation to complete a task that had proved so unexpectedly problematic, the deputies now began discussing and revising this minimal text clause by clause. Within a week, little of the original wording of its articles was left; much had been sacrificed to language taken from other drafts or hammered out in discussion on the Assembly floor. Few members of the Assembly would probably have wished to claim for the resulting document more than that "relative perfection" Démeunier urged them again to accept.[97] But the representatives of the French nation had nevertheless arrived by 27 August, after so much hesitation and difficulty, at a Declaration of the Rights of Man and of the Citizen.

The preamble to the draft declaration first proposed so unenthusiastically by the Committee of Five, and then rejected so easily by the National Assembly, suddenly became the basis for the definitive text. Several possible preambles were proposed on 20 August. There was even a call for the Declaration to be preceded by the Decalogue (just as Duquesnoy had suggested earlier that it be preceded by the text of the *Social Contract*).[98] Many deputies expressed the importance of invoking the name of the Supreme Being, which was indeed added to the eventual text. But it was the preamble of the Committee of Five and its Genevan ghostwriters – adroitly presented by Démeunier with minor modifications suggested by the tenor of the preceding debate[99] – that suddenly regained favor during a discussion in which, even "at the last minute, one was far from foreseeing the solution."[100] Of all the passages proposed to the National Assembly in the various versions of a declaration of rights submitted to it, this luminous preamble – with its promise of political transparency – found its way into the final document in a form most remarkably close to its initial formulation.

Even so, the text the Assembly had hammered out by 27 August was not yet definitive; nor was it formally adopted as complete. Instead, discussion of further articles was simply suspended on that date, their consideration now being postponed until "after the constitution."[101] The deputies had arrived at a provisional text adequate for the moment to satisfy the philosophical imperative of a prior declaration; they could no longer defer the practical imperative of fixing the French constitution in the light of its principles. "The order of the day had been to deal with articles to be added to the declaration of rights," reported the *Point du jour*; "but the order of needs was to work on the constitution."[102] Long before that constitution was completed, however, the Declaration of the Rights of Man and of the Citizen had taken on a separate and definitive life of its own.

A PROBLEMATIC CHOICE

Though it has often been seen as at once the most striking proof and almost inevitable product of a notorious French rationalism, the text of the Declaration of Rights of Man and of the Citizen – indeed its very appearance – was far from being a foregone conclusion in 1789. To the contrary, the story of its composition is one of profound uncertainty and conflict over the meaning and essential purpose of any declaration of rights; over its necessity or desirability over its benefits or potential dangers; over the form it should take; over the procedures by which it might be composed; over the precise relationship it would bear to the constitution the National Assembly had committed itself to "fix"; over the relative place within it of rights and duties; over the claims of eternal, universal principles as opposed to particular considerations of time and place. Several times, the project of a declaration of rights seemed destined simply to founder in the face of these difficulties and uncertainties. Remarkably, it survived to be realized in a text composed by an assembly of twelve hundred persons in a final week of passionate public debate.

It is scarcely surprising, then, that the resulting document bore the marks of its difficult birth. Though it rapidly assumed a virtually sacred status, it was left by its authors as a text still provisional and incomplete. Though it appealed to eternal principles, it was shaped by acute conflicts over the exigencies of the political moment. Though it held out the ideal of political transparency, it emerged as a work of textual compromise and conceptual ambiguity. In adopting the language of the Declaration of the Rights of Man and of the Citizen, the deputies had not decisively resolved many of the issues dividing them so much as they had arrived at a series of linguistic compromises upon the basis of which they could now turn to debate the constitution. Many of the provisions of the Declaration remained profoundly ambiguous – their meaning left to be determined in subsequent arguments over the constitutional provisions that would give them effect.

129

The Declaration nevertheless answered enough of the needs of the particular moment, and satisfied enough of the competing political strategies formulated in response to it, to gain the acceptance of a body that had been so profoundly divided over its production. First and foremost, it gave the National Assembly a statement of universal, eternal, natural principles to legitimate its defiance of an absolute monarch.[103] General truths were held out against the despotism of arbitrary, particular will. Truths valid for all times and places were invoked to end the injustices and vicissitudes of a political order now implicitly emptied of the authority of historical prescription and reduced to a regime of power constantly destabilized by the play of vicious interests. The imprescriptible rights of individuals, the inalienable sovereignty of the nation, the natural order of society: these conceptions justified the deputies in their resistance against a monarchical power hitherto constituted as the sole point of unity within a particularistic regime of orders and Estates, the political vehicle by which the transcendent claims of the divine became the norms of earthly existence.

But this revolution carried out in the name of national sovereignty was not, strictly speaking, a revolution of the nation. More precisely, it was a revolution of deputies acting in the name of the nation. Moreover, it was a revolution of deputies who had initially received powers very different from those they soon found themselves exercising – and from a nation defined very differently from the one they were summoning into existence. Recurring debate over the nature of the "mandates" the deputies had received from their constituents constantly revealed the aporia between representation and national sovereignty in the revolutionary situation. The deputies had to legitimate representation even as they broke with the forms that had constituted them as representatives. They had to justify what Sieyes had so frankly called their "usurpation," a usurpation not only in relation to the monarch but in relation to the nation itself. The principles of publicity, immediacy, and transparency set forth in the preamble to the Declaration of the Rights of Man and of the Citizen offered an essential solution to this problem. This declaration that would be *constantly present* to all members of society promised the closing of the gap between the people and its representatives. It promised a world of instantaneous communication in which the deputies would be directly and immediately linked to the nation they served: a world in which the people could therefore assure itself, *at each moment*, that it was at one with its representatives. The physiocratic circuit of knowledge now closed the gap in the Rousseauian circuit of power.

Enough deputies were therefore convinced of the necessity of a statement of universal, eternal principles – and of a promise of political transparency – to make these indispensable features of the Declaration of the Rights of Man and of the Citizen. But many were also fearful of the dangerous implications that might be drawn from abstract principles in a situation of widespread unrest. They feared that disorder would arise from popular insurrection justified by appeal to the primitive rights of man, that anarchy would result from the dissolution of social bonds in the name of individualistic principles of liberty and equality. They were offered some recognition of these concerns in the preamble's promise that the Declaration would ceaselessly remind all members of the social body of their duties as well as their rights, while constantly ensuring respect for the acts of the legislative and executive bodies. But they sought their principal safeguards against anarchy and disorder in language more immediately controlling the implications of the successive rights the Declaration announced. They wanted rights contained by the positive provisions of the law.

This concern for social order became one of the principal motivations behind the markedly "legicentric" provisions of many articles of the Declaration of the Rights of Man and of the Citizen.[104] Time and again, the more conservative or moderate members of the Assembly insisted on the need to qualify the general statement of a right by immediate reference to the constraints of the law and the needs of civil society. The *Courier de Provence* observed of the Assembly's final debates over the declaration:

Each step it takes in the exposition of the rights of man, it appears struck by the abuse that the citizen may make of them – abuse that prudence will often even exaggerate. Hence these multiple restrictions, these minute precautions, these conditions laboriously applied to all the articles to follow: restrictions, precautions, conditions which almost everywhere substitute duties for rights, hindrances for liberty, and which, encroaching in more than one respect on

131

the most taxing details of legislation, will present man bound by the civil state and not the free man of nature.[105]

But a convergence was possible here between fear of social disorder and fear of despotism. Fear of social disorder required that the subversive potential implications of rights be limited by the law. Fear of despotism required that rights remain free from abridgment by any arbitrary personal power, which is to say that their exercise be limited *only* by the law. With this *"only,"* the law could be established as the solid reality exorcising the competing specters of disorder and despotism. Liberty could be defined as "being able to do anything that does not injure another," with the limits necessary to fulfill this latter condition safely left to be "determined *only* by law" (Article 4). The law, but only the law, could fix the point at which religious opinion troubled the public order (Article 10); the law, but only the law, could determine the cases in which speech or action constituted an abuse of the right to freedom of expression (Article 11). By way of this *only*, the discourse of justice found its place in the text of the Declaration.

Nevertheless, it did so in a curiously alloyed form. For the law the Declaration invoked was henceforth to be understood as "the expression of the general will" (Article 6), that impersonal collective power emanating from all and applying to all. Understood in this way, the law would have the right "to forbid *only* actions harmful to society" (Article 5), and to "lay down *only* those penalties that are strictly and evidently necessary" (Article 8). But the judgment as to which forbidden actions were or were not harmful to society – and which penalties were or were not necessary for their punishment – could not be left to individuals, even though these latter were held to be endowed with an inalienable right of "resistance to oppression" (Article 2). Since the law was the expression of the general will, it followed that "every citizen summoned or seized by virtue of the law must obey at once; he makes himself guilty by resistance" (Article 7). It followed, in short, that *only* the law could decide the limits of the law. But this meant, in effect, that the law – even if *only* the law – could indeed fix the meanings and limit the exercise of the rights of man and of the citizen. It meant that political will – even if only the general will – could ultimately limit the exercise of rights. It meant legislative sovereignty, the sovereignty of the Rousseauian discourse of will.

132

By such linguistic compromises and conceptual transpositions, the divided deputies finally reached a measure of agreement on a text for a Declaration of the Rights of Man and of the Citizen. But they did so at the cost of accepting a document that blended competing discourses into a volatile compound, a document producing profound ambiguities that would henceforth drive the revolutionary dynamic. The deputies agreed in adopting Article 16 of the Declaration, for example, that "a society in which the guarantee of rights is not secured, or the separation of powers not clearly established, has no constitution." But in the context of the political languages of 1789, the phrase "separation of powers" was susceptible of two quite different interpretations. Within the discourse of justice, it could be understood as applying to a system of checks and balances on the Anglo-American model favored by Mounier and the Monarchiens. Within the discourse of will, however, it could be construed according to the Rousseauian distinction between legislative and executive power, the former constituting the formal expression of the general will by the sovereign body of the people, the latter its application to particular persons and cases by the act of government. This distinction entailed a clear separation of powers, but proscribed any system of checks and balances; it operated simply to make the executive clearly subordinate to the general will. The language of Article 16 therefore glossed over the differences between two fundamentally antithetical conceptions of a division of powers. It was as compatible with an English model of government as it was with the Rousseauian notion of the general will.

Much, then, depended on the constitutional application of the language of Article 6 to the effect that "the law is the expression of the general will." Was it to be construed as implying the strong Rousseauian notion of a direct and immediate sovereignty that could ultimately have no limits outside itself, no restrictions other than those inherent in its very generality? Or might it imply some less demanding conception of sovereignty? Once again the Declaration was ambiguous. For, having declared the law to be the general will, Article 6 went on to say that all citizens have the right to participate personally or through their representatives in its formation. How, then, was this article to be understood if it admitted the possibility of representation so emphatically denied by Rousseau on the grounds that it was fundamentally incompatible with the notion of the general will? Little clarification could be found in Article 3 of the Declaration proclaiming that "the source of all sovereignty resides essentially in the nation. No body, no individual can exercise authority that does not explicitly proceed from it." To assert that the nation was the ultimate *source* of all sovereignty was not necessarily to say that the nation must exercise that sovereignty directly and immediately. Indeed, it was the specific virtue of this formulation that it glossed over the considerable difference between a strong Rousseauian version of the principle of national sovereignty (embraced by its more radical members) and the weaker one espoused by the moderates led by Mounier.

The choice between these competing definitions of sovereignty lay at the heart of the arguments that immediately occurred when the deputies finally turned, at the end of August, to debate the issue of the constitution. In the course of these debates, the assembly opted for a Rousseauian gloss on the notion of the separation of powers enunciated in Article 16 of the Declaration. It abandoned and repudiated the idea of checks and balances, favoring instead the idea of a binary separation between the legislative power – exercised by a unitary representative assembly, understood as expressing the general will – and an executive power responsible for applying that will to particular cases. This is to say that the Assembly opted, in effect, for a Rousseauian interpretation of the idea of the general will enunciated in Article 6, as of the principle of national sovereignty proclaimed in Article 3. It thus fell back upon a conception of political right that ultimately found individuals protected by the inherent generality of the general will itself rather than by any external, institutional limitations upon it.

But it was a condition of the generality of the general will, in Rousseau's conception, that it be neither alienated nor represented. How then could the deputies avoid profound contradiction when they found themselves compelled to combine the theory of the general will with the practice of representation unavoidable in a large state? Nothing was to prove more problematic for the revolutionaries – more volatile in its implications – than this notion of representing the general will, which opened up the constant risk that the will represented might be the particular will of the representative body rather than the general will of the nation. The suspensive royal veto adopted by the National Assembly in September 1789 was seen as a mechanism to close this gap between sovereignty and representation by offering a procedure through which legislative decisions could be appealed to the general will.[106]

In the event, it served to widen that gap and to exacerbate the tension between sovereignty and representation. Against the will of the deputies, the royal veto was swept away on 10 August 1792 (and, with it, the very constitution of which it formed part) by a new revolution justified and carried out in the name of popular sovereignty. With that revolution, the dynamic established by the attempt to combine sovereignty and representation became clear. The problematic relation between the people's two bodies – the insoluble problem of making the will of its representative body consubstantial with the will of its sovereign collective body (or those outside the National Assembly who claimed to express that will) – became the critical center of revolutionary politics. The Terror took form as the "people" and its representatives sought, in turn, to purge and purify one another to secure their unity and mutual identity.

The Terror took form, too, as the revolutionaries continued the struggle to realize, *at each moment*, that impossible transparence of will and understanding between the nation and its representatives that had been promised by the preamble of the Declaration of the Rights of Man and of the Citizen in 1789. The principles of that document had been enunciated in the name of universal reason and a common humanity. But its ambiguities served to inaugurate a radical dynamic that subverted representation in the name of the general will, constitutionalism in the name of political transparence, the rights of individuals in the name of the right of the nation.

NOTES

Source Reprinted from *The French Idea of Freedom: The Old Regime and the Declaration of Rights of 1789*, ed. Dale Van Kley (Stanford: Stanford University Press, 1994), pp. 154–96, 388–92.

1 Georg Jellinek, *The Declaration of the Rights of Man and of the Citizen. A Contribution to Modern Constitutional History*, trans. Max Ferrand (New York, 1901), p. 11.
2 *Ibid.*
3 *Ibid.*, p. 44.
4 *Ibid.*, p. 50.

5 Emile Boutmy, "*La Déclaration des droits de l'homme et du citoyen* et M. Jellinek," *Annales des sciences politiques* 17 (1902): 415–43, at 416. Jellinek replied, quoting copiously in support of his position from an impeccably French Aulard. See Jellinek, "*La Déclaration des droits de l'homme et du citoyen*," *Revue du droit public et de la science politique en France et à l'étranger, 18 (1902) 385–400*.

6 *Ibid.*, p. 443.

7 Franco Venturi, *The End of the Old Regime in Europe, 1776–1789. I. The Great States of the West*, trans. R. Burr Litchfield (Princeton, NJ, 1991), pp. 3–143. See also Claude Fohlen, "La filiation américaine de la Déclaration des droits de l'homme," in Claude-Albert Colliard, *et al.*, *La Déclaration des droits de l'homme et du citoyen de 1789: ses origines – sa pérennité* (Paris, 1990), pp. 21–9.

8 Gauchet; Rials. The bicentennial of the French Revolution was particularly fertile for study of the Declaration of the Rights of Man. Other valuable works include de Baecque; Christine Fauré, *Les Déclarations des droits de l'homme* (Paris, 1988); Denis Lacorne, *L'Invention de la République. Le modèle américain* (Paris, 1991). Rials, de Baecque, and Fauré reprint substantial collections of documents relating to the composition of the Declaration.

9 Gauchet, p. 107.

10 Sieyes, "Manuscrit inédit sur les Déclarations des droits de l'homme," in Fauré, *Les Déclarations*, p. 321. The date of this note is uncertain, though Fauré plausibly ascribes it to the Year III. Unless indicated otherwise, translations from the French are my own.

11 *Ibid.*

12 *Ibid.*, p. 322.

13 *Federalist* no. 84, as printed in Philip B. Kurland and Ralph Lerner eds, *The Founders' Constitution*, 5 vols (Chicago 1987), 5, p. 10.

14 [Alexander Hamilton], *Farmer Refuted*, as quoted in Gordon S. Wood, *The Creation of the American Republic* (Chapel Hill, NC, 1969), p. 271.

15 [Moses Mather], *America's Appeal*, as quoted in Wood, *American Republic*, p. 271.

16 *Founders' Constitution* 5, p. 7–9.

17 Declaration of the Parlement of Paris, 3 May 1788, as printed from Flammermont, *Remontrances du parlement de Paris*, in Rials, pp. 522–8. Rials offers a particularly convenient compendium of French versions of, and drafts for, a declaration of rights.

18 Rials, pp. 275–6, 277.

19 Lafayette, first draft for a declaration of rights (January 1789), as reprinted in Rials, p. 528.

20 *Ibid.* Compare Lafayette's second draft (June 1789) and the version finally presented to the National Assembly (11 July 1789), *ibid.*, pp. 567, 591. The composition of Lafayette's successive drafts, composed in consultation with Thomas Jefferson, is thoroughly discussed in Louis Gottschalk and Margaret Maddox, *Lafayette in the French Revolution: Through the October Days* (Chicago, 1969).

21 Rials, p. 528. Emphases added.

22 *Ibid.*, p. 591.

23 *Archives Parlementaires* (hereafter *AP*) (11 July 1789), 8:221.

24 *Ibid.*, (9 July 1789), 8:215.

25 Mounier, *Déclaration des droits de l'homme et du citoyen* (Versailles, s.d.), as reprinted in Rials, p. 606.

26 Rials, pp. 613–14.

27 [John Stevens], *Examen du gouvernement d'Angleterre, comparé aux constitutions des Etats-Unis. Où l'on réfute quelques assertions contenus dans l'ouvrage de M. Adams, intitulé: Apologie des constitutions des Etats-Unis d'Amérique, et dans celui de M. Delolme, intitulé, De la constitution d'Angleterre. Par un cultivateur de New Jersey* (London, 1789).

28 *Ibid.*, p. 201.

29 Eugène Daire, ed., *Physiocrates*, 2 vols (Paris, 1846), 1, p. 54. Dupont had set this essay at the head of the collection of Quesnay's writings he published in 1767 as an introduction to *Physiocratie, ou constitution naturelle du gouvernement le plus avantageux au genre humain*, 2 vols (Leyden and Paris, 1767–8). The physiocratic origins of the Declaration of the Rights of Man and of the Citizen are brought out particularly in V. Marcaggi, *Les Origines de la Déclaration des droits de l'homme et du citoyen de 1789*, 2nd edn (Paris, 1912).

30 *Maximes générales du gouvernement économique d'un royaume agricole*, in Daire, *Physiocrates* 1, p. 81; italics in original.

31 *Droit naturel*, in *ibid.* 1, p. 54.

32 Baudeau, *Introduction à la philosophie économique*, in *ibid.*, 2, p. 777.

33 *ibid.* 1, p. 795.

34 *Oeuvres de Condorcet*, ed. A. Condorcet-O'Connor and F. Arago, 12 vols (Paris, 1847–49), 9, pp. 165, 172.

35 Condorcet's reservations regarding the calling of the Estates-General are discussed in my *Condorcet. From Natural Philosophy to Social Mathematics* (Chicago, 1975), pp. 250–2, 264–5.

36 *Examen du gouvernement d'Angleterre*, p. 180.

37 Rials, p. 538.

38 *Ibid.* On the importance of this function of the Declaration of the Rights of Man in filling the National Assembly's need for legitimacy, see esp. Gauchet.

39 On this feature of Sieyes's thinking, see my "Sieyes," in François Furet and Mona Ozouf, eds, *Critical Dictionary of the French Revolution*, trans. Arthur Goldhammer (Cambridge, MA, 1989), pp. 313–23.

40 Rials., p. 538.

41 *Ibid.*

42 In what follows, I have drawn on, developed, and occasionally corrected the discussion of the National Assembly's constitutional debates in my *Inventing the French Revolution* (Cambridge, 1990), pp. 252–305.

43 [Barère] *Le Point du jour, ou Résultat de ce qui s'est passé aux Etats Généraux* 1(2):71–2 (27 June 1789).

44 *AP* (20 June 1789), 8:138.

45 *Ibid.* (27 July 1789), 283.

46 *Ibid.*

47 *Ibid.* (9 July 1789), 215.

48 *Ibid.*, 216.

49 *Ibid.* (11 July 1789), 222. Barère's response was acid. "Must consideration for ancient prejudices make us forget the imprescriptible rights of man?" he demanded. "Must fear of damaging ideas established till now ever compromise the eternal rights of humanity?" *Le Point du jour* (12 July 1789), 1(2):174–5.

50 *AP* (11 July 1789), 8:222.

51 *Le Point du jour* (14 July 1789), 1(2):187.

52 *AP* (27 July 1789), 8:281. But this praise of the New World prompted a vigorous defense of the originality of the Old – and particularly of Rousseau – in Mirabeau's *Courier de Provence*: "Let us observe that before the independence of English America the *Contrat social* had appeared. . . . No, one must never speak of liberty without paying a tribute of homage to this immortal avenger of human nature," *Le Courier de Provence*, no. 20 (24–27 July 1789).

53 *AP* (27 July 1789), 8:281.

54 See Sieyes, *Préliminaire de la constitution. Reconnaissance et exposition raisonnée des droits de l'homme et du citoyen. Lu les 20 et 21 juillet 1789, au comité de constitution*, in Rials, p. 591–606.

55 *AP* (27 July 1789), 8:282.

56 As Champion de Cicé makes clear, Sieyes had added a summary list of rights to his "systematic exposition" only when pressed to do so by the constitutional committee.

57 [Le Hodey de Sault Chevreuil,] *Journal des Etats Généraux* (30 July 1789), 2:270.

58 Adrien Duquesnoy, for one, was convinced that this motion was the scheme of those who, "seeing that the abbé de Sieyes's constitutional project is not finding favor in the *bureaux*, where it is being coldly examined, wish to carry it into full battle in the Assembly, which is fatigued by long discussion." See Robert de Crèvecoeur, ed., *Journal d'Adrien Duquesnoy, député du tiers-état de Bar-le-Duc, sur l'Assemblée constituante (3 mai 1789–3 avril 1790)*, 2 vols (Paris, 1894), 1: p. 57.

59 The reasoning behind his motion was frankly reported in the *Journal des Etats Généraux* edited by Le Hodey de Sault Chevreuil. "The military, ecclesiastical, and judicial aristocrats craftily develop their ideas in these meetings; they would have kept their silence in an assembly of twelve hundred. They speak boldly before thirty, half of whom encourage them. The good patriots find themselves isolated . . . the obligation of certain kinds of respect, the habit of an ancient deference, regain their empire proportionately, the closer one approaches a bishop or a noble; the latter perorates and the other [the good patriot] falls silent." *Journal des Etats Généraux* (30 July 1789), 2:277–8.

60 *AP* (30 July 1789), 8:307.

61 *Ibid.* (1 August 1789), 315.

62 Anxious to move the debate to a conclusion, and claiming that at least 200 deputies wanted to present their views, Bouche proposed a five-minute limit on the second day of the debate (3 August). The proposal was rejected in response to vigorous claims for unrestrained

deliberation as the essence of liberty. The assembly agreed only that speeches would be given alternately in favor of the motion and against it. For a passionate report on this debate, see *Le Point du jour* (4 August 1789), 2:9–13.

63 *Journal des Etats Généraux* (1 August 1789), 2:306–7.

64 *Le Point du jour* (2 August 1789), 1(2):377.

65 *AP* (1 August 1789), 8:322.

66 *Ibid.*, 324.

67 *Ibid.*, 323.

68 *Ibid.*, 319.

69 However, the comte d'Antraigues did indeed invoke Rousseau in demonstrating that a declaration of rights would sustain rather than subvert respect for property – on the grounds that "in the state of nature, man has the right to all that force can procure for him. In the state of society, man has the right only to what he possesses." *AP* (3 August 1789), 8:335.

70 *Ibid.* (1 August 1789), 320.

71 *Ibid.*

72 *Ibid.*, 321.

73 *Le Point du jour* (3 August 1789), 2:6; *AP* (1 August 1789), 8:322.

74 *Le Point du jour* (4 August 1789), 2:20.

75 *Journal des Etats Généraux* (4 August 1789), 2:352–60.

76 *AP* (4 August 1789), 8:340.

77 *Le Point du jour* (4 August 1789), 2:22.

78 "He stubbornly insisted on deliberation on this motion," Duquesnoy recalled. "It was rejected, but this pigheadedness caused an immense loss of time, and it was noticed with sorrow that M. Camus maintained with a kind of furious determination a proposition upon which the clergy seemed to set so much importance," *Journal d'Adrien Duquesnoy* 1:264.

79 On this point, see de Baecque, p. 20.

80 *Le Courier de Provence*, no. 23 (3–5 August 1789).

81 See Patrick Kessel, *La Nuit du 4 août 1789* (Paris, 1969), pp. 127–33.

82 *AP* (4 August 1789), 8:345.

83 *Ibid.* (12 August 1789), 399, 434. The committee, composed of deputies who had not submitted a draft declaration to the assembly, included the comte de Mirabeau, Jean-Nicolas Démeunier, François-Denis Tronchet, Claude Rhédon, and the bishop of Langres, César-Guillaume de La Luzerne.

84 Etienne Dumont, *Souvenirs sur Mirabeau et sur les deux premières assemblées législatives*, ed. J. Bénétruy (Paris, 1951), p. 97, On Mirabeau's "workshop" more generally, see Bénétruy, *L'Atelier de Mirabeau. Quatre proscrits genevois dans la tourmente révolutionnaire* (Paris, 1962).

85 On these points, see Marcel Thomann, "Le 'Préambule' de la Déclaration des droits de l'homme (1789)," *Tijdschrift voor Rechtsgeschiedenis* 55 (1987): 375–82; "Origines et sources doctrinales de la Déclaration des droits," *Droits* 8 (1988): 55–69.

86 *AP* (17 August 1789), 8:438.

87 *Le Courier de Provence*, no. 28 (17–18 August 1789). On the composition of the journal, see Dumont, *Souvenirs*, pp. 89–93.

88 *Le Courier de Provence*, no. 28 (17–18 August 1789).

89 *AP* (17 August 1789), 8:438.

90 *Ibid.*

91 The point is made by Marcaggi, *Les Origines de la Délaration des droits*, pp. 167–8.

92 *AP* (18 August 1789), 8:453.

93 *Ibid.* (17 August 1789), 438–9.

94 *Ibid.* (18 August 1789),454.

95 *Ibid.* (19 August 1789), 458–9.

96 For the text of this draft, see Rials, pp. 621–4. Its character and origins are well described in Philip Dawson, "Le 6ᵉ bureau de l'Assemblée nationale et son projet de Déclaration des droits de l'homme," *AHRF* 50 (1978): 161–79.

97 *AP* (20 August 1789), 8:462.

98 *Journal d'Adrien Duquesnoy*: p. 303.

99 *AP* (20 August 1789), 8:463.

100 *Journal des Etats Généraux* (20 August 1789), 3:19.

101 *AP* (27 August 1789), 8:492.

102 *Le Point du jour* (28 August 1789), 2:222–3.

103 This point has been forcefully made by Gauchet.

104 On this point, see particularly Rials, pp. 236, 369–73, 396–403.

105 *Le Courier de Provence*, no. 31 (22–23 August 1789).

106 For an analysis of the arguments over the suspensive veto, see my *Inventing the French Revolution*, pp. 281–305.

Part III

NEO-LIBERAL RESPONSES TO REVISIONISM

The revolutions that have taken place in other European countries, have been excited by personal hatred. The rage was against the man, and he became the victim. But, in the instance of France, we see a revolution generated in the rational contemplation of the rights of man, and distinguishing from the beginning between persons and principles.

Tom Paine
Rights of Man

5

A RHETORIC OF BOURGEOIS REVOLUTION

William H. Sewell, Jr

In the excerpts below from William H. Sewell, Jr's recent book,
A Rhetoric of Bourgeois Revolution: The Abbé Sieyes and "What
Is the Third Estate?", *the bold ideas of Furet and Baker are challenged
through an analysis of the major theorist of the Revolution's early years,
the Abbé Sieyes. It was his 1789 pamphlet,* What Is the Third Estate?,
*after all, that helped to transform the political crisis from a struggle
between crown and aristocracy to one among the privileged orders
and the leaders of the Third Estate, or in Sieyes terminology, between
parasitic noblemen and the French nation.*

*As he admits here, Sewell's criticism is meant to be a friendly
amendment. He accepts much of Furet and Baker's critique of the old
Marxist orthodoxy. But he faults them for accepting Marxist definitions
of social categories and thereby dismissing social explanations in favor of
intellectual ones. Sewell suggests turning such a method on its head by
viewing the writing and publishing of a pamphlet or book as itself a
social activity, involving an array of social interests and processes. Seen
in this light, he argues that Sieyes's pamphlet represented a bourgeois
ideology, indeed, "the most thoroughly 'bourgeois' vision of any of the
great revolutionaries." But such a vision, thinks Sewell, became irrelevant during the radical years of war and counter-revolution, when
Sieyes's language of political economy could not stir much national
sentiment. Even after 1794, middle-class deputies rejected Sieyes's
bourgeois rhetoric. By isolating the early period of the Constituent
Assembly as a moment when leading statesmen were willing to adopt
Sieyes's vision, Sewell illustrates how different that period was from
those that came after it.*

* * *

INTRODUCTION

It should be clear from the very subject of this book that I too have been influenced by the turn from social to intellectual interpretations of the French Revolution. I fully accept the [Revisionist] critique of [Marxist historians Georges] Lefebvre and [Albert] Soboul and am convinced that the Revolution cannot be understood apart from the language and conceptual vocabulary of the revolutionaries. This book is resolutely textual in method and focus; in many respects it is yet another example of the French Revolution as intellectual history. Indeed, many of the arguments developed in the book were first worked out for a series of lectures that I gave in Furet's seminar in Paris. But at the same time, I am attempting to mount a modest challenge to what I regard as a mistaken tendency in the current historiographical school to eliminate social considerations from revolutionary history and from the study of revolutionary texts.

This tendency is present in even the most impressive works in the new genre. François Furet's *Penser la Révolution française* is a particularly clear case. In this book, Furet was locked in mortal combat against the classical social interpretation. One of his major efforts was to establish that social determinations of the sort that preoccupied Lefebvre, Soboul, and Mazauric – that is, class interests derived from relations to the mode of production – were essentially irrelevant to the major issues of revolutionary history. As we have seen, he argued that the semiotic dynamic of revolutionary political rhetoric completely displaced such social determinations during the crucial period from 1789 to 1794. But as often happens in polemic, Furet in effect accepted his enemies' definition of the terrain: he implicitly defined the social in the same narrow and reductionist way as it was understood by his Marxist opponents. Because social determinants as posited by a reductionist form of Marxism proved irrelevant to revolutionary history, Furet made the unwarranted inference that the explanations lay solely in politics and ideas, to the exclusion of social considerations.

It may well be that class interests in an orthodox Marxist sense were only tangential to the political struggles of the French Revolution, although the massive peasant uprisings of the summer of 1789 stand as a continuing challenge to this claim. But orthodox Marxism has no monopoly on conceptualizing the social. The human sciences, including their Marxian variants, have developed many ways of thinking about humans as social beings: not only Marx's concepts of class and mode of production but also Weber's status hierarchies and forms of rationality, Malinowski's social structures, Gramsci's hegemony, Goffman's interaction rituals, Thompson's experience and agency, Foucault's power/knowledge and disciplinary regimes, Durkheim's social integration and collective representations, Braudel's structures, conjunctures, and events, Giddens's duality of structure, Geertz's cultural systems, and Bourdieu's habitus and symbolic capital, to name only a few. If we adopt a broader definition of the social, then the French Revolution fairly bristles with social determinations and social consequences that in the work of Furet and his school are either ignored or reduced to political ideology.

Keith Baker, in his pathbreaking *Inventing the French Revolution*, is more aware than Furet of alternative concepts of the social. But he too, in the end, reduces the social to the intellectual. Baker, however, has the merit of performing this reduction by explicit argument rather than simply by fiat. He posits what he calls "political culture" as the object of his investigation and offers a "linguistic" definition of the term. His definition

sees politics as about making claims; as the activity through which individuals and groups in any society articulate, negotiate, implement, and enforce the competing claims they make upon one another and upon the whole. Political culture is, in this sense, the set of discourses or symbolic practices by which these claims are made. . . . It constitutes the meanings of the terms in which these claims are framed, the nature of the contexts to which they pertain, and the authority of the principles according to which they are made binding. It shapes the constitutions and powers of the agencies and procedures by which contestations are resolved, competing claims authoritatively adjudicated, and binding decisions enforced. Thus political authority is, in this view, essentially a matter of linguistic authority: first in the sense that political functions are defined and allocated within the framework of a given political discourse; and second, in the sense that their exercise takes the form of upholding authoritative definitions of the terms within that discourse.[1]

145

Baker's definition of political culture develops a powerful argument for the fundamental significance of political language. But one might question whether the incontestable fact that political claims are elaborated in language necessarily implies that political authority is *"essentially* a matter of linguistic authority." This definition, in short, contains a hint of linguistic reductionism.

The hint is expanded to a matter of principle in the following paragraph, where Baker explicitly considers the anticipated objection that such a definition "denies the relevance of social interests to political practice, seeking instead to privilege a symbolic realm over the realities of social life." He answers this objection by denying

> that there are social realities independent of symbolic meanings: All social activity has a symbolic dimension that gives it meaning, just as all symbolic activity has a social dimension that gives it point. This is to argue that claims to delimit the field of discourse in relation to nondiscursive social realities that lie beyond it invariably point to a domain of action that is itself discursively constituted. They distinguish, in effect, between different discursive practices – different language games – rather than between discursive and nondiscursive phenomena.[2]

Here Baker begins with a point I fully endorse: that there are no social realities independent of symbolic meanings. But, from this premise, he derives the reductive conclusion that social realities can adequately be characterized as "discursive practices" or "language games." This, it seems to me, does not follow. The fact that all human activities are structured by and bring into play linguistic or paralinguistic meanings does not imply that those activities are *nothing but* the production of meaning, or that a linguistic conceptual vocabulary can describe them adequately. Indeed, Baker's own language of social and symbolic "dimensions" of activities seems to imply that there is more to the human world than making meaning: "All social activity has a symbolic dimension that gives it meaning, just as all symbolic activity has a social dimension that gives it point." I take the second clause of this sentence as meaning that symbolic activity typically both shapes and is shaped by phenomena not reducible to symbolic meanings – for example, interpersonal communication networks, direct coercion, competition for scarce resources, or patterns of spatial contiguity and dispersion. To me, Baker's language of dimensions implies that all domains of action are constituted simultaneously and indissolubly by both "social" and "symbolic" considerations – that the shaping of the social by the symbolic and the symbolic by the social is fully mutual and reciprocal.

The problem is that Baker follows up only one side of this reciprocal relationship. In the sentence quoted above, the social and the symbolic are contrasted as two distinct but interdependent dimensions of action. But in the two sentences that follow, Baker transmogrifies the social into the symbolic. He asserts that what are usually thought of as "social realities" are themselves "discursively constituted," but he does not add that what are usually thought of as discursive realities are themselves socially constituted. By this means, he effectively reduces the social to the discursive and turns the claim that all symbolic activity has a social dimension into a tautology: that all symbolic activity has a symbolic dimension. In this way, Baker erases the social dimension of human action that he initially introduced into his account, freeing himself to conceptualize the French Revolution as fully constituted by an evolving counterpoint of linguistic claims.

This evacuation of the social from the Revolution is combined, in both Furet and Baker, with a particular strategy of textual analysis. If they reduce the complexities of social life to language, they tend to reduce the political texts they study to their logic. At a time when literary critics and a vocal minority of intellectual historians are calling for deconstructive readings of texts, readings that try to undermine or disperse what have been taken to be the texts' clear, normative, and intended meanings, the Furet school remains true to an older style of textual analysis.[3] At their best, these analyses are extremely powerful; they bring into sharp focus the texts' major contributions to the ongoing political debate and illuminate their authors' fundamental philosophical assumptions. But rather than bringing to the surface the partially suppressed multiplicity of voices that always coexist in a text, they try to discern each text's central tendency, its essential intellectual argument. Even in Baker's *Inventing the French Revolution*, which takes great pains to recapture the multiplicity of prerevolutionary political debate, the complexity of the whole is achieved by reanimating a clamoring diversity of individually coherent political voices.

Texts should be seen as social products that have social consequences. They are linked to extra-textual realities both through their authors, who creatively use existing linguistic conventions to carry out their socially formed intentions, and by readers, who are influenced by texts but who also interpret them – again, creatively – in terms of their own socially specific identities and interests. The meanings of texts, and therefore their social effects, are never securely and unambiguously inscribed in their language but depend on the ambiguous motives and contradictory social locations of both authors and readers. An approach that sees texts as media of social action can both profit from deconstructive strategies in analyzing the multiple social meanings of texts and show how the social situations in which texts are produced and interpreted lead to the multiplication of linguistic meaning. Indeed, I believe that the impossibility of fixing meaning arises as much from the contested character of the social actions in which language inevitably is employed as from any internal mechanics. The instability of language seems to me inseparable from the inherent contradictions of motivated social action.

AN UNCONTROLLABLE REVOLUTION

What Is the Third Estate? It did much to set the tone and direction of the French Revolution in the fateful year of 1789, but its author could hardly control the Revolution's course over the longer run. In his pamphlet, Sieyes succeeded in scripting both the triumph of the National Assembly on 17 June and its radical abolition of privileges on 4 August. He did this by joining a rhetoric of political revolution that pointed toward a seizure of power by the delegates of the Third Estate with a rhetoric of social revolution that inflamed bourgeois resentment against the aristocracy. From August 1789 forward, however, the Revolution veered increasingly out of his control. There was, to be sure, much in the constitutional work of the National Assembly that Sieyes not only supported but influenced. His ideas were significantly reflected in the Declaration of the Rights of Man and Citizen, the administrative reorganization of the country, the civil constitution of the clergy, and the distinction between active and passive citizens that was written into the Constitution of 1791. But in spite of his continuing influence on certain constitutional issues, the political culture of the Revolution developed in directions that Sieyes found antipathetic.

A Failed Bourgeois Vision?

The abbé Sieyes gained his initial fame by expressing in a novel and brilliantly conceived rhetoric the aspirations and resentments of the French bourgeoisie – the diverse class of well-to-do officials, merchants, lawyers, professionals, rentiers, men of letters, and landowners who made up the politicized segment of the Third Estate. By simultaneously telling them that they were the real leaders of the nation and reminding them of the countless petty humiliations they had suffered at the hands of aristocrats, Sieyes harnessed the energies of the bourgeoisie to a project of political and social revolution – a project that triumphed in the summer of 1789, when the deputies of the Third Estate declared themselves the National Assembly, abolished the privileges of the aristocracy, and laid the foundations of a new social and political order based on the sovereignty of the nation and equality before the law. In *What Is the Third Estate?* Sieyes represented the bourgeoisie to itself as a class of producers, whose useful private and public activities assured the prosperity of the country. It was this quality that set the bourgeoisie off from the nobility, whom Sieyes's rhetoric banished from the nation as a class of idlers and parasites. To judge from the extraordinary reception of the pamphlet, the politically active segments of the French bourgeoisie passionately embraced a self-definition that drew its fundamental terms from a political-economic view of the human condition.

But bourgeois acceptance of the discourse of political economy turned out to be provisional. In the context of a political struggle against the nobility, political economy supplied a perfect argument. The opening chapters of *What Is the Third Estate?* used the language of political economy to transform the Third Estate from the lowliest of the three orders that made up the kingdom into the whole of the nation – and to transform the nobility from superiors deserving deference to parasites and enemies. Political economy provided a language of exclusion that severed the nobility from the body of the nation, thereby avenging the thousands of petty acts by which the nobles had previously excluded the bourgeoisie

149

from its rightful place of honor. But when Sieyes moved from this negative usage of political economy as a language of exclusion to a positive portrayal of the social order as an association for the creation of wealth, he was unable to win general assent for his arguments.

Sieyes had what was perhaps the most thoroughly "bourgeois" vision of any of the great revolutionaries. He broke thoroughly and explicitly not only with the aristocratic view that men of superior breeding and ancient family traditions should govern the state, but with the classical Greek and Roman model of civic simplicity and military virtue. He believed that the modern states of Europe had abandoned such archaic notions and had embraced instead the peaceful pursuit of material well-being. He celebrated the growing complexity of society as the most potent source of prosperity and liberty and fashioned a theory of representative government based on these "modern" trends. He advocated administrative and juridical reforms that would abolish all forms of legal privilege and open to merit all careers in public service. He elaborated a political and social theory that cast the élites of the former Third Estate as the prime movers of economic activity, public reason, and social well-being. And he enunciated a theory of political representation meant to ensure that these élites would maintain a firm grip on state power.

There are reasons to think that this vision should have been widely attractive to the French bourgeoisie. As Colin Jones has recently reminded us, France at the end of the eighteenth century was a highly commercialized society.[4] It had experienced a substantial increase in wealth and trade over the past three-quarters of a century, and its people, particularly its well-to-do urban dwellers, had developed an expanding taste for a whole range of consumer goods: clocks, books, coffee, sugar, chocolate, furniture, cutlery, glassware, textiles, and minor luxuries of all kinds. Manufacturers, commerce, and public and private services had all expanded impressively, opening ever greater opportunities for those with the requisite wealth or education to make profitable employment of their capital and talent. Sieyes's political and social vision would seem to have been perfectly calculated to win an enduring endorsement from the bourgeoisie of late-eighteenth-century France.

In fact, the new constitutional order elaborated between the summer of 1789 and the summer of 1791 seems on the whole to have been consonant with Sieyes's views. The Assembly dismantled privileges and venal offices, decreed that careers in public service were open to talent, abolished guilds, established a unified market, made the first steps toward a new uniform legal code, replaced the provinces with uniform departments, made priests into public functionaries, and established an electoral system that distinguished between active and passive citizens and assured that only members of what Sieyes called the available classes could be elected to the Legislative Assembly. It is true that many of Sieyes's pet projects were rejected: the National Assembly chose another's draft of the Declaration of the Rights of Man and Citizen, seized the lands of the church over his protests, overwhelmingly rejected his position on the royal veto, modified his scheme for the establishment of geometrically uniform departments, and never seriously considered the establishment of tributes of electors and eligibles. Nevertheless, the constitutional and legislative work of the National Assembly not only was consistent with the general outlines of Sieyes's vision but was profoundly influenced by many of his specific proposals.

It was only in the following years, when France was wracked by war on the frontiers, the overthrow of the monarchy, and the onset of violent civil strife, that the Revolution diverged sharply from Sieyes's "bourgeois" ideals. This was in part, as Soboul (and before him Mathiez) insisted, a consequence of the alliance between the Jacobin faction in the National Convention and the Parisian sans-culottes; who campaigned openly for direct democracy and for the reimposition of controls on the economy.[5] But only in part. The bourgeois deputies associated with the Jacobin factions diverged from Sieyes's vision not only by reimposing economic controls but by passionately embracing classical Greek and Roman notions of virtue. The values of classical republicanism had been prevalent in French and European political culture well before 1789 and had constituted a major theme in political debate during the early years of the Revolution.[6] But it was only from 1792 forward that the passion for classical republicanism became hegemonic in the political culture of the French Revolution. This passion was hardly imposed on the Jacobins by the sans-culottes, it was, rather, a specialty of the classically educated bourgeois Jacobins. As the storms engulfing the Republic intensified in 1792 and 1793, left-wing orators and publicists styled themselves tribunes and invoked Solon, Pericles, Brutus, Cato, the Gracchi, and Caesar; they imagined their Republic as a modern replica of Roman history. This classicizing mode, moreover, outlasted the Terror and even the Republic: Napoleon, after all, made himself a modern Caesar, replacing the Republic with an Empire in 1804 and administering its provinces with prefects.

Karl Marx, in *The Eighteenth Brumaire of Louis Bonaparte*, wrote astutely about the revolutionaries' obsession with Rome, which he saw as a mask hiding from them their tawdry bourgeois objectives:

> releasing and setting up modern *bourgeois* society [which would be] wholly absorbed in the production of wealth and in the peaceful struggle of competition. [The] classically austere traditions of the Roman republic, [provided the revolutionaries with] the self-deceptions that they needed in order to conceal from themselves the bourgeois limitations of the content of their struggles and to keep their passion at the height of the great historical tragedy.[7]

Although I think Marx's interpretation gets at some of the attraction of the classical model, it cannot be accepted whole. During the relative calm of 1789 to 1791, the revolutionaries needed no self-deception to mask their establishment of the legal conditions for capitalist enterprise. They promulgated revolutionary transformations of the nation's administrative, constitutional, and juridical structures under the banner of enlightened reason, efficiency, and natural law, without significant recourse to Roman and Greek masks.

But when the affairs of the Revolution grew desperate, when the very survival of the Revolution was threatened by external war and internal revolts and the legislature was faced with the awful task of trying and executing the king for treason, the language of political economy – indeed, the language of Enlightenment rationalism more generally – no longer sufficed. Political economy, whose leading advocate in the French Revolution was Sieyes, lacked a heroic vision. Political economy had been developed to explain the peaceful arts of production and exchange; it extolled efficiency, self-interest, and the rational division of labor, rather than virtue, solidarity, and selfless sacrifice for the common good. It assumed a bland linear narrative of gradual and anonymous improvement rather than a perilous narrative of danger, heroism, tragedy, and triumph. Political

economy provided a plausible language for thinking about juridical and constitutional relations among citizens – not about
fateful decisions or struggles to the death. Classical antiquity,
by contrast, offered a host of heroes and tragic plots – and,
given the dominance of the classics in contemporary education,
heroes and plots intimately familiar to the revolutionary politicians. Faced with genuinely herculean tasks and historic
decisions, it is not surprising that revolutionary actors identified
themselves and their times with Greek and Roman history.
Although I do not agree with Marx that the bourgeois revolutionary leadership needed classical draping to conceal from
themselves their establishment of a social and juridical order
consistent with a capitalist economy, their classical obsessions
did serve to "keep their passion at the height of the great historical tragedy" during the most desperate moments of the
Revolution.

Marx saw the recourse to classical models as the choice of an
imaginary but heroic vision over a humdrum but accurate recognition of the Revolution's real tasks, which were to erect a state
apparatus and legal system appropriate to a rising "bourgeois"
social and economic order. Yet it is far from obvious that Sieyes's
political-economic view of the Revolution and its tasks was any
more realistic than the Revolution's Roman drapery. Because
capitalism and political economy triumphed in the nineteenth
century, we tend to credit the eighteenth-century inventors of
political economy with a realism far in advance of the aims of
their contemporaries, who were steeped in classical rhetoric,
utopian longings, or aristocratic fantasies and failed to see with
steely clarity the actual historical trends of their time. But this
assumption is dangerously anachronistic. Political economy was
a visionary enterprise, not the product of painstaking empirical
investigations into the workings of the economy. Adam Smith,
for example, was an absent-minded professor whose lack of
touch with the daily world was legendary; his distracted
unconcern for quotidian problems casts some doubt on the
assumption that his system was especially realistic. Moreover, the
highly deductive, logical, and closed character of his doctrine
bears the marks of a totalizing philosophical vision, not of a
down-to-earth empiricism.

Whatever we may think about Smith, Sieyes is certainly an odd
candidate for the mantle of "worldly philosopher."[8] After all, he

had been a sickly and scholarly child who spent his entire youth in the seminary of Saint-Sulpice and lived out his pre-revolutionary adult years in the clergy. In the seminary he rebelled against ecclesiastical discipline not by indulging in the fleshly pleasures of Paris but by reading incessantly in the texts of the philosophes and scribbling reams of notes. Throughout his life he remained an aloof intellectual, a spinner of systems and ideal constitutions. He was taciturn and solitary; his friends were few and his favorite occupation was reading. He had no firsthand experience of day-to-day economic life and little empirical curiosity about commercial and industrial matters. His view of political economy was drawn entirely from the texts of economic philosophers, both the French Physiocrats and the Scottish political economists. We have seen that some of his ideas about his country's economy were absurdly inaccurate. He imagined that a small intellectual élite organized and set in motion French economic activity, when both entrepreneurship and technical knowledge were actually the province of artisans and peasants – whom Sieyes dismissed as ignorant and passive working machines. His cognitive map of the French economy was logical, but it was also delusionary. Sieyes was nothing if not a visionary, and he was at his most visionary, not his most realistic, when he thought about economic questions.

The French bourgeoisie at large and the bourgeois political activists who manned the revolutionary legislative bodies may therefore be excused for failing to recognize themselves consistently in the mirror held up to them by Sieyes. He certainly shared important motivations and worries with his bourgeois contemporaries. Both his resentment against the aristocracy and his profound antipathy toward urban and rural laboring people struck responsive chords. The National Assembly did abolish the privileges of the nobility and adopt Sieyes's distinction between active and passive citizens and a pyramidal system of electoral filtering. But neither the National Assembly, nor the Convention, nor any other of the revolutionary legislative bodies embraced his ideas about representation and division of labor. Like all political actors everywhere, they had a choice not between an imaginary and a real political project, but between alternative imaginative constructions of the social and political world. It should not be surprising that the French revolutionaries eventually preferred a Romanizing vision, which drew on images familiar since their school days, to the novel and idiosyncratic political-economic vision of the abbé Sieyes.

Nor should it be a surprise that the French bourgeoisie of the Old Regime, dominated as it was by rent-taking property owners, professionals, and state officials, was ultimately unmoved by a social and political vision based on the primacy of production. Sieyes may have contributed much to the launching of a bourgeois revolution, a revolution spearheaded by the well-to-do élite of the Third Estate. But this bourgeoisie was not the entrepreneurial class imagined by either Marx or Sieyes, and its identity as producers was neither deep nor lasting. This self-definition faded after 4 August 1789, when the privileges of the aristocracy were annihilated. From that point forward, a rhetoric that excluded idlers from members of the nation not only lost much of its utility for the bourgeoisie but might even have proved dangerous to the bourgeois rentiers who made up the most "available" of "the available classes." The politicized elements of the bourgeoisie accepted Sieyes's productivist vision only provisionally, as a language of exclusion that served them in a particular political and social struggle, not as a fundamental and enduring identity.

NOTES

Source Excerpted from William H. Sewell, Jr, *A Rhetoric of Bourgeois Revolution: The Abbé Sieyes and* What Is the Third Estate? (Durham, NC: Duke University Press, 1994), pp. 29–40, 185–97.

1 Baker, *Inventing the French Revolution: Essays on French Political Culture in the Eighteenth Century* (Cambridge, 1990), pp. 4–5.
2 *Ibid., p. 5.*
3 The most vocal of this minority of intellectual historians has been Dominick LaCapra. See his *Rethinking Intellectual History: Texts, Contexts, Language* (Ithaca: Cornell University Press, 1983); *History and Criticism* (Ithaca: Cornell University Press, 1985); *History, Politics, and the Novel* (Ithaca: Cornell University Press, 1987); and *Soundings in Critical Theory* (Ithaca: Cornell University Press, 1987).
4 Colin Jones, "Bourgeois Revolution Revivified: 1789 and Social Change," in *Rewriting the French Revolution*, ed. Colin Lucas (Oxford: Oxford University Press, 1991), pp. 69–118 [reprinted as Chapter 6 of this volume].
5 Albert Soboul, *Les Sans-Culottes parisiens en l'an II; Mouvement populaire et gouvernement révolutionnaire, 2 juin 1793–9 thermidor an II* (Paris: Librairie Clavreuil, 1962); Albert Mathiez, *La Vie chère et le mouvement social sous la terreur* (Paris: Payot, 1927).

6 See, e.g., Baker, *Inventing the French Revolution,* esp. "A Script for the French Revolution: The Political Consciousness of the Abbé Mably," Chap. 4, pp. 86–106, and "A Classical Republican in Eighteenth-Century Bordeaux: Guillaume-Joseph Saige," Chap. 6, pp. 128–52; and J.G.A. Pocock, *The Machiavellian Moment* (Princeton: Princeton University Press, 1975).

7 Karl Marx, *The Eighteenth Brumaire of Louis Bonaparte* (New York: International Publishers, n.d.), p. 14.

8 I take the expression from Robert L. Heilbroner's *The Worldly Philosophers: The Lives, Times and Ideas of the Great Economic Thinkers* (New York: Simon and Schuster, 1961). Heilbroner's discussion of Smith seems to me quite contradictory. On the one hand he paints a portrait of the philosopher as an extraordinary eccentric oblivious to the surrounding world and given to fits of abstraction; on the other, he portrays Smith's theory as an accurate representation of the eighteenth-century English economy as it really was. Heilbroner never asks how so removed a philosopher achieved such a mimetic representation of the real world (pp. 28–57).

6

BOURGEOIS REVOLUTION REVIVIFIED
1789 and social change

Colin Jones

One of the most interesting features of the new challenges to Revision-
ism is how much the challengers are indebted to the Revisionists them-
selves. Not only do they accept much of Revisionist work, but their
closest colleagues, mentors, and teachers are often the same Revisionists
whose work they are critiquing. Their debate, then, is more in the spirit
of the Enlightenment philosophes than the fratricidal struggles between
Jacobins and Girondins. Just as this was the case for William Sewell's
critique of his colleagues Furet and Baker, so it is here with British
historian Colin Jones, who combines sarcasm and humor with a percep-
tive analysis of the eighteenth-century French economy.

One of the hallmarks of Revisionism has been its rejection of an
ascendant capitalist bourgeoisie hostile to privileged noblemen. On the
eve of the Revolution, as Colin Lucas claimed earlier in this volume, the
ruling élite was composed of both commoners and noblemen, and the
most important social distinction did not concern birth, but rather,
whether one performed manual labor. Colin Jones accepts parts of this
analysis, but insists that it ignores the complexity of the late eighteenth-
century economy, in which many parts of what we might call the
privileged orders had become immersed in market capitalism. For
example, Jones identifies the buying and selling of public offices as being
a capitalist enterprise with its own national market. Such new forms of
capitalism created sharp social antagonisms. The bourgeoisie may not
have constituted a distinct class with its own sense of its potential, but
that does not mean that large sections of the ruling élite were not
influenced by bourgeois interests that stemmed from a nascent form of
capitalism. In this sense, Jones agrees with Sewell that the French
Revolution was truly a bourgeois revolution.

* * *

COLIN JONES

The decision on 16 July 1789 to demolish the Bastille presented a wonderful opportunity to Pierre-François Palloy.[1] The 34-year-old building contractor, who – so he said – had helped to storm the Bastille on 14 July, took on the job of demolition. The grim medieval fortress was soon a building site, offering much-needed employment to about 1,000 hungry Parisian laborers and providing a diverting and edifying spectacle for the leisured élite. The famous Latude, who had made his name by publishing an account of his imprisonment in the state fortress, was on hand to act as tourist guide to the site. Latude's publishers rushed out extra editions of his work, and Bastille commemorative volumes were soon among the bestsellers. A further wave of popular interest accompanied the discovery by Palloy's workmen in early 1790 of subterranean cells filled with chains and skeletons. This was not the Man in the Iron Mask, but it was something.

Palloy, however, was attracting some unwanted attention. When he presented accounts to the National Assembly in October 1790, certain right-wing deputies suggested that he had made a huge profit from the whole enterprise. Bertrand Barère, the future colleague of Robespierre in the great Committee of Public Safety, sprang to Palloy's defence. "It's not some deal that he made. . . . It's political destruction; it's something truly revolutionary. . . . So the Bastille's demolition turns a profit for the nation and provides honor for liberty."[2] Fine words and flattery: but Palloy's books seem not to have balanced. Although he managed to avoid investigation, he seems to have made a considerable profit from merely selling off the stones of the Bastille; many went, for example, into the construction of the Pont de la Concorde. He went further than this, moreover, setting up a manufactory in his home in which huge numbers of the stones were carved into little replicas of the Bastille. Chains and irons found on the site were created into similar memorabilia: medals, dice-boxes, paper-weights, snuff-boxes, inkpots, and the like. Palloy enrolled a host of fellow *Vainqueurs de la Bastille* to act as his travelling salesmen – he called them his apostles of liberty – taking stocks around the departments to meet what was clearly a great demand. Three parcels of Bastille memorabilia were presented gratis to each of France's eighty-three departments – though the latter did pay the transport costs, which allowed a profit to be made, and doubtless further stimulated local demand.

As he protests at his stone Bastille models being undercut by cheap plaster imitations, we should perhaps tiptoe quietly away from this interesting entrepreneurial figure who clearly awaits his Samuel Smiles – or better still, his Richard Cobb. From the vantage-point of the Bicentenary in 1989, with its chocolate guillotines and Bastille boxer shorts, his story nevertheless neatly demonstrates that the commercialization of the French Revolution is as old as the Revolution itself. The character sketch does, moreover, illustrate some of the themes I wish to develop here: namely, the Revolution and economic opportunities; bourgeois entrepreneuralism; consumerism and fashion; civic sensibilities; the interlocking of business and rhetoric.

To bring a bourgeois to the centre of the stage may, however, appear gloriously *dépassé*. After all, 1989 marked not just the bicentenary of the Revolution, but also the twenty-fifth anniversary of the publication, in 1964, of Alfred Cobban's *Social Interpretation of the French Revolution*, the classic text of the Revolutionist school which has come to dominate French Revolutionary historiography.[3] Over the last quarter of a century, the Revisionist current has virtually swept from the board what is now identified as the Orthodox Marxist view. The idea, almost axiomatic to the historians whom Cobban attacked – Mathiez, Lefebvre, Soboul – that the Revolution marked a key episode in the passage from feudalism to capitalism is now either widely discounted or else viewed as a *question mal posée*. And the idea – regarded as a truism before the 1960s – that the Revolution was a bourgeois revolution is now held up to ridicule. Indeed, George V. Taylor, one of the Grand Old Men of Revisionism, recently warned off historians from using the term "bourgeois" which is, he contends, "freighted with too many ambiguities to serve in research as a general analytical tool or operational category."[4]

In the place of the old Marxist orthodoxy – the Revisionists always talk of the Marxist interpretation in the singular, as if Marxists never disagreed, or else robotically took their cue from the Politburo – a New Revisionist Orthodoxy has gradually sprung up, which by now has permeated into general interpretations and views, in much of French publishing as well as in English and American scholarship. The New Orthodoxy will have little truck with social interpretations in general, and the bourgeois revolution in particular. Far from being the heroic, world-historical, almost transcendental force which Karl Marx had seen him as, the bourgeois now cuts a shabby figure. Revisionist historians view him as pathetically insecure, anaemic, transitional – zombie-esque, in the view of Simon Schama.[5] The Old Regime bourgeoisie, so the New Orthodoxy goes, burnt its candle at both ends. At the top, merchants and manufacturers who built up sufficient wealth were swift to disinvest from productive activities and sink their capital in land, seigneuries, and venal office. Their propensity to ape their social betters was exemplified by their wish to achieve noble status, and indeed many former traders and manufacturers referred to themselves as *bourgeois vivant noblement*. The preference for status over profit which this behavior is alleged to exemplify can be dated back centuries, as Colin Lucas and William Doyle have reminded us, and may thus be dubbed, as George Taylor would have it, atavistic.[6] At its bottom end, the Revisionists tell us, the bourgeoisie was equally undynamic. Peasants who might have enriched themselves by production for the market preferred risk-avoidance and subsistence strategies, and coralled themselves away from their bourgeois betters in the ghetto of a "popular culture" they shared with guild-dominated, and equally "traditionalist" urban workers.[7]

This was a bourgeoisie more deeply riven by internal schisms than by class antagonisms – and indeed the Revisionists reserve some of their sharpest barbs for those starry-eyed "Marxist" idealists who retain some attachment to the concept of class struggle. Indeed, the New Orthodoxy has it that there was less unity shown by the bourgeoisie as a class than, for example, by the inter-class élite of upper bourgeois and nobles. One must admire the Revisionists' sleight of hand, for the Old Regime nobility, normally portrayed (they tell us) as monolithically parasitic and feudal in its outlook, are nowadays viewed as hyper-dynamic and entrepreneurial. The nobility dominated the key sectors of the economy, Guy Chaussinand-Nogaret assures us, exercised overwhelming cultural hegemony, and generously held out a co-operative hand to those awestricken bourgeois wishing to enter France's social élite.[8] Once viewed as the agents of a "feudal reaction" which shut out talented commoners, the nobility is now seen as the leading partner in an enlightened élite, entry into which through venal office was still surprisingly easy.[9] The term "open élite" is now being used less in regard to eighteenth-century England, following the broadsides of

Lawrence and Jeanne Stone, than to Old Regime France.[10] The Revolution's persecution of this enlightened noble-dominated group can only, in its injustice, its economic irrationality, and its lack of humanity, be compared to anti-Semitism (the comparison is Chaussinand-Nogaret's).[11] Yet the nobility would have the last laugh, for once the Revolution was over, they formed the backbone of the class of landowning and professional notables which dominated nineteenth-century France.[12]

The idea that France's late eighteenth- and nineteenth-century history essentially concerns the formation of an élite of notables (the latter, incidentally, every bit as much a portmanteau term as that of "bourgeois," against whose vagueness Cobban inveighed), with the Revolution as an unwelcome intrusion or even an irrelevant footnote, has become a keystone of the New Revisionist Orthodoxy.[13] It fits in very snugly with the systematic disparagement of the economic significance of the Revolution. Far from marking the passage from feudalism to capitalism, the Revolution could not even transform the economic structures and shortcomings of the economy: agrarian productivity only registered progress, Michel Morineau tells us, after 1840, and industrial capitalism had generally to await the railway age.[14] Late eighteenth-century France was in any case only just emerging from *l'histoire immobile*, Emmanuel Le Roy Ladurie's description of a kind of neo-Malthusian prison-camp in which French society had been interned since the fourteenth century.[15] The Revolution thus becomes little more than a minor fold in the flowing fabric of that *longue durée* so beloved of the *Annales* school.

This tendency within the Revisionist camp to minimize the social changes associated with the Revolution has led to most recent historiographical running being made by historians of politics and culture. Lynn Hunt has chided social historians for concentrating their interest on mere "origins and outcomes,"[16] and for failing to recognize that the revolutionary character of the 1790s resides in the fabrication of a new political culture. The outstanding work of Keith Baker, and the 1987 Chicago conference proceedings, *The Political Culture of the Old Régime*, which have been published under his direction, buttresses that view.[17] In the Brave New Revisionist World, discourse reigns supreme and social factors bulk exceeding small. It often seems, for example, as if the new political culture had no long-term social roots, but emerged in a process of inspired and semi-spontaneous politico-cultural *bricolage* in 1788–9. François Furet, for example, the verit-able pope of contemporary Revisionism, sees 1789 as ushering in a political logic and a proto-totalitarian discourse which lead in unilinear fashion to the Terror.[18] The idea that the Revolution's shift to the left in the early 1790s might have something to do with the counter-revolution is roundly dismissed: the revolutionaries are diagnosed as suffering from a plot psychosis predating any real threat to their work. The Revolution was on the track to Terror from the summer of 1789, socio-political circumstances notwithstanding.[19]

François Furet has been a devastating critic of the unreflective sociologism of the old Marxist approach as exemplified in some of the writings of Albert Soboul.[20] The pendulum has now swung to the other extreme, however, and many Revisionists seem to wish to reduce the history of the Revolution to political history with society left out. A typical recent example of the way in which discourse analysis and high politics over-ride the social angle is the treatment which a number of recent authors have given to the famous Night of 4 August 1789, when the National Assembly issued a decree formally abolishing feudalism. Overlooking or discounting evidence about the blatant fixing of this session, ignoring the ridiculously high rates of compensation for losses of feudal rights the deputies awarded, turning a blind eye to stories of violent peasant revolution which, magnified by rumor, were pouring into Paris and Versailles at the time, William Doyle, Norman Hampson, Michael Fitzsimmons, and Simon Schama all view the explanation of the behavior of the deputies as lying in the altruism of the old "enlightened" élite.[21] One of the key moments in the social transformation of France, the zenith of peasant influence on the course of events, thus merely becomes a vacuous chapter in group psychology, with the Assembly acting as if hermetically sealed from outside social influences. What Simon Schama characterizes as a "patriotic rhapsody" becomes for Michael Fitzsimmons a kind of beautific vision, a Close Encounter of the 4 August Kind, in which the deputies self-denyingly pledged themselves to "the sublimity of the Nation."[22] The Revolution as a whole thus becomes "the reaction of groups and individuals to the imposition by the National Assembly of its new vision of France," an approach congruent with George Taylor's famous characterization of the Revolution as a "political revolution with social consequences rather than a social revolution with political consequences."[23]

This denigration of the popular and collectivist aspects of the Revolution and the downplaying of social origins to the political crisis of 1789 keys in with some other recent accounts, moreover, which view French society as largely the opponent or the victim of the new political culture. From Donald Sutherland's account, for example, one gains the impression that nine-tenths of French society in the 1790s was objectively counter-revolutionary.[24] (This, incidentally, is a view which calls into question François Furet's diagnosis of plot psychosis.) If there was a popular revolution at all, Douglas Johnson tells us, it was the Counter-Revolution.[25] From evacuating the Revolution of all positive social content to viewing the repression of counter-revolution as "genocide" by a "totalitarian" power is only a short step – and one which certain historians have not been afraid to take.[26]

Perhaps we are wrong to judge the views of the New Revisionist Orthodoxy by the uses to which they are being put by the political Right; after all, the Old Marxist Orthodoxy was shamelessly exploited by the Left. What is, however, worrying for a social historian is the extent to which social change is disparaged in or omitted from the New Revisionist Orthodoxy. It is not my intention to pose as King Canute, vainly bidding the Revisionist wave to recede. On the contrary, I would contend that a great deal of Revisionist research being done in fact subverts the main, rather brittle assumptions around which the New Revisionist Orthodoxy has hardened.[27] In this essay, I would like to mine that seam in a way which suggests that we need to rethink our attitudes towards some of the key problems associated with the relationship of the Revolution to social change. While many may prefer cosily to relax in the platitudes of the New Revisionist Orthodoxy, we may in fact be moving towards a situation in which new research allows us to relate afresh to some of the problems of causation which concerned Marxist French Revolutionary historiography. This may come as a shock to many Revisionists, who tend to relate to that historiographical tradition by presenting a knockabout pastiche of the views of the alleged Old Marxist Orthodoxy, a kind of pantomime in which a succession of Revisionist Prince Charmings rescue Marianne from the clutches of a wicked, mean-spirited old Stalinist Baron – a part reserved in most scripts for the late Albert Soboul. Using the research of both

Revisionist and Marxist scholars, I am going to be foolhardy enough to suggest that the Revolution did have long-term social origins. I will go on to suggest that these related directly to the development of capitalism and indeed that the much-disparaged term "bourgeois revolution" retains much of its force and utility.

One of the cardinal tenets of the New Revisionist Orthodoxy is that eighteenth-century France was – with the possible exception of the enlightened élite – "traditionalist," preferring a flight from capitalism rather than its warm embrace. Much of the force of this view has in the past resided in unfavorable comparisons made with the allegedly more mature capitalist economy of Great Britain, undergoing in the period from 1780 the classic Rostovian "take-off" into self-sustained economic growth. Against this, the argument runs, the French economy can only seem "backward" or "retarded."[28]

One has only to scratch the surface of this approach today to realize that it lies in tatters. The work of François Crouzet, Nicholas Crafts, Patrick O'Brien and others have pointed up the buoyancy of French economic performance over the eighteenth century, and shown that in many respects it even may have outdistanced Great Britain.[29] Annual averages of both agricultural and industrial growth were higher in France than in Great Britain.[30] If we are to believe Patrick O'Brien and Caglar Keyder, a broad comparability between the British and the French economies continued into the early twentieth century. France's per capita physical product tripled between the early nineteenth and early twentieth centuries, and the authors see this as part of a development which stretches back into the eighteenth century. Perhaps Britain's priority in emergence as First Industrial Nation owed less to her economic performance over the eighteenth century than to factors which predated 1700 – the stability of Britain's financial institutions grounded in the establishment of the Bank of England in 1694, and Britain's early switch to mineral fuel, which stimulated the emergence of a coal-fuel technology which would contribute importantly to the industrialization process.[31] But rather than talk in terms of retardation or backwardness, perhaps we should just accept that there is more than one way towards industrialization, and that the British route, though first – or perhaps because it was first – was not necessarily the most appropriate for others. France did not have the sudden spurt in industrial performance which England enjoyed, but her more balanced and drawn-out pathway to industrialization was no less effective in the longer term, and may indeed be particularly deserving of attention in that it avoided many of the direst social costs which accompanied Britain's Industrial Revolution.[32]

I have thus far portrayed eighteenth-century France as a more and more commercial society, increasingly sensitive to the market, very different from the stagnating, traditionalist society encountered in the New Revisionist Orthodoxy. Seen from this viewpoint, it seems clear that the main intermediaries and beneficiaries of this growing commercialization were the allegedly "traditional" bourgeoisie. Merchants, artisans, shopkeepers, and the *paysannerie marchande* were in the fore, with only a sprinkling of the nobility. The size of the bourgeoisie grew over the century from 700,000 or 800,000 individuals in 1700 to perhaps 2.3 million in 1789 – getting on for 10 per cent of the global population.[33] The New Revisionist Orthodoxy that bourgeoisie and nobility were somehow identical in economic terms thus seems rather wide of the mark: even were we to take all of the 120,000 nobles Chaussinand-Nogaret claims to have been in existence in 1789 as engaged in entrepreneurial activity – a hypothesis very far from the mark, as Chaussinand-Nogaret would admit – they would still be sinking without trace in a bourgeois sea.[34] Entrepreneurial nobles were anyway more likely to be involved in monopoly capitalist ventures or financial dealing than in the more humdrum bread-and-butter mercantile and manufacturing activities which were the staple of French commercial capitalism.

In the New Revisionist Orthodoxy, the professions are usually patronizingly labeled the "traditional élites," the assumption being that they remained locked in the rigidities of the Society of Orders until 4 August 1789. In fact, they were in a state of institutional and intellectual ferment in the eighteenth century. Each seems to have undergone important institutional changes over the century, and developed in self-esteem, self-definition, and commitment. This was accompanied by a certain consumerism – one might say a bourgeoisification – in their lifestyles which reflects the extent to which they were adjusting to the inroads and the potentialities of commercial capitalism.

To look at any one of the professions in the late eighteenth century is to uncover a welter of ongoing debates – grounded, I would contend, in the changing size and nature of demand – on the nature of professionalism. In these debates, issues fundamental to the role of the service sector in a capitalist economy – the provision of services, rational organization, public accountability, market forces, quality control, and so on – were addressed. These are matters which we can as yet glimpse only darkly, and on whose exact nature we can at this stage only hazard guesses. To make an outrageously bald generalization, however, it seems helpful to classify the arguments utilized into two broad camps. On the one hand there were arguments for professionalization which adopted a corporative framework, and which sought changes on a "vertical," internalist, and hierarchical basis. Expertise, internal discipline, and segregation from the wider society was the key. On the other hand, there were arguments which adopted a civic dimension, where the framework for professionalism was transcorporative, egalitarian, "horizontal." The profession should be opened up on to the wider society. Both sets of arguments utilized the same kinds of language, though if proponents of the corporative professionalism tended to think in terms of "subjects" of the "state" (sometimes even personalized still as "the king") the civic professionalizers referred to "citizen" and the "Nation" or, sometimes, "the public."[35] It is a language which in its most democratic and egalitarian formulations prefigured the debates in the National Assembly in the summer of 1789.

Let us take the profession of arms as an example. David Bien, in a brilliant Revisionist article, has familiarized us with the notion of the professionalization of the army officer corps.[36] This took the form of measures aimed to produce an effective army, Spartan in its virtues (though Prussia was the real blueprint), operating within more bureaucratic and hierarchical structures, and enjoying more efficient training and a more articulated career structure. Even the infamous Ségur ordinance of 1781 which limited high command to officers enjoying four quarters of nobility can be regarded as a professionalizing measure.[37] The aim of the ordinance was to exclude not commoners so much as recently ennobled bourgeois who had bought their way into the corps through the system of venal office and were thought to lack the sense of inbred honor which only dynasties of military nobility could produce in young recruits. What has tended to be seen as a

flagrant instance of feudal reaction thus takes on the more ano-
dyne colors of military professionalization; privilege is legitimized by service, high birth by social utility. Unfortunately, this is
only half of the story. Though Bien does not tell us so, in fact there
was more than one way of construing professionalization. The
corporative model of the old nobility was matched by a very
different, civic model, reflected and furthered by the writings of
Rousseau, but transcending any narrow lineages of literary influences.[38] Embraced by many younger officers, this model was
grounded in the belief that professionalism could best be
achieved through opening up the army on the wider society. The
military man was a citizen before he was a soldier: this basic
message comes through in a whole host of writings from the
1770s onwards, rising in a crescendo, as one might expect, with
the American War of Independence. Guibert's *Essai de tactique*
(dedicated *A ma patrie*) (1772) and Joseph Servan's *Le Soldat citoy-
en* (1780) may serve as instances of the genre.[39] Consider in this
respect too the early career of Lazare Carnot, the "Organizer of
Victory" in Year II, and a military engineer in the last years of the
Old Regime. Carnot's prize-winning "Eloge de Vauban" (1784) is
a fine example of civic professionalism. Writing self-proclaimedly
as a *militaire philosophe et citoyen*, Carnot praises the technical
skills of Vauban as a servant, but he also sees him as a friend of
the people, whose professional artistry was intended to defend *la
Nation* from the sufferings of war. In this civic version, the professional ethic was combined with a critique of Ségur-style privilege,
and the corporative professionalism which camouflaged it.[40]

Antagonistic strands of civic and corporative professionalism
are to be found in the secular clergy prior to 1789 too, as Timothy
Tackett has shown.[41] The corporative model owed much to the
continuing post-Tridentine reforms of the Catholic hierarchy,
which aimed to make of parish priests spiritual gendarmes working obediently under their bishops. Intensive training, through
seminaries and apprenticeship as *vicaires*, bade fair to make the
Catholic clergy a force quite as disciplined, quite as *pur et dur* as
the professionalized army corps. The equation of professionalism
with the wearing of the clerical cassock highlighted the congru-
ity.[42] This conception of the parish priest had increasingly to
compete, however, with a more civic view which stressed the
duties the clergy owed to the Nation. The citizen-clergy, often
fuelled by Richerist ideas, resented the overly hierarchical and

disciplinarian character of the Church, as well as its social dominance by the high nobility; practised the virtues of charity and
consolation to their fellow citizens; and invoked the rights of the
Nation. Their lifestyle as well as their outlook became increasingly bourgeois: the watches, clocks, mirrors, books, and other
decorative bric-à-brac found in their homes revealed them as very
much part of the new consumer culture.[43] The large number of
civic-minded lower clergy elected to the Estates-General were to
play a crucial role in helping to win the political initiative for their
bourgeois fellow deputies in the Third Estate.[44]

Schoolteachers – very largely within the aegis of the church –
were a group amongst which this civic ideology made a particular mark.[45] The pedagogy of the last decades of the Old Regime
was thoroughly infused with civic values. Schoolteachers
included some of the most eloquent and persuasive members of
the revolutionary assemblies: Lanjuinais, Fouché Billaud-
Varenne, Daunou, François de Neufchâteau, Manuel, and
Lakanal are a representative crop.

There was to be a good admixture of medical men among the
deputies of the revolutionary assemblies too, the good doctor
Guillotin not least.[46] Debates over professionalism in the world of
medicine were complicated by the traditional split between
university-trained physicians and the more artisanal surgeons.
Medicine was a jungle: the physicians cordially despised the surgeons, and the major medical faculties were perennially at dag-
gers drawn. Over the course of the century, however, important
changes took place. Surgeons hoisted up their prestige, wealth,
and status: a liberal education came to be required for a surgical
career.[47] A growing professionalization on their part, grounded in
their highly centralized organization – the King's First Surgeon
was effectively "King of Surgery" throughout France – was
helped by their proven utility in their service of the royal armies.[48]
As the century wore on, many physicians also tried to transcend
the corporative petty-mindedness for which they were famous,
and to stress the public benefits of medical professionalism.[49] The
foundation of the Royal Society of Medicine in 1776 was viewed
as an attempt to give some corporative structure to the straggling
bands of physicians throughout France; but it also made a great
play of its mission as recorder and diagnostician of epidemics
and as information network on disease and the environment.[50]
Above all, it stood as the scourge of medical "charlatanism," and

argued that social utility and public health required the enforcement of a monopoly of medical services by trained physicians.[51] Even before 1789, medical eulogists were portraying the dedicated physician as a bastion of citizenship, a cross between an altruistic notable and a secular saint devoted to his ailing flock.[52]

The legal profession seems in many respects to have been the least professionalized of the traditional professions prior to 1789. Though riddled with corruption and the object of tremendous popular hostility, as the *cahiers* were to make clear in 1789, legal practitioners still maintained a high estimation of their constitutional importance. They sometimes claimed to comprise a kind of Fourth Estate, for example, a position which clearly chimed in with the constitutional pretensions of the parlements.[53] As Sarah Maza and Keith Baker have shown, many legal practitioners came to exploit civil and criminal cases so as to develop significant civic and political arguments, which were widely followed by the literate public – as well as by others not so literate.[54] The Calas affair is only one example – there are many – in which a contentious lawsuit led to an outpouring of pamphlets and polemical writings, normally the work of lawyers or attorneys, which invoked *l'opinion publique* as a kind of supreme arbiter.[55] The sociological supports of this powerful concept clearly lay in the growing market for cultural products and services over the eighteenth century which I have already described.[56] Be that as it may, "public concern" in the mouths of pre-revolutionary lawyers and polemicists predicated a feel for natural justice soon to receive more famous embodiment in the Rights of Man and the Nation, promulgated by a National Assembly in which were to sit some 151 lawyers.[57] The "heap of blabbers, lawyers, prosecutors, notaries, bailiffs and other such vermin" who, in the charmingly unlovely language of the *Père Duchesne*,[58] dominated every subsequent revolutionary assembly owed much to their exposure before 1789 to the problems inherent in exercising their profession in a fast-changing commercial society whose service sector was being transformed.

The debate over professionalism, civic and corporative, is particularly interesting to follow in the state bureaucracy, where it is complicated by the system of venal office. Classic Weberian reforms were increasingly introduced over the last decades of the Old Regime, to limit the rampant patrimonialism which characterized the service generally. The most hated branch of the service, the General Farm, was most advanced in its corporative professionalism, having introduced a wide range of rational bureaucratic procedures, and also having installed a career structure for employees which included a contributory pensions fund.[59] Elsewhere, there was a reaction against the prevalence of venal office. The latter was widely blamed for, as one critic put it, "this insulting separation that sits between the administration and the Nation."[60] Venality was in fact reduced or abolished in a number of services in the last decades of the Old Regime, including the *maréchaussée*, the postal system, and the saltpetre service.[61] Necker attempted to centralize the multiple treasuries of the financial bureaucracy.[62] There were some valiantly civic-minded administrators who endeavored to move the popular imagination into believing them citizens as well as Crown servants. But bureaucrats continued to be seen essentially as peddlars of hope and protection, little despots, insolent petty kings, the very embodiment of privilege, without any social utility or public benefit.[63] One can understand why the revolutionary assemblies would desire to debureaucratize French society – familiar phantasm.[64]

Showing an awareness of the interpenetration of political and economic factors which is in itself an object-lesson to historians, many critics of venal office in the late Old Regime attacked the way in which such posts could entail what might be seen as unfair market advantage. This whole question of venal office has been reopened in recent years by a number of important Revisionist articles. In an article in the *Historical Journal* in 1984, for example, William Doyle demonstrated that the market for venal office was more buoyant than Marxists and indeed many Revisionists had held. The price of some offices falls, but far more rise, and Doyle concludes in general that overall the price of office was rising; he ascribes this to the traditionalism of the Old Regime bourgeoisie, who were failing to give up their secular preference for status over profit.[65]

Before this view finds its niche within the canon of the New Revisionist Orthodoxy, however, let us consider how this rise in the value of venal office might relate to the growth of the market for services. The post of court physician (*médecin du roi*), on which I have done some research, is an interesting starting-point. In 1720, only seventeen physicians could claim this title, while in 1789, eighty-eight, to whom might be added quite as many court

170

surgeons and apothecaries.[66] The price of these posts seems to have been pretty buoyant. As only a handful of the individuals who could style themselves *médecin du roi* came near the person of the monarch, or even resided at Versailles, it might be concluded that here was a title that meant prestige and little else. In fact, this was far from the case. The purchase of a post was a means of circumventing the monopoly which the Paris Medical Faculty had on medical services within the capital. One has only to remember the wild enthusiasm of Parisians for every medical fad and fancy in the eighteenth century to see how valuable that access could be: Paris rocked to, and *médecins du roi* made money out of, the crazes for vapours, male midwives, smallpox inocula-tion, Mesmerism, and a good many forms of treatment for ven-ereal disease – the most exotic of which must surely have been Lefebvre de Saint-Ildephont's anti-venereal chocolate drops. This particular court physician claimed that one could medicate one's wife against venereal infection by providing her with an unend-ing supply of boxes of chocolates.[67]

Crudely put, purchase of a post within the royal medical Household was a means of cashing in on medical consumerism. It represented a headlong rush towards a market – even an entre-preneurial interest in stimulating it – rather than a flight from it. One wonders whether there are similar stories to tell about many of the other venal offices. Indeed, if we turn again to William Doyle's list of venal offices for which prices were rising, we find that a good number of them – attorneys, notaries, legal clerks, auctioneers, and wigmakers – do indeed relate to expanding markets for professional services or fashionable lifestyle.[68] Venal office (and perhaps a similar case might be mounted for land purchase) begins to look less like an option for status than a shrewd investment aimed to give the purchaser access to a mar-ket or edge within it.[69] Money bought privilege within this market as well as within the polity and within the social hierarchy.

Attacked by their co-professionals as the embodiment of privil-ege and social inutility, many venal officers themselves grew pro-gressively disenchanted by their posts. The advantages of market edge plus the returns on the initial investment palled as the mon-archy, increasingly beset by financial problems, came to interfere with the venal office market in a number of ways. The value of the investment was reduced by a series of injudicious decisions by the monarch to levy forced loans, for example (on the *corps* of financial officials in particular), to increase the number of offices in a particular *corps,* or to reduce wages.[70] The downturn in the economy from the 1770s may also have diminished the buoyancy of many markets for services. Economies in the state bureaucracy – pursued by all controllers-general in the last years of the Old Regime, but with no greater vigour than by Loménie de Brienne in 1787–8 – must have helped venal officers to see the writing on the wall.[71] In any event, with state bankruptcy on the horizon, it was a pretty shrewd move, on the Night of 4 August 1789, to agree to the abolition of all venal offices. For the abolition was agreed on the basis of compensation which, it was hoped, would be financially more advantageous than forcible expropriation or sale in depressed market conditions.[72] So much for the "patriotic rhapsodies" of altruism!

In the question of venal office were encapsulated many of the problems of the absolute monarchy. The state operated the most extraordinarily ornate system whereby it sold offices which thereby became the private property of their owners. The holders could not be bought out altogether – the expense was too colossal; so kings turned disadvantage to advantage by levying forced loans on the main bodies of venal office-holders to help it in its financial difficulties. The king was thereby to a certain extent digging his own grave, in that these loans ran up the National Debt to colossal proportions. In addition, the royal demands amplified the corporate awareness of the bodies of venal office-holders. This was particularly marked in the case of the towns, as Gail Bossenga has recently shown.[73] Venal municipal offices, constantly chopped and changed over the course of the century, bred discontent both within the charmed circle of municipal officials, and outside in sectional groups wanting to get in. This provided a seed-plot in which – over all sorts of issues, from street lighting to local taxes – could grow a civic awareness quite as cogent as that developing within the professions.

A growing sensitivity to civic issues is found elsewhere in Old Regime society too. Even at village level, Hilton Root finds Burgundian peasants deciding on local matters utilizing, in pretty sophisticated fashion, the concept of the General Will long before the latter term was dreamed up by Jean-Jacques Rousseau.[74] Urban guilds were often too the micro-sites for similar exercises in political education and the exercise of political democracy. They too, like Hilton Root's peasants, utilized the courts as means of redress, with lawyers playing the part of cultural intermediary between legal form and social issues.[75] If we suspend the New Revisionist Orthodoxy's certainty that modern political culture was born in 1789, we can glimpse within Old Regime society, even at these lowly levels supposedly locked away into the bromides of a "popular culture," a vibrant and developing political sensibility which cries out to be inventoried, classified, and understood.

Although what came to be at issue often had far wider ramifications, these burgeoning debates within the professions and other corporative cells of the Society of Orders were at first often localized and sectional. The courts and, by way of the press, the notion of "public opinion" provided a conduit along which civic sensibilities could penetrate the body social, as we have seen. A number of other institutions came to act as a crucible in which these fragmented disputes were fused into a supra-corporative consciousness. The Enlightenment Academies were a case in point.[76] Their internally democratic practices favored such fusion, for the niceties of the social hierarchy were normally not observed within them, and bourgeois rubbed shoulders with noble, as well as doctor with lawyer. To be frank, the Academies were often dominated by local nobles and dignitaries, and consequently stuffy, if worthy, in their procedures. The egalitarian, meritocratic sharing of experience which they embodied was doubtless important for some. Even more important, however, were the Masonic lodges.[77] The cult of Masonry had its adepts throughout the social pyramid; yet the numerical predominance among the body of 50,000 French Masons was clearly with the professional classes and with their social equivalents. Businessmen – often excluded from Academies for being lacking in tone and breeding – were here in massive numbers: they represented 36 per cent of members in major cities, and the proportion was often well over 50 per cent in numerous localities. Soldiers were the main professional category, although lawyers, administrators, and doctors – if few priests – were also there in bulk.[78] The same elements – in a slightly different mix – were found in reading clubs, small lending libraries and their like.[79]

These new forums for egalitarian mixing and discussion were as much organs of sociability as anything else. In his recent work on Masonry, Ran Halévi has dubbed this a "democratic sociability."[80] Halévi, like his close collaborator François Furet, is in fact particularly interested in the lodges as lineal ancestors of the Jacobin Clubs, and so chooses a narrowly political term. I prefer the term "civic sociability," which I think expresses rather better the urban and wider cultural implications of this form of social mixing, and has the additional merit of making explicit the clear affinities it has with the civic ideologies and practices exuded by the professional and corporative institutions of the Old Regime.

In the light of the previous discussion, we can now revisit the debate on the social origins of the Revolution of 1789. Given the development of commercial capitalism in eighteenth-century France, the spread of a consumer society, the development of professionalization within the service sector of the economy which this helped to spawn, and the appearance of associated forms of civic sociability, it no longer looks realistic to disparage the vitality nor indeed the ideological autonomy of the Old Regime bourgeoisie. Far from the social structure of Old Regime France being locked remorselessly into "traditional," "pre-capitalist," "archaic" forms, the progress of commercialization and the spread of a consumer society suggests a relative "bour-geoisification" of Old Regime society. Far from an élite of "not-ables" melding harmoniously and cosily together in the last years of the Old Regime, moreover, conflict over the role of privilege and the implications of citizenship was endemic and established an explosive agenda beneath the surface calm of the Society of Orders. Yet though civic sociability had achieved much, it had signally failed to capture control of the state apparatus. This was to be the achievement of the men of 1789.

Who, then, were the "revolutionary bourgeoisie" (if we can now assume there was one)?[81] Alfred Cobban characterized it as a mixture of landowners, venal officers, and professional men. To a certain degree he was correct. Yet he saw both the professions and the venal office-holders as declining, inferiority-complexed classes, so many shrinking violets easily written off as "trad-itional élites." What I have argued here is that the professions and indeed a great many venal office-holders, far from being sectional and "traditionalist" in their orientation and outlook, were in fact responding to and very much part of the development of capital-ism in the Old Regime. These groups were more genuinely bour-geois than ever before, and exuded a new civic professionalism which had its roots in a developing "market-consciousness" and which clashed with the corporative values espoused by many of their fellows. They shared the vision and the reflexes of the commercial bourgeoisie of the Old Regime in a far more direct way than has hitherto been recognized. Moreover, although they thought through these problems at first perhaps largely through the corporative framework, the ongoing debts on professionalization nurtured widening perspectives. Masonic lodges, *sociétés de pensée*, and the like further elaborated and refined the debate and also opened it up so that it included sections of the economic bourgeoisie in the years leading up to 1789. Professionalization was thus not simply a part of the noble reaction, as David Bien might have us believe. In its civic form, professionalism legitimated the attack on privilege, even when the latter was defended by corporative values. It stimulated a conception of the state as something which was not so much embodied in the dynast as present in the "Nation," an ideological construct which developed *pari passu* with the growth and elaboration of the market. The organs of civic sociability, finally, provided forums in which new ideas of equality, democracy, and civic concern could take material form among an increasingly homogeneous bourgeoisie and their allies among the liberal aristocracy.

In his notorious *Qu'est-ce que le Tiers Etat?*, Sieyes showed himself very much the apologist for this new civic consciousness. He argued that the "Nation" was composed of useful classes and groups which with great lucidity he itemized as including agriculture, industry, the mercantile interest, services "pleasant to the person," and the public services of the army, the law, the Church, and the bureaucracy.[82] His thinking was not as much the early appearance of a revolutionary ideology which sprang out fully developed from the political context, as the Revisionists are prone to argue. Rather, as the list of groups suggests, the new ideology of the Third Estate was in essence the ideology of pre-revolutionary civic professionalism. Its presence in one of the cardinal texts of the Revolution of 1789 indicates something of the contribution this new and increasingly aggressive civic ideology made to the downfall of the Old Regime. The civic sociability which had developed among this fraction of the bourgeoisie in the last decades of the Old Regime was corrosive of the deferentialism and hierarchical structures of the Society of Orders.

The ability of the Old Regime state to provide social and political conditions free from privilege and corporatism was in question long before its financial shipwreck in 1787–8. In the decades which preceded 1789, successive ministers had found themselves trying to float public loans by appeals to a general public increasingly impregnated with civic consciousness. The mercantile and professional bourgeoisie – together with the liberal fraction of the noble class – were, however, loath to go on extending moral or financial credit to a state which continued to conjugate public interest with the entrenched privileges of the aristocracy. As a social force, public opinion stretched out and reached every corner of this increasingly commercialized society. As an intellectual construct, moreover, "public opinion" was too closely tied into the cultural hegemony established by the professions and the new organs of civic sociability to be plausibly invoked by a monarch who seemed to be indissolubly wedded to the maintenance of the institutions of privilege.[83] The Nation, credit, public opinion, professionalism, and civic sociability had become woven into a spider's web in which privilege became helplessly stuck – and was then devoured. Far from the financial crisis of 1789 being, as the Revisionists contend, somehow extrinsic to earlier social developments,[84] it was in many ways the apotheosis of the social, political, and cultural developments I have been outlining.

The influence of the professional classes upon the Revolution was not only at the level of cultural hegemony. When one looks at political participation in 1789 and in the following revolutionary decade, what strikes one at once is the importance of the professional classes at every level and their interpenetration with other branches of the bourgeoisie. Cobban's original perception that declining venal officers and liberal professions dominated the Constituent Assembly is at least a starting-point,[85] though his analysis is misguided: venal office-holders were not necessarily a declining group; and anyway further research has shown that their representation in later revolutionary assemblies fell drastically, while that of professional men (including, increasingly, what one might call career or professional politicians) stayed consistently high. Moreover, as Lynn Hunt has brilliantly shown, local administration was very much in the hands of lawyers, physicians, notaries, and local bureaucrats, often with a good admixture of the merchants and manufacturers found only rather rarely at national level. In 1793 and 1794, a bigger input of petty bourgeois elements – shopkeepers, artisans, and minor clerks – is often visible, and in the countryside wealthier peasants got a look in.[86] But this really only underlines the bourgeois and professional orientation. Recent work on Parisian local politics confirms the general picture: the districts of 1789–90, as R.B. Rose has shown, were a fairly representative bourgeois cross-section; while incisive work on the Parisian sans-culottes of Year II, conducted by Richard Cobb and others in his wake, has revealed the more solidly bourgeois backgrounds of many militants who, for reasons of political expediency, deflated their social rank in the democratic atmosphere of the Terror.[87]

The analysis of Edmund Burke, cited Lynn Hunt, that the Revolution was the work of "moneyed men, merchants, principal tradesmen and men of letters" thus seems pretty accurate, as a description of both the key participants in the political process after 1789 and many of the major proponents of "civic sociability" before that date.[88] It is important, in the light of my earlier arguments, however, to view Burke's "men of letters" not as an autonomous, free-standing group, but rather as the vocal representatives of the professions. This interpretation clashes, I am aware, with Robert Darnton's fine studies of men of letters as a significant influence on the revolutionary process.[89] However, to classify men of letters as an autonomous group seems to distort and to underplay the professional and corporative framework within which such men had done – and maybe continued to do – their thinking. Clearly the concept had an important role in revolutionary ideology and myth-making. In particular, there is a brand of counter-revolutionary interpretation which rejoices at seeing the Revolution allegedly in the hands of an anomic pack of Grub Street low-life, seedy intellectuals cut off from any experience of real-life political problems, and consequently wild and utopian in their aims. The professional prism puts quite a different, more solid, more pragmatic, more market-orientated view on the revolutionary bourgeoisie. The latter is no more synonymous with Darnton's riff-raff intelligentsia than Old Regime professionals are with David Bien's reactionary army officers.

I have suggested that there was a far closer, organic link between the development of capitalism in the eighteenth century and the emergence of more "market-conscious," and public-spirited intellectual élites than historians have normally allowed. The attractiveness of this hypothesis is amplified when we look at much of the social and economic legislation carried out by successive revolutionary assemblies which would do so much to shape nineteenth-century France. If one assumes that the liberal professionals who made up such an important constitutive part of the assemblies are socially autonomous from the economic bourgeoisie, then reforms as classically capitalistic in their character as the formation of a national market, the abolition of guilds, the introduction of uniform weights and measures, the removal of seigneurial excrescences, the redefinition of property rights come to be seen as the product of conspiracy, accident, or a hidden hand. The impregnation of the bourgeoisie with market values, the "bourgeoisification" of the professions, and the organic links developing between the professions and mercantile groups prior to 1789, on the other hand, help to provide a more viable political and cultural framework for understanding why such reforms were introduced. These phenomena constitute a "silent bourgeois revolution" which was the essential precursor of the noisier, messier, and better-known events of 1789.[90] They also help to explain why one of the most durable and toughest legislative legacies of the revolutionary years should be the so-called "career open to talents," a principle which was indeed tailored to the career interests and civic sense of the liberal professions by, precisely, the members of the liberal professions who dominated the assemblies.

A great deal more work still needs to be done on relations between the different branches of the bourgeoisie – the different types of professionals, the landed and commercial bourgeoisie, and so on – as well as what Colin Lucas has called the "stress zones" between them. These relationships, moreover, shifted, sometimes radically as a result of the revolutionary experience. The quotation by Barère with which I began [see above, p. 158] is symptomatic of the problem: Barère attacks commerce and speculation from a political viewpoint; yet, on the other hand, his rhetoric connives in a good commercial operation. We need to know more about how the Revolution affected the professions, and the arguments about professional standards, quality control, educational requirements, and public interest which had percolated within them throughout the late Enlightenment. The events of 1789 moved these debates which had gripped the professions under the Old Regime on to a new level, and their subsequent history highlighted the mixed and sometimes contradictory legacy of the revolutionary experience.

There was to be, it seems, no single trajectory for the professions in the 1790s, nor any common destiny for their members. The abolition of venal office on 4 August and the enunciation of the principle of the career open to talent in the Declaration of the Rights of Man on 26 August 1789 left a great deal of room for debate and disagreement of how professionalism should be conjugated with the exigencies of citizenship. The response of each of the professions differed, and new fault-lines emerged out of the process. The furore within the army is relatively well-known.[91] How far did the rights of soldiers as citizens entitle them to political activities which, in the opinion of many of their supporters, nullified professional *esprit de corps*? The path towards the patriotic citizen-soldier of Year II passed by way of the Nancy mutiny and its repression and the emigration of 60 per cent of the putatively "professional" noble officer corps. The late 1790s and the Napoleonic period were to see the reassertion of a more corporative version of professionalism, with the sacrifice of many of the more democratic procedures of Year II, such as election of officers.

The experience of the clergy was rather different.[92] The Civil Constitution of the Clergy may in many respects be viewed as the charter of a professionalized secular clergy, establishing as it did democratic procedures, rational hierarchies, and a well-founded career structure. Yet civic professionalism fell foul of corporative professionalism: many priests found it difficult to accept the loss of their monopoly of spiritual services consequent on the enunciation of the principle of freedom of conscience, and jibbed at National Assembly's failure to consult either the Church as a corporate entity or its hierarchical head, the Pope. The 1790s was to prove an often tragic backcloth against which the clergy rethought their attitudes towards ecclesiastical hierarchy, conscience, and civic responsibility.

A similar reassessment was necessary for the medical and legal professions and for the state bureaucracy.[93] The career open to talents and the attack on privilege within corporate hierarchies justified the attack on the Old Regime bureaucracy, the abolition of many of its services (such as the General Farm, probably the most corporatively professionalized of all state services,) the closure of legal and medical faculties, and the dissolution of first attorneys, then barristers. By the late 1790s, however, a barrage of complaints emerged from all quarters which highlighted how the opening up of a free field for medical and legal practice had damaged public interest and (so it was said) standards of professional competence. The public was, it was argued, prey to medical charlatans, legal sharks, and corrupt and ill-trained clerks. The reassertion of a corporative hierarchy and the reintroduction of better training methods under the Thermidorian Convention, the Directory, and the Consulate attested to a reworking of the relationship between profession, state, and public.

There is much about the civic-inspired deregulation of many of the professions in the 1790s and their corporative reprofessionalization later in the decade which remains obscure. Certainly the professions were transformed in the Revolutionary decade – a fact palpable in the disappearance of many pre-revolutionary titles such as *procureur, avocat, chirurgien,* and so on. After the perils of the "free field" had been exposed, it looked as though for most the best guarantee of professional success after 1789 was state utility. Hence the unrivalled prestige of the armed forces from the late 1790s; hence the formidable strengthening of the state bureaucracy; hence the emergence of a prestigious scientific profession, very much under the wing of the state; hence too the arguments of state utility advanced by doctors and lawyers in their attempts to win government support.[94] The civic and corporative models of professionalization which had emerged in the Ancien Régime were transformed by the experience of the 1790s; but in broad terms, it was something akin to the corporative model which often prevailed, while maintaining the career open to talent which the civic model had required. The Revolution had changed both the context of and the protagonists in the debate over professionalism. And the transformed professions were to make a massive and well-documented contribution to the character of nineteenth-century France.

The professions remained after 1800, finally, still very much tributary to the market for their services. Though the state was often a valued client, most depended very considerably on the overall situation of the economy. As the Revisionists have pointed out with an often wearisome frequency, the Revolution did not mark a transition to industrialism in the French economy. (Actually, Georges Lefebvre and Albert Soboul seem to have been pretty much aware of that fact too, as their balanced assessments of the sometimes contradictory social and economic legacy of the Revolution should make clear.)[95] France's economy was still in the commercial mould, and the professions inevitably reflected that fact.[96] *Pace* many Revisionists, however, the French economy was not irredeemably traditionalist nor stagnatingly precapitalist. France continued its measured and balanced way towards industrialization. Indeed, growth in the early nineteenth century, even before the creation of a national rail network, is now being recognized as having been far stronger than has often been thought. In that progress, the Revolution had been perhaps a less heroic and dramatic episode than the Old Marxist Orthodoxy would maintain; though it certainly had far more importance, and positive influence, than the New Revolutionist Orthodoxy would allow. The legislative achievement of successive Revolutionary assemblies and the eradication of Old Regime privilege provided a more appropriate environment for commercial capitalism in general to develop, and the bourgeoisie in particular to prosper. France moved slowly towards its industrializing goal at the end of a bourgeois nineteenth century for which the stage had been set by a bourgeois revolution, Revisionist reports of whose sad demise I persist in finding greatly exaggerated.

NOTES

Source Reprinted in an abridged format from *The French Revolution and Social Change*, ed. Colin Lucas (Oxford: Oxford University Press, 1990), pp. 69–118.

Acknowledgment Alfred Cobban, launching his famous broadside against the so-called "Marxist interpretation" of the French Revolution in 1964, regretted that "one cannot criticise an historical interpretation without appearing to criticise the historians who have held it." As I am sure was the case with Cobban, it is not my intention to launch *ad hominem* (or *ad feminam*) attacks – all the more in that numbers of the historians whose arguments I here criticize offered helpful and constructive comments following earlier versions of this paper read in Oxford, London, and Washington, DC. Particular thanks are due to Jonathan Barry, Bill Doyle, Colin Lucas, and Michael Sonenscher.

1 For a brilliantly written account of some of Palloy's activities, see S. Schama, *Citizens: A Chronology of the French Revolution* (London, 1989), pp. 408–16. Cf. Romi [pseud. Robert Miquel] *Le Livre de raison du patriote Palloy* (Paris, 1962); and H. Lemoine, "Les Comptes de démolition de la Bastille," *Bulletin de la Société de l'histoire de Paris et de l'Ile de France*, 1929.

2 *Archives parlementaires de 1787 à 1860*, 1st ser., 19 (1884), 433 (session 4 October 1790).

3 A. Cobban, *The Social Interpretation of the French Revolution* (London,

1964). Cobban's line of argument can be traced back to his Inaugural Lecture in 1954, "The Myth of the French Revolution," reprinted along with other of his polemical and scholarly pieces in *Aspects of the French Revolution* (London, 1968).

4 G.V. Taylor, "Bourgeoisie,", in B. Rothaus and S.F. Scott, *Historical Dictionary of the French Revolution*, 2 vols (Westport, Conn., 1985), i. p. 122.

5 Schama, *Citizens*, p. xiv for the zombies. This is little improvement on Colin Lucas's reference to 'indeterminate social mutants': C. Lucas, "Nobles, Bourgeois and the Origins of the French Revolution," *Past and Present* (henceforth *P&P*), 60 (1973), 90. [Reprinted as Chapter 2 in this volume.]

6 G.V. Taylor, "Noncapitalist Wealth and the Origins of the French Revolution," *American Historical Review* (henceforth *AmHR*), 72 (1967), 482; Lucas, "Nobles, Bourgeois and Origins," 89–92 and *passim*; W. Doyle, "The Price of Offices in pre-Revolutionary France," *Historical Journal*, 27 (1984), 844. These are major articles within a relatively small range of classic texts which together form the much remasticated pabulum of Revisionist argument. Other key works in the litany include G.V. Taylor, "Types of Capitalism in Eighteenth-Century France," *English Historical Review*, 79 (1964); *id*. Revolutionary and Non-Revolutionary Content in the *Cahiers* of 1789; An Interim Report," *French Historical Studies* (henceforth *FHS*), 7 (1972–3); E. Eisenstein, "Who Intervened in 1788?," *AmHR*, 71 (1965); C.B.A. Behrens, *The Ancien Régime* (London, 1967); *id*., "Nobles, Privileges and Taxes in France at the End of the Ancien Régime," *Economic History Review* (henceforth *EcHR*), 15 (1962–3); W. Doyle, *Origins of the French Revolution* (Oxford, 1980) F. Furet and D. Richet, *The French Revolution* (London, 1970); F. Furet, *Interpreting the French Revolution* (London, 1981). T.C.W. Blanning, *The French Revolution: Aristocrats versus Bourgeois?* (London, 1987) is a brilliant summation of the debate and itself stands as a major contribution to Revisionism.

7 A good example of a "traditionalist" reading of Old Regime society from an authoritative Revisionist source in W. Doyle, *The Oxford History of the French Revolution* (Oxford, 1989), esp. ch. 1. Cf. *id*., *The Ancien Régime* (London, 1986), 20 ff. For popular culture, see the classic R. Mandrou, *De la culture populaire aux XVIIe et XVIIIe siècles* (Paris, 1964); and, as a recent example, T. Brennan, *Public Drinking and Popular Culture in Eighteenth-Century Paris* (Princeton, NJ, 1988). For spirited onslaughts on the conceptual framework of much research on "traditional society" and "popular culture," see M. Sonenscher, *Work and Wages: Natural Law, Politics and the Eighteenth-Century French Trades* (Cambridge, 1989), pp. 44–6; and R. Chartier, "Culture as Appropriation: Popular Cultural Uses in Early Modern France," in S.L. Kaplan (ed.), *Understanding Popular Culture* (Paris, 1984).

8 G. Chaussinand-Nogaret, *The French Nobility in the Eighteenth Century: From Feudalism to Enlightenment* (Cambridge, 1985). Much of Chaussinand-Nogaret's evidence on entrepreneurship is culled from

the (refreshingly unrevisionist) scholarship of Guy Richard, notably the latter's *La Noblesse d'affaires au XVIIIe siècle* (Paris, 1975). See too Chaussinand-Nogaret, *Une Histoire des élites, 1770–1848* (Paris, 1975); R. Forster, "The Provincial Noble: A Reappraisal," *AmHR*, 78 (1968); and D. Sutherland's trenchant views on the social élite in his *France 1789–1815: Revolution and Counter-Revolution* (London, 1985), pp. 19–21. A good counter-argument to Chaussinand-Nogaret is mounted by P. Goujard, "Féodalité et lumières au XVIIIe siècle: L'Exemple de la noblesse," *Annales historiques de la Révolution française* (henceforth *AhRf*), 227 (1977).

9 See W. Doyle, "Was There an Aristocratic Reaction in pre-Revolutionary France?" *P&P*, 57 (1972); D. Bien. "La Réaction aristocratique avant 1789: L'Exemple de l'armée," *Annales: Economies, sociétés, civilisations* (henceforth *AnnESC*), 29 (1974).

10 L. and J. Stone, *An Open Elite? England, 1540–1880* (Oxford, 1984). Cf. A. Milward and S.B. Saul, *The Economic Development of Continental Europe, 1780–1870* (London, 1973), esp. pp. 30–1. On the French side, note the important calculations on social mobility in Bien, "Réaction aristocratique," pp. 505–14.

11 Chaussinand-Nogaret, *French Nobility*, p. 1.

12 An authoritative overview of this widely held perspective in Doyle, *Ancien Régime*, pp. 25–6.

13 W.G. Runciman, "Unnecessary Revolution: The Case of France," *Archives européennes de sociologie*, 23 (1983).

14 M. Morineau, "Was There an Agricultural Revolution in Eighteenth-Century France?," in R. Cameron (ed.), *Essays in French Economic History* (London, 1970); and *id.*, *Les Faux-semblants d'un démarrage économique: Agriculture et démographie en France au dix-huitième siècle* (Paris, 1970) – both key texts for the Revisionists' case which is also buttressed on this point by socio-economic historians who view structural economic change in France as a post-railway phenomenon. See, for example, R. Price, *The Economic Modernization of France, 1730–1914* (London, 1981); and E. Weber, *Peasants into Frenchmen: The Modernisation of Rural France, 1870–1914* (London, 1979). The gloomy diagnosis is confirmed in the non-scholarly but well-argued R. Sedillot, *Le Coût de la Révolution française* (Paris, 1987).

15 E. Le Roy Ladurie, "L'Histoire immobile," *AnnESC*, 29 (1974). This influential article, highly symptomatic of much contemporary writing on rural history, is available in English translation as "History that Stands Still," in *id.*, *The Mind and Method of the Historian* (London, 1981).

16 L. Hunt, *Politics, Culture and Class in the French Revolution* (London, 1986), p. 9.

17 K.M. Baker (ed.), *The French Revolution and the Creation of Modern Political Culture*, i. *The Political Culture of the Old Regime* (Oxford, 1987). Reviews of this important work by J. Censer, "The Coming of a New Interpretation of the French Revolution?," *Journal of Social History*, 21 (1987); and P.R. Campbell, "Old Régime Politics and the New

183

Interpretation of the French Revolution," *Renaissance and Modern Studies*, 32 (1989). The second volume of the series, ed. Colin Lucas, was *The Political Culture of the French Revolution* (Oxford, 1988).

18 Furet, *Interpreting the French Revolution*, esp. p. 47 ff., p. 61 ff.

19 *Ibid.* p. 53 ff. Cf. F. Furet and R. Halévi, "L'Année 1789," *AnnESC*, 44 (1989), esp. p. 21. This view by Furet contrasts with his own views as expressed in Furet and Richet, *The French Revolution* – where the Terror is seen as taking place as a result of the Revolution "skidding" unpredictably to the Left. Cf. the forceful statement of much of the Furet case (Mark II) in Schama, *Citizens*, esp. pp. 446–7, 623, 792, etc.

20 Notably Furet's essay "The Revolutionary Catechism" in *Interpreting the French Revolution*, Ch. 2.1.

21 M. Fitzsimmons, "Privilege and Polity in France, 1786–9," *AmHR*, 92 (1987); and *id.*, *The Parisian Order of Barristers and the French Revolution* (Cambridge, Mass., 1987), pp. 41–2, 193–4; N. Hampson, *Prelude to Terror: The Constituent Assembly and the Failure of Consensus, 1789–1791* (Oxford, 1989), p. 56; Doyle, 'Price of Offices,' pp. 859–60; Schama, *Citizens*, p. 439.

22 Schama, *Citizens*, p. 439 Fitzsimmons, *Parisian Order of Barristers*, pp. 41–2.

23 Fitzsimmons, *Parisian Order of Barristers*, p. 197; Taylor, "Noncapitalist Wealth," p. 491.

24 Sutherland, *France, 1789–1815*: see esp. pp. 333–5, 438–42.

25 D. Johnson, "Fire in the Mind," *Times Educational Supplement*, 14 October 1988, p. 24.

26 See in particular the recent work of R. Sécher, *Le Génocide franco-français: La Vendée-Vengé* (Paris, 1986) and *La Chapelle-Basse-Mer: Révolution et contre-révolution* (Paris, 1986), dealing in highly contentious fashion with the repression of revolt in western France in the 1790s. For a sober assessment of some of the statistics involved, cf. F. Lebrun, "Reynald Sécher et les morts de la guerre de Vendée," *Annales de Bretagne* (henceforth *AB*), 93 (1986).

27 There are clear signs that historians are becoming increasingly dissatisfied with many Revisionist arguments. See, as a sampler, B. Edmonds, "Successes and Excesses of Revisionist Writing about the French Revolution," *European History Quarterly*, 17 (1987); P.M. Jones, *The Peasantry in the French Revolution* (Cambridge, 1988), esp. ch. 2; and P. McPhee, "The French Revolution, Peasants and Capitalism," *AmHR*, 94 (1989). Cf. too M.D. Sibalis, "Corporatism and the Corporation: The Debate on Restoring the Guilds under Napoleon I and the Restoration," *FHS* 15 (1987–8), esp. p. 720. It is noticeable that even Schama, who espouses most of Furet's arguments on the Revolution, is still often critical of Revisionist stances: *Citizens*, e.g. p. 188 ff.

28 Cf. Doyle, *Origins*, p. 32; *id.*, *Ancien Régime*, 26–8; W.W. Rostow, *The Stages of Economic Growth: A Non-Communist Manifesto* (Cambridge, 1960). The "backwardness" thesis is stated with great force in the influential D. Landes, *The Unbound Prometheus: Technological Change*

and Industrial Development in Western Europe from 1750 to the Present (Cambridge, 1972).

29 F. Crouzet's numerous articles around this point are conveniently collected in his *De la supériorité de l'Angleterre sur la France: L'Economique et l'imaginaire (XVIIᵉ–XXᵉ siècle)* (Paris, 1985). See too P. O'Brien and C. Keyder, *Economic Growth in Britain and France, 1780–1914: Two Paths to the Twentieth Century* (London, 1978); *id.*, "Les Voies de passage vers la société industrielle en Grande-Bretagne et en France (1780–1914)," *AnnESC*, 34 (1979); N. Crafts, "England and France: Some Thoughts on the Question 'Why was England first?'," *EcHR*, 30 (1977); *id.*, "British and French Economic Growth, 1700–1831: A Review of the Evidence," *EcHR*, 36 (1983); *id.*, "British Industrialisation in an International Context," *Journal of Interdisciplinary History*, 19 (1989); R. Roehl, "French Industrialization: A Reconsideration," *Explorations in Economic History*, 15 (1976); J.L. Goldsmith, "The Agrarian History of Pre-Industrial France: Where do We Go from here?," *Journal of European Economic History* (henceforth *JEEH*), 13 (1984); R. Aldrich, "Late-Comer or Early Starter? New Views on French Economic History," *JEEH*, 16 (1987). These are only a sampler from a list which could be considerably extended. The chorus does not sing in unison, there being a number of major differences of opinion between them. However, all are critical of the classic account, as is the wide-ranging C. Sabel and J. Zeitlin, "Historical Alternatives to Mass Production: Political Markets and Technology in Nineteenth-Century Industrialisation," *P&P*, 108 (1985). Overall it seems a fascinating historiographical paradox that Anglo-Saxon scholarship on Old Regime French society settled into a "traditionalist," "backward-orientated" mold just as economic historians of Britain, working comparatively, called into question the economic dynamism of the "First Industrial Nation." The edifice of French "backwardness" is thus a lot shakier than the confident tone of the Revisionists would suggest.

30 O'Brien and Keyder, *Economic Growth in Britain and France*, p. 57.

31 C.P. Kindleberger, "Financial Institutions and Economic Development: A Comparison of Great Britain and France in the Eighteenth and Nineteenth Centuries," *Explorations in Economic History*, 23 (1984); J.R. Harris, "Skills, Coal and British Industry in the Eighteenth Century," *History*, 61 (1976).

32 O'Brien and Keyder, *Economic Growth in Britain and France*, esp. pp. 186–8, 191–3. Cf. C. Heywood, "The Role of the Peasantry in French Industrialisation, 1815–80," *EcHR*, 34 (1981).

33 These figures are from Pierre Léon's contribution to Braudel and Labrousse, *Histoire économique et sociale* and are accepted by Doyle, who suggests they might even be revised upwards: *Origins*, pp. 129, 231.

34 Chaussinand-Nogaret, *French Nobility*, pp. 28–30, 87–8.

35 J. Merrick, "Conscience and Citizenship in Eighteenth-Century France," *Eighteenth-Century Studies*, 4 (1987); R. Robin, *La Société*

française en 1789: Semuren-Auxois (Paris, 1970); and cf. J. Revel, "Les Corps et communautés," in Baker, *Political Culture of the Old Régime*, pp. 539–41. Those who have read W. Sewell, *Work and Revolution in France* will know how much I owe on some of what follows to this marvellous book (for a helpful, if critical review of which, see L. Hunt and G. Sheridan, "Corporatism, Association and the Language of Labor in France, 1750–1850," *JMH*, 58 (1986)). There remains a whole area of socio-cultural linguistic study to be done on the shifting meanings of key terms in these debates.

36 Bien, "Réaction aristocratique" (see above, n. 9). Cf. *id.*, "The Army in the French Enlightenment: Reform, Reaction and Revolution," *P&P*, 85 (1979). Incidentally, as Bien admits, the artillery was both one of the most highly professional of all sectors of the armed forces in the late eighteenth century and one sector in which noble dominance was least marked. See too S.F. Scott, "The French Revolution and the Professionalisation of the French Officer Corps," in M. Janowitz and J. van Doorn, *On Military Ideology* (London, 1971).

37 Bien, "Réaction aristocratique," pp. 519–22; E.C. Léonard, *L'Armée et ses problèmes au XVIIIe siècle* (Paris, 1958), pp. 286 ff.

38 See Léonard, *Armée*, Chs 12–14. There is relevant material too in J. Chagniot, *Paris et l'armée au XVIIIe siècle: Etude politique et sociale* (Paris, 1985), particularly useful for not being orientated around the rural nobility. Chagniot also emphasizes the importance of lower non-noble officers in entrepreneurial activity (moneylending, petty trading, etc.).

39 J.A.H. de Guibert, *Essai général de tactique*; J. Servan de Gerbay, *Le Soldat citoyen*; and others discussed in Léonard, *Armée*, pp. 251 ff.

40 L. Carnot, "Eloge de Vauban," discussed in M. Reinhard, *Le Grand Carnot*, 2 vols (Paris, 1950–2), i. pp. 76–86. See too Ch.16, entitled "Le civisme du militaire."

41 T. Tackett, "The Citizen-Priest: Politics and Ideology among the Parish Clergy of Eighteenth-Century Dauphiné," *Studies in Eighteenth-Century Culture*, 7 (1978); B. Plongeron, *La Vie quotidienne du clergé français au XVIIIe siècle* (Paris, 1974). See also Tackett's *Priest and Parish in Eighteenth-Century France: A Social and Political Study of the Curé in a Diocese of Dauphiné, 1750–97* (Princeton, NJ, 1977) and his *Religion, Revolution and Regional Culture in Eighteenth-Century France: The Ecclesiastical Oath of 1791* (Princeton, NJ, 1986); D. Julia, "Les Deux Puissances: Chronique d'une séparation de corps," in Baker, *Political Culture of the Old Régime*.

42 Plongeron, *Vie quotidienne du clergé*, p. 75.

43 Supporting older, anecdotal scholarship on this point, are recent studies based on post-mortem inventories: e.g. A. Pardailhé-Galabrun. "L'Habitat et le cadre de vie des prêtres à Paris au XVIIIe siècle" and R. Plessix, "Les Inventaires après décès: Une piste d'approche de la culture matérielle des curés du Haut-Maine au XVIIIe siècle," both *AB*, 95 (1988).

44 R.F. Necheles, "The Curés in the Estates General of 1789," *JMH*, 46

(1974); M.G. Hutt, "The Role of the Curés in the Estates General," *Journal of Ecclesiastical History*, 6 (1955).

45 A great deal on schoolteachers and civic values in this classic work of D. Mornet, *Les Origines intellectuelles de la Révolution française* (Paris, 1933), esp. pp. 319 ff. and 419 ff.

46 G. Saucerotte, *Les Médecins pendant la Révolution* (Paris, 1887).

47 T. Gelfand, *Professionalizing Modern Medicine: Paris Surgeons and Medical Science and Institutions in the Eighteenth Century* (Westport, Conn., 1980).

48 *Ibid.* pp. 43–4; and J. Guillermaud (ed.), *Histoire de la médecine aux armées; De l'Antiquité à Révolution* (Paris, 1982).

49 The history of medical practice is marvellously illuminated in M. Ramsey, *Professional and Popular Medicine in France, 1770–1830: The Social World of Medical Practice* (Cambridge, 1988). See too "La Médicalisation en France du XVIIIᵉ au début du XXᵉ siècle," *AB*, 86 (1979); J.P. Goubert (ed.), *La Médicalisation de la société française, 1770–1830* (Waterloo, Ontario, 1982); and C. Jones, "The Medicalisation of Eighteenth-Century France," in R. Porter and A. Weare (eds), *Problems and Methods in the History of Medicine* (London, 1987). For medical training, see L.W.B. Brockliss, *French Higher Education in the Seventeenth and Eighteenth Centuries: A Cultural Study* (Oxford, 1987).

50 C. Hannaway, *Medicine, Public Welfare and the State of Eighteenth-Century France: The Société Royale de Médecine (1776–93)*, University Microfilms edn (1975) of Johns Hopkins Ph.D. thesis (1974). See *id.*, "The Société Royale de Médecine and Epidemics in Ancien Régime France," *Bulletin of the History of Medicine*, 40 (1972); and J. Meyer, "L'Enquête de l'Académie de médecine sur les epidémies, 1774–94," *Etudes rurales*, 9 (1969).

51 Ramsey, *Professional and Popular Medicine; id.*, "Traditional Medicine and Medical Enlightenment: The Regulation of Secret Remedies in the Ancien Régime," in Goubert, *Médicalisation;* and T. Gelfand, "Medical Professionals and Charlatans: The *Comité de salubrité enquête*, 1790–1," *Histoire sociale/Social History*, 8 (1978).

52 D. Roche, "Talents, raison et sacrifice: L'Image du médecin des Lumières d'après les Eloges de la Société Royale de Médecine (I776–89)," *AnnESC*, 32 (1977); J.P. Goubert and D. Lorillot, 1789, *le corps médical et le changement: Cahiers de doléances (médecins, chirurgiens et apothicaires)* (Toulouse, 1984), pp. 25–6.

53 Berlanstein, "Lawyers," p. 164 ff.

54 S. Maza, "Le Tribunal de la Nation: Les Mémoires judiciaries et l'opinion publique à la fin de l'Ancien Régime," and K. Baker, "Politique et opinion publique sous l'Ancien Régime," both *AnnESC*, 42 (1987). Cf. M. Ozouf, "L'Opinion publique," in Baker, *Political Culture of the Old Régime*; and W. Doyle, "Dupaty (1746–88): A Career in the Late Enlightenment," *Studies in Voltaire and the Eighteenth Century*, 230 (1985), esp. p. 82 ff.

55 For Calas, see D. Bien, *The Calas Affair: Persecution, Toleration and Heresy in Eighteenth-Century Toulouse* (Princeton, NJ, 1961).

56 Maza, Baker, and Ozouf (see references at note 54) draw heavily on J. Habermas, *L'Espace public: Archéologie de la publicité comme dimension constitutive de la société bourgeoise* (Paris, 1978). It is symptomatic of the Revisionist approach that they neglect the aspects of Habermas's work which deal with the infrastructural aspects of the growth of a public, and also its bourgeois dimension, both of which are directly related to the present essay.

57 E.H. Lemay, "La Composition de l'Assemblée nationale constituante: Les Hommes de la continuité," *RHMC*, 24 (1977). The assembly also contained 315 office-holders, a great many of whom had legal training too.

58 Cited in F. Brunot, *Histoire de la langue française des origines à nos jours* (Paris, 1930), ix (1967), pp. 944–5.

59 G. Matthews, *The Royal General Farms in the Eighteenth Century* (New York, 1958); and V. Azimi, *Un modèle administratif de l'Ancien Régime: Les Commis de la ferme générale et de la régie des aides* (Paris, 1987). On the bureaucracy in general, see too C. Church, *Revolution and Red Tape: The French Ministerial Bureaucracy, 1770–1850* (Oxford, 1981); Doyle, "Price of Offices"; M. Antoine, "La Monarchie absolue," in Baker, *Political Culture of the Old Régime*; J.F. Bosher, *French Finances, 1770–1795: From Business to Bureaucracy* (Cambridge, 1970); and G. Bossenga, "From *Corps* to Citizenship: The *Bureau des Finances* before the French Revolution," *JMH*, 58 (1986).

60 V. Azimi, "1789: L'Echo des employés ou le nouveau discours administratif," *XVIIIᵉ Siècle*, 21 (1989), p. 34.

61 Church, *Revolution and Red Tape*, p. 28.

62 Bosher, *French Finances*, pp. 142–65; R.D. Harris, *Necker, Reform Statesman of the Ancien Régime* (Berkeley, Calif., 1979); Bossenga, "From *Corps* to Citizenship," *passim*.

63 Azimi, "1789," p. 134.

64 Church, *Revolution and Red Tape*, p. 46.

65 Doyle, "Price of Offices," p. 844.

66 C. Jones, "The *Médecins du Roi* at the End of the Ancien Régime and in the French Revolution," in V. Nutton (ed.), *Medicine at Court, 1500–1800* (London, 1989).

67 *ibid.*, plus P. Delaunay, *Le Monde médical parisien au XVIIIᵉ siècle (1906)* (p. 100 for Lefebvre), and R. Darnton's classic *Mesmerism and the End of the Enlightenment in France* (Cambridge, Mass., 1968), for insights into the general atmosphere.

68 Doyle, "Price of Offices," pp. 852–4, 856–7. See R. Giesey, "State-Building in Early Modern France: The Role of Royal Officialdom," *JMH*, 55 (1983) for some interesting ideas on office and markets.

69 Cf. in this respect the arguments of R.C. Allen on the economic rationality behind land purchase, allegedly for status reasons, in eighteenth-century England: "The Price of Freehold Land and the Interest Rate in the Seventeenth and Eighteenth Centuries", *EcHR*, 41 (1988).

70 Bossenga, "From *Corps* to Citizenship"; and D. Bien, "Office, Corps

and a System of State Credit: The Uses of Privilege under the Old Régime," in Baker, *Political Culture of Old Régime*.

71 Bosher, *French Finances*; J. Egret, *The French Pre-Revolution, 1787–8* (Chicago, 1977), pp. 43–61, 95–9; Harris, *Necker*, pp. 107–15.

72 Carey, *Judicial Reform*, p. 105.

73 G. Bossenga, "City and State: An Urban Perspective on the Origins of the French Revolution," in Baker, *Political Culture of the Old Régime*.

74 Root, *Peasants and King*, esp. Ch. 3. Cf. K. Tonnesson, "La Démocratie directe sous la Révolution française: Le Cas des districts et sections de Paris," in Lucas, *Political Culture of the Revolution*, pp. 295–6.

75 The outstanding work of Michael Sonenscher is especially illuminating of this theme: besides his *Work and Wages*, see too his article "Journeymen, the Courts and the French Trades, 1781–91," *P&P*, 114 (1987). Cf. Revel, "Corps et comunautés," pp. 239–41.

76 D. Roche, *Le Siècle des Lumières en province: Académies et académiciens provinciaux, 1680–1789*, 2 vols (Paris, 1978); *id.*, "Académies et politique au siècle des Lumières: Les Enjeux pratiques de l'immortalité," in Baker, *Political Culture of the Old Régime*.

77 Roche, *Siècle des Lumières en province*, i. p. 257 ff.; R. Halévi, *Les Loges maçonniques dans la France d'Ancien Régime: Aux origines de la sociabilité démocratique* (Paris, 1984); D. Roche, "Négoce et culture dans la France du XVIIIᵉ siècle," *RHMC*, 25 (1978); Hunt, *Politics, Class and Culture*, pp. 198–200; and the classic M. Agulhon, *Pénitent et franc-maçons dans l'ancienne Provence* (Paris, 1965). Cf. too the general overview of E. François and R. Reichhardt, "Les Formes de sociabilité en France du milieu du XVIIIᵉ siècle," au milieu du XIXᵉ siècle," *RHMC*, 34 (1987).

78 Roche, *Le Siècle des Lumières en province*, ii. pp. 419–24; and cf. François and Reichhardt, "Formes de sociabilité," pp. 465 ff.

79 For a general overview, see M. Agulhon, "Les Sociétés de pensée," in M. Vovelle (ed.), *Etat de la France pendant la Révolution, 1789–99* (Paris, 1988), pp. 44–8.

80 Halévi, *Les Loges maçonniques*. Cf. Furet, *Interpreting the French Revolution*, pp. 37 ff.

81 Cf. W. Reddy, *Money and Liberty in Western Europe: A Critique of Historical Understanding* (Cambridge, 1987), p. 5: "There was no revolutionary bourgeoisie."

82 E.J. Sieyes, *Qu'est-ce que le Tiers Etat?*, ed. S.E. Finer (Chicago, 1963), pp. 63–4. Cf. Sewel, *Work and Revolution*, 79.

83 See e.g. the highly illuminating recent study of D.R. Weir "Tontines, Public Finance and Revolution in France and England, 1688–1789," *Journal of Economic History*, 49 (1989). On a different tack, see too the interesting perspective on the problem opened up in J. de Viguerie, "Le Roi, le 'public' et l'exemple de Louis XV," *Revue historique*, 278 (1987).

84 Reddy, *Money and Liberty*, pp. 128–9, for arguments along the same lines as here.

85 Cobban, *Aspects*, pp. 109–11.

86 Hunt, *Politics, Class and Culture*, Ch. 5; and L. Hunt, P. Hansen and D. Lansky." The Failure of the Liberal Republic in France, 1795–9: The Road to Brumaire," *JMH*, 51 (1979).

87 R.B. Rose, *The Making of the Sans-Culottes* (Manchester, 1983); R. Cobb, *The Police and the People: French Popular Protest, 1789–1820* (Oxford, 1970), pp. 178–9; R. Andrews, "Social Structures, Political Elites and Ideology in Revolutionary Paris," *Journal of Social History*, 19 (1985); M. Sonenscher, "The Sans-Culottes of the Year II: Rethinking the Language of Labour in Revolutionary France," *Social History*, 9 (1984).

88 Hunt, *Politics, Culture and Class*, p. 161, citing E. Burke, "Thoughts on French Affairs," in R.A. Smith (ed.), *Burke on Revolution* (New York, 1968) p. 190.

89 Most famously in R. Darnton, "The High Enlightenment and the Low Life of Literature in pre-Revolutionary France," *P&P*, 51 (1971); and more recently in "The Facts of Literary Life in Eighteenth-Century France," in Baker, *Political Culture of the Old Régime*. Cf. too Furet, *Interpreting the French Revolution*, pp. 36–7.

90 The phrase "silent bourgeois revolution" comes from D. Blackbourn and G. Eley, *The Peculiarities of German History: Bourgeois Society and Politics in Nineteenth-Century Germany* (Oxford, 1982), a work which has a number of similarities of approach to those outlined here, but which I unfortunately encountered only when writing the final draft of this essay.

91 S. Scott, *The Response of the Royal Army to the French Revolution: The Role and Development of the Line Army, 1787–1793* (Oxford, 1978); J.P. Bertaud, *The Army of the French Revolution: From Citizen Soldiers to Instrument of Power* (Princeton, NJ, 1989). Cf. too J. Godechot, *Les Institutions de la France sous la Révolution et l'Empire* (Paris, l968), pp. 113–38, 353–74, 494–5.

92 Tackett, *Religion, Revolution and Regional Culture*; and J. McManners, *The French Revolution and the Church* (London, 1969) for introductions to this massive topic.

93 D.M. Vess, *Medical Revolution in France, 1789–96* (Gainesville, Fla., 1975) and D.B. Weiner, "French Doctors Face the War, 1792–1815" in C.K. Warner (ed.), *From the Ancien Régime to the Popular Front: Essays in the History of Modern France in Honor of S. B. Clough* (New York, 1969); Fitzsimmons, *Parisian Order of Barristers*, esp. p. 116 ff.; I. Woloch, "The Fall and Resurrection of the Civil Bar, 1789–1820s," *FHS*, 15 (1987–8). See too Godechot, *Institutions*, pp. 154–5, 449–53, 704–5 and *passim*.

94 C.C. Gillispie, "Politics and Science, with Special Reference to Revolutionary and Napoleonic France," *History and Technology*, 4 (1987); Bosher, *French Finances*; Church, *Revolution and Red Tape*; M. Brugière, *Gestionnaires et profiteurs de la Révolution* (Paris, 1986); *id.*, "Les Finances et l'Etat," in Lucas, *Political Culture of the French Revolution*.

95 See, for example, G. Lefebvre, *The French Revolution*, 2 vols (New York, 1962, 1964), ii. p. 303 ff.; and A. Soboul, *The French Revolution*,

1787–1799 (London, 1974), p. 553 ff. Cf. Edmonds, "Successes and Excesses," pp. 198–200.

96 See generally the works cited above, n. 29, by O'Brien and Keyder, Crafts, Roehl, Goldsmith, and Aldrich, plus Heywood, "Role of the peasantry" and Lemarchand, "Du féodalisme au capitalisme." See too M. Lévy-Leboyer, "La Croissance économique en France au XIXe siècle," *AnnESC*, 28 (1973); W. H. Newell, "The Agrarian Revolution in Nineteenth-Century France," *Journal of Economic History*, 33 (1973); and J. Marczewski, "Economic Fluctuations in France, 1815–1938," *JEEH*, 17 (1988).

7

NOBLES AND THIRD ESTATE IN THE REVOLUTIONARY DYNAMIC OF THE NATIONAL ASSEMBLY, 1789–90

Timothy Tackett

In this richly detailed analysis of factional struggle within the Constituent Assembly, Timothy Tackett addresses many of the assumptions that the Revisionists have had regarding this early stage of the Revolution. In his view, the period 1789–90 was not some radical precursor to the Terror, but dominated by moderates who did what was required to avoid counter-revolution and make the country safe for constitutional government. Based in part on an unusually comprehensive grasp of correspondence between deputies and their constituents, Tackett argues that factions within the assembly broke out not simply over modes of thought or discourses (as Furet and Baker emphasize), but over fundamental cleavages. Deputies moved to the Left, not so much because they became more influenced by Rousseau's ideas, but rather because they became convinced that a group of powerful deputies on the Right were scheming to halt the Revolution and bring back absolute monarchy. Nor does Tackett think these were the images of some paranoic delusion: he provides evidence that for many months in 1789 and 1790, the danger of counter-revolution was a viable threat that patriotic deputies needed to take seriously. Moreover, Tackett argues that this political division reflected a genuine social hostility between commoners (who championed the Left) and former noblemen (who supported Right-wing efforts to roll back the clock). Like Sewell and Jones, Tackett challenges the Revisionist consensus by claiming that even in its first months, the French Revolution reflected not merely semiotic or ideological differences but more fundamentally, deep-rooted social conflicts.

* * *

192

For over two decades now, debate has raged between "Marxists" and "revisionists" over the question of the French Revolution.[1] The outlines of this debate have become familiar even to historians with no particular expertise in eighteenth-century French studies. In place of the Marxist or Marxist-inspired vision of a revolution arising out of class conflict between nobility and bourgeoisie, most revisionists would stipulate a revolution, "caused" ultimately by the internal collapse of the monarchy. In this view, the nobles and the upper-class commoners were converging in the, late eighteenth century into a single "élite" group, bound by common economic interests and cultural experiences and by the substantial possibilities of social mobility into the nobility. When the two groups fell into conflict in 1789, it was either a kind of accidental aberration arising from misunderstandings, a difference in "style," or a failure of imagination and leadership.

Although most of the controversy to date has hinged on the question of revolutionary origins, François Furet, the leading French representative of revisionism, has also pushed a reconsideration of the revolutionary dynamic after the opening of the Estates-General in May 1789. In his widely read and influential book, *Penser la Révolution*, Furet argued that, once the Revolution had begun, it was impelled forward through the workings not of a class struggle but of a power struggle.[2] By June of 1789 and the creation of the National Assembly, the privileged orders, like the monarchy itself, had essentially "capitulated," and, by October, as Furet and Denis Richet wrote elsewhere, "the battlefield had essentially been conquered, the fight was over: the revolution had been won."[3] Thereafter, conflict within the National Assembly pitted various elements of the Third Estate against one other. The Revolution was progressively democratized and radicalized as successive factions of Patriots each claimed to be the authentic voice of popular sovereignty, the true mouthpiece of the general will. Political struggle thus became a battle of rhetoric and of ideology – but with no class content. It also became a battle of denunciations, as each faction tried to outdo its opponents in its condemnations of "aristocratic plots" and counter-revolutionary conspiracies. But, in Furet's view, these denunciations were largely contrived and the plots "imaginary," "the figment of a frenzied pre-occupation with power," and the indication also of an incipient terrorist mentality in evidence among the Patriots as early as 1789.[4]

But did the "aristocrats" really capitulate and abandon the political struggle so soon? And were early revolutionary developments so totally devoid of social dimensions? I have no intention of considering Furet's complex and suggestive thesis in all its ramifications, or of attempting to treat every aspect of the Revolution. Here, I would only present some of the results of recent research into factional organization and the revolutionary dynamic at the vital core of political life during the early Revolution, the Constituent Assembly. In fact, despite the revisionist call for a return to politics – and despite the awesome number of studies devoted to this period in French history – the internal political life of France's first National Assembly is still rather poorly understood. This is true in part for historiographical reasons. Interest in the process and functioning of the Constituent Assembly has frequently been overshadowed by historians' tenacious fascination with the problem of the origins of the Republic and the Terror. But research has also been hampered by difficulties with sources. The official accounts of events within the assembly halls are often incomplete and tendentious. No minutes at all were maintained by the Third Estate through the second week in June,[5] and, even after the appearance of official recordkeeping, minutes were commonly sanitized and abridged by the secretaries in power to promote a desired public impression of assembly activities.[6] Moreover, the near absence of nominal roll-call votes – the principal meat of what once was called the "new" history of parliamentary behavior – renders the careful quantitative assessment of deputy alignments all but impossible.[7] Nevertheless, if it is not feasible to reconstitute voting records or follow the manifold, day-to-day fluctuations of every deputy, one can at least take note of such glimpses of collective behavior as revealed by the lists of adhesions to political clubs and the signatures on petitions.[8] One can also make use of the incomplete records of the periodic elections of National Assembly officers – presidents, secretaries, and committee members. And, perhaps most important, one can examine the considerable number of accounts – many of them still only in manuscript – written by the deputies themselves in letters and memoirs to their families and home constituencies.[9]

The earliest formation of political groupings within the Estates-General will probably always remain somewhat uncertain.[10] Yet the most important and influential of these could clearly trace their genealogies to the pre-revolutionary period. Within days of their arrival in Versailles, groups of liberal deputies of the second estate were regularly congregating at the residences of the Duc de La Rochefoucauld or the Marquis de Montesquiou or in the "Viro-flay Society" on the estates of the Duc de Piennes.[11] A substantial number of the participants, perhaps the majority, were veterans of the Paris-based association of Patriots, the so-called Society of Thirty – from whose membership no fewer than twenty-six had successfully sought election to the Estates-General.[12] Most of these men were Parisians who had long known each other and who were linked through a dense network of association in Masonic lodges, mesmerist groups, and a variety of Enlightenment and philanthropic societies. Many Nobles of the Sword in the group were also bound together as outsiders to the clique of courtiers then in favor in Versailles.[13] With considerable previous experience in political organization, young noblemen such as Adrien Duport, Charles and Alexandre de Lameth, the Marquis de Lafayette and the Comte de Clermont-Tonnerre mapped the strategy that ultimately led to the secession of the liberal nobles from their order and their union with the Third Estate.[14]

Several members of the "Commoners" – Antoine Barnave, Jean-Paul Rabaut-Saint-Etienne, abbé Emmanuel-Joseph Sieyes, for example – seem also to have attended meetings of the liberal noblemen.[15] But the most celebrated and influential of the early Versailles clubs was in fact indigenous to the Third Estate. There is no need to repeat here the well-known history of the Breton Club.[16] It should be emphasized, however, that many and perhaps most of the Breton deputies had previously participated in provincial estates or in the local committees that had co-ordinated opposition against the privileged orders and their attempts to dominate Breton affairs.[17] Even before arriving in Versailles, the newly elected Third Estate delegations had met in Rennes to discuss strategy, and many of the deputies then traveled to the capital together. After the opening of the Estates-General, they followed a procedure apparently already practiced during the last Estates of Brittany, debating important issues in a café each evening, arriving at a majority decision, deciding who would speak the next day in favor of that decision, and urging all participants to vote as a bloc. It was also the specific provincial context – coupled with the absence of all Nobles and bishops from the delegation –

that rendered the Breton representatives so exceptionally radical.[18] From the earliest days of the Estates-General, they advocated a unilateral transformation of the Third Estate into a "salle nationale" or "assemblée nationale" – anticipating by some six weeks the famous motions by abbé Sieyes to this effect.[19] Indeed, for many in the Breton group, such a strategy was conceived not as a ploy for forcing joint deliberation with the Nobles and Clergy but as the first step in creating a constitution *without* the participation of the privileged orders.[20] They soon came to be identified with an unrestrained hatred of all nobles: "an extreme violence," "an implacable hatred of the nobility," as two of the more moderate deputies described it.[21]

Yet the Bretons' rapid rise to prominence in early June was by no means inevitable and was rarely anticipated by contemporaries. Although the Breton delegation began inviting representatives from other provinces to participate in its meetings early on, many deputies expressed their aversion and mistrust of the very idea of factions or "cabals" or an "esprit de parti," widely viewed as warping the representative process. The Lorraine landholder and sometime scholar Adrien Duquesnoy spoke harshly of the Breton delegation as "hotheads without measure and without moderation." For the Bordeaux merchant Pierre-Paul Nairac, they were "always moving toward extreme positions," while the Alsatian Etienne-François Schwendt sharply criticized them for attempting to "exercise a kind of domination over all opinions."[22] Others were clearly disconcerted by the Bretons' abrasive attitude toward the nobility. In this, they reflected the fears and ambiguities of men who were often socially and juridically at the very frontier between noblemen and commoners. The majority had probably spent many years of their lives imitating aristocratic values and patiently working within the aristocratic system. Whatever their views – and perhaps rage – against the injustice or irrationality of such a society, few had even dreamed that the system and its values could themselves be changed.[23] In any case, on 18 May, the motion by the Breton Isaac-René-Guy Le Chapelier, declaring that the deputies of the "National Assembly" did not represent specific orders but the whole nation, seems to have won the support of only sixty-six deputies – of whom forty-three were from Le Chapelier's own provincial delegation.[24]

The spectacular success of the Bretons in early June was probably the result of a number of factors. But, to believe the letters and diaries of the deputies themselves, no single factor was more important than the growing intransigence of the majority of the privileged deputies and their ultimate refusal to consider compromise or reconciliation in any form over the crucial question of voting procedure. For, in point of fact, the defenders of privilege and tradition among the deputies, no less than the deputy-Patriots, had also begun organizing in support of their positions. By the end of May – and probably a good deal earlier – bishops in the first estate were meeting with some regularity in the church of Notre-Dame in Versailles. Many of the prelates had known one another for years and were linked by ties of family as well as by a common educational experience at the seminary of Saint-Sulpice.[25] They readily reactivated a miniature version of the General Assembly of the Clergy – on which most of them had long collaborated – and they were notably effective in countering the activities of the more liberal curé-deputies, frustrating their efforts to unite with the Third Estate until after the unilateral decision of that estate to verify credentials in common.[26]

Unlike the Clergy, the conservative and reactionary Nobles – the great majority within the order – had no real institutional base on which to build an effective organization. Nevertheless, a substantial number of the nobles undoubtedly knew one another prior to the convocation of the Estates-General. Historians have not previously noted that almost 40 per cent of the Nobles were actually residents of Paris who had scattered into the provinces to seek election in districts where their families owned land and seigneuries.[27] At least 78 per cent of the Nobles had been educated for the military and were or had previously been commissioned officers in the army or navy. Close to two-thirds, moreover, could trace their families back to at least the sixteenth century, while over half could apparently prove lineage dating to the fourteenth century or earlier.[28] They represented most of the great families of France, and many were closely related to one another – and to the equally aristocratic episcopal families – and had long associated with one another at court and in Parisian societies. In short, the Nobles of 1789 were an extraordinarily "aristocratic" body in the full sense of the word – considerably more so than their counterparts in the Estates-General of 1614. As a corps, they occupied a dramatically different sphere of status and prestige – and probably of wealth – from that occupied by the Third Estate.[29] Although we know relatively few details about the political

197

workings of the Nobles during this period, the substantial blocs of votes given to the winning candidates in the secret ballots for officers of the order in June 1789 strongly suggest some measure of organization.[30] Indeed, the Marquis de Ferrières spoke of the "club" of conservative noblemen, led by Jean-Jacques Duval d'Eprémesnil – judge in Parlement and renegade ex-associate of the Committee of Thirty – the Marquis de Bouthillier, and the Vicomte de La Queuille.[31] With the strong support and patronage of the Comte d'Artois and the reactionary court faction, this group proved remarkably successful through the end of June in maintaining the disciplined intransigence of the great majority of noble deputies. Indeed, several of the originally "liberal-leaning" noblemen, including some with statements of grievances (*cahiers de doléances*) mandating a vote by head in the Estates-General, are known to have been won over to the hard-line position .[32]

In any case, many of the Third Estate deputies became increasingly convinced of the threat of such organization to the reforming desires of the nation. The Breton deputy Jean-Pierre Boullé warned his constituents on 9 June that the "aristocratic committee" led by Eprémesnil was meeting daily to plot its strategy and that organized action by the Patriots was necessary if the "desires of the nation" were ever to triumph.[33] Even many of the normally moderate and prudent deputies – "les hommes sages," as they liked to call themselves – began commenting on the hopeless resistance to compromise on the part of the bishops and Nobles. With the "aristocrats" of the first and second estates rejecting any form of conciliation, the Third ultimately had no choice, it was argued, but to pull together and go it alone. The self-consciously moderate Antoine Durand, a lawyer from Cahors, was outraged by the Nobles' statement of 28 May, which accepted royal mediation but rejected in advance any discussion of a vote by head: the Nobles "refuse to yield an inch of ground." "Those who have led the Nobles," wrote the usually cautious judge Jean-Baptiste Grellet de Beauregard, "have blocked all roads to compromise"; while his colleague from Toul, the *lieutenant général* Claude-Pierre Maillot, concluded that "the violence of the Nobles' decisions have increased rather than weakened the determined resolution of the Third." The wealthy landholder and mayor of Laon, Laurent de Visme, noted in his diary that under normal circumstances he would never have accepted Sieyes's motion of 10 June, but now he was inclined to do so: "The Nobles' actions have justified it."[34]

The Breton Club probably reached the pinnacle of its ascendancy toward the middle and end of June. Boullé wrote on 9 June that "during the last few days our salon has become the rallying point for all good citizens. . . . All the best citizens from all of the provinces are assembling there." On that evening, the Breton group seems to have sent out delegates to argue its case within the individual *bureaux* – the small discussion groups into which the Assembly had recently divided itself – thus measurably contributing to the development of opinion in favor of the motion to be voted on the next day.[35] To be sure, one should not underestimate the role played by the abbé Sieyes himself, whose prestige and eloquent articulation of revolutionary objectives had an enormous impact on many of the deputies.[36] But, in fact, each of Sieyes's motions seems to have been discussed and debated in the Breton Club before being brought to the full assembly of the Third Estate, and the principles in question had been continuously advocated by the Breton delegation for well over a month.[37] Once viewed with considerable mistrust by the majority of deputies, the Breton "committee" now became the center of all political activity in the Third Estate. Impelled by the absolute intransigence of the Nobles and the apparent deadlock of the Clergy, buoyed and invigorated by the support of the Versailles crowds, the Third Estate achieved a remarkable consensus around the Tennis Court Oath and the revolutionary declarations of 10, 17, and 23 June: a new definition of sovereignty and political legitimacy in open defiance of the monarchy that would probably have seemed impossible or unthinkable to most of the deputies just a few weeks earlier.[38]

By all accounts, the period from late June to early August witnessed a substantial transformation of the political chemistry of the Assembly, a restructuring of many of the positions and alliances of the middle of June. Two developments in particular seem to have contributed to cracking the solidarity and apparent consensus of the nascent National Assembly. The first was the popular violence that exploded in the capital in mid-July but that continued in both Paris and the provinces well into August. In short order, the image of the "people" held by many of the deputies – as revealed in their letters and diaries – was dramatically altered. The Rousseauist conception of the Common Man as repository of goodness and truth was frequently replaced, or at least strongly modified, by the image of the violent, unpredictable, and dangerous classes of July and August.[39] To judge by the deputies' own writings, the most shocking event was usually not the storming of the Bastille on 14 July but the popular executions about a week later of the royal officials Joseph Foulon de Doué and Louis Berthier de Sauvigny, the details of which were luridly recounted in the Assembly by deputies who had witnessed them.[40] Although several of the radicals revealed obvious sympathy for the past suffering of the people, and others were pushed by events toward a new, more expansive definition of the electorate they represented,[41] the overall reaction was one of outrage and horror: "barbarous and atrocious violence" (Visme), "scenes of cruelty and horror" (the Third Estate deputies from Marseille), "arbitrary executions that arouse horror" (Joseph Delaville Le Roulx From Brittany).[42] In any case, the July violence is known to have been a key factor in the movement of many deputies away from the more democratic vision of the new regime that had garnered increasing favor in June. It was certainly a major element in the changing position of the "Monarchien" Jean-Joseph Mounier and his liberal noble ally, the Comte de Clermont-Tonnerre. Looking back on this event, Clermont-Tonnerre wrote in 1791: "I feared that we were inciting atrocities; I remembered the St. Bartholomew's Day Massacre . . . and I sadly asked myself, 'Are we even worthy of being free?' "[43]

The second development that contributed to breaking down the earlier consensus within the Third Estate was the entry of the privileged orders into the National Assembly. In point of fact, the process of integrating the first two estates into the Assembly was long and difficult. Even though a majority of the Clergy and a small minority of the Nobles came over to the Third of their own accord between 22 and 26 June, the forced union of the remainder was nothing short of traumatic. Many of the recalcitrants were even ready to refuse the king's request for union on 27 June, and it was only after receiving a warning from the Comte d'Artois that the king's life was in danger that they sullenly marched into the National Assembly, "tears in their eyes, and rage and despair in their hearts."[44] For the next three weeks, a significant minority of both the Nobles and the Clergy continued to boycott all votes and discussions and returned daily to their own meeting halls, frequently voting formal protests of decrees made in the Assembly.[45] It was only after the Parisian insurrections of mid-July that the "parti protestant" agreed to take part in the proceedings.[46] "Severed heads," as one caustic deputy remarked, "were frightfully instructive."[47] But, even at that, it was early August before Jacques-Antoine-Marie de Cazalès and the abbé Jean-Siffrein Maury and several other of the most conservative deputies who had fled – and, in many cases, been chased back by their own constituencies – formally announced their intention of participating in the National Assembly.[48] Yet prolonged opposition of this kind was almost certainly not the norm. After the initial shock of 27 June, the majority of the newly arrived clergy and noblemen seemed to adapt themselves to the situation with surprising grace. After a two-day break in late June, according to the Comte de La Gallissonnière, "the deputies had calmed down a bit and were less frightened, and a new order of things seemed to appear."[49] The Baron de Pinteville described the sharp reversal in sentiment of many of his colleagues who had long held back because of fear and pride and pressure from the reactionary "party" but who were now swept by sentiments of patriotism and duty to the Nation: "all was forgotten as they came forward with this act of self-sacrifice."[50] For the Marquis de Ferrières, the experience was a revelation: nervous at first, he soon discovered that he was far more at ease with the commoners of the Third Estate than with the great court nobles, whom he had always detested. The Marquis de Guilhem-Clermont-Lodève, the Chevalier de Boufflers, Bishop Talleyrand, the bishop of Nancy, the archbishop of Aix, and numerous others made the transition with relative ease and were soon participating in the debates, some simply "bending to the circumstances," as Boufflers described it, others with a real measure of idealism and enthusiasm, convinced that "the nobles . . . could be equally useful within the common hall of the Assembly."[51]

It was not only these new recruits to the National Assembly who were affected. The entry of the privileged orders into their midst also had a profound effect on the deputies of the Third Estate. Numerous letters give expression to the explosion of joy and the feelings of fraternity with which the Third progressively welcomed the new arrivals. Whatever their rhetoric in late May and early June against the "aristocrats," the majority of the commoners were still awed by the great nobles and flattered that they might sit with them in the same assembly. Adrien Duquesnoy was effusive with praise for "the finest names in the kingdom,"

201

"the most virtuous men in the kingdom," who now gave the Assembly "an aura of seriousness ... that was previously lacking." François-René-Pierre Ménard de la Groye, who had felt almost ashamed of his growing anger with the aristocrats in early June, again felt at ease when he dined with them and was delighted to observe "a great deal of unity and cordiality among all the members of the Assembly."[52]

Members of the Third Estate clearly went out of their way to encourage the participation of their new colleagues. The Vicomte de Malartic noted with evident satisfaction the deferential efforts of the commoners in his *bureau* to elicit his opinions on Saint-Domingue, where he had once lived.[53] Félix Faulcon waxed poetic as he described the camaraderie of nobles and commoners spending the night together in the assembly hall during the mid-July crisis: "These proud nobles, who once so greatly profited from their alleged privileges and the chance occurrence of their birth, now sleep or walk side by side with the commoners."[54] The astute Ferrières rapidly sized up the new situation. "The Upper Third will be flattered," he wrote his sister, "by the consideration shown them by the Nobles. ... Let the Nobles take a single step and the Third will take ten."[55] Despite their suspicions of the "aristocrats" and the latter's pretensions of social superiority and political dominance, the Commoners' ultimate desire at this stage in events was not to destroy the Nobles but to be treated by that body as equals. Indeed, this surge of fraternal sentiments among the orders should not be underestimated in evaluating the night of 4 August, the dramatic session during which substantial portions of Old Regime institutions were swept away in the space of a few hours. Even though most interpretations of the event emphasize the behind-the-scenes manipulations of the Breton Club, it is doubtful that such tactics would have been effective without the short-lived atmosphere of brotherhood that permeated much of the Assembly in early August.[56]

Only a few of the Third Estate deputies, several of them future Jacobins, seem to have viewed the situation with a more cynical eye. The Breton deputy Delaville Le Roulx despaired that the Assembly would be "captivated by the seductive manners" of the Nobles and bishops and wondered how the Patriots might "bring fresh energy to the Assembly and prevent it from slipping into error." Maillot noted that the "flattery and familiarity" of the privileged were more dangerous than their previous "arrogance and pride." And Jacques-Antoine Creuzé-Latouche, who had never wanted a union of the three orders in the first place, and who would have preferred that the Third Estate act on its own to write a constitution, saw only divisions ahead in the Assembly. "Feeble individuals," he wrote, previously brought into conformity with correct principles by the "vigorous and virile" in the Assembly would now be won over by the nobles, and "aristocratic and antipatriotic maxims" would become the order of the day.[57]

Creuzé's fears were probably not unfounded. After the heroic days of the early Revolution, there is considerable evidence that the Breton Club's influence went into decline. Whether or not the number of adherents actually diminished, the entry of 600 new deputies into the National Assembly – most of whom were clearly conservatives or moderates[58] – invariably decreased the proportionate size of the radical contingent and reduced their hold on the large bloc of moderate Patriots within the Third Estate. In fact, by September, the "comité breton" seems to have reverted to an exclusively provincial organization, no longer attended by deputies from other provinces. It was apparently badly divided over the issue of the royal veto and was meeting less frequently than before.[59] Undoubtedly, the Patriots continued to meet to plan strategy in one way or another, but the meetings probably took place outside any formal organization. The Provençal deputy, Jacques-Athanase de Lombard-Taradeau, who openly aligned himself with the most advanced faction of the Patriots, never referred to the "Breton Club" after July but only to "what we call the 'Palais royal' of the Assembly" or simply "our party." And his descriptions of the group's operations portray an extremely loose factional organization improvised on the spot, "in the morning, before the beginning of the session, after much discussion among groups in the hall." Indeed, if Lombard's accounts are at all typical, it seems likely that the lengthy hours passed in the National Assembly and in the various discussion groups and committees throughout the months of August and September, the sheer fatigue from the work involved, made nightly club meetings substantially more difficult.[60]

One indication of the decline in the Breton group's fortunes and the general movement of deputy opinion during this period comes – in the absence of roll-call records – from the various elections of officers to the National Assembly. The organizational regulations of the Assembly specified that every two weeks the deputies would meet in their *bureaux* – the thirty discussion groups, to which all members were assigned – to vote for a president and three secretaries. The president would serve for a two-week period and would be chosen in multiple ballots if necessary – in an effort to obtain a winner by absolute majority; the secretaries would be chosen by simple plurality on a single vote and would hold office for a month (so that there were always six secretaries in service at a given moment).[61] Although a great deal depended on the personalities of the individuals holding the posts, all the officers had considerable potential power: the president to set the order of debate and designate – or reject – speakers, the secretaries to control the minutes of the meetings and to sort correspondence and decide which letters and petitions went to which committees. Since the votes were organized through the thirty individual *bureaux* – in isolation from the pressures of the galleries – and were apparently taken by secret ballot, they can be interpreted as a useful index of the evolution of deputy sentiment and perhaps also of the degree of organization of the various political factions.[62]

The earliest elections seem generally to confirm the atmosphere of a united front previously identified for this period. To be sure, with the possible exception of the abbé de Montesquiou Agent-General of the Clergy, all fourteen of the individuals elected as officers between 3 July and 3 August had earlier reputations as Patriots.[63] But while four of these – Le Chapelier, Sieyes, the abbé Henri Grégoire, and Jérôme Pétion de Villeneuve – were probably considered radicals and later became members of the Jacobin Club, six others would undoubtedly have been classed as moderates, and four – Clermont-Tonnerre, Mounier, the Comte de Lally-Tollendal, and the abbé de Montesquiou – soon embraced the more conservative "Monarchiens" position.[64] Perhaps equally significant, no less than ten of the fourteen were members of the privileged orders – though not all had actually been elected by their "natural" estates. This marked preference for nobles and clergymen as assembly officers continued throughout the entire first year of the Constituent Assembly with nineteen of twenty-seven presidents and fifty-one of eighty-eight secretaries being drawn from members of the first two estates.[65] The first three presidential contests were scarcely contests at all, with votes going overwhelmingly to the Duc d'Orléans (who declined), the archbishop of Vienne, and the Duc de Liancourt. The first and only Breton Club president, the Rennes lawyer Le Chapelier, obtained the post almost by accident in early August. In fact, he had come in third in the initial contest and was chosen in a second election only after the victor, the moderate Jacques-Guillaume Thouret, had resigned.[66] And it was to be the last time a member of the Left would control the rostrum for almost seven months. Through the end of the year, the future Jacobins were largely an insignificant force in the presidential tallies, their candidates unable to muster more than 183 votes (out of over a thousand) in any of the elections for which voting totals are preserved.[67] Indeed, to judge by the deputies elected to office from mid-August to mid-October, the best organized and most influential faction within the Assembly was not on the Left at all but on the Right.[68]

Throughout the month of July, the organization of the recalcitrant privileged action seems never entirely to have dissolved, despite the popular upheavals and the temporary flight of many of its adherents. Even after the meeting halls of the Nobles and the Clergy had been closed and converted into offices by Jacques Necker, director-general of finance, a core of the most conservative noblemen and bishops continued to meet in the homes of individuals. They were clearly acting as a corps on 16 July when they announced to the Assembly that they would henceforth join in the votes and the debates.[69] It was most likely this same coalition that then co-ordinated the considerable deputy discipline involved in placing several of its numbers on the new Committee on Research at the end of July and in the election of Thouret to the presidency at the beginning of August.[70] Significantly, it was toward the beginning of August that several Patriots first took note of the "cabal" of Nobles and Clergy that was opposing them and voting as a bloc.[71]

An initial turning point in the new evolution was undoubtedly the night of 4 August. While in some respects this sweeping attack on privilege marked the ultimate fruition of the earlier flowering of fraternal generosity, it also carried with it the seeds of renewed factional strife. To judge by the reflections of the deputy letter-writers, the suppression of seigneurial rights was accepted with resignation and sometimes with enthusiasm. "If it leads to advantages for the public good," wrote Ferrières to his wife, "I will easily be able to console myself for my losses as a noble and as a seigneurial lord." The chevalier Garron de la Bévière was more morose about the economic prospects of his order, but he, too, in a letter to his wife, accepted the inevitable: "In the end, if it will promote general happiness, I have no regrets. . . . One must yield to necessity."[72] Yet large numbers of the clerical deputies were clearly upset by the suppression of the tithes without reimbursement and by the first proposals for the nationalization of church property. According to numerous witnesses, however, the key issue that united many of the nobles and clergymen as a solid and cohesive group was the debate two weeks later over including religious toleration in the Declaration of the Rights of Man and the Citizen and the counter-proposal that Catholicism be made the state religion. In what were widely described as the most tumultuous debates to date, a number of deputies in all three estates seem to have dramatically crystallized their opposition to the Revolution.[73] Thus curé Emmanuel Barbotin, previously a strong supporter of the Third Estate, now became convinced that many Third Estate deputies were "philosophers who have neither faith nor discipline"; while Guilluame Gontier de Biran, a chief *bailliage* magistrate from Bergerac, first came to perceive a dual menace to religion and the throne. For the Baron de Gauville – who had been irritated by the loss of his hunting rights on 4 August but who had generally accepted the abolition of seigneurial dues – it was precisely during these debates of late August that "we began to recognize one another" and that he and his colleagues began sitting together consistently on the right side of the president's table.[74]

Nevertheless, the critical achievement in the organization of the Right was to be the work of a new coalition of more moderate conservatives, a number of them recruited from the Third Estate. The formation and general character of the "Monarchiens" have been described in some detail by Jean Egret and, more recently, by Robert Griffiths.[75] Unlike the extreme right of the recalcitrant Nobles and Clergy, who sought either a return to the Old Regime or a system of reforms based on the king's declaration of 23 June, the Monarchiens sought to affirm the transformations of that summer but to ensure that ultimate sovereignty remained in the hands of the king as a buttress against the dangers of popular violence. Centered on the delegation from Dauphiné – the only provincial delegation that could match the Bretons in its cohesiveness and its tradition of group action – but also including important contingents from Auvergne and Normandy and a bevy of moderate nobles, the group resolved sometime in late July or early August to beat the Breton Club at its own game.[76] In relatively short order, the Monarchiens had surpassed the Patriots in their level of factional organization. While the Breton Club had operated in an essentially democratic fashion, with relatively loose discipline and public debates in a café to which all were invited, the Monarchiens followed their more authoritarian and hierarchical penchant by establishing a small decision-making "central committee," which convened in private at one of the member's homes – and sometimes in the château of Versailles itself – and which then sent out directives through a system of subcommittees to all its potential adherents. Before votes in the *bureaux* for committee members or National Assembly officers, someone passed out notes listing the names that deputies were to inscribe on their ballots.[77] On the floor of the National Assembly, Mounier's friend and colleague from Dauphiné, the Comte de Virieu, assumed the role of a veritable party whip: "he can be seen in every corner of the hall, speaking, entreating, shouting, peering to see who will vote for or against."[78] By early September, the progressively tighter coalition between moderate and extreme right was clearly in place, with Cazalès, Eprémesnil, and the abbé Maury participating in the Monarchien central committee and speaking frequently in the Assembly in defense of Monarchien positions.[79] On 17 September, the radical printer-deputy from Lyon, Jean-André Périsse-Duluc, wrote that "the coalition of nearly all of the Clergy and the Nobles, along with a lesser number of Commoners, has become so strong that the deputies involved never differ on their votes: without exception, all of them rise together or remain seated [in order to vote]."[80] Clearly, many of the "aristocrats" were increasingly prepared to follow the rules of the game and work within the newly evolved parliamentary system, convinced of the real possibility of halting and perhaps reversing the revolution through political organization and majority votes.

The growing power of this new coalition was apparent in the choice of Assembly officers. After the middle of August, the Monarchiens not only won four successive presidential elections but also largely dominated the secretariat's table as well. In the election of 31 August, they even obtained a clean sweep of the president – the bishop of Langres – and all three secretaries. Indeed, there is good evidence that the Monarchien coalition was the only group systematically organizing for elections during this period. The scraps of voting records remaining reveal that, in September, the Monarchien candidates alone received significant blocs of votes in every *bureau*, the remainder of the votes being spread out over an enormous range of individual deputies.[81] "For three weeks now," wrote Virieu after the election of the bishop of Langres, "the reasonable and upright deputies have quietly reclaimed the majority. The *enragés* have been beaten back on all fronts. In spite of their efforts, we have chosen the president and all three secretaries."[82] The election in mid-September of the Monarchien Comte de Clermont-Tonnerre was perhaps even more galling to the Left in that, by the rotation procedure tacitly agreed on since July, the post should normally have gone to a member of the Third Estate.[83]

To be sure, the coalition was frequently more successful in the electoral *bureaux* than on the floor of the Assembly itself, and it came up short on several of the key constitutional votes for which it militated with particular fervor – above all, the effort in early September to obtain a two-house legislature and an absolute royal veto on all legislation. Indeed, the alliance would seem to have broken down entirely on the issue of the number of chambers, with the extreme right apparently following a *politique du pire* and voting with the Patriots. But most of the deputies perceived the veto decision as a compromise vote between the Right's desire for an absolute veto and the Left's desire for no veto at all. And the Monarchiens and their allies won a considerable victory later in the month when it was decided that three successive legislatures would have to pass the same law in order to override a royal veto – a complication considered by some as tantamount to an absolute veto.[84]

In any event, the deputies of the Left clearly believed themselves under siege from late August to early October. Lombard wrote home that "our party is absolutely in the minority." Louis-Prosper Lofficiel was convinced that, without the support of about forty clergymen and a hundred or so liberal nobles, "we would certainly be defeated" on every vote. Périsse estimated that as many as two-thirds of all the deputies were influenced by the "cabal" – although fortunately half of these were open-minded and could sometimes be won over.[85] For the celebrated writer, Constantin-François Chassebeuf de Volney, deputy from Anjou, the Assembly was now so divided and in danger of being won over by the aristocrats that it was necessary to elect a whole new assembly and a new set of deputies, chosen this time to represent the true social composition of the French population – notably, by eliminating most of the noble and clerical deputies. And after losing the vote on the manner of overriding a royal veto, the delegation from Brittany seriously discussed abandoning the Assembly altogether, an Assembly now deemed to be entirely dominated by the "aristocrats."[86]

The political history of the Constituent Assembly after the dramatic events of 5–6 October – the march on Versailles that led to the transfer of both monarchy and Assembly to Paris – is generally less well known than the earlier period of the Revolution. Many series of correspondence ended in the later half of 1789 or toward the beginning of the following year, as deputies found themselves burdened with ever-increasing demands on their time and as a growing national distribution of newspapers removed one of the principal *raisons d'être* for the letters home.

Nevertheless, it seems clear that the October Days did not mark the demise of the Right as a meaningful force in the National Assembly. The mass desertion of the conservative deputies – 300 are sometimes said to have taken out passports[87] – is apparently a myth, altogether unsubstantiated by the evidence available.[88] Although four of the Monarchien leaders did indeed leave the Assembly,[89] Pierre-Victor Malouet, Clermont-Tonnerre, Virieu, and their associates continued their efforts on behalf of the Monarchien platform to the very end of the Constituent Assembly. Together, they formed first a "Club des Impartiaux" and later a "Club Monarchique."[90] Despite his initial despondency over the October events, Virieu ultimately repudiated the desertion of his friend Mounier and vowed to fight on: "the sacred flame that burns within me is not yet extinguished, and is reviving . . ." "I will stay with the Assembly," wrote Archbishop Boisgelin, "and I will go with it [to Paris]." Gontier de Biran also affirmed his determination to stay on despite his anguish and disappointment over the events: "I think that if it were not for the honor and desire of doing our duty, few of us would remain here."[91]

For the next few months, the focus of power seemed to shift back toward the center of the political spectrum, with the unaligned "Center" Patriots – Emmanuel-Marie Fréteau de Saint-Just, Armand-Gaston Camus, Thouret, and Jean-Nicolas

Démeunier – picking up five of the six presidencies to the end of the year.[92] Yet the factional organization, the very considerable coordinating capabilities created by the Monarchiens, seem to have been maintained. On occasion, the group was still able to elect its candidates as president: Boisgelin in November and the abbé de Montesquiou in early January.[93] Basking in his recent victory, the prelate congratulated himself for having rejected all the predictions of doom by Mounier and Lally-Tollendal and for having stayed on to fight. Where would he be now, he mused, "if I had listened to the advice everyone was giving me?"[94] Like many other deputies, he was convinced that the decree of 2 November placing ecclesiastical lands "at the disposal of the Nation" was actually a victory for his side. Everyone knew that some church lands would have to be sold, he wrote, but they had succeeded in simply admitting the principle without in any way turning all lands over to the state: "They will perhaps be satisfied to sell off monastic property."[95] The Monarchiens and their allies also continued to obtain election of their adherents to various committees, culminating in a dramatic vote in late November that gave them effective control of the powerful organ of investigation and repression, the Committee on Research.[96]

Yet the October Days may well have marked the beginning of a certain shift within the Right coalition in favor of the more reactionary elements. This evolution is particularly evident if one examines the breakdown of those deputies actually participating in Assembly debates – as suggested by entries in the index to the proceedings and debates of the Constituent Assembly. (See Figure 7.1.[97]) The frequency of participation of the Monarchiens dropped precipitously from September to March, continuing downward even after the departure of the four Monarchien leaders in October. During the same period, the most notable speakers of the extreme Right were participating ever more frequently, so that from early 1790 to the end of the Constituent Assembly they had become the principal spokesmen for the Right. Unfortunately, much less is known of the factional organization of the extreme Right during this period. But the religious issue, and particularly the question of church property seems increasingly to have become the central rallying point in binding together the most conservative elements of the Nobles, the Clergy, and the Commoners – or such, at least, was the opinion of the conservative Baron de Gauville.[98]

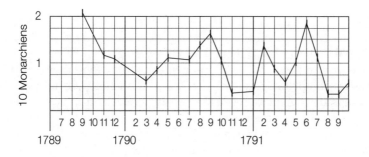

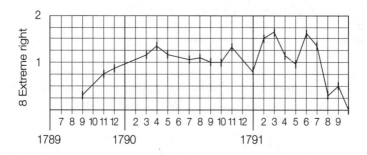

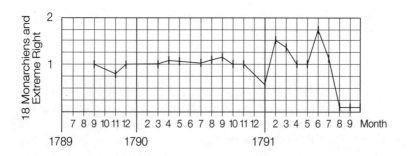

Figure 7.1 Index of participation of Monarchiens and Extreme Right speakers in the proceedings and debates of the Constituent Assembly

Significantly – in the midst of the debates over ecclesiastical land and monastic vows – the group began holding its meetings in the Grands Augustins, in the same hall where the bishops had been accustomed to holding their *Assemblées générales* for generations. Here, according to the elderly Patriot lawyer René-Antoine-Hyacinthe Thibaudeau, "They begin by preparing in their committees the insidious measures that they then try to push through the Assembly.[99] When the faction was forced to leave under the pressures of the Parisian crowds, they took refuge in the Capuchin monastery, which was directly attached to the assembly hall and which allowed the deputies to enter through a private passageway unseen by the crowds outside.[100] It was here that the "Capuchin Society" as they came to be known, drew up their declaration of 19 April 1790, adhering to Dom Christophe-Antoine Gerle's motion six days earlier that Roman Catholicism be declared the state religion.[101] Chased away once again by the Parisian crowds, the group seems to have continued its coordination in more secretive fashion through a series of small "committees" that met in the homes of individuals, each committee delegating one of its members as liaison with a central steering committee. On occasion, they seem also to have met jointly with the Club des Impartiaux – confirming a continued loose alliance between the two alignments on the Right.[102]

By the spring of 1790, there were already numerous signs of a shift of the Assembly's center of gravity in the direction of the Left. To believe the analysis of Visme, at the beginning of December the deputies were divided almost exactly into two equal parts. In the important vote of 7 December, when the radicals attempted to revise the election laws to promote broader political participation, "the Assembly divided into two almost equal parts sitting at opposite ends of the hall."[103] And Périsse-Duluc noted the hesitancy of the Left to have any of its adherents sent out as *commissaires du roi* to organize the new local governments, for fear that the absence of even a few Patriots would tip the balance in favor of the Right.[104] But, by late December and early January, a number of deputies from various points on the political spectrum were becoming aware of an evident erosion of the Right. By the year's end, the Protestant banker from Lyon, Guillaume-Benoît Couderc, was convinced that "the aristocratic influence in the hall is declining appreciably from day to day." The Patriot curé Thomas Lindet concurred: "The opposition party is diminishing. . . .

It is winning some small victories, but it is losing the major questions." And Delaville, so pessimistic for the Left the previous September, now suggested, for the first time, that his "party" was clearly in control of the situation: "les hommes forts," as he described them. "Those who know anything of the Assembly," wrote Duquesnoy, "cannot help but notice the progressive desertion and depopulation of that part of the hall where the abbé Maury sits, and that there is no longer a sufficient number of seats at the other side of the hall." By mid-January, the Assembly staff was having to install more benches on the Left to accommodate all the new arrivals.[105] To be sure, the Right retained a considerable residual strength through at least the middle of 1790 and was able to attract enough votes from the still rather volatile uncommitted deputies to win several presidential elections and a certain number of constitutional votes. Indeed, from late February through the middle of July, the elections suggest an Assembly more polarized than ever before. One might be tempted to speak of a veritable two-party system during this period, with nine of the eleven presidential victories going to either the Jacobin or the Capuchin candidates.[106] But, by and large, the momentum and the initiative within the Assembly were increasingly passing to the left of hall.[107]

The reasons for this evolution at this particular moment in the Assembly's history are not entirely clear. It was related in part, no doubt, to the increasing dominance within the Right of the most reactionary strand of conservatism, the strand associated in the minds of most deputies with the trio of Maury, Cazalès, and Eprémesnil. Many of the Monarchiens had built earlier reputations as patriots and reformist leaders. But the leaders of the opposition most in evidence by the end of 1789 had been identified from the beginning with a complete return to the Old Regime. As Duquesnoy suggested, far fewer people wanted to sit on the Right when the abbé Maury became the central figure on his side of the hall.[108] The situation was compounded in that the geography of the new meeting hall in Paris no longer provided any intermediate places in which to sit. The hall in Versailles had been essentially oval in its layout, while the long, narrow "Manège," divided in the middle by the speaker's platform and the president's table, forced every deputy to make a daily symbolic affirmation as to which side he was on.[109]

Yet perhaps the single most important development in the

resurgence of the Left was the formation in late November or early December of the Jacobin Club and the rapid emergence of this association as a highly organized political force. In fact, the new *société* was not – as is often suggested – the simple continuation of the Breton Club, transferred from Versailles to Paris. By the end of the summer, the Breton group had already lost its character as the central rallying point for all Patriots. Once in Paris, the Bretons apparently continued their separate meetings for a time even after the creation of the Friends of the Constitution.[110] Although a great many of the members of the new association had probably also been members of the earlier Breton Club, the Jacobins created a new kind of Patriot structure, more highly centralized and organized, patterned in many respects after the organization of the Right. Indeed, according to Louis-Marie de La Revellière-Lépeaux, the initial formation of the Jacobin Club in late November was in direct response to the organizational offensive of the Right. Everyone knew, wrote La Revellière, that "the aristocratic party normally chose the Assembly officers because it held meetings in which it was decided in advance who was to be elected." For this reason, the Left "decided to hold meetings of their own so that they could ensure the Patriots' control of the bureau."[111]

The details of this organization are still poorly known. It seems certain, however, that in addition to their general public meetings in the Dominican convent, the Jacobins created a central committee with prime responsibilities for guiding the general direction of the club and set up a far more efficient means of disciplining voting. But if, in many respects, they simply emulated the organization of the Monarchiens, the Jacobins also went beyond the Right in their efforts to systematically mobilize public opinion in favor of their initiatives through the creation of a correspondence committee as liaison with affiliated clubs in the provinces.[112] It was almost certainly this new organization that allowed the Jacobins to increase their influence in the election of Assembly officers – first, from November onward, the secretaries and, by March 1790, the presidents as well. The same organization enabled the Left to begin systematically taking control of most of the committees. Thus, in the December election of the Committee on Research, the club engineered a dramatic turnabout, with the elimination of all the deputies on the Right and their replacement by twelve known Patriots, eight of whom were Jacobins.[113] While in 1789 they obtained only a fourth of the committee assignments, in 1790 the

Jacobin group was able to gain half of all new positions. Over the same period, the deputies on the Right saw their share of committee posts decline from one-fifth to less than one-tenth of all assignments.[114]

By the early weeks of 1790, both outside observers and the deputies themselves were aware of the growing polarization of the National Assembly and of the extent to which developments in that assembly were increasingly dominated by two politicized and well-organized "parties." As *L'Observateur* remarked, "For the last month, two associations have existed in Paris. Each is composed of members of the National Assembly. The first . . . meets in the Jacobins of the *rue Saint-Honoré*; the second . . . meets in the *Grands-Augustins*. Both have a numerous membership; both are a source of uneasiness for Parisians from the influence they may have over the National Assembly."[115] Lindet, in a letter to his brother, expressed it even more simply, "A singular division reigns in the Assembly: the hall has become a battlefield where two enemy armies face one another."[116]

But who were these two armies? What differences can one find in the character and composition of their respective contingents? Unfortunately, the participants in the Breton Club and the Monarchien group will probably never be known for certain. Membership in the Jacobin group can be generally reconstructed, however, through the research of Alphonse Aulard.[117] Based on this source, 205 Constituent Assembly deputies would seem to have adhered to the "Amis de la Constitution" in the months following December 1790. Although membership had undoubtedly varied somewhat since the club first formed in late 1789, this number is surprisingly close to the round figure of 200 who were supporting Jacobin candidates for committee assignments in April 1790.[118] As for the "Capuchins Society," a substantial portion of its participation can be ascertained from the petition signed during the faction's meeting on 19 April.[119] Even though the specific object of the petition, the maintenance of Catholicism as the sole state religion, may have prevented the association of a few anticlerical conservatives – like the Marquis de Ferrières – the petition remains the best single record of factional adhesion to the Capuchins for the first half of 1790. In all, 292 deputies signed this document – suggesting an alignment on the Right significantly larger than the Jacobin group.[120]

A preliminary analysis of the two groups of deputies suggests that the collective biographies of the Capuchins, on the one hand, and the Jacobins, on the other, were in certain respects dramatically different.[121] Without a doubt, the most salient distinction was the remarkable alignment by Old Regime estate. More than eight out of ten Jacobins were deputies of the Third Estate, while more than nine out of ten Capuchins represented the two privileged orders.[122] Indeed, among the handful of twenty-three Third Estate deputies belonging to the Capuchins, a third were actually nobles or clergymen who had been elected by the commoners.[123] To be sure, the single largest contingent of Capuchins – slightly over half – were clergymen. They included almost all of the bishops, as well as some 40 per cent of the parish priests in the Assembly.[124] We have already noted the importance of opposition to the Constituent Assembly's religious policies in the general cohesion of the group. It is not surprising that the coalition soon came generally to be known as "les noirs." Yet if one includes the deputies from all three estates, some 54 per cent of the Capuchins are found to have come from noble families. And of these, two-thirds were true "aristocrats" who could trace back their lineage to the sixteenth century or earlier.[125] Much can be made of the relatively modest family backgrounds of the three most visible leaders of the Right: Maury, Cazalès, and Eprémesnil – the first a commoner, the second two of first-generation nobility. Yet one should also not overlook the strong "aristocratic" imprint on the Capuchins as a whole – aristocratic not only in the revolutionary meaning of "conservative ideology" but with the older implication of ancient social or caste origins. Beyond Maury, Cazalès, and Eprémesnil, seven of the ten most common Capuchin speakers originated in families of this kind.[126]

As for the Jacobins in the Assembly, the commoners among them – the vast majority – differed very little in their social contours from the Third Estate deputies as a whole.[127] There was, however, a distinct over-representation of those calling themselves "avocats" and a corresponding under-representation of the various categories of royal officeholders.[128] Unfortunately, the socioeconomic position of the "lawyers" in question is difficult to define and was almost certainly very diverse – from practicing court lawyers to wealthy landowners who had never set foot in a court and whose law degrees were essentially symbols of status.[129] The paucity of officeholders among the Jacobins is not insignificant, however, in that many of them – particularly the royal magistrates – occupied what was perhaps the highest status level of the entire Third Estate. They were also among those Commoners deputies with the greatest vested interests in the Old Regime. In all, only eleven clergymen and forty-two noblemen – representing any of the three estates – had thrown in their lots with the Jacobins. A few of the nobles – the Duc d'Aiguillon, the Vicomte de Noailles, the brothers Lameth, for example – were from among the greatest families of the kingdom. Of the central club leadership, both Alexandre Lameth and the parlementary magistrate Adrien Duport had been members of the second estate. It is significant, nevertheless, that this small group of Jacobin nobles was distinctly less "aristocratic" than the large contingent of Capuchin nobles, with only a little over one-third holding titles dating before the seventeenth century.[130] Indeed, almost half of all the newly ennobled Third Estate deputies – eighteen of thirty-eight – joined the Jacobins. Among the twelve most important leaders of the Constituent Assembly from the Jacobin deputies, those participating most frequently in National Assembly debates, only one – the Comte de Mirabeau – was an "aristocrat" by birth.[131]

Beyond the question of social differences, a preliminary prosopography would suggest two other ways in which the two political factions can be distinguished. In the first place, Capuchins and Jacobins would seem to have had somewhat differing residences. A full 26 per cent of the Capuchins, compared to only 11 per cent of the Jacobins, are known to have lived in Paris. Most of the Parisian Capuchins in question were in fact from great noble families who had won election in provincial *bailliages* by virtue of their names and status. Half of the Jacobins, by contrast – compared to only 30 per cent of the Capuchins – came from small to medium-size provincial towns, with populations of from 2,000 to 50,000 inhabitants. Among those Capuchins who did come from the provinces, however, a significantly larger proportion came from southern France – south of a line between La Rochelle and Geneva – and notably from the Massif Central and other interior provinces of the Midi, regions that were among the most isolated and economically backward in the kingdom.[132]

In the second place, the Capuchins were distinctly older, on the average, than their opponents. Among those deputies for whom dates of birth are known, the Jacobins averaged 43.2 years old in

1790, three years younger than the average for all deputies, while the Capuchins averaged 49.5.[133] Indeed, among totality of the youngest deputies, those under thirty at the beginning of the revolution, no less than 40 per cent adhered to the Jacobins – compared to 11 per cent who associated with the Capuchins. Among those deputies over sixty-five at the opening of the Estates-General, 28 per cent became Capuchins and only 5 per cent became Jacobins. Moreover, such differences cut across all three orders: the average ages of Jacobin clergymen, Jacobin noblemen, and Jacobin commoners were all lower than their respective counterparts within the rival faction. The differences were particularly dramatic among the small group of radical nobles, whose mean age was nearly ten years younger than that of their noble colleagues on the right side of the hall.[134] A generational effect was clearly operational in the radicalism and conservatism of many of the deputies.

Factional confrontations between Left and Right continued as a characteristic feature of the Constituent Assembly to the very end of that body's existence in September 1791. Indeed, to judge by the participation index (see Figure 7.1) the principal speakers on the Right were never more active than during the spring of 1791.[135] Yet the political influence of the conservative coalition within the Assembly was ebbing sharply by the middle of 1790. Two extraordinary successes by the Patriots at the beginning of the summer undoubtedly contributed to breaking the momentum and the energy of the Capuchin–Impartial alliance: the formal suppression of the nobility on 20 June and the passage of the Civil Constitution of the Clergy three weeks later. Taken together, the two measures fostered a deep sense of fatalism and demoralization on the part of many of the deputies of the Clergy and the Nobles.[136] The last president elected by the Right retired from office in the middle of July. From September of that year – after a succession of moderate Patriots – the Jacobins effectively came to dominate the presidency, as they already controlled the secretariat, through the end of the Constituent Assembly. By November, the Jacobin curé Lindet could write to his brother, "The aristocracy no longer has an influence, it seems to me, on the choice of Assembly officers."[137]

Yet the rise of the Jacobins to pre-eminence within the National Assembly had been neither rapid nor inevitable. Their triumph, if triumph it was, came not in 1789, as is usually suggested, but only in the second half of 1790.[138] And the chronology is significant. Events during that first formative year of the Revolution helped set the tone of the parliamentary process and establish many of the basic political presuppositions for years to come. Far from capitulating, the representatives of privilege and conservatism had asserted a dynamic presence within the Estates-General and the National Assembly from the very beginning. Many of the reactionary deputies of the Clergy and the Nobles, whose initial intransigence had greatly contributed in crystallizing the revolutionary sentiment of June 1789, had eventually been won over by the successful organizational achievements of the Monarchiens and, rapidly adapting to circumstances, had set out in an alliance with the more moderate conservatives to exploit to their advantage the new system and its rules. Learning from the methods of the Breton Club, this coalition had soon taken the initiative, pioneering many of the electoral tactics usually attributed to the Jacobins, and playing a key role in the transformation of the more archaic Old Regime faction into a first sketch of the modern political party. In their heyday, their numbers closely matched – actually somewhat superior to – those of the Jacobins, and they could feel justified in their ambition to win over a sufficient number of the non-aligned moderate majority to seize control of the Assembly. The Monarchien Malouet certainly believed this was possible, and he speculated, many years later, on what might have happened if a relatively small number of deputies on the Right had not decided to abandon the battle so early in the Revolution. The Jacobin leader Alexandre Lameth made much the same argument, musing that the presence in the Estates-General of deputies from the Breton nobility and upper clergy – groups that had boycotted the elections in the spring of 1789 – might have entirely transformed the situation.[139]

Inevitably, the Patriots were intensely aware of the offensive of the Right and often, understandably, felt harried and besieged. They were also clearly conscious of the social composition of the group that opposed them at the other end of the hall. It was not a question of mere rhetoric, of the Jacobins concocting imaginary machinations by the aristocrats. In fact they faced genuine, genealogically certified aristocrats, swords at their sides, day after day in the Assembly itself: aristocrats who, for a time, were prominent elements in a highly organized political faction or alliance of factions, and who, for a time, could harbor the plausible hope of a "legal" counter-revolution engineered through the Constituent Assembly itself.[140] Little wonder that the Patriots on the Left soon felt compelled to match the organization of the Right with their own, highly centralized party organization. Little wonder that many deputies on the Left came to view all opposition parties as dangerous and illegal, and that the very concept of a "loyal opposition" failed to develop in the early revolution. Obviously, a close "internal" analysis of this kind does not answer all the questions about the dynamics of the Revolution, or even about the dynamics of the National Assembly. A more general synthesis will have to take into account those exogenous factors – economic trends, crowd activities, international relations, and the pressures of newspapers, clubs, home constituencies, and Parisian assemblies – all those forces that exerted an overwhelming impact on revolutionary developments as a whole. A broader account will also have to confront the seemingly intractable problem of the influence of pre-revolutionary ideologies on the men of 1789.

But the approach taken here does reveal the extent to which the political behavior of a significant and highly influential – if minority – segment of the National Assembly was associated with social divisions among the deputies. To be sure, the social divisions operative were not those of class. Most of the Nobles and most of the wealthy commoners who represented the Third Estate – as revisionist historians never tire of demonstrating – had basically similar relationships to the means of production.[141] A Marxian analysis, whatever its utility for explaining other aspects of the Revolution, is ultimately not very useful for the problems of the National Assembly. It seems likely that, for understanding social interaction within the Constituent Assembly, an analysis based on a complex of categories – such as wealth, status, education, and previous political experience – will prove far more helpful. In terms of the subjective element of status within the traditional value system – a value system with which the deputies, as revealed in their letters, long maintained an ambiguous relationship – there was clearly a world of difference between the majority of those individuals participating in the two major factional divisions of the Assembly.[142] And it seems evident that the political-social dialectic between Left and Right, a dialectic whose origins can be traced to the earliest days of the

Estates-General and the National Assembly, would exert a major influence on the development of the new political culture of the French Revolution and of modern France.

NOTES

Source Reprinted from the *American Historical Review* 94 (April 1989): 271–301.

Acknowledgment Much of the research on which this article is based was supported by a fellowship from the John Simon Guggenheim Memorial Foundation. Earlier versions were presented at the Washington/ Baltimore French history study group and at the 1988 meeting of the Society for French Historical Studies. May I express my particular appreciation to Jack Censer and Donald Sutherland for their careful readings and criticisms.

1 Perhaps the best general summaries of the debate are in William Doyle, *Origins of the French Revolution* (Oxford, 1980), pp. 7–40; Lynn Hunt, *Politics, Culture, and Class in the French Revolution* (Berkeley, Calif., 1984), pp. 3–10; and D.M.G. Sutherland, *France, 1789–1815: Revolution and Counterrevolution* (Oxford, 1985), pp. 15–18. See also the recent articles by Michael P. Fitzsimmons, "Privilege and the Polity in France, 1786–1791," *AHR*, 92 (April 1987): 269–95; and Michel Vovelle, "L'historiographie de la Révolution française à la veille du bicentenaire," *Annales historiques de la Révolution française*, 272 (1988): 113–26. Vovelle would substitute "Jacobins" for "Marxists," since not all historians embracing the synthesis of Jean Jaurès and Georges Lefebvre were themselves Marxists. There is also, of course, a wide variety of nuances and approaches among the various scholars in the "revisionist" line.

2 François Furet, *Penser la Révolution* (Paris, 1978). In citations, I will use the English version, *Interpreting the Revolution*, trans. Elborg Forster (Cambridge, 1981). Translated into several languages, Furet's work has become standard reading in university courses on the Revolution and provided a central theme for discussion in a recent international conference. See also Keith Michael Baker (ed.), *The French Revolution and the Creation of Modern Political Culture*, vol. 1, *The Political Culture of the Old Regime* (Oxford, 1987), esp. the introduction by Baker; and Jack R. Censer, "The Coming of a New Interpretation of the French Revolution," *Journal of Social History*, 21 (1987): 295–309. Among the few other revisionist or quasi-revisionist works treating the revolutionary period itself, see esp. Patrice Higonnet, *Class, Ideology, and the Rights of the Nobles during the French Revolution* (Oxford, 1981); and Norman Hampson, *Prelude to Terror: The Constituent Assembly and the Failure of Consensus* (Oxford, 1988).

3 Furet, *Interpreting the Revolution*, p. 46; François Furet and Denis Richet, *La Révolution française* (Paris, 1973), p. 99.

4 Furet, *Interpreting the Revolution*, p. 54.

5 The first official minutes of the Third Estate seem to have been taken on 12 June; Jérôme Mavidal, *et al.*, (eds.), *Archives parlementaires, Première série*, 82 vols (Paris, 1867–1913), 8:94. (Hereafter, *AP*.) The early minutes were partially reconstructed several weeks later.

6 See, for example, the Assembly's decision on 29 April 1790, to expunge the Comte de Virieu's speech resigning the presidency because it was deemed "injurieuse" to the Assembly; *Réimpression de l'ancien Moniteur (mai 1789–novembre 1799)*, 31 vols (Paris, 1858–63), 4:241.

7 Motions to create such lists were rejected on 9 July, 29 August, and again on 8 December 1789; *AP*, 8:510 and 10:776–77; Philip Dawson, *Provincial Magistrates and Revolutionary Politics in France, 1789–1795* (Cambridge, Mass., 1972), p. 194; and Jean-François Gaultier de Biauzat *Gaultier de Biauzat, député du Tiers-Etat aux Etats-Généraux de 1789: Sa vie et sa correspondance*, ed. Francisque Mège, 2 vols (Clermont-Ferrand, 1890), 2:168.

8 The present study is based on a new computerized prosopography of the 1,315 deputies who sat at any time during the Constituent Assembly. See also the works of Harriet B. Applewhite: "Political Legitimacy in Revolutionary France, 1788–1791," *Journal of Interdisciplinary History*, 9 (1978): 245–73; and "Political Alignment in the French National Assembly, 1789 to 1791," *Proceedings of the Annual Meeting of the Western Society for French History*, 8 (1980): 265–75. For a complementary study based on a linguistic analysis of newspaper accounts, see Pierre Rétat, "Partis et factions en 1789: Emergence des désignants politiques." *Mots*, 16 (1988): 69–89.

9 To date, I have located memoirs, letters, or diaries describing the events of the Constituent Assembly, written by a total of 114 deputies. About half of these are in manuscript. Edna Hindie Lemay has consulted some of these materials in her *La vie quotidienne des députés aux Etats généraux, 1789* (Paris, 1987).

10 Among the few general studies, see Rudolf Von Albertini, "Parteiorganisation und Parteibegriff in Frankreich, 1789–1940," *Historische Zeitschrift*, 193 (1961): esp. 529–46.

11 See Alexandre Lameth, *Histoire de l'Assemblée constituante*, 2 vols (Paris, 1828–29), 1:34–6; G. Michon, *Essai sur l'histoire du part Feuillant: Adrien Duport* (Paris, 1924), p. 48; Augustin Challamel, *Les clubs contre-révolutionnaires, cercles, comités, sociétés, salons, réunions, cafés, restaurants, et librairies* (Paris, 1895), pp. 129, 133; Charles Du Bus, *Stanislas de Clermont-Tonnerre et l'échec de la Révolution monarchique 1757–92* (Paris, 1931), p. 84.

12 Daniel L. Wick, *A Conspiracy of Well-Intentioned Men: The Society of Thirty and the French Revolution* (New York, 1987). pp. 342–7, 354–5. The list given by Wick on pp. 354–5 includes one *suppléant* deputy and overlooks the Duc de Luxembourg. The "thirty" seem actually to have consisted of about fifty-five individuals.

13 See Ran Yadid-Halévi, "La sociabilité maçonnique et les origines de la pratique démocratique" (thèse de 3ᵉ cycle, Paris, Ecole des Hautes

Etudes en Sciences Sociales, 1981). Among the known Mesmer enthusiasts were Nicolas Bergasse, Jean-Jacques Duval d'Eprémesnil, Pierre-Victor Maclouet, François-Dominique de Reynaud de Montlosier, Adrien Duport, Jérôme Pétion de Villeneuve, Jean-André Périsse-Duluc, the Marquis de Lafayette, the Duc de Coigny, and perhaps the Comte de Virieu. See Robert Darnton, *Mesmerism and the End of the Enlightenment in France* (New York, 1970), pp. 68, 74, 78–9; Etienne Lamy, *Un défenseur des principes traditionnels sous la Révolution: N. Bergasse* (Paris, 1910), p. 46; François-Dominique de Reynaud de Montlosier, *Mémoires*, 2 vols (Paris, 1830), 1: pp. 133, 324–7; Pierre-Victor Malouet, *Mémoires*, 2 vols (Paris, 1874), 1: p. 195. The Viroflay Society was said to have had a distinctly Masonic character. See also Wick, *Conspiracy of Well-Intentioned Men*, pp. 49, 90–9; and Daniel L. Wick, "The Court Nobility and the French Revolution: The Example of the Society of Thirty," *Eighteenth-Century Studies*, 13 (1979–80): 263–84.

14 Lameth, *Histoire de l'Assemblée constituante*, 1: pp. 420–1; Michon, *Essai sur l'histoire du parti Feuillant*, pp. 48–52.

15 Michon, *Essai sur l'histoire du parti Feuillant*, p. 48.

16 See, for example. F.-A. Aulard, *La Société des Jacobins*, 6 vols (Paris, 1889–97), 1: "Introduction"; Gérard Walter, *Histoire des Jacobins* (Paris, 1946), pp. 1–55; A. Bouchard, *Le club breton: Origine, composition, rôle à l'Assemblée constituante* (Paris, 1920); and Lemay, *La vie quotidienne*, Part 2, Chap. 4.

17 Bouchard, *Le club breton*, pp. 21–3.

18 Walter, *Histoire des Jacobins* pp. 12–15; Bouchard, *Le club breton*, pp. 21–2; Lemay, *La vie quotidienne*, pp. 212–13; Jean-Pierre Boullé, "Ouverture des Etats généraux de 1789," ed. Albert Macé, *Revue de la Révolution: Documents inédits*, 10 (1887): 162–65; Léon Dubreuil, "Le clergé de Bretagne aux Etats généraux," *La Révolution française*, 70 (1917): 483–84. Joseph Delaville Le Roulx to Municipality of Lorient, 15 May 1789, BB 12, Archives Communales de Lorient (hereafter, AC, Lorient), describes the voting procedures followed. The Breton nobles and upper clergy had boycotted the elections in the spring of 1789 and had consequently sent no deputies to Versailles.

19 Delaville Le Roulx, 3 and 8 May 1789, BB 12, AC, Lorient; Boullé, *Revue de la Révolution*, 10 (1887), p. 169. Sieyes had proposed an "Assemblée nationale" the previous January. See his *Qu'est-ce que le Tiers Etat?*, ed. Edme Champion (Paris, 1889). p. 79.

20 Reported by Antoine Durand to Delcamp-Boytré in Gourdan, 6 May 1789, carton 5–56, Archives diocésaines de Cahors; François-René-Pierre Ménard de la Groye to his wife, 19 May 1789, 10 J 122, Archives Départementales de la Sarthe (hereafter, AD, Sarthe); and Jacques-Antoine Creuzé-Latouche, *Journal des Etats généraux et du début de l'Assemblée nationale, 18 mai–29 juillet 1789*, ed. Jean Marchand (Paris, 1946), p. 130.

21 Adrien Duquesnoy, *Journal d'Adrien Duquesnoy*, ed. R. de Crèvecoeur, 2 vols (Paris, 1894), 1: p. 13; Laurent de Visme, 14 May 1789, ms. "Journal des Etats généraux," Nouv. acq. fr. 12938, Bibliothèque Nationale.

22 Duquesnoy, *Journal*, 1: p. 2; Pierre-Paul Nairac, 19 May 1789, ms.

"Journal," 5 F 63, Archives Départementales de l'Eure; Etienne-François Schwendt in Rodolphe Reuss, (ed.), *L'Alsace pendant la Révolution française*, 2 vols (Paris, 1880–94), 1: p. 108. See also Gaultier de Biauzat, *Correspondance*, 2: p. 118; and Jean-Baptiste Poncet-Delpech, *La première année de la Révolution vue par un témoin*, ed. Daniel Ligou (Paris, 1961) pp. 11–12.

23 Many remained wary of the nobles' power and fearful of jeopardizing even minimal gains by overly bold action. Thus the Poitevin deputy René-Antoine-Hyacinthe Thibaudeau had warned his son earlier against "un acte de hardiesse qui n'aurait eu d'autre effet que de nous attirer à dos le clergé et la noblesse." And Durand would recall to a friend how cautious and prudent they had to be in drawing up their *cahiers*: "Il fallait encore se garder de trop alarmer le despotisme"; Durand, 4 September 1789, carton 5–56, Archives diocésaines de Cahors; Antoine-Claude Thibaudeau, *Biographie, Mémoires, 1765–92* (Paris, 1875), p. 64. Research on the social origins of the Third Estate deputies will be published subsequently. See also Edna Hindie Lemay, "La composition de l'Assemblée nationale constituante: Les hommes de la continuité," *Revue d'histoire moderne et contemporaine*, 24 (1977): 340–63; and Colin Lucas, "Nobles, Bourgeois, and the Origins of the French Revolution," *Past and Present*, 60 (August 1973): 90. [Published as Chapter 2 in this volume.]

24 Michel-René Maupetit, "Lettres de Michel-René Maupetit," ed. E. Quéruau-Lamerie, in *Bulletin de la Commission historique et archéologique de la Mayenne*, 2e serie, 18 (1902): 136. Le Chapelier's motion was made on 13 May; *AP*, 8:36–7. See also the Vicomte de Mirabeau's interpretation of this motion; *AP*, 8:42.

25 Michel Peronnet, *Les évêques de l'ancienne France* (Lille, 1977), esp. pp. 1337–43.

26 The first curés came over to the Third Estate on 13 June. Many had originally hoped to join much earlier. See my article, "Les députés du premier ordre: Le Clergé aux Etats généraux et à l'Assemblée constituante, 1789–1791," in *Croyances, pouvoirs et sociétés: Des Limousins aux Français: Etudes offertes à Louis Pérouas* (Treignac, 1988), pp. 85–99.

27 Based on *Almanach de Paris, Première partie, contenant les noms et qualités des personnes de condition pour l'année 1789* (Paris, 1789). Only about 20 per cent of the Nobles were country gentlemen known to have resided in their chateaus. See also James Murphy and Patrice Higonnet, "Les députés de la noblesse aux Etats généraux de 1789," *Revue d'histoire moderne et contemporaine*, 20 (1973): 230–47.

28 For military experience, I have used Armand Brette, *Recueil de documents relatifs à la convocation des Etats généraux de 1789*, 4 vols (1894–1915), vol. 2; and Adolphe Robert, *et al.*, *Dictionnaire des parlementaires français*, 5 vols (Paris, 1891). For the approximate dates of ennoblement, I have used Henri Jougla de Morenas, *Grand armorial de France*, 6 vols (Paris, 1934–49); and François Bluche, *Les honneurs de la cours* (Paris, 1957). More precise conclusions must await the biographical dictionary of the Constituent Assembly to be edited by Edna Lemay. Such proportions would, of course, have been largely

similar for the liberal nobility. Within this group, as we shall see below, age was probably the critical factor.

29 J. Michael Hayden, *France and the Estates General of 1614* (Cambridge, 1974), esp. pp. 82–5. See also Sutherland, *France, 1789–1815*, pp. 19–21.

30 The Duc de Luxembourg won on the first ballot for president, with 145 out of 251. The Duc du Croy won the vice-presidency with 160 out of 239; the Marquis de Bouthillier was elected secretary with 139 out of 184. See Ambroise-Eulalie de Maurès de Malartic, 12, 15, and 16 June 1789, "Journal de ma députation aux Etats généraux," MS. 21, Bibliothèque Municipale de la Rochelle (hereafter, BM, La Rochelle).

31 Marquis de Ferrières, *Mémoires*, 3 vols (Paris, 1825), 1: pp. 37, 60.

32 Among those won over to a position of intransigence were the Marquis de Guilhem-Clermont-Lodève and the Duc de Châtelet: Guilhem to the Municipality of Arles, 21 May 1789, AA 23, Archives Communales d'Arles. Note also the interpretation of the Marquis de Ferrières, *Mémoires, passim*. Malartic claimed that, on 25 June, six noble deputies with mandates for votes by head were refusing to join the Third Estate and were writing home for new mandates supporting their intransigence: see Malartic's entry for that date, "Journal," MS. 21, BM, La Rochelle. Of the twenty-seven Noble deputies from *bailliages* indicated by Guy Chaussinand-Nogaret to have had imperative mandates for a vote by head, only fifteen actually joined the Third Estate before 27 June; *La noblesse au XVIIIe siècle* (Paris, 1976), pp. 184–5 and Murphy and Higonnet, "Les députés de la noblesse," pp. 244–6.

33 Boullé, *Revue de la Révolution*, 12 (1888), p. 50.

34 Durand, 30 May 1789, carton 5–56. Archives diocésaines de Cahors; Jean-Baptiste Grellet de Beauregard. "Lettres de M. Grellet de Beauregard," ed. Abbé Dardy, *Mémoires de la Société des sciences naturelles et archéologiques de la Creuse*, 2e sér., 7 (1899): 10 July 1789; Claude-Pierre Maillot to an unnamed municipal official of de Toul, 3 June 1789, JJ 7. Archives Communales de Toul (hereafter, AC, Toul); and Visme, "Journal des Etats généraux," 26 May and 10 June 1789. All four men were moderates who never joined the Jacobin Club. See also Pierre-Joseph Meifrund, 10 June 1789, ms. journal; copy in Institut de la Révolution française (Paris).

35 Nairac, "Journal," 9 June 1789, 5 F 63, Archives Départementales de l'Eure; Boullé, *Revue de la Révolution*, 12 (1888), pp. 40, 49. Visme also described "une grande conférence tenue par les Bretons et leurs partisans"; "Journal des Etats généraux," 10 June 1789.

36 See Maupetit, "Lettres," 18 (1902), pp. 157–8.

37 Walter, *Histoire des Jacobins*, p. 22, Henri Grégoire, *Mémoires*, ed. H. Carnot, 2 vols (Paris, 1837–40), 1: p. 380. According to Gaultier de Biauzat, the motion had already been decided by the Breton group when it was voted to have Sieyes present it: "pour donner plus de poids à la motion"; Gaultier de Biauzat, *Correspondance*, p. 102.

38 There was a near-perfect consensus in the Tennis Court Oath of 20 June. While eighty-nine Third Estate deputies voted against Sieyes's

motion on 17 June, this was primarily a disagreement over the specific name to be given to the new assembly. On the very next vote that day, the National Assembly unanimously decided that all taxes would be subject to reorganization; see, for example, Jean-Sylvain Bailly, *Mémoires*, 3 vols (Paris, 1821–2). 1: pp. 179–80; Maupetit, "Lettres," 19 (1903), p. 215; Nairac, "Journal," 17 June 1789, 5 F 63, Archives Départementales de l'Eure; and Meifrund, ms. journal, 17 June, 1789, Institut de la Révolution française. The evidence does not seem to sustain Georges Lefebvre's assertion that the eighty-nine deputies "disavowed the juridical Revolution"; *The Coming of the French Revolution* (Princeton, N.J., 1947) p. 82.

39 In general, the Constituent deputies' attitudes toward the people were very complex. But, through the end of June, the Third Estate deputies' views of the crowds in Versailles were almost universally favorable; see, for example, Jean-Baptiste Poncet-Delpech, "Documents sur les premiers mois de la Révolution." Daniel Ligou (ed.), *Annales historiques de la Révolution française*, 38 (1966): pp. 430; Duquesnoy, *Journal*, 1: pp. 133–4; Creuzé-Latouche, *Journal*. pp. 25–6: Boullé; *Revue de la Révolution*, 11 (1888), p. l8. Afterward, many of the deputies, not only of the Clergy and the Nobles but of the Commoners as well, seem to have felt directly threatened. See, for example, Félix Faulcon, *Correspondance*, vol. 2, *1789–91* ed. G. Debien (Poitiers, 1953), journal entry of 13 July 1789; Grellet, "Lettres," pp. 76–7.

40 *AP*, 8:263–67.

41 For examples, see Creuzé-Latouche, *Journal des Etats généraux*, pp. 270–1; Ménard de la Grove, 24 July 1789, 10 J 122, AD, Sarthe; Maximillien Robespierre, *Correspondance*, (ed.) Georges Michon, 2 vols (Paris, 1926–41), p. 50; François-Joseph Bouchette, *Lettres*, (ed.) C. Looten (Lille, 1909), p. 234.

42 Visme "Journal des Etats généraux," 22 July 1789; letter of the deputies of Marseille, 27 July 1789, BB 361, Archives Communales de Marseille; Delaville Le Roulx, 24 July 1789, BB 12, AC, Lorient. Numerous other examples could be given.

43 Du Bus, *Stanislas de Clermont-Tonnerre*, p. 123. See also Jean Egret, *La révolution des notables: Mounier et les monarchiens* (Paris, 1950), pp. 92–103; and Montlosier, *Mémoires*, 1: p. 251.

44 August-Félix-Elizabeth Barin de La Gallissonnière, 27 June 1789, ms. journal, A4 LVI, Archives de la Guerre, also Louis-Henri-Charles de Gauville, *Journal*, (ed.) Edouard de Barthélémy (Paris, 1864), p. 8. On the Nobles' initial refusal to obey the king, see Malartic, "Journal," 27 June 1789, MS. 21, BM, La Rochelle; and Jean-Baptiste de Cernon de Pinteville to his brother, undated letter of *ca.* 27 June, J 2286, Archives Départementales de la Marne.

45 La Gallissonnière, ms. journal, A4 LVI, folio 155, Archives de la Guerre; Durand, 30 June 1789, carton 5–56. Archives diocésaines de Cahors; Malartic, "Journal." 9 and 11 July 1789, MS. 21, BM, La Rochelle; Delaville Le Roulx, 11 July 1789, BB 12, AC, Lorient.

46 The term was used by Maupetit on 11 July; "Lettres," 18 (1902): p. 461.

47 Maillot, 18 July 1789, JJ 7, AC, Toul. For a nobleman's interpretation, see Malartic, "Journal," 16 July 1789, MS. 21, BM, La Rochelle.
48 Visme, "Journal des Etats généraux," 10 August 1789; see also Dominique-Georges-Frédéric du Four de Pradt, "Quelques lettres de l'Abbé de Pradt, 1789–92," (ed.) Michel Leymarie, *Revue de la Haute-Auvergne*, 56ᵉ année, 34 (1954): introduction, pp. 89–91; and Charles-Elie de Ferrières, *Correspondance inédite*, (ed.) Henri Carré (Paris, 1932), pp. 82, 87, 108.
49 La Gallissonnière, ms. journal, A4 LVI, folio 154, Archives de la Guerre.
50 Pinteville, 27 June 1789, J 2286, Archives Départementales de la Marne.
51 La Gallissonnière, ms. journal, 27 June 1789, A4 LVI, Archives de la Guerre; also Ferrières, *Correspondance*, 3 July 1789; Guilhem-Clermont-Lodève, 2 August 1789. AA 23, Archives Communales d'Arles. Also Bernard de Brye, *Un évêque d'ancien régime à l'épreuve de la Révolution: Le cardinal A. L. H. de La Fare (1752–1829)* (Paris, 1985), pp. 249–59; Charles-Maurice de Talleyrand, *Mémoires*, (ed.) Duc de Broglie, 5 vols (Paris, 1891–2), 1: pp. l23–4; Eugène Lavaquery, *Le Cardinal de Boisgelin. 1732–1804*, 2 vols (Paris, 1920), 2: pp. 13–15.
52 Duquesnoy, *Journal*, 26 June 1789; Ménard de la Groye, 7 July 1789, 10 J 122, AD, Sarthe.
53 Malartic, "Journal," 7 July 1789, MS. 21, BM, La Rochelle. Note also Visme's entry of 6 July "j'ai vu avec plaisir ... que les idées d'un membre de la noblesse n'aient point été négligées"; "Journal des Etats généraux."
54 Faulcon, *Correspondance*, journal entry of 3 a.m., 15 July 1789, p. 69.
55 Ferrières, *Correspondance*, 10 August 1789. Compare the analysis of Talleyrand, *Mémoires*, 1: p. 124.
56 Numerous deputies commented on the unity and concord in the Assembly in the days before the event; see Maillot, 1 August 1789, JJ 7, AC, Toul; Charles-François Bouche to the Commissaires de communautés de Provence, 2 August, 1789, C 1046, Archives Départementales des Bouches-du-Rhône; Charles Francoville to the Municipality of Ardres. 3 August 1789, in François de Saint-Just, *Chronique intime des Garnier d'Ardres* (Paris, 1973), p. 118. Newspaper accounts of the period also placed enormous emphasis on the intense "désir d'union, ... de la 'fraternité' retrouvée dans l'élan du coeur" just prior to 4 August; Rétat, "Partis et factions en 1789," p. 76. This is in no way to underestimate the influence of the Great Fear and the general anarchy of late July 1789 in the psychology of the deputies. See also Fitzsimmons, "Privilege and the Polity in France," pp. 286–91.
57 Delaville Le Roulx, 29 July 1789, BB 12, AC, Lorient; Maillot, 1 August 1789, JJ 7, AC, Toul; Creuzé-Latouche, *Journal des Etats généraux*, pp. 165–66. See also Durand, 29 June 1789, carton 5–56, Archives diocésaines de Cahors.
58 See the discussion of "party" composition below.
59 Bouchard, *Le club breton*, pp. 90–2. On approximately September 2. Boullé, deputy from Pontivy, mentioned a special request by the

Rennes representatives that the provincial delegation meet again to discuss a petition from the town of Rennes. The other Breton deputies apparently rejected the request; Boullé, *Revue de la Révolution*, 15 (1889), pp. 117 (the letter is incorrectly dated 28 September by the editor). Delaville Le Roulx, 18 September 1789, BB 13, AC, Lorient, wrote that the Breton delegation had "de nouveau" opened its doors to deputies of other delegations as "avant et après le 17 juin," clearly suggesting that the doors had previously been closed. But there is no indication in Delaville's later letters that anything came of this initiative. Neither Walter, *Histoire des Jacobins*, nor Aulard, *Le Société des Jacobins*, mention the Breton Club between 4 August and late November or early December.

60 Jacques-Athanase de Lombard-Taradeau, "Lettres (1789–91)," (ed.) L. Honoré, *Le Var historique et géographique*, 2 (1925–27): pp. 245, 247, 261, 274–5, 324.

61 See the *règlement* of 29 July 1789; AP, 8:300–3.

62 *AP*, 33:88–91, lists the winners, but it is not entirely complete. To complete the list and to locate information about votes cast and opposition candidates, one must consult a wide range of sources, notably the minutes of the meetings in the *AP*, the *Moniteur*, and the official *Procès-verbaux*, as well as various newspaper accounts and deputy memoirs and letters. There were apparently sixty-three presidential elections, if one counts those replacing presidents who refused their elections or who resigned immediately. The generally perceptive deputy Duquesnoy was convinced that the votes for president mirrored his colleagues' political affiliations at a given point in time; Duquesnoy, *Journal*, 2: p. 127.

63 Note that several of the fourteen were chosen more than once. Lafayette is included for his election as vice-president on 13 July – the only time such an office was filled.

64 On Monarchien and Jacobin membership, see below.

65 This deference shown toward the privileged classes was equally in evidence in the choice of presidents for the thirty *bureaux* elected at intervals during the summer: at least twenty-seven of the thirty in early July and fifteen of sixteen for which data exist in mid-September were either Nobles or bishops; *AP*, 8: 185; and C 83, dossier 818 (14), Archives Nationales (hereafter, AN). Note that the family of Le Chapelier was newly ennobled. Sieyes was, of course, a clergyman.

66 On the election of 1–3 August, see Boullé, *Revue de la Révolution*, 15 (1889), p. 101; Gaultier de Biauzat, *Correspondance*, 2: p. 221; Ernest Lebègue, *La vie et l'oeuvre d'un constituant: Thouret* (Paris, 1910), pp. 142–3; Paul Bastid, *Sieyes et sa pensée* (Paris, 1939), p. 78.

67 Pétion received 183 votes on 12 September and 143 on 28 September – although some of the votes of the Left may have gone to Jacques-Guillaume Target, who received thirty-seven and fifty-two votes, respectively. On 23 November, the Duc d'Aiguillon received 166; AN, C 83, dossier 818 (1–3); Comte de Virieu to the Marquis de Viennois, 29 September 1789. Archives of the Château de Viennois, from a

copy kindly loaned to me by Jean-Louis Flandrin: and Daniel Ligou, *La première année de la Révolution vue par un témoin* (Paris, 1961), p. 169.

68 On the general problem of the Right in the early revolution, see Paul Beik, *The French Revolution Seen from the Right in Transactions of the American Philosophical Society*, 46 (1956), part 1; Philip Kolody, "The Right in the French National Assembly, 1789–91" (Ph.D. dissertation, Princeton University, 1967); Jean-Paul Bertaud, *Les Amis du roi: Journaux et journalistes royalistes en France de 1789 à 1792* (Paris, 1984); William James Murray, *The Right-Wing Press in the French Revolution, 1789–1792* (London, 1986).

69 La Gallissonnière, undated entry, ms. journal, A4 LVI, folio 155, Archives de la Guerre. Several deputies noted the presence of Eprémesnil – one of the key leaders of the reactionary group – among the nobles making the announcement that day; see Delaville Le Roulx, 17 July 1789, BB 12, AC, Lorient.

70 Jacques Jallet, *Journal inédit* (ed.) J.-J. Brethé (Fontenay-le-Comte, 1871), 28 July 1789, was impressed by the unusually large number of "aristocrats" who appeared on 28 July for the committee elections. See also Maillot, 1 August 1789, JJ 7, AC, Toul.

71 Maillot, 1 August 1789, JJ 7, AC, Toul; Delaville Le Roulx, 4 August 1789, BB 12, AC, Lorient; Lombard-Taradeau, "Lettres (1789–91)," 5 August 1789, Boullé, *Revue de la Révolution*, 14 August 1789.

72 Ferrières, *Correspondance*, 6 August 1789; Claude-Jean-Baptiste Garron de la Bévière to his wife, 5 August 1789, 1 Mi 1, Archives Départementales de l'Ain.

73 On the violence and intensity of the debates in mid-August, see Boullé, *Revue de la Révolution*, 14 (1889), p. 104; and Maupetit, "Lettres," 19 (1903): p. 226. The original motion of 4 August had called for suppression of the tithes with some form of reimbursement, but this was changed in the days that followed. The earliest motions for the expropriation of church lands had been made on 8 August by the Marquis de Lacoste and Alexandre Lameth.

74 Guillaume Gontier de Biran to the Municipality of Bergerac, retrospective letter of 22 May 1790, carton 1, Archives Communales de Bergerac, Fonds Faugère; Emmanuel Barbotin, *Lettres de l'abbé Barbotin*, (ed.) A. Aulard (Paris, 1910), 23 and 29 August 1789; Gauville, *Journal*, 16–20. A similar picture is confirmed by the patriots Lombard-Taradeau. "Lettres (1789–9l)," p. 263; Gaultier de Biauzat, *Correspondance*, 2: pp. 269–70; and François-Antoine Boissy d'Anglas, "Lettres inédites sur la Révolution française," (ed.) René Puaux, *Bulletin de la Société de l'histoire du Protestantisme français*, 75 (1926): 433. It was also in August that the newspapers first began mentioning "cabals" and "coalitions" in the Assembly; Rétat, "Partis et factions en 1789," p. 77.

75 Egret, *La révolution des notables*; Robert Griffiths, *Le centre perdu: Malouet et les "monarchiens" dans la Révolution française* (Grenoble, 1988). Griffiths placed the Monarchiens in the "center." However, the group is known to have allied itself with the extreme right and, on most issues, to have voted to the "right" of the large group of

unaligned deputies. I would prefer to use the term "center" for the latter group.

76 Jean-André Périsse-Duluc to J. B. Willermoz, 17 September 1789, MS. 5430, Bibliothèque Municipale de Lyon (hereafter, BM, Lyon), claimed the Normans led by Thouret were initially part of the coalition. There were at least seven deputies from Auvergne, led by Malouet; Egret, *La révolution des notables*, pp. 126–8; Griffiths, *Le centre perdu*, pp. 109–10.

77 Montlosier, *Mémoires*, 1: p. 277; Malouet, *Mémoires*, 1: 301–2. Gaultier de Biauzat also observed this; *Correspondance*, 2: pp. 269–70.

78 Périsse-Duluc, 17 September 1789, MS. 5430, BM, Lyon. Virieu himself described his role in similar terms: "je me suis promis de faire toutes les avant gardes dangereuses et difficiles dont d'autres ne se seront pas chargés"; Virieu to the Marquis de Viennois, 25 August 1789, Archives of the Château de Viennois.

79 Montlosier, *Mémoires*, 1: p. 277; Périsse-Duluc, 17 September 1789, MS. 5430, BM, Lyon; Albert Mathiez, "Etudes critiques sur les journées des 5 et 6 octobre 1789." *Revue historique*, 67 (1898): 266, 273. On the general question of an alliance between the extreme right and the Monarchiens, see especially Kolody, "The Right in the French National Assembly," pp. 122–34.

80 Périsse-Duluc, 17 September 1789, MS. 5430, BM, Lyon.

81 Thus, in the secretarial election of 29 August 1789, only the three Monarchien candidates, Claude Redon, Pierre-Suzanne Deschamps, and Jean-Louis Henry de Longuève, obtained large blocs of votes; the remainder of the votes apparently represented individual, uninstructed choices; AN, C 83, dossier 818 (6–7).

82 Virieu, 1 September 1789, Archives of the Château de Viennois. See also the analysis of Théodore Vernier to the Municipality of Lons-le-Saunier, 30 August; 1789, "Lettres de Vernier," Archives Communales de Bletterans (non-classé).

83 The rotation system arranged by verbal agreement was described by Bouche, 31 August 1789, C 1046, Archives Départementales des Bouches-du-Rhône. He also noted his anticipation that the mid-September election would go to a commoner. See also La Gallissonnière, undated entry, ms. journal, A4 LVI, folio 153, Archives de la Guerre. It is clear that most of the deputies were still voting by the rotation system in the previous election: 802 out of 834 votes were cast for clergymen; AN, C 83 (1–3).

84 Delaville Le Roulx, 22 September 1789, BB 13, AC, Lorient; and Jean-François-Marie Goupilleau to his cousin, senechal in Rochefervière, undated letter of late September, Collection Dugast-Matifeux, no. 98, Bibliothèque Municipale de Nantes.

85 Lombard-Taradeau, "Lettres (1789–91)," p. 271; Louis-Prosper Lofficiel, "Lettres de Lofficiel," (ed.) M. Leroux-Cesbron, *La nouvelle revue rétrospective*, 7 (1897): 111; Périsse-Duluc, 2 September 1789, MS 5430, BM, Lyon. Note also Durand: "il y a dans l'Assemblée une telle division . . . qu'il est encore bien problématique lequel aura le dessus"; 5 September 1789, carton 5–56, Archives diocésaines de Cahors.

Maillot spoke of the patriots as "le parti de la minorité"; 30 August 1789, JJ 7, AC, Toul. See also the letter of Robespierre, *Correspondance*, p. 51; and of Goupilleau, undated, *ca.* late September, Collection Dugast-Matifuex, no. 98, BM, Nantes.

86 On the Volney motion, see Lofficiel, "Letters," 14 and 18 September 1789, pp. 111–13; and Visme, "Journal des Etats généraux," 18 September 1789. On the Breton discussion, Delaville Le Roulx, 22 September 1789, BB 13, AC, Lorient; and Barbotin, *Lettres*, p. 61.

87 Apparently first reported by Hippolyte Taine and followed by numerous other historians. See Eric Thompson, *Popular Sovereignty and the French Constituent Assembly, 1789–91* (Manchester, 1952), p. 24.

88 Malouet wrote that the Monarchien leadership hoped for 300 resignations; perhaps this is the origin of the myth. But he admitted that only twenty-six deputies actually requested passports; *Mémoires*, 2: pp. 4–5. This is approximately confirmed by the records of the National Assembly itself; AN, C 32, dossier 266. Mirabeau spoke of 300 *requests* on 9 October, but this was probably an exaggeration; *AP*, 9:389.

89 Mounier and Lally-Tollendal resigned almost immediately; Bishop La Luzerne resigned within a month; Bergasse abandoned the Assembly without ever formally resigning.

90 In early January 1790, the group met with Lafayette, La Rochefoucauld, and a faction of the moderate patriots – and perhaps secretly with Mirabeau – and almost succeeded in engineering a new "coalition" on the center right. See Malouet, *Mémoires*, 2: pp. 45–8; Montlosier, *Mémoires*, 2: p. 35; *Mercure de France*, January 1790, p. 164.

91 Virieu, 12 and 16 October 1789, Archives of the Château de Viennois; Jean-de-Dieu Boisgelin de Cucé to Comtesse de Gramont, 6 October 1789, AN, M 788; Gontier de Biran, 12 October 1789, carton 1, Archives Communales de Bergerac, Fond Faugère.

92 None of the four would be members of the Jacobin Club during the period of the Constituent Assembly or sign the petition of the "Capuchin" group; see below.

93 Note also that, in the election of 13 November, Boisgelin came within seven votes of a victory on the second round; Boisgelin de Cucé, undated, *c.* 13 November 1789, *pièce* 136, AN, M 788.

94 Boisgelin de Cucé, undated, *c.* mid-November 1789, *pièce* 141, AN, M 788.

95 Boisgelin de Cucé, 3 November 1789; also 7 and 23 November, AN, M 788. Similar views were also expressed by the moderates; Maupetit, "Lettres," 19 (1903): p. 371; Visme, "Journal des Etats généraux," 2 November 1789; André-Marie Merle to the Municipality of Mâcon, 4 November 1789, D2 no. 13 (carton 21 *bis*), Archives Communales de Mâcon; Jean-François Begouen-Demeaux to municipal officers of Le Harvre, 31 October 1789, D (3) 38–39, Archives Communales du Harvre and by the future Jacobin, Vernier, Archives Communales de Bletterans, 3 November 1789. Not all deputies agreed, however; see, for example, Robespierre. *Correspondance*, p. 57; and Goupilleau, 2 November 1789, Collection Dugast-Matifeux, no. 98, BM, Nantes.

96 Visme, "Journal des Etats généraux," 21 November 1789. Seven of the twelve members elected were future "Capuchins" (see below); AN, C 32, dossier 274.

97 I have used vol. 33 of the *AP*, which is the index to vols 8–32, dealing with the Constituent Assembly. Represented are the leading speakers of the Monarchiens and the extreme right as determined by the length of the entries for each deputy in the index: for the Monarchiens: Jean-Joseph Mounier, Comte de Lally-Tollendal, Nicolas Bergasse, Bishop La Luzerne, Comte de Virieu, Clermont-Tonnerre, Malouet, Pierre-Joseph de Lachèse, Amable-Gilbert Dufraisse-Duchey, and Noël-Joseph Madier de Montjau; for the extreme right: Abbé Maury, Cazalès, Eprémesnil, Marquis de Foucauld Lardimalie, Marquis de Bonnay, Marquis de Folleville, Reynaud de Montlosier, and Vicomte de Mirabeau. Displayed on the graph [Figure 7.1] is the average weekly frequency of participation plotted as an index around the overall mean for the entire period of the Constituent Assembly, where the mean is set at 1.0. Although the index does not give precise dates, these can be extrapolated from the volume numbers – which are given. The *Archives parlementaires* is undoubtedly the best single source for debates in the National Assembly, but unfortunately it does not include all speeches given in the Constituent Assembly, and approximately 5 to 10 per cent of those that it does mention seem to be missing in the index – probably through the carelessness of the editors.

98 Gauville, *Journal*, p. 59.

99 Thibaudeau to Faulcon, undated but probably early January 1791; printed in Faulcon, *Correspondance*, p. 141.

100 Lavaquery, *Le Cardinal de Boisgelin*, 2: pp. 74–6. Du Bus, *Stanislas de Clermont-Tonnerre*, p. 224, equated the Grands Augustins meetings with the Club des Impartiaux. This is probably not correct, although there was a substantial overlap between the two groups.

101 Thomas Lindet, *Correspondance de Thomas Lindet pendant la Constituante et la Législative (1789–92)*, (ed.) A. Montier, (Paris, 1889), pp. 115–16; Lameth, *Histoire de l'Assemblée constituante*, 2: pp. 148–9; Gaultier de Biauzat, *Correspondance*, 2: pp. 307–12. Also, Louis-Jean-Baptiste Leclerc de Lassigny de Juigné to his wife, 14 April 1790, Archives of the Château de Saint-Martin (Taradeau, Var).

102 Lavaquery, *Le Cardinal de Boisgelin*, 2: pp. 74–6. The home of Eprémesnil seems to have been one of the central meeting places; Montlosier, *Mémoires*, 2: pp. 328, 334.

103 Visme, 7 December 1789, "Journal des Etats généraux." The vote was 453 for the Right and 443 for the Left. See *AP*, 10: 414–15.

104 Périsse-Duluc, 27 December 1789, MS. 5340, BM, Lyon.

105 Guillaume-Benoît Couderc, "Lettres de Guillaume-Benoît Couderc (1781–92)," ed. M.O. Monod, *Revue d'histoire de Lyon*, p. 420; Lindet, *Correspondance*, p. 38; Delaville Le Roulx, 18 January 1790, BB 13, AC, Lorient; Duquesnoy, *Journal*, 2: pp. 196–7, 269. See also Faulcon, *Correspondance*, 2: pp. 140–1; Ménard de la Grove, 1 January 1790, 10

J 122, AD, Sarthe; and Goupilleau, 11 January 1790, Collection Dugast-Matifeux, no. 98, BM, Nantes.

106 The presidents on the Right: Abbé de Montesquiou, the Marquis de Bonnay (twice), and the Comte de Virieu; on the Left: Rabaut-Saint-Etienne, Baron de Menou, Bon-Albert Briois de Beaumez, Abbé Sieyes, and Louis-Michel Le Pelletier de Saint-Fargeau.

107 This was particularly the case in the series of major decrees concerning the reorganization of the church, culminating in the Civil Constitution of the Clergy. But the Left also won major victories in votes on the judicial system and the right to declare war.

108 Duquesnoy, *Journal*, 2: p. 269. See also Jean-François Campmas to his brother, vicaire in Carmaux, 24 December 1789, MS. 177, Bibliothèque Municipale d'Albi.

109 Armand Brette, *Histoire des édifices où ont siégé les assemblées parlementaires de la Révolution* (Paris, 1902).

110 Bouchard, *Le club breton*, p. 94; and Lemay, *La vie quotidienne*, p. 216. Delaville Le Roulx, 30 November 1789, BB 12, AC, Lorient, and others, mentions Breton Committee meetings in Paris discussing general subjects.

111 Louis-Marie de La Revellière-Lépeaux, *Mémoires*, 3 vols (Paris, 1895), 1: p. 85.

112 Walter, *Histoire des Jacobins*, p. 55. Grégoire describes the importance of mobilizing petitions from Jacobins throughout France in order to pressure the decisions of the National Assembly; *Mémoires*, 1: p. 387. See also Michael L. Kennedy, *The Jacobin Clubs in the French Revolution: The First Years* (Princeton, N.J., 1982). esp. Chap. 1.

113 *AP*, 32:564. At the last and final election of the Comité, in April 1790, nine of the twelve men elected – all Jacobins or known Patriots – received almost exactly the same number of votes – between 196 and 206, a sure sign of the collusion involved; AN, C 38, dossier 334.

114 In 1789, future Jacobins obtained 160 (25 per cent) and future Capuchins obtained 118 (19 per cent) of a total of 636 committee assignments; in the first six months of 1790, Jacobins obtained eighty-six (48 per cent) and Capuchins twenty-one (12 per cent) of a total of 180 new assignments. Faulcon thought that it was impossible to be named to a committee in 1790 unless one belonged to a club; *Correspondance*, 29 May 1789, p. 236.

115 Quoted in Walter, *Histoire des Jacobins*, pp. 93–4

116 Lindet, *Correspondance*, p. 38.

117 The most complete list of the Jacobins – as Aulard himself indicates – is to be culled from the index at the end of his *La Société des Jacobins*, vol. 6. This must be used to complement the list of December 1790, published in the introduction of his vol. 1.

118 See above, note 112.

119 *Déclaration d'une partie de l'Assemblée nationale sur le décret rendu le 13 avril concernant la religion* (Paris, 1790).

120 The petition was signed by 293, but one deputy later retracted his signature. A part of the group around Malouet and Clermont-

Tonnerre seems also to have remained aloof from the Capuchins for tactical reasons; Malouet, *Mémoires*, 2: pp. 41–3. Of the core group of Monarchiens listed by Egret who were still active as deputies in April 1790, eleven of seventeen signed the petition.

121 More detailed analysis must await the completion of Edna Lemay's biographical dictionary.

122 One hundred sixty-eight (82 per cent) of 205 Jacobins. Two hundred sixty-nine (92 per cent) of 292 Capuchins. The importance of the deputies' estate in Left/Right alignments has been noted by Applewhite, "Political Alignment," pp. 267–8

123 Seven nobles and one *chanoine* (canon).

124 One hundred sixty-two (55 per cent) of the signers were clergymen. This included 102 (49 per cent) of all 207 curés sitting at this time, and thirty-four (87 per cent) of the thirty-nine bishops.

125 One hundred sixty-seven (57 per cent) of the 292 are known to have been nobles. One hundred and seven (64 per cent) of the 167 could trace their lineage before 1600. Of course, the non-aligned nobles in the Assembly would have had much the same lineage breakdowns. I am not arguing that aristocratic origins determined political options but that they may have been a factor in such options, and that the social origins of the Capuchins were strongly weighted by a large bloc of aristocratic deputies, a bloc that was clearly in evidence to contemporaries.

126 Marquis de Folleville, Vicomte de Mirabeau, Comte de Virieu, Marquis de Foucauld-Lardimalie, Chevalier de Murinais, Marquis d'Ambly, and Bishop de Bonal. Among the Capuchin group, by my count, Maury spoke the most, Folleville was second, and Cazalès was third, while Eprémesnil was eighth.

127 For instance, the proportion of all Third Estate deputies with agriculturally related professions was 12 per cent; it was the same for Jacobin deputies from the Third. For all deputies from commercial professions: 12 per cent for Jacobin deputies: 14 per cent.

128 Thirty-two per cent of all deputies called themselves "avocats," while 42 per cent of Third Estate deputies in the Jacobins described themselves in this way. Thirty-five per cent of all deputies were officeholders – including 17 per cent who were judges; while 26 per cent of the Jacobins were officeholders – including 12 per cent who were judges.

129 See Lenard R. Berlanstein, *The Barristers of Toulouse in the Eighteenth Century, 1740–1793* (Baltimore, 1975), pp. 11, 16.

130 Sixteen (38 per cent) of 42.

131 The others, in order, were Charles-François Bouche, Le Chapelier, Jean-Denis Lanjuinais, Gaultier de Biauzat, Barnave, Jacques Defermon, Guillaume-François-Charles Goupil de Prefelne, Jean-François Reubell, Duport, Philippe-Antoine Merlin, Pierre-Louis Prieur, and Robespierre.

132 By my count, 48 per cent of the Capuchins and 30 per cent of the Jacobins represented districts south of this line. Approximately 30 per cent of all deputies seem to have come from southern France;

Edna Lemay, "La composition de l'Assemblée constituante: Les hommes de la continuité?" *Revue d'histoire moderne et contemporaine*, 24 (1977): 349.

133 Ages are taken primarily from Robert, *Dictionnaire*.

134 Among the Clergy the Jacobins averaged 45.4 years, the Capuchins averaged 50.7; among the Nobles, the Jacobins were 37.0, the Capuchins 46.5; among the Third Estate, the Jacobins were 42.3, the Capuchins 43.7. Murphy and Higonnet, "Les députés de la noblesse," p. 240, noted the relative youth of the "liberal" nobles.

135 After Louis XVI's attempted flight from the kingdom in June 1791 and the majority's decision to suspend the king's powers, however, much of the Right boycotted the debates.

136 There are many comments on the demoralization of the bishops; Bouchette on the archbishop of Aix, *Lettres*, p. 484; and Boisgelin, speaking for himself in his letter of late June, Boisgelin de Cucé, *pièce* 114, AN, M 788; Ménard de la Graye on the bishop of Le Mans, 28 May 1790, 10 J 122, AD, Sarthe; also Brye. *Un évêque d'ancien regime*, pp. 269–70, on the bishop of Nancy. Among the Capuchins in general, eight are known to have left the Assembly in the first half of 1790, thirteen in the second half of 1790, and twenty-eight in the first half of 1791.

137 Lindet, *Correspondance*, 22 November 1790, p. 247.

138 It is not possible here to follow the political developments of the Assembly through its completion in September 1791. Significantly, it was only *after* the Right had effectively collapsed as a power within the Assembly that major splits began to appear within the Left coalition – splits that were clearly in evidence before the king's attempted flight. See, especially, Michon, *Essai sur l'histoire du parti Feuillant*, pp. 182–5.

139 Malouet, *Mémoires*, 2: p. 36; Lameth, *Histoire de l'Assemblée constituante*, 1: p. 421. Lindet said much the same thing in a letter of 8 May 1790; *Correspondance*, p. 155.

140 Compare the thesis of Sutherland in his *France, 1789–1815*. As I have argued here, I would push back the inception of the revolutionary-counter-revolutionary dialectic to the very beginning of the Estates-General and the National Assembly.

141 See the classic study of Alfred Cobban in *Aspects of the French Revolution* (New York, 1968), pp. 100–2, 109–11. See also George V. Taylor, "Noncapitalist Wealth and the Origins of the French Revolution," *AHR*, 72 (January 1967): 469–96; and Lemay, "La composition de l'Assemblée constituante."

142 We have seen above that Capuchins and Jacobins also represented, in part, different generations. Although it would be impossible to demonstrate here, they probably also differed significantly in education and overall wealth.

8

VIOLENCE, EMANCIPATION, AND DEMOCRACY

The countryside and the French Revolution

John Markoff

With the ascendancy of intellectual history, recent Revisionists have minimized the role peasants played in the Revolution. For the most part, they have seen the peasants as bystanders during much of the Revolutionary struggle. After the summer of 1789, having won the abolition of feudalism and the right to own private property, they pretty much sat out the rest of the ordeal. When they became involved, it was usually trying to resist revolutionary programs (such as military conscription) and keeping the new government at bay. The peasants, recent historians tell us, were at best lukewarm supporters of a Revolution that never was especially popular in the countryside.

John Markoff argues against such an interpretation. "There was a peasant revolution that was emancipatory and egalitarian in its consequences," he writes. Such liberation, he emphasizes, "was not achievable in the 1790s without this violence." Away with the Neo-Conservative dismissal of revolution as an inherently oppressive process. Markoff's perspective returns us to a Liberal perspective that sees revolutions as doing much good, especially for the poor and rural folk. Peasant violence was not irrational; it was a way to overcome the oppression of aristocratic landlords whose privileges yielded despotic power over their peasants. However disparate their subjects, Markoff's article nicely dovetails with Tackett's in seeing a class of privileged noblemen standing in the way of a new political culture based upon the values expressed in the Declaration of the Rights of Man.

* * *

As heads of state gathered in Paris in the summer of 1989 for the celebration of the French Revolution's bicentennial, Prime Minister Margaret Thatcher faced a question in Parliament about her own imminent crossing of the English Channel. Comparing the changes brought about in her administration to those of France in the 1790s, she commented that "our revolution in the past ten years . . . has been managed more quietly and very well." A Tory MP then advised her to consider the historical dimensions of British superiority: while visiting Paris, she ought to bear in mind the "virtually bloodless" character of the Glorious Revolution, whose tricentennial had been celebrated the previous year. An unnecessary admonition: Thatcher had already explained to interviewers for *Le monde* that the British had considerably preceded the French in institutionalizing a respect for human rights and had done so "calmly, without a bloodbath." Even the way the British commemorated their historical turning points was calmer.[1]

Although her remarks earned her a public history lesson from Christopher Hill,[2] it could hardly be said that the prime minister was out of touch with the current wisdom of students of French history. Two hundred years after the Revolution, it was not only a political personality of the Right who doubted that plebeian violence had contributed to human advance. Many a historian was thinking the same thing. The Revolution's effects are now widely seen as perverse (as in the claim that the Revolution so damaged the French economy that it assured British economic dominance)[3] or non-existent (as in the claim that the advances often attributed to the Revolution were already being carried out by the reforming élites of the Old Regime).[4] Recent writing is particularly critical of the claim that revolutionary violence made much of a contribution to the history of democracy. In line with the debunking just described, either the contribution to democracy is taken to be negative or, alternately, that contribution is attributed primarily to mutations in élite political culture rather than to mass action.[5]

Not that popular insurrection has been shunted aside as an arena for historical research; rather, the connection between plebeian actions and revolutionary outcomes has come to be seen as extremely complex in the recent literature. Where George Rudé's work had suggested that plebeian violence was a conceivably rational means to a morally defensible end, much recent writing has focused on violence as having its own logic: we are alerted by Brian Singer to the ritual characteristics of violent confrontations

237

or led by Roger Chartier to see popular violence as a symptom of the incompleteness of what Norbert Elias called "the civilizing process."[6] And, where popular action is seen as purposive, an important theme in the recent literature has been "resistances to the Revolution," to use a now common phrase that denotes the many ways in which people in villages and urban neighborhoods evaded revolutionary tax collectors and recruiting sergeants, rejected the symbols and personnel of the Revolution's Constitutional Church, deserted from the Revolution's armed forces, as well as engaged in armed and open counter-revolution.[7] So deeply has the recent literature been permeated by the notion of popular resistance, some writers are suggesting that historians should see overt counter-revolution as merely the most dramatic form taken by a profoundly widespread resistance to a visionary and brutal revolutionary élite.[8] It was an important advance to be able to see the disorderly actions of insurrectionary people as having a culture, as being part of, in Charles Tilly's fine phrase, a "repertoire of contention," just as it was an advance to rediscover the ways in which plebeians were injured by a revolution to which they sometimes responded with violence.[9]

In summary, much recent literature has focused on popular hostility to the Revolution, on the expressive and traditional aspects of popular violence, and on the dynamic role played by the Revolution's élites in creating a modern society. Nonspecialists of the 1990s, coming to much of this recent literature, will probably readily find the French Revolution to be another buttress for the current multi-continental disillusion with revolutionary projects of any sort. Yet the prevailing picture, itself in part a corrective to an earlier oversimplification, will be a seriously misleading one. There *was* a peasant revolution that was emancipatory and egalitarian in its consequences, that did more than accept the reforms of élite power-holders, that pushed those power-holders far beyond their initial positions, that was not merely a ritualized expression of violence but exhibited choices of targets and tactics guided by reason. I refer to the struggle waged in the countryside against the lords. It is hard to see how there could have been much in the way of democratic advance in France without the full emancipation of the French countryside from the "odious remains of the tyranny of the powerful," as the Third Estate of Etampes put it in the spring of 1789.[10]

There is little dispute that this emancipation was achieved with a great deal of insurrectionary violence;[11] but if a revolutionary élite, steeped in the enlightened ideas of the late Old Regime, was fully committed to the reform of rural social relations and capable of organizing it through legislative action, such violence would have to be regarded as a tragically unnecessary sideshow. In spite of an opposition to feudalism from that revolutionary élite, however, an emancipation in the countryside was not achievable in the 1790s without this violence. This is to restate a proposition central to Georges Lefebvre's analysis of the part played by the people of the countryside in the Revolution, elaborated in more detail by Anatoly Ado.[12] To demonstrate it, I shall be examining two bodies of evidence and glancing at a third: the grievances expressed at the onset of revolution, the targets and timing of insurrectionary events in the countryside, and then the legislative debates.

I have three main points. First, élite proposals for reorganizing the seigneurial rights, widely expressed in the spring of 1789, were real and significant but were also significantly limited. Second, the subsequent legislative action that alleviated peasant burdens was in large degree a response to rural violence. Third, a look at projects for reform of roughly comparable social relationships elsewhere on the European continent, at least into the middle of the nineteenth century, also suggests that popular violence or the fear of it was a major element of rural emancipation elsewhere.[13]

In the 1780s, a French lord could collect a variety of monetary and material payments from his peasants, could insist that nearby villagers grind their grain in the seigneurial mill, bake their bread in the seigneurial oven, press their grapes in the seigneurial wine press, could set the date of the grape harvest, could have local cases tried in his own court, could claim favored benches in church for his family and proudly point to the family tombs below the church floor, could take pleasures forbidden the peasants – hunting, raising rabbits or pigeons – in the pursuit of which pleasures the peasants' fields were sometimes devastated.[14]

How did the French respond to these privileges at the onset of revolution? To begin with the positions being staked out by the élites in the spring of 1789: the grievance lists that assemblies around France provided their deputies in the complex, multi-stage elections to the Estates-General yield national data of unparalleled richness. Let us focus particularly on what are known as the general *cahiers* of the Third Estate, those documents adopted by assemblies in county-sized electoral districts whose deputies were to convene in Versailles, where they were to meet with the separately chosen deputies of the clergy and nobility. Roughly speaking, the assemblies adopting these Third Estate *cahiers* were dominated by the urban notables. The electoral rules, as modified in practice by local conflict and central confusion, meant that these Third Estate assemblies chose rather more than half of what became the National Assembly.

Table 1 displays the broad lines of proposals on those seigneurial rights that were commonly discussed.[15] While there is almost no support in the *cahiers* for retaining the seigneurial rights as they were at the time, proposals for uncompensated abolition are distinctly in the minority, and a small minority at that, for one important class of rights, the periodic dues. Contrasting the views expressed on serfdom, tolls, or compulsory labor, we can see that the urban notables were capable of taking a much tougher position on other aspects of the seigneurial regime. Not only is some sort of indemnification the favored position on periodic dues but uncompensated abolition is not even the second choice: a significant minority of Third Estate assemblies favors reform proposals. This is particularly interesting, since seigneurial rights generally tended not to attract reform proposals at all.[16]

We may compare these figures with those the deputies of the nobility carried to Versailles on the one hand and those adopted by preliminary assemblies in the countryside on the other. While the most striking noble trait is an avoidance of discussing seigneurial rights, those *cahiers* with such discussions include a significant number that both demand the continuation of some seigneurial rights and lack any reform proposal. Twenty-one per cent of noble *cahiers* made no mention of the seigneurial regime. Of those that do so, some 13 per cent of the demands favor maintaining at least one seigneurial right substantially unaltered, as compared to 1 per cent for the Third Estate. In the same vein, noble demands to abolish a seigneurial right without indemnification amount to some 10 per cent of their grievances, which may be contrasted with 27 per cent for the Third Estate.[17] The noble presence in the soon-to-be-created National Assembly included a significant body of representatives who carried *cahiers* that, by silence or open advocacy, were notably less disposed to the abolition of seigneurial rights than those carried by the

Table 8.1 Percentages of Third Estate *cahiers* with various positions on seigneurial rights

Right[a]	Maintain	Reform	Abolish without compensation	Abolish with indemnification	(Number of cahiers discussing right)
Periodic dues					
Cens (a cash payment)	7	32	4	57	(28)
Champart (a portion of the crop)	2	26	13	60	(61)
Cens et rentes (a cash payment)	3	35	0	59	(37)
Periodic dues in general	0	23	7	55	(30)
Miscellaneous periodic dues	0	36	7	9	(22)
Seigneurial monopolies					
Monopoly on ovens	2	8	56	29	(50)
Monopoly on milling	0	13	44	25	(70)
Monopoly on wine press	0	5	59	31	(44)
Monopolies in general	0	15	40	43	(103)
Assessments on economic activity					
Seigneurial tolls	0	9	53	27	(117)
Dues on fairs and markets	0	16	36	33	(45)
Property transfer rights					
Dues on property transfers	0	39	37	12	(49)
Retrait (substitution of lord for purchaser of property)	4	25	44	0	(48)

Table 8.1 cont.

Justice				
Seigneurial courts in general	3	19	53	10	(90)
Seigneurial courts, miscellaneous	2	18	23	0	(56)
Recreational privileges				
Hunting rights	2	39	14	2	(107)
Right to raise pigeons	0	18	38	0	(96)
Right to raise rabbits	0	13	51	0	(39)
Fishing rights	0	21	21	0	(24)
Symbolic deference				
Right to bear arms	0	5	24	0	(41)
Serfdom				
Mainmorte (extreme restriction on property transfers)	0	17	56	30	(36)
Serfdom in general	0	4	69	15	(26)
Other				
Compulsory labor services	0	14	51	32	(109)
Miscellaneous rights	3	9	44	27	(79)
Regime in general	2	18	18	22	(91)

[a] Rights discussed in at least twenty documents

delegates of the Third Estate. The distinctiveness of the *cahiers* of the urban notables on seigneurial rights is their emphasis on the indemnification option where periodic payments were concerned.

Among the élite, then, some notion of a gradual buy-out rather than simple abolition of seigneurial rights was in the air. It was the course that had been advocated in Pierre-François Boncerf's notorious pamphlet on "feudal rights," condemned by the Paris Parlement in 1776.[18] And, perhaps even more important, it was the course being followed in neighboring Savoy.[19] The *cahiers* show that the assemblies electing the Third Estate delegates were not prepared to stray far from Savoy's model. Those noble assemblies that cared or dared to express themselves at all sometimes did not want to go even that far. Delegates elected to the National Assembly by the assemblies that adopted these documents could not be expected easily to support the more radical option of abolition.

The indemnification option had many appealing aspects, and it may well have seemed more, rather than less, attractive, when those elected in the spring found themselves responsible for enacting legislation to deal with the financial crisis. To members of the Third Estate who were themselves seigneurs, a matter made much of by Alfred Cobban, indemnification was a way to eliminate seigneurialism and thereby march into the modern world at minimal personal cost (or even to gain if the indemnification terms were set high enough). Cobban sees the National Assembly as trying to limit change under an anti-feudal smoke screen.[20] But Cobban does not take note of a less personally interested motive: those concerned about the finances of the state were also likely to worry about the consequences of simply abolishing the king's own seigneurial dues at a time of crisis. This would be even more important for those who saw some sort of royal land sale as a step toward raising funds: abolition would plainly lower the value of royal properties whose purchasers would be counting on acquiring the associated seigneurial rights. It would also eliminate a minor source of state revenue.[21] For those advocating a state takeover of church landholdings to fill the empty fisc, the seigneurial rights of ecclesiastical institutions would also have to be taken into account.[22] For those interested in a compromise that might pacify the peasants without sparking the lords to rebel, the indemnification option could appear the moderate, reasonable, centrist position.[23] And, for those who simply wished to stall, the social impact of indemnification would depend on the rates – which could be set later.[24]

Far closer to the people of the countryside, the preliminary *cahiers* of the rural parishes are less enthusiastic than the Third Estate documents for indemnification, even for periodic dues, and correspondingly more prone to advocate an uncompensated abolition.[25] In contrast, for example, to the 60 per cent of Third Estate *cahiers* proposing to indemnify the *champart* (an annual payment of a portion of the crop), the 21 per cent of parish *cahiers* that do so appears meager.[26] It is in their support for indemnification that the Third Estate *cahiers* differ most sharply from the parish texts, a difference with great consequences for the subsequent relationship of revolutionary legislature and revolutionary village.[27] In the debates and discussion around the drafting of *cahiers* and the election of deputies, village France had many opportunities to discover both the strength and the limits of the anti-seigneurial program of the urban élites.[28]

On "the eternally memorable night of 4 August," as it was almost instantly known, and during the discussions of the following week, many dramas were taking place, but one of the most important was establishing the distinction between those rights to be abolished outright and those to be compensated. In the final decree of 11 August, which announced the abolition of "the feudal regime," and in the detailed legislation of March and May 1790, it was clear that the National Assembly was prepared to move within the conceptual framework of the Third Estate *cahiers*, devoting considerable energy to the question of precisely which rights were to be in which group, working out the rates of indemnification, and developing a complex set of historical and legal arguments to justify the structure. These actions of the Assembly help explain why the targets of peasant violence were even more likely to be aspects of the seigneurial regime after that initial legislation than they had been up to that point. And without that peasant violence, in part a response to the legislators' actions, the further legislative actions would be difficult to understand. Although the 11 August decree spoke of the destruction of the feudal regime "in its entirety," many peasant obligations continued, pending indemnification. Until well into 1792, indeed, revolutionary legislation combined conceptually radical statements of the termination of one historical epoch with detailed prescriptions for the indefinite continuation of much of what peasants had always paid. The fusion of the two was effected rhetorically by Merlin de Douai, who argued that precisely because "the feudal regime is abolished," peasants were now morally as well as legally obliged to pay whatever was not abolished.[29]

In the dialogue between legislators and peasants, the relevant evidence on the legislative side is relatively unproblematic. We have the laws enacted, the debates on the floor of the legislatures, and a good number of letters and memoirs of the legislators to ponder. On the peasant side, however, we do not have an enumeration of the time, place, and nature of rural actions on a national scale. There are excellent and invaluable monographic studies of particular regions, forms of conflict, and time periods but nothing that approximates what is needed here.[30] Even the Herculean triumph of Anatoly Ado, invaluable in its documentation of the spatiotemporal aspects of anti-feudal action as well as conflicts over food supply, needs supplementation.[31] The archival exploration of rural conflict from 1661 through the spring of 1789 being carried out by the team directed by Jean Nicolas and Guy Lemarchand is an inspiring but also daunting model.[32] Rather than attempt to follow these models of archival exploration, I opted for the more limited task of assembling as complete a set of data as possible from already published accounts.[33] Such a data set carries with it the limitations and selection biases of historians of France; yet it also has the considerable virtue of being a far more modest undertaking than the multi-year, transatlantic archival search to be carried out by a research team requiring training and supervision. It is essential to recognize the biases. The collective research of historians is likely to under-report smaller incidents, is likely to over-count events that took place in the much-studied summer of 1789 relative to events in 1790 or 1791, is likely to under-count taxation conflicts compared to the anti-feudal events central to important historical interpretations, and is likely to over-count events in the rural zones around the cities that are pleasant to live in while doing research. (I recall Richard Cobb observing something to the effect that the Muse of History was no closer in Paris than in the Massif Central but that everything else was a lot closer.) But, as justification for such an enterprise, even a rough tracing of the flow of insurrection as it unfolds in time and space permits a fuller appreciation of the richness of rural political action and helps fill in an important context for the behavior of other parties to revolutionary struggles.

I put together a file on events in which people from the countryside, acting publicly as a group, directly engaged in the seizing or damaging of the resources of another party (including an attack on persons) or in defending themselves against another party's claims on them. Such a definition includes many forms of anti-seigneurial, anti-tithe, or anti-tax actions, a variety of subsistence-oriented events, invasions of land, labor conflicts, and even many panics (such as the Great Fear) induced by the belief that one is under attack. I identified some 4,700 such events from June 1788 through June 1793 and recorded what I could learn of the geographic location, the date the event commenced, the target and nature of the action.

Among the incidents identified from the summer of 1788 to the summer of 1793, there was considerable variation in the level of detail reported. Sometimes, all that was clear was that there had been some sort of clash; at other times, one could say that a group of peasants entered the lord's château, but one had no idea of what they did there; in still other instances, there was a rich account. The date could often be discovered; but, sometimes, I could date an event only roughly (for example, an anxious report to the National Assembly on food riots over the preceding few months). In general, the published literature on which I relied is clearer about when a conflict commenced than when it ended, to the degree, indeed, that I abandoned the attempt to analyze the duration of actions altogether. Nor were these sources usable for the reconstruction of sequences of action within a single event: I was far more likely to get a catalog of the various things the invaders did in the château, monastery, or tax office than any clear sense of the order in which they did those things; still less often did I arrive at a clear picture of the process that brought them to the château. Did they assemble elsewhere? Did they come from church or parish assembly? Had they been working in the fields or chatting in the tavern? Did they converge individually before the lord's dwelling? And what happened next? Did they disperse to their homes? Did they plan another attack? I often had only the vaguest indication of which members of the rural community participated. Were they landless laborers, sharecroppers, rural textile-workers, smallholders? Only rarely was there any indication of gender. I recorded the level of detail I did have concerning the character of the event and, in the case of dates, the approximate level of precision. Indications of the number of participants in an action were vague, when they existed at all. While I was sure that a "very large" group was at least twenty, I was often less sure if two hundred or two thousand was closer to the mark. Far more successful, however, was the discovery of the targets of the action: that one gathering stormed a monastery while another looted a household's grain was usually clear enough. Given these limitations, my analyses must focus on places, dates, targets, and tactics.

An examination of the targets of these actions, aggregating together all events from June 1788 through June 1793 that meet the criteria, offers a sense of the multifarious nature of rural mobilizations during the revolutionary crisis. The anti-seigneurial events formed a very large group – somewhat more than one third of all events found – and were quite widespread. Their diversity is depicted in Table 8.2, which shows the percentages of anti-seigneurial actions of various sorts. Note that the categories are not exclusive: a single event could involve a crowd that invades the lord's wine cellar and manhandles him prior to seizing his papers. Such an event would fall under several of the rubrics used in this table.[34] Some of the categories used are sub-categories of others: to choose the first three figures as an example, more than half of all anti-seigneurial events involved some violence against persons or property, but a much smaller number involved personal violence, and a somewhat smaller number still, violence against the lord.

Peasants invaded the lord's fields, destroyed his crops, felled his trees, pastured communal animals on his property, destroyed his fences, and attempted to redraw the boundaries of communal and seigneurial property (often insisting that usurped land was being reclaimed). The lord's château could be broken into and, once entered, a variety of actions undertaken: furniture could be seized or damaged, the lord's archives could be ransacked in search of seigneurial titles or – particularly if the search was resisted – the documents could be set on fire. The invaders could demand food or drink, even, in a tense parody of some old norm of hospitality, compel the lord to have them served a feast right then and there.

There was also plenty of damage to be done outside the château. Lords were dragged outside and forced to make public

Table 8.2 Types of anti-seigneurial insurrection

Targets and modes of action	Percentage of anti-seigneurial events
Violence	
Violence against persons or property	54.2
Violence against persons	4.7
Violence against lord	3.1
Château penetrated and interior invaded, with varying degrees of damage	27.3
Château a target; interior penetrated or exterior damaged	52.5
Destruction of food sources, rather than seizure (killing pigeons, fish, or rabbits; destruction of lord's crop; destruction of lord's trees)	5.2
Claims to rights	
Coerced renunciation of rights	7.7
Searches, seizures, and demands for documents (at château or at notary's office)	16.3
Subsistence	
Search for food stores, seizure of goods in wine cellar, compelling lord to feed the invaders	7.1
Recreational privileges	
Attacks on lord's right to hunt, raise pigeons or rabbits, or to maintain a fishpond (includes both acts or seizure and of destruction)	9.4
Hunting only	2.9
Lord–Church nexus	4.3
Dues	
Collective and public statement of refusal to pay	10.2
Public refusals to pay, demands for restitution, attacks on scales	18.4
Coerced restitution only	9.1
Land conflict	
All land conflicts	10.7
Conflicts over ownership or use rights in woods	4.9
Monopolies	0.5
Agents	3.9
King as Lord	0.7
Symbolics	
Honorific symbols of seigneurial status (weather vanes, coats of arms, gallows, turrets, battlements)	11.9

renunciations of their rights, often recorded by a notary (himself sometimes under compulsion). The lord's amusements were the targets of some actions: his rabbits or pigeons killed (or sometimes seized for food) and their habitations destroyed, his fishpond emptied or fouled, his compulsory mill or oven destroyed. Sometimes, the focus was specifically the lord's collection of dues: he was forced to make restitution of dues, the scales used to measure his portion of the crops was smashed, or the community openly announced its solidarity in future non-payment, sometimes backed by coercive measures taken (or at least threatened) against any who chose to continue paying. At times, the agents of the lord were the target: his judge, his notary, his rent collector, or his guard who had often engaged in a battle of wits with would-be poachers and violators of hunting rights; sometimes, the lord himself was beaten, an action usually (but not always) halted short of his death.

An important group of actions was the attacks on the lord–church nexus: the lord's family bench in the local church was sometimes dramatically torn out and unceremoniously dumped outside – and on occasion smashed or set on fire; more rarely but even more dramatically, the family tombs in the church were desecrated. As the Revolution grew more radical, in one of the many inversions of the old order by which the Revolution continually demonstrated its reality, the lord's (or later on, ex-lord's) dwelling might be searched for firearms or hidden counter-revolutionaries, just as lords had once joined the state in searching peasant homes for forbidden weapons or concealed criminals.

In all these ways, the lord's prerogatives were challenged, his material accumulations reclaimed, damaged, or desecrated, the legal basis of his authority seized from his archives as a text or from his mouth as a sworn renunciation, his connection with the sacred grounding of the community severed just as the family tomb or family bench was torn from the local church. Assaults also took place on the symbols of seigneurialism that made the lord more than another man. The weather vane was one likely target, as were turrets and battlements. Although the advance of the central state had long since rendered the fortress aspect of the medieval castle out of date, many a lord maintained reminders of a warrior identity in the form of architectural motifs of a decorative sort in his elegant lodgings, only to have these pretty turrets and graceful battlements attract the rage of peasant communities.

Any display of the family coat of arms was a tempting target as well. With its turrets knocked down and its coat of arms destroyed, the château was just a house.

One interesting cluster of actions involves the destruction of food sources. Some peasant communities obtained meat by defying the lord's exclusive rights and hunting on his preserves; others appear to have killed the game and left the carcasses.[35] Some forced the lord to feed them, and others destroyed the lord's crop.[36] Some made use of the products of the lord's forests, and others appear to have primarily damaged the trees.[37] Some seized the creatures the lord was privileged to raise (pigeons, rabbits, fish), and others seem to have been primarily concerned to destroy dovecotes, warrens, and ponds (and their feathered, furry, or finny inhabitants).[38] It is striking that these acts of destruction are scarcely less numerous in the data than are seizures of food from the lord.

Perhaps such actions arose from the blind anger of those for whom adequate diets were uncertain, while among them lived lords who made provisioning a form of play. Perhaps they were an assertion of a claim to a social order in which peasants, like lords, could defend their productive labors against pests.[39] Perhaps they were an assertion of peasant dignity, of the right to define their own activities as valuable and the lords' game – and games – as nuisances (which merely eating the rabbits would not do).[40]

It is also worth pausing over the relatively small number of incidents in which seigneurial agents are targets. It is commonly asserted that the lord's agents, in acting as intermediaries – whether as dues collectors, judges, estate managers, or legal advisers – became, for the peasants, the personification of the ills inflicted by the seigneurial regime. These agents thereby absorbed blows that might otherwise have been directed at the more distant lord.[41] The evidence of the actual insurrections (as well as the evidence of the parish *cahiers*)[42] suggests that, on a national scale, these intermediaries, these dwellers in the world between the lord and the peasant, were in fact of relatively minor concern to the country people. While the French peasants may not have loved the lord's agents, the agents did not constitute a major target of grievance or rebellion.[43] The peasants' target seems to have been a social institution and not, primarily, its human beneficiaries.[44] The country people were not, as some of the literature has it, sidetracked by the lord's agents, nor were they blinded by the search for revenge on the lord himself. The pattern of violent action, like the pattern of expressed grievances, suggests that peasants had an abstract conception of a social system. Their actions were violent, to be sure, and often inherently violent, not merely by-products of resistance to peaceable protests – although resistance might well augment the violence. But to be angry does not mean that one is blinded by anger, and to be violent does not mean that one's actions are unreasoned.

Finally, there was a striking bit of by-play around the meaning of a wooden pole. Lords who had proudly demonstrated their claims to possess the rights of "high justice" often decorated their lawns with gallows,[45] whose lack of utility did not spare them destruction in some parishes and replacement by a different pole, by which rural communities indicated their own power and their newly seized freedoms. In early 1790, anti-seigneurial events in Périgord and Quercy began to include the installation of the trimmed trunk of a very straight tree, often decorated with anti-seigneurial mockery and warnings, in place of the front-lawn gallows. Sometimes, indeed, the new pole was itself conceived as a gallows, but now it was the peasants' gibbet rather than the lord's.[46]

In considering the relative frequency of the different ways of challenging the seigneurial regime, it must be remembered that the nature of these sources makes it certain that many incidents are not fully described and that, therefore, many of the figures for the percentage of events with particular characteristics err on the low side. One would think that, with regard to the scale of violence in particular, the reverse would be the case. The more frightening aspects of these events would be the most likely to be reported in the first place, and historians searching for the dramatic anecdote would be more likely to recover from their archival locations accounts of severe damage to property and persons than respectful petitioning. (If we accept Simon Schama's indictment of the historical profession as squeamish, however, there might be a powerful countervailing tendency.) If one is willing to lend credence to the data (or to regard them as likely to overstate violence), the results are fascinating. While more than half the incidents involved overt violence (injuries to persons or property) in contrast to public declarations, demands, or threats, almost all of the violence was property damage. While lords may have been terrified by these events – some were hurt or killed and many

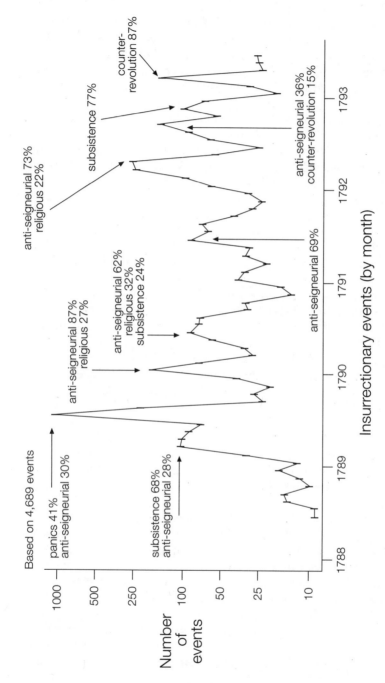

Figure 8.1 Number and character of insurrectionary events, June 1788 through June 1793 (based on 4,689 events)

threatened – revenge on the person of the lord played a fairly small role.[47]

The aggregated statistics, however, conceal at least as much as they reveal. What is most obscured is that revolution is not so much a state as a process involving an ebb and flow of events and alterations in the nature of those events. Figure 8.1 shows the number of incidents in each month from June 1788 through June 1793 as well as something of the changing character of the events at the moment of peak intensity. For example, in March 1789, about two-thirds of the incidents involved subsistence issues.[48]

The anti-seigneurial activity is far from being a constant from beginning to end. It is dominant in the waves of revolt that peaked in February 1790, June 1790, June 1791, and April 1792; but earlier and later, the story is different. In March and July 1789 and again in November 1792, anti-seigneurial events share the spotlight with other sorts of actions, and earlier and later still they are even less salient.

This is evident from a different angle when comparing the rhythms of anti-seigneurial actions with other kinds of actions. Figure 8.2 displays the trajectories of eight kinds of events. Each graph charts the changing proportions of events falling into various rough categories. The upper left graph shows the anti-seigneurial actions to have a clear rise and fall. Rather than an indiscriminate rural violence, attacks on varying targets have varying histories. In the summer of 1788, there are hardly any anti-seigneurial events. Subsistence events are the opening wedge of rural insurrection. In late 1788, anti-seigneurial events assume increasing significance and climb through 1789, remaining high – apart from a dip late in 1791 – until well into 1792, when they are eclipsed by other rural actions. It is worth pausing over this pattern. I suggest that in the course of the convocation of the Estates-General, and then in the patterns of debate and legislation, the anti-seigneurial character of the new revolutionary élites is becoming apparent to the peasants. Although the deputies of the Third Estate were more gradualist than the countryside wished – note their support for indemnifying the lords – peasants had come to believe that rural action against seigneurial rights had a good chance of paying off.

Peasant action against seigneurial rights continued until substantial gains were made. To the frustration of many deputies in the various legislatures, many villagers did not consider as a

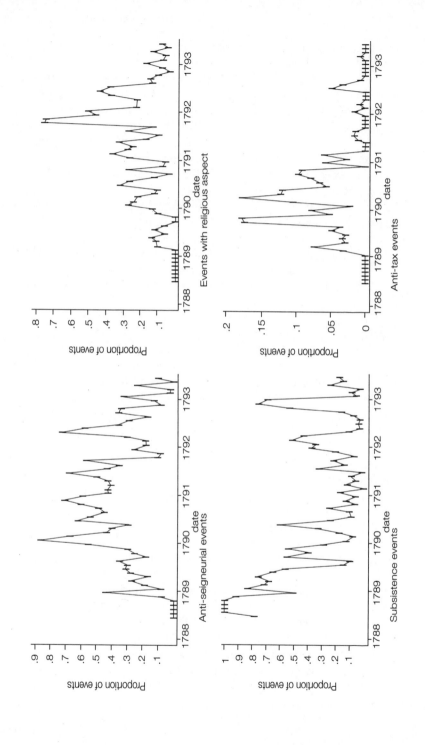

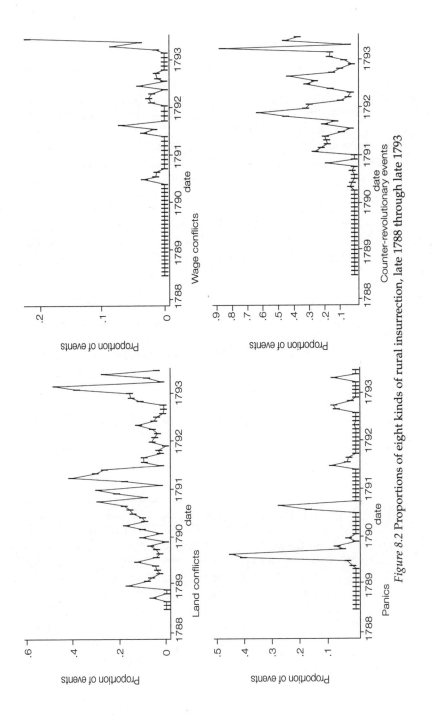

Figure 8.2 Proportions of eight kinds of rural insurrection, late 1788 through late 1793

substantial gain the ringing declaration of 4 August 1789, that the feudal regime was destroyed but would accept only significant alterations in what had to be paid to whom and in how disputes over such claims were to be resolved. The outright abolition of many seigneurial rights was not enough, in village France, if payments to the lords were to continue, pending an indemnification. The country people were fighting the claims of the lords, not an esoteric conception of "feudalism" defined by the National Assembly.[49] The significant achievements as far as the dues were concerned awaited piecemeal enactments of the spring of 1792, which culminated in a new law in late August of that year – after which anti-seigneurial actions plummeted. The trajectory of anti-seigneurial actions shows that rural action was not merely a blind and angry reflex. There may have been anger, but the uprisings developed as the moment seemed opportune and faded as goals were achieved.

I will not recount here the story of how rural insurrection persuaded the deputies to whittle away at the initial detailed legislation of March 1790, except to pause at one crucial moment in early 1792.[50] The legislators, from the initial language of the night of 4 August onward, had spoken in self-congratulation of the radicalism of their abolition of the feudal regime, while French villagers, from late in 1789 on, were mounting wave after wave of insurrection. February through April of 1792 was the largest such wave after the summer of 1789; it was also the eve of war with Europe, and it was within this context that peasant action was especially efficacious.

Seigneurial rights had become a central element of interstate tension on the night of 4 August. German princes, whose seigneurial claims in Alsace were guaranteed in the Treaty of Westphalia in 1648, hoped to find a powerful backer in the Holy Roman Empire. The landgrave of Hesse-Darmstadt, the bishop of Spire, and the duke of Württemberg had already been at odds with the French government over the flurry of institutional innovation of the pre-revolutionary period. For these princes, the new local and regional assemblies set up in 1787 raised the specter of popular sovereignty. The tax reform proposals of 1787 and 1788, the judicial reorganization of 1788 that threatened seigneurial courts, and the anti-feudal discourse in which public affairs were already being discussed were issues in Alsace even before the Estates-General met.[51] On 4 August these tensions were raised, on the French side, from a problem to a national commitment. From a problem that pitted local privileges against monarchical reform and state centralization, this conflict was transmuted into a struggle of the new epoch being born against the lay and clerical lords who fought to keep humanity in chains.

What may have appeared at first as simply the conflicting claims of France and the empire appeared to some in the Assembly as a question of whether the sovereignty of the French people (which the legislators took themselves to embody) could be assigned limits under the treaties of past monarchs. Merlin de Douai, speaking for the Committee on Feudal Rights, found a legal principle to sustain the jurisdiction of the National Assembly: the social contract took precedence over all. Since the people of Alsace had never consented to the Treaty of Westphalia but had participated in the election of the deputies that enacted the 4–11 August decree, the "treaties of princes" were illegal.[52] By implication, all interstate treaties were illegitimate, and no European structure of authority, except France's, had the basis in popular consent that made it worthy of respect.[53] Here, as in other pronouncements on seigneurial rights, Merlin's sharp and absolute statement of principle was as radical as the totality of concrete measures was moderate. The Diplomatic Committee, appropriate to its mission, took a more diplomatic view and proposed compensating the princes, but the princes refused.[54] Because the empire was unwilling to back the princes, there was no immediate threat of military action, but the rhetorical linkage of anti-feudalism in France and hostility toward the European monarchies had been forged.[55]

As tensions between states increased, those in France who favored war convinced themselves that not only would the conscript armies of their enemies crumble when confronting a free people but that the subject peoples of Europe would rise in emulation of the liberated French. Maximin Isnard's inflammatory speech of late November 1791 linked French émigrés and German princes in a common concern with lost rights and warned that, "if foreign courts try to raise a war of kings against France, we will raise a war of peoples against kings."[56] When a Prussian radical told the Legislative Assembly in December 1791 that interstate conflict would prompt peasants in Germany and Bohemia to rise against their lords, he was only reaffirming what many were already prepared to hear.[57] Jacques-Pierre Brissot and his political associates persistently defined the war they advocated as a war against feudalism.[58] There were, to be sure, some who proposed cooling the rhetorical temperature. As war neared in February 1792, the Diplomatic Committee of the Legislative Assembly reiterated the conciliatory proposal of indemnifying the German princes, a proposal dismissed by Jean-Baptiste Mailhe for its weakness.[59] (If it was wrong to indemnify lords across the Rhine, did some of the listeners wonder why was it proper to do so on their side?) And Robespierre's attempted deflation of the yoking of liberation and European war is well known.[60] Nonetheless, the sense of national mission prevailed.

Until the approach of actual war, most of the legislation on the seigneurial regime still amounted to tinkering with the basic structure embodied in the declarations of 4–11 August 1789, as given detailed elaboration by the enactments of March and May 1790. As interstate tensions become more ominous, peasant insurrection began to suggest a dangerous failure of the existing scheme. When rural incidents mounted in February 1792 – they were to reach the second largest insurrectionary peak of the Revolution in April – Georges Couthon urged a new course in the Legislative Assembly. He reminded his fellow deputies of the great size of the French army. But he urged them to recall that sheer size was far less significant than the moral unity of army and nation. The benefits of the Revolution, unfortunately, had not yet been fully received in the French countryside; village France had largely received fine words.

> Each of us has seen that ever-memorable night of August 4, 1789, when the Constituent Assembly ... pronounced in a holy enthusiasm the abolition of the feudal regime ... But these striking decisions were soon to present nothing more to the people than the idea of a beautiful dream, whose deceitful illusion left nothing but regrets. It was ... on August 4, 1789, that a decree was joyously received in all parts of the empire that abolished ... the feudal regime. Eight months later, a second decree preserved everything of value of this regime, so that far from having served the people, the Constituent Assembly could not even retain for them the consoling hope of being able to one day free themselves from the despotism of the former lords and the exaction of their agents.

Couthon alluded to the earlier work of abolishing the honorific aspects of the regime while insisting on indemnities for lucrative rights: "You will surely understand, gentlemen, that it was not exactly the honorific aspects of the feudal regime that weighed on the people." And he summed up: "We want [the people] to believe in the reign of liberty when they rest chained in dependence beneath their former lord."[61]

In the months that followed, a series of critical attacks occurred on the anti-seigneurial edifice as conceived by Merlin, and the war with Europe continued to be identified as a war about feudalism.[62] With the war came the overturning of the assumptions of the initial legislation, a process culminating in the August decrees of the Legislative Assembly.[63] By virtue of these new enactments, the burden of proof in disputes between peasant communities and lords was dramatically shifted. One of the most important aspects of the legislation that had initially spelled out what was to be abolished outright and what indemnified (and at what rates), starting with the spring of 1790, had been its allocation to the peasants of the burden of proof in the event of a dispute over the legitimacy of particular claims. A community had the right to challenge the lord's claim to payment pending indemnification, but that community was required to furnish evidence that the right in dispute had originated in an initial act of coercion, a formidable legal hurdle. The new enactments of August 1792 reversed this: it would now be up to the lords to demonstrate that a contested right had been initiated in an uncoerced contract. Even if a lord actually had some relevant documentation, how many would run the risk of attempting to make good such a claim in the threatening climate of the fall of 1792, a claim that would have to be pressed in a revolutionary court not likely to be very sympathetic?[64] Although the legislature had not yet declared the entire seigneurial regime illegitimate in principle, the August legislation made it nearly impossible for the lords to make claims on peasants in practice. It is striking that anti-seigneurial actions in the countryside declined sharply in the fall; with the lords no longer able to collect, peasant attention turned elsewhere.[65]

Even after the new anti-seigneurial legislation of August 1792, anti-feudal language surrounding the war continued to outrun the law in France. The Convention continued to expound the fusion of anti-feudalism and the struggle against foreign kings. In

November 1792, the Convention discussed "the principles," as Brissot put it, "under which France must grant her protection to all the peoples who ask it," Mailhe interjected that, whatever else these principles might be, they must include instructing other peoples "in the natural rights on which the destruction of feudal rights in France was based." And he went on to speak of a national mission: "Citizens, it is in France that feudal rights and their consequences unhappily were born: it is from France that enlightenment must come; it is the French who must raise the thick veil which, among all our neighbors, still conceals the fundamental rights of nature."[66]

Pierre-Joseph Cambon, urging on behalf of the finance, war, and diplomatic committees, the policies to be pursued by French forces, advanced a famous slogan: "[The committees have asked first of all] what is the purpose of the war you have undertaken. It is surely the abolition of all privileges. War against the châteaux, peace to the cottages."[67] On 15 December 1792, the Convention decreed the abolition of seigneurial rights in French-controlled areas of Belgium and Germany with no mention of any provision for appeal.[68] Peasants outside of France were to be promised French support for insurrection: "show yourselves free men and we will guarantee you against their vengeance." Although the seigneurial regime was no longer a primary target of French peasant action, the wartime Convention could hardly ignore the turbulent countryside, particularly with the radical increase in the frequency and scale of rural mobilization in March 1793. One symptom of the gravity with which the rural situation was viewed is Bertrand Barère's speech of 18 March. Advocating a complex package of proposals that combined repression with benefits for both the rural poor and the well-off, he urged the creation of a (not yet "the") "committee of public safety."[69] Three months later, the Convention proclaimed the entire seigneurial regime illegitimate.[70]

The wartime discussions of seigneurial rights were rooted in the war-promoting rhetoric of the Girondins, in statements of war aims, in policy declarations by generals in Belgium, in inspirational pep talks to the troops. The rhetorical climate was changing. If the sons of French villagers were to die in order to free German or Piedmontese villagers from feudal oppression, could the legislators stick to a definition of feudal rights so narrow that it appeared an utter fraud in rural France? Couthon's bitter observation in February 1792 that much of the anti-seigneurial legislation was "like that which the former lords would have dictated themselves" did no more than echo the claims of share-croppers in the countryside around Gourdon as early as the fall of 1790.[71] If the Convention encouraged anti-feudal insurrection in France's neighbors, could it manage to prosecute anti-feudal peasants at home? Mailhe went beyond supporting the wartime proclamation of liberation of occupied territories from feudal rights and protecting peasants against their lords; on 15 December, he proposed abolishing nobility itself where French arms triumphed. It seems but a matter of consistency for him to have advocated, ten days later, that legal proceedings against French peasants rebelling against seigneurialism be dropped.[72] (After the counter-revolutionary explosion in the western countryside of March 1793, in the name of what ideal were French peasants to be ordered into the vicious counter-insurgency campaign against other French peasants?)

The war made it impossible to maintain the disjunction between the sense of a radical rupture in history and a detailed specification that altered little of what peasants owed lords. In presenting the French armies as the agents of liberty in battle against the slave armies of the crowned tyrants, the legislators had to accept the victory of defiant French villagers who doggedly refused the coexistence of the narrow and the broad senses of the abolition of the feudal regime.[73] It took years of rural violence to push the revolutionary legislatures to make of the dismantling of feudalism a reality recognizable in the villages. And it is far from obvious that they would have done so without the wartime stresses.

Was a more peaceful termination of seigneurial rights, carefully controlled by a forward-looking élite, possible? The question demands speculation about the consequences of an élite-driven anti-seigneurial program pursued without the threat of effective peasant disruption. Such counter-factual speculation is fraught with hazards, but a failure to pose the question has its own hazard, namely, the ignoring of an important perspective on the rural revolts. Some parallel experiences are available to draw on in other European efforts to remove broadly similar rights.

Élite desires partially or wholly to dismantle anti-seigneurialism drew on many sources apart from fears of rebellion: the conviction that agricultural productivity could be advanced, that state revenues would increase, that an emancipated peasantry was more reliable in wartime, that a "civilized" country required a juridicial commitment to personal freedom, and that at least some seigneurial claims cost more to extract than they were worth even to the seigneurs. As discussed above, French élites did have an anti-seigneurial program at the onset of revolution, though one well short of what many French villagers would accept. Were there rural emancipations pushed by similar élite reformers in which fear of rural plebeians was minimal?

Jerome Blum's comparative survey of the formal emancipations of continental Europe's rural populations shows that almost everywhere emancipation was a protracted process.[74] Three states preceded France. Savoy's duke freed his own serfs in 1762 and went beyond the later similar act of Louis XVI by decreeing an indemnified redemption for other peasants. In 1772, the indemnification terms were altered in favor of the peasants, but the incapacity of the country people to buy their freedom caused the process to drag on until the French army entered two decades later and ordered an immediate and unindemnified abolition.[75] Baden's initial proclamation dates from 1783, but seigneurial claims did not definitively end until 1848.[76] After a series of false starts as early as 1702, Denmark proclaimed an effective abolition in 1788 but did not complete the process until 1861.[77]

Emancipations hardly proceeded any more rapidly in those many instances in which reform began in the wake of the revolution. Emancipation decrees were issued in Prussia, Württemberg, Mecklenberg, Bavaria, and Hesse between 1807 and 1820, but the processes were not completed until the revolutionary wave of 1848. Still other emancipatory processes did not even commence until the pressures of the agitated early 1830s (Hannover and Saxony), and others awaited the still more intense pressures of 1848 (Austria, Saxe-Weimar and Anhalt-Dessau-Köthen). Austrian officials were keenly affected by a Galician revolt in 1846.[78]

All of these emancipations outside France involved indemnifications. Many were limited to certain categories of peasants. Denmark's 1788 law, for example, did not free serfs between fourteen and thirty-six years old; its 1791 law denied landless farm workers the right to seek other employment.[79] Some of these indemnified emancipations required the consent of both lord and peasant, a measure that enabled those lords who wished to retain their rights to do so, at least until, as invariably happened, subsequent legislation removed the voluntary element.[80] The rapidity of the French transition from a process in large part indemnificatory to one thoroughly abolitionist stands out as unique among all European cases that commenced before 1848.

Apart from Savoy, Baden, and Denmark, moreover, the initial impulse for all the pre-1815 cases was French. French arms sometimes brought varying degrees of rural emancipation, as in Belgium at the start of the long war, the Helvetic Republic, and various western German states in 1798, the Grand Duchy of Warsaw in 1807, and various north German states in 1811; these actions in turn triggered pre-emptive emancipation by fearful neighbors, as in a number of German instances in 1807. Beyond the direct use of force, however, the knowledge of the dangers of revolution in which French peasants instructed the world certainly helped spur some reform even after Napoleon's armies went down to defeat.[81] And in 1848 itself, insurrectionary peasants may have more rapidly won concessions in German-speaking lands because many governments had learned from 1789–93 the futility of half-measures in the countryside: thus the termination of several decades-long emancipatory processes and the commencement and rapid completion of others in 1848–9. (In Hungary in 1848, the Diet appears to have been panicked into abolishing serfdom by a false report of 40,000 mobilized peasants.)[82] In other words, in Central and Western Europe through the mid-nineteenth century, there are many instances of élite-driven emancipations, but, if we credit Blum's survey, not a single one that came to completion without the presence of the French army, the specter of popular insurrection, or both.

This glance to the east strengthens the view that without the determined, violent, and frightening popular battle, French peasants would still have been responsible for seigneurial obligations at the midpoint of the nineteenth century – at the very least. The Third Estate's delegates did carry indemnificatory proposals to the Estates-General, where they joined with nobles, some of whom represented more conservative constituencies. Considering the role of popular uprising in promoting the initial decrees of 4–11 August 1789, one might well wonder if emancipation would have taken place at all without further pressure from the peasants.[83] Even the positions expressed in the general *cahiers* of the spring of 1789 were surely taken with an awareness of the riots rising in the French countryside; the assemblies, moreover, though dominated by urban notables, had a significant number of village delegates. The positions taken in the Third Estate *cahiers* already reflect rural pressures.

The years of disruptive insurrection of the French countryside in revolution are a part of the modern history of democracy, despite the view expressed in much of the recent literature that emancipation from the chains of the past was largely the work of highly educated élites, that plebeian violence only helped to emphasize the illiberal leanings of those élites, and that much rural mobilization was directed against the revolutionary regime rather than in tacit alliance with it. Democracy is a highly charged and profoundly contested notion,[84] but essential to virtually all conceptions is some sense of "self-rule," not a state of affairs one could readily imagine extending to those in relations of dependence on others. This has been a continuing and potent rationale for the exclusion from public life and full political rights of many – of the poor, servants, and women at various points during the Revolution, of a variety of groups at other times and in other places, of the continuing exclusion of children from active citizenship everywhere. A rural world of lords and peasants is a world of very limited democratic possibilities: the attack on seigneurial rights was therefore an important component of creating the possibility of a democratic future.

A case can be made that the essential ingredient in this attack was a revolution in thought, largely promoted by the revolutionary élite and enunciated as early as the summer of 1789. François Furet remarked, on the conceptual achievement of the National Assembly,

the decrees of August 4 to August 11 number among the founding texts of modern France. They destroyed aristocratic society from top to bottom, along with its structure of dependencies and privileges. For this structure they substituted the modern, autonomous individual, free to do whatever was not prohibited by law. August 4 wiped the slate clean by eliminating whatever remained of intrasocial powers between the individual and the social body as a whole.[85]

We ought to question the real extent of these individual rights. Women were hardly emancipated from structures of dependence by 4–11 August, to take one very important example.[86] Conflict over the definition of who is seen as autonomous and free, in fact, has been a central but not always noticed feature of democracy for the past two centuries. Even if we may not wish to take the next step to equate a conception with the actual experience of social relationships, we may, nevertheless, agree on the radicalism of a conception of a society in which all dependence and privilege have given way before autonomous individuals. But is the National Assembly to be credited with the destruction of rural structures of dependence because it issued a text in which it credited itself? We may wonder, first of all, whether the National Assembly, which added a considerable dose of noble conservatism to the clear but clearly limited anti-feudal program of the Third Estate, would have even gone as far as it did in early August without the social explosion of July 1789. And we may ask whether this conceptual break would be easy to see as anything other than hypocrisy without the measures taken later, in 1792, to gain the support of peasants unwilling to settle for the removal of the symbols of deference without a far more dramatic change in material obligation. Even on the level of such symbolics, how quickly would the legislatures have acted, looking ahead from 4–11 August, without the vast destruction of church benches, weather vanes, and coats of arms carried out by the country people?

The rural popular violence and the élite conceptual radicalism, moreover, were hard to separate, for each sustained the other. Not only did violent peasants push the legislature forward, but conceptually radical legislators showed peasants that if they pushed, they could win.

Does any of this argument indicate that the élite's own anti-feudal program, which I have not treated in any detail here, was an insignificant matter? Not at all. The people of the countryside rose against different targets at various times and places, and those in a position to write laws or command armed force responded in various ways. Consider the two contrasting cases: overt rejection of the central institutions and symbols of the Revolution in the west was met by savage violence on the part of the authorities; rejection of the revolutionary freeing of the grain trade (in which rural people were joined by urban popular forces) led to the spectacular, but only temporary, reimposition of controls. If the anti-seigneurial campaign, though difficult, was such a success, was it not in considerable part because revolutionary legislators had their own anti-feudal agenda?

Furthermore, insurrectionary peasants were responding to the élites just as the legislators were responding to rural disruption. Consider again the trajectory of peasant insurrection (see Figure 8.1): it was not, at first, predominantly anti-seigneurial, but it became so. As the elections to the Estates-General approached, the struggle for the hearts and minds of the country people could not have failed to have made them aware of urban élite sympathies for significant alterations in the seigneurial regime; the night of 4 August was even more instructive. And, the data show, it is following 4 August that rural turbulence became predominantly focused on seigneurial rights. The debates in the spring over the contents of the *cahiers* and the legislative events of early August were demonstrations that an assault on the seigneurial regime might not quite be, as the French say, kicking in an open door, but it surely was not a stoutly defended oaken door, either. The dealings of villagers and legislators with each other over the rights of the lords radicalized both parties, but this is another story.

Let us speculate for a moment about a less violent revolution, in which a conceptually radical National Assembly abolishes feudalism but manages to obtain peasant compliance in paying what they have always paid, no doubt inspiring a host of programs by which all manner of states, following France, Savoy, Baden, and Denmark, discovered how to be modern without expropriating a landed upper class. We would have fewer documents that tell us of the terrors of the countryside in revolution. Yet it is hard to see how such a state of affairs would have advanced democracy. No doubt, for many, such an outcome would nevertheless be preferable to all the pain that occurred.

The structures that made one man more than another, grounded in force, were abolished in principle by the National Assembly, helped along by rural violence against the visible signs of honor for the lords and the counterpart humiliations for the villagers. But the initial legislative program, more or less following the intentions voiced by the urban notables in the spring of 1789, was not accepted in much of rural France; it took years of battle in the countryside and the pressure of war with Europe for the legislators to translate their own sense of a break with a feudal past into terms recognizable in the villages. While the idea of a world of contractual relations among juridically equal persons may be an essential component that underlies evolving democratic practice, in which no one governs by age-old right and governors are accountable for their performances to citizenries, many in the French countryside plainly did not accept the claim that they had in some sense consented to their material obligations to their now former lords. Without the genuine end to those payments, there might as well be lords in village France, regardless of what the lawyers wrote in Paris. Merlin held early on that the Treaty of Westphalia to which the people had not consented could not obligate them to continue to pay lords across the Rhine; but the revolutionary legislatures tried for three years to act as though the same country people had consented to pay French lords. It took considerable violence to go beyond a gradual phase-out. Such violence had many consequences: the counter-mobilizations of the terrorized (the nineteenth-century Right and ultra-right fed off French revolutionary terrors), the repressive measures of a revolutionary state eager to remove initiative from the village and the street, and the sufferings of the victims (whose complicity in the earlier sufferings of their own now-violent tormentors varied greatly). So the revolution, and its popular insurrections, opened the way for new forms of non-democratic and even anti-democratic politics. But they also made a more democratic social order possible. To the extent that over the past two centuries those in command in France had to take into consideration their accountability to the French people (rather than, like Louis XV, only their responsibilities before God),[87] the thousands of violent incidents of rural France in revolution made an essential contribution.

NOTES

Source Reprinted from the *American Historical Review* 100 (April 1995): 360–386.

Acknowledgement An earlier version of this article was presented at the conference "Violence and the Democratic Tradition in France," University of California, Irvine, February 1994. The essay benefited from the comments of participants in that event, particularly Colin Lucas, as well as from suggestions by Seymour Drescher, Jeremy Popkin, Donald Sutherland, and Isser Woloch.

1 *The London Times* (12 July 1989): l2: *Le monde* (12 July 1989): 1, 4.

2 "Mrs. Thatcher Set to Rights." *Guardian*, 15 July 1989.

3 See François Crouzet, *De la supériorité de l'Angleterre sur la France: L'économique et l'imaginaire, XVIIe–XXe siècles* (Paris, 1985). esp. pp. 248–98; Pierre Chaunu, *Le grand déclassement: A propos d'une commémoration* (Paris, 1989), pp. 265–84; and René Sédillot, *Le coût de la Révolution* (Paris, 1987).

4 From Simon Schama's preface to *Citizens*: "The drastic social changes imputed to the Revolution seem less clear-cut or actually not apparent at all . . . [T]he modernization of French society and institutions seem to have been anticipated by the reform of the 'old regime.'" Schama, *Citizens: A Chronicle of the French Revolution* (New York, 1989), p. xiv.

5 For John Mueller, the Revolution's contribution to the history of democracy was a "disastrous" bad example; and Jack A. Goldstone stresses the revolutionary violence "that systematically destroys the political space necessary for freedom and liberty to flourish." See Mueller, "Democracy and Ralph's Pretty Good Grocery: Elections, Equality and the Minimal Human Being." *American Journal of Political Science*, 36 (1992): 994; Goldstone, "Révolutions dans l'histoire et histoire des révolutions," in *Revue français de sociologie*, 30 (1989): 421. For surveys of the recent stress on élite political culture, see Sarah Maza, "Politics, Culture and the Origins of the French Revolution," *Journal of Modern History*, 61 (1989): 704–23; and Jack Censer, "The Coming of a New Interpretation of the French Revolution," *Journal of Social History*, 21 (1987): 295–309.

6 Brian Singer. "Violence in the French Revolution: Forms of Ingestion/Forms of Expulsion," in Ferenc Fehér, *The French Revolution and the Birth of Modernity* (Berkeley, Calif., 1990), pp. 150–73. To argue that violence is not fully explained as a means to an end outside itself, as Singer brilliantly does, is by no means the same as demonstrating that violence never has an instrumental aspect. The leap that identifies violence with the gratuitously anti-rational is an important element of Schama's rhetoric. If the revolution is violence and violence is senseless, a reader can easily draw the implied conclusion about all revolutionary action. See also Roger Chartier, *The Cultural Origins of the French Revolution* (Durham, N.C., 1991), pp. 193–4: Norbert Elias, "The Civilizing Process: Sociogenetic and Psychogenetic Investigations (New York, 1982).

7 The recent literature on resistance is voluminous beyond ready citation: there is a useful survey in Michel Vovelle, *La découverte de la politique: Géopolitique de la Révolution française* (Paris, 1993).

8 The most compelling portrait along these lines is Donald Sutherland, *France 1789–1815: Revolution and Counterrevolution* (New York, 1986). Sutherland's preview of his argument: "The history of the entire period can be understood as the struggle against a counterrevolution that was not so much aristocratic as massive, extensive, durable and popular" (p. 10).

9 Charles Tilly, *The Contentious French* (Cambridge, Mass., l986), p. 2.

10 J. Mavidal and E. Laurent, *Archives parlementaires de 1787 à 1860* (*première série*) (Paris, 1879), 3: 285. (This series will be abbreviated *AP* in subsequent references.)

11 Hilton Root has expressed some skepticism on this point. See Root, "The Case against Georges Lefebvre's Peasant Revolution," *History Workshop*, 28 (1989): 88–102; and the reply by Peter Jones in the same number.

12 Georges Lefebvre *The Coming of the French Revolution* (New York, 1947), pp. 127–45; Anatoly Ado, *Krest'ianskoe dvizhenie vo frantsii vo vremia velikoi burzhuaznoi revoliutsii kontsa XVIII veka* (Moscow, 1971).

13 There were many other targets of rural insurrection besides the seigneurial regime that are not treated in this essay; there are also important regional differences in the types and timing of anti-seigneurial actions. On these matters, as well as more on the legislative context, see John Markoff, *The Abolition of Feudalism: Peasants, Lords and Legislators in the French Revolution* (University Park, Pa., forthcoming).

14 The search for a precise evaluation of the weight of the seigneurial regime has generated a large and complex literature because there were many different sorts of seigneurial rights, much variation from region to region and even *seigneurie* to *seigneurie*, difficulty in adequately measuring the total revenues of peasants and lords against which the place of the seigneurial rights is to be weighed, and many problems in making judgments about the role of seigneurialism in conferring power and honor as well as income. It is clear from this literature, however, that there were many French peasants on whom the lord's claims were heavy and many lords for whom these rights were a significant component of income; it is also evident from the grievance lists of 1789 that many a lord took the honor attached to some of the rights with the greatest seriousness, while others in France took with equal seriousness the associated dishonor. For one example of an attempted monetary evaluation of seigneurial revenues, see M. Leymairie, "Les redevances foncières seigneuriales en Haute-Auvergne," *Annals historiques de la Révolution française*, 40 (1968): 299–380; the issue of honor and dishonor is treated in Markoff, *Abolition of Feudalism*.

15 The figures presented are drawn from a quantitative content analysis of the *cahiers* carried out with Gilbert Shapiro. Our code distinguishes more than one thousand institutions under discussion and hundreds of actions demanded. We coded virtually all the extant general *cahiers* of the Third Estate and nobility as well as a sample of 748 of the parish *cahiers*. Since we did not code the clerical *cahiers*, there is a missing part of this picture. The procedures for counting demands in the *cahiers* are spelled out in detail in Gilbert Shapiro and John Markoff, *Revolutionary Demands: A Content Analysis of the Cahiers de Doléances of 1789* (Stanford. Calif., forthcoming); a briefer account may be found in John Markoff, Gilbert Shapiro, and Sasha Weitman, "Towards the Integration of Content Analysis with General Methodology," David Heise (ed.), *Sociological Methodology* (San Francisco, 1974), pp. 1–58.

16 By contrast, taxation was an arena that attracted many reform pro-
    posals. By one measure, 16 per cent of Third Estate grievances about
    seigneurial rights called for reform, compared to 39 per cent when
    taxation was at issue. See John Markoff, "Peasants Protest: The
    Claims of Lord, Church and State in the *Cahiers de Doléances* of 1789,"
    Comparative Studies in Society and History, 32 (1990): 428–9.
17 Markoff, "Peasants Protest." pp. 428–9,: Markoff, *Abolition of Feudal-
    ism*, Chap. 2.
18 Pierre-François Boncerf, *Les inconvéniens des droits féodaux* (London,
    1776).
19 Max Bruchet, *l'abolition des droits seigneuriaux en Savoie* (1761–1793)
    (Annecy, 1908).
20 Alfred Cobban, *The Social Interpretation of the French Revolution*
    (Cambridge, 1965), pp. 27, 43–8, 39.
21 George T. Matthews, *The Royal General Farms in Eighteenth-Century
    France* (New York, 1958), p. 175.
22 As the legislative reconstruction of France proceeded, concern
    among the deputies for the continued collection of seigneurial rights
    on former royal or church property was evident. When the depart-
    mental and district administrations, to whom the supervision of
    "national property" was originally entrusted, proved lax in the
    collection of seigneurial rights, the National Assembly assigned
    this responsibility elsewhere. See Jean Noël Luc, "Le rachat des
    droits féodaux dans le département de la Charente-Intérieure (1789–
    1793)," in Albert Soboul (ed.), *Contributions á l'histoire paysanne de la
    Révolution française* (Paris, 1977), pp. 314–15.
23 Merlin de Douai introduced his committee's report on the feudal
    rights to the National Assembly on 8 February 1790: "it is high time
    that we present the people a law whose justice will silence the selfish
    feudatory who has been screaming so indecently about spoliation for
    the past six months, a law whose wisdom may lead the peasant to
    return his duty, that peasant whom resentment over a long oppres-
    sion could temporarily lead astray." *AP*, 11: 498–9.
24 The National Assembly voted on which rights to indemnify in March
    1790 but did not settle on the rates until May. The rates of indemnifi-
    cation discussed varied and, over time, became more favorable to the
    peasants. Boncerf's pamphlet of 1776 proposed fifty or sixty times
    their annual value, the duke d'Aiguillon suggested thirty times on 4
    August 1789, and the rate established in May 1790 was twenty to
    twenty-five, depending on the particular right. See Boncerf, *Les
    inconvéniens*, p. 11; *AP*, 8: 344, *AP*, 15: 365–6.
25 The extent to which rural France authentically speaks through the
    parish *cahiers* has been debated among historians for a long time. For
    a detailed treatment of this issue, see Gilbert Shapiro and John
    Markoff, "L'authenticité des cahiers de doléances," *Bulletin d'histoire
    de la Révolution française* (1990–1): 17–70.
26 Markoff, "Peasants Protest," p. 433.
27 The peasants rarely paid the indemnities. In some places, very few
    took advantage of the indemnificatory aspects of the new laws; in

others, some people did, but these were largely not peasants. In Charente-Inférieure, merchants, legal professionals, administrators, and urban *seigneurs* were the main users of the elaborate indemnification procedures. Similarly in the *départements* studied in Brittany, Normandy, Franche-Comté, Champagne, and Limousin, indemnification seems hardly to have taken place at all. The *département* of Corrèze appears unusual in the extent of peasant utilization of the legal route (at least in the hill country – lowland Corrèze refused participation). See Luc, "Le rachat des droits féodaux," pp, 332–3, 345; and J.N. Luc, *Paysans et droits féodaux en Charente-Inférieure pendant la Révolution française* (Paris, 1984), pp. 125–59; André Ferradou, *Le rachat des droits féodaux en Haut-Vienne* (Limoges, 1939); Jean Millot, *L'abolition des droits seigneuriaux dans le département du Doubs et la région comtoise* (Besançon, 1941), pp. 172–96; Georges Lefebvre, *Les paysans du Nord pendant la Révolution française* (Paris, 1972), pp. 387–90; Philippe Goujard, "L'abolition de la féodalité dans le district de Neuchâtel (Seine-Inférieure)," in Soboul, (ed.), *Contributions à l'histoire paysanne*, pp. 366–73; Donald Sutherland, *The Chouans: The Social Origins of Popular Counter-revolution in Upper Brittany, 1770–1796* (Oxford, 1982), pp. 139–41; Jean-Jacques Clère, *Les paysans de la Haute-Marne et la Révolution française: Recherches sur les structures foncières de la communauté villageoise (1780–1825)* (Paris, 1988), pp. 189–91; Jean Boutier, *Campagnes en émoi: Révoltes et Révolution en bas-Limousin, 1789–1800* (Treignac, 1987), pp. 146–51.

28   A country lawyer representing his parish at the electoral assembly in Ploërmel recalled in his memoirs how he first gained and then lost the support of other rural delegates in the course of debating the *cahier*. An initial denunciation of privilege brought him considerable notice and made him a front runner for election to the Estates General: a later, judicious speech on behalf of indemnification as a compromise could not even be finished in the face of shouts, threats, and clenched fists. See Roger Dupuy, "Les émeutes anti-féodales de Haute-Bretagne (janvier 1790 et janvier 1791): Meneurs improvisés ou agitateurs politisés?" in Jean Nicolas (ed.), *Mouvements populaires et conscience sociale, XVIᵉ–XIXᵉ siècles* (Paris, 1985), p. 452.

29   *AP*, 11: 500.

30   For a few instances among many, see Boutier, *Campagnes en émoi*; Clère, *Paysans de la Haute-Marne*; Hubert C. Johnson, *The Midi in Revolution: A Study of Regional Political Diversity, 1789–93* (Princeton. N. J., 1986); Michel Vovelle, "Les campagnes à l'assaut des villes sous la révolution," in Vovelle (ed.), *Ville et campagne au 18ᵉ siècle: Chartres et la Beauce* (Paris, 1980), pp. 227–76.

31   Ado, *Krest'ianskoe dvizhenie vo frantsii.*

32   Jean Nicolas, "Les émotions dans l'ordinateur: Premiers résultats d'une enquête collective" (paper presented at Université Paris VII, 1986); "Une jeunesse montée sur le plus grand ton d'insolence," in Robert Chagny (ed.), *Aux origines provinciales de la Révolution* (Grenoble, 1990); Guy Lemarchand, "Troubles populaires aux XVIIIᵉ siècle et

271

conscience de classe: Une préface à la Révolution française," *Annales historiques de la Révolution française*, no. 279 (1990): 32–48.

33 The sources for the data file on insurrection included reports to the revolutionary legislatures found in *Archives parlementaires* as well as the monographic research of later historians, more than one hundred of which were used. The ultimate sources for nineteenth and twentieth-century publications are usually administrators' reports, police and judicial records, and the letters or memoirs of witnesses (who were often victims).

34 If a group of country people invades the lord's château and menacingly insist that he feed them, is this primarily an invocation of a rule of hospitality, mockingly parodied in order to demonstrate that the lord's former dependents are now the enforcers of the rules? Or are these essentially hungry people seeking food? Is it an "anti-seigneurial" or a "subsistence" action? We cannot reconstruct the state of mind of the participants, but there were no doubt diverse motives within a group insisting that the lord feed them. Some (or all) of the participants may have had a mixture of motives. It is, in any event, improbable that we can discover the precise mix in any particular crowd. Nor are the attributions of motive by participants and observers necessarily more credible than those of historians. One should not take a frightened lord's testimony or the hastily penned letter of a local official as authoritative on such a matter – even when the reporter comments on motive. Rather than attempt to decide whether to regard such an event as essentially anti-seigneurial or essentially subsistence in character, I regard it as both.

35 For instance, at the same time that neighboring villages in Cambrésis were breaking into local abbeys to seize grain, in early May 1789 a dozen communities around Oisy exterminated a lord's game. Georges Lefebvre, *Les paysans du Nord pendant la Révolution française* (Paris, 1972), p. 356.

36 For example, on 26 March 1789, the holdings of the count de Gallifet near Draguignan were attacked by peasants who drove their livestock onto his sown fields, ruining them. Jules Viguier, *La convocation des Etats-Généraux en Provence* (Paris, 1896), pp. 269–70.

37 Local officials reported on 25 November 1790, that fruit trees of the abbey of Beaubec in Normandy were cut down, a rather late date for collecting fruit. See Philippe Goujard, *L'abolition de la "féodalité" dans le pays de Bray (1789–1793)* (Paris, 1979), p. 99.

38 To take one large group of instances: in the spring of 1791, peasant communities around Uzerche, Tulle, and Brive fought what Jean Boutier calls "the war against the ponds," in which large numbers of peasants seized the lords' fish and, in the process, destroyed them, a point seen favorably by local urban radicals who regarded the ponds as environmentally damaging. See Boutier, *Campagnes en émoi*, pp. 118–24.

39 Keeping rabbits and pigeons and hunting were often, in principle, activities constrained by customary legal codes, a set of codes often violated, however. A typical rule might be that all lords in the

province could have "closed" warrens (surrounded by walls or water-filled moats), but "open" warrens were only permitted to those with enough land so that neighbors' crops were not ravaged. See Marcel Garaud, *La révolution et la propreté foncière* (Paris, 1958), p. 92.

40 In a similar vein, Jean-Pierre Hirsch distinguishes between those for whom hunting in the summer of 1789 was "a pleasure long forbidden," those who experienced "the sensation of at last achieving the dignity of bearing arms," and those "moved simply by hunger." See Hirsch, *La nuit du 4 août* (Paris, 1978), p. 234. Jean-Sylvain Bailly, first mayor of revolutionary Paris, believed that the "disastrous" outpouring of hunting that first summer spared the lands of "patriot princes" such as the duke of Orléans. If this claim could be confirmed, it also would assign hunger a reduced place as motive. See *Mémoires de Bailly* (Paris, 1821), 2: p. 244.

41 See, for example, Saint-Jacob, *Les paysans de la Bourgogne du Nord*, pp. 428–34: Cobban, *Social Interpretation of the French Revolution*, pp. 47–9.

42 See Markoff, *Abolition of Feudalism.*

43 Indeed, in some places, the agents may have turned into the local leadership once the lord was pushed aside, as Jean-Pierre Jessenne found in the most detailed study to date of the revolution's transformation of village politics. In Artois, those whose power had been conferred by the lords before 1789 did well in the municipal elections of 1790, unless the local community was at legal loggerheads with the lord – a situation that identified the agent too closely, Jessenne contends, with his master. The lord's appointed *lieutenant* became the revolution's elected mayor. The 1790 elections were no fluke, for the same groups did well in 1791. While the 1792 upheaval brought in mid-size landowners, urbanites, and artisans, these newcomers continued the same policies locally; and the post-Thermidor era saw the triumphant and long-lived return of the village élite. Perhaps future research may reveal whether the success of the former seigneurial agents of Artois was duplicated elsewhere – especially in the zones of staunch early anti-seigneurial activism such as around Mâçon, in Franche-Comté, Dauphiné, and coastal Provence or in later anti-seigneurial epicenters such as Quercy, Périgord, and upper Brittany. At present, the *cahiers* data show how rare verbal attacks on these agents were. See Jessenne, *Pouvoir au village et Révolution: Artois 1760–1848* (Lille, 1987).

44 For a similar judgment, see Jessenne, *Pouvoir au village*, p. 59.

45 Even Voltaire had the right to display an elaborate gallows when he climbed his way to the proper status. See Fernand Caussy, *Voltaire, seigneur de village* (Paris, 1912), p. 3.

46 Mona Ozouf, *La fête révolutionnaire 1789–1799* (Paris, 1976), pp. 280–3I6.

47 Schama recognizes how little violence there was in the countryside against the lord's person, as opposed to the emblems of his authority, but that does not lead him to a more complex analysis of violence. See Schama, *Citizens*, p. 434.

48 I remind the reader that these classifications are not exclusive ones. In

early 1790, Figure 2 shows 87 per cent of incidents having an anti-seigneurial character, while 27 per cent have a religious aspect. This comes about because some of those anti-seigneurial events are attacks on ecclesiastical lords (usually monasteries).

49 Régine Robin, "Fief et seigneurie dans le droit et l'idéologie juridique à la fin du XVIIIᵉ siècle, *Annales historiques de la Révolution française*, 43 (1971): 554–602; Claude Mazauric, "Note sur l'emploi du 'régime féodal' et de 'féodalité' pendant la Révolution française," in his *Sur la Révolution française: Contributions à l'histoire de la révolution bourgeoise* (Paris, 1970), pp. 119–34; Alain Guerreau, "Fief, féodalité, féodalisme: Enjeux sociaux et réflexion historienne," *Annales: Economies, sociétés, civilisations*, 45 (1990): 134–66; Rolf Reichardt and Eberhard Schmitt, "La Révolution française – rupture ou continuité? Pour une conceptualisation plus nuancée," in Reichardt and Schmitt (eds.), *Ancien Regime: Aufklärung und Revolution* (Munich, 1983), pp. 4–71; Diego Veinturino. "La naissance de l'Ancien Régime," in Colin Lucas (ed.), *The French Revolution and the Creation of a Modern Political Culture* (New York, 1987), 2: pp. 11–40; John Markoff, "Burżuazja rewolucyjna definiuje system feudalny," in Andrzej Zybertowicz and Adam Czarnota (eds.), *Interpretacje Wielkiej Transformacji: Geneza kapitalizmu jako geneza współczesności* (Warsaw, 1989), pp. 357–89.

50 The history of the revolutionary legislation is treated in Henri Doniol, *La Révolution française et la féodalité* (Paris, 1876); Emile Chénon, *Les démembrements de la propriété foncière avant et après la Révolution* (Paris, 1923); Philippe Sagnac, *La législation civile de la Révolution française* (Paris, 1898); Alphonse Aulard, *La Révolution française et le régime féodal* (Paris, 1919); Garaud, *La Révolution et la propriété foncière*; Peter M. Jones, *The Peasantry in the French Revolution* (Cambridge, 1988).

51 Pierre Muret, "L'affaire des princes possessionés d'Alsace et les origines du conflit entre la Révolution et l'Empire," *Revue d'histoire moderne et contemporaine*, 1 (1899–1900): 433–56, 566–92.

52 *AP*, 20: 81.

53 T. C. W. Blanning, *The Origins of the French Revolutionary Wars* (London, 1986), pp. 74–5.

54 *AP*, 20: 84.

55 Sydney Seymour Biro, *The German Policy of Revolutionary France* (Cambridge, Mass., 1957), 1: pp. 39–42. See also T.C.W. Blanning, *The French Revolution in Germany: Occupation and Resistance in the Rhineland, 1792–1802* (Oxford, 1983), pp. 59–69; Muret, "L'affaire des princes possessionés."

56 *AP*, 35: 441–3.

57 *AP*, 36: 79. The speaker, Anacharsis Cloots, might have been buoyed by thoughts of the recent peasant uprising, in August 1790, in Saxony. See Jerome Blum, *The End of the Old Order in Rural Europe* (Princeton, N.J., 1978). pp. 337–8.

58 For example, Louvet in December 1791 (*AP*, 36: 381).

59 *AP*, 39: 89–90, *AP*, 39: 97.

60 Maximilien Robespierre. *Oeuvres* (Paris, 1950), 8, p. 81.

61 Georges Couthon, *Discours sur le rachat des droits seigneuriaux prononcé*

à la séance du mercredi 29 février 1792 (Paris, 1792), pp. 2–3, 3, 7.

62 *AP*, 39: 595, 41: 470–74, 42: 21, 45: 17–18, 119–23, 53: 473, 55: 70, 75, 101.

63 *AP*, 45: pp. 119–23.

64 It seems a reasonable assumption that few peasant challengers availed themselves of the opportunity to mount a legal challenge under the earlier legislation and that fewer lords did so after August 1792. Withholding payments would seem to have been a more promising action for peasants in the earlier phase and despair the most likely response of the lords later on. But scholarly research into the utilization (or presumed lack of it) of the judicial arena in peasant/lord conflict during the revolution is too inadequate to permit certainty.

65 This is in accord with the notion of a peasantry engaged in aggressive actions for instrumental ends; but note that just before this sharp decline, there is a short, sharp rise in anti-seigneurial acts. In this latter group of actions, which are among the most destructive of property in the entire data series, we are probably seeing acts of vengeance against the now politically vulnerable fomer lords.

66 *AP*, 53: 473.

67 *AP*, 55: 70.

68 *AP*, 55: 76.

69 *AP*, 60: 290–94.

70 *AP*, 66: 4, *AP*, 69: 98.

71 Couthon, *Discours*, p. 5. A puzzled National Assembly was told that the rural National Guards would not enforce decrees held to be fraudulent, that the new laws were not believed to be the work of the Assembly at all but of the former lords. *AP*, 21: 457.

72 *AP*, 55: 72–73, *AP*, 56: 65, 74.

73 The other European powers, when triumphant over French arms, sometimes showed an acceptance of the French definition of the international struggle as a war over feudalism by attempting to undo the emancipatory reforms, as in Hannover, Hesse-Cassel, or the Napoleonic Kingdom of Westphalia. Blum, *End of the Old Order*, pp. 362–70. The most interesting such restoration attempt was in the Austrian-occupied portion of northern France in 1793–94. With the half-hearted support of the Austrian army, lords and ecclesiastics attempted to collect but were largely stymied by peasant evasion of payment. Lefebvre, *Paysans du Nord*, pp. 551–5.

74 Given the variety of rights lords held over peasants, there is some ambiguity in defining just which measure should be taken as initiating effective emancipation. Does one date France's process from the decree of 4–11 August 1789, for example, or from the king's limited abolition of serfdom on his own holdings in 1779? The ambiguities of dating the end points of emancipation are even more hazardous: many emancipatory processes trailed off with monopoly rights or tolls or sometimes other claims still alive and well, for example. As a guide through these and other difficulties in comparative observation, I have largely relied on Blum.

75 Max Bruchet, *L'abolition des droits seigneuriaux en Savoie (1761–1793)* (Annecy, 1908).
76 Blum, *End of the Old Order*, p. 386.
77 Blum, *End of the Old Order*, pp. 219–20, 385–6. Unmarried male servants, for instance, could not leave their employer until 1840 and then only if they were over twenty-eight.
78 Blum, *End of the Old Order*, p. 364.
79 Blum, *End of the Old Order*, pp. 384–5.
80 Blum, *End of the Old Order*, p. 406.
81 This is not to deny that, at points, élites made fearful by the French example may well have delayed or aborted emancipation processes. In Austria, for example, the French Revolution further energized a conservative current that was already successfully combating the reforms of Joseph II. See Ernest Wangermann, *From Joseph II to the Jacobin Trials: Government Policy and Public Opinion in the Habsburg Dominions in the Period of the French Revolution* (Oxford, 1969).
82 G. Spira. "La dernière génération des serfs de Hongrie: L'exemple du comitat de Pest," *Annales: Economies, sociétes, civilisations*, 23 (1968): 366–2.
83 Readers might object, following Figure 8.2, that the great peak of rural unrest immediately preceding the August decrees was not primarily anti-seigneurial. True enough, but the crescendo of rural violence of the second half of July surely concentrated the legislators' minds on taking some action to pacify the countryside.
84 Robert R. Palmer, "Notes on the Use of the Word 'Democracy,' 1789–1799," *Political Science Quarterly*, 68 (1953): 203–26; Otto Brunner, Werner Conze, and Reinhart Koselleck (eds.), *Geschichtlich Grundbegriffe: Historisches Lexikon zur politisch-sozialen Sprach in Deutschland* (Stuttgart, 1972–84), Vol. 1, pp. 821–99; John Dunn, *Western Political Theory in the Face of the Future* (Cambridge, 1993), pp. 1–28.
85 "Night of August 4," in François Furet and Mona Ozouf (eds.), *A Critical Dictionary of the French Revolution* (Cambridge, Mass., 1989), p. 131.
86 On this topic, see Carol Pateman, *The Disorder of Women: Democracy, Feminism and Political Theory* (Stanford, Calif., 1989).
87 Michel Antoine, *Le Conseil du Roi sous le règne de Louis XV* (Paris, 1970), pp. 7–9.

Part IV

GENDER STUDIES

Women, wake up; the tocsin of reason sounds throughout the universe; recognize your rights. The powerful empire of nature is no longer surrounded by prejudice, fanaticism, superstition, and lies. The torch of truth has dispersed all the clouds of folly and usurpation. Enslaved man has multiplied his force and needs yours to break his chains.

Olympe de Gouges
The Declaration of the Rights of Women

9

THE MANY BODIES OF MARIE ANTOINETTE

Political pornography and the problem of the feminine in the French Revolution

Lynn Hunt

Lynn Hunt formulates a new question for historians to ponder, and the answers she develops take scholarship in an exciting direction. She does not ask whether Marie Antoinette was guilty or innocent of the crimes charged against her; nor is she interested per se in why the queen was so hated by the French people even before the Revolution began. Rather, she wonders why such a rich pornographic literature about the queen – reaching as many as 126 pamphlets – infiltrated the country both before and during the revolutionary epoch.

Armed with both feminist and literary criticism at her side, and echoing current debates over the ways in which obscene literature exploits women in our own society, Hunt uses the case of Queen Marie Antoinette to reveal Jacobin attitudes towards gender and sexuality. The queen became emblematic of any woman's attempt to play a public and political role. The revolutionaries tended to view republican politics as an ordinary man's game: not only were monarchs excluded, but all women as well. Here Hunt offers a sharp indictment of revolutionary political culture as being self-consciously masculinist.

* * *

It has long been known that Marie Antoinette was the subject of a substantial erotic and pornographic literature in the last decades of the Old Regime and during the Revolution itself. Royal figures at many times and in many places have been the subject of such writing, but not all royal figures at all times. When royal bodies become the focus of such interest, we can be sure that something is at issue in the larger body politic. As Robert Darnton has

279

shown, for example, the sexual sensationalism of Old Regime *libelles* was a choice means of attacking the entire "establishment" – the court, the church, the aristocracy, the academies, the salons, and the monarchy itself.[1] Marie Antoinette occupies a curious place in this literature; she was not only lampooned and demeaned in an increasingly ferocious pornographic outpouring, but she was also tried and executed.

A few other women, such as Louis XV's notorious mistress Madame Du Barry, suffered a similar fate during the Revolution, but no other trial attracted the same attention or aired the same range of issues as that of the ill-fated queen. The king's trial, in contrast, remained entirely restricted to a consideration of his political crimes. As a consequence, the trial of the queen, especially in its strange refractions of the pornographic literature, offers a unique and fascinating perspective on the unselfconscious presumptions of the revolutionary political imagination. It makes manifest, more perhaps than any other single event of the Revolution, the underlying interconnections between pornography and politics.

When Marie Antoinette was finally brought to trial in October 1793, the notorious public prosecutor, Antoine-Quentin Fouquier-Tinville, delivered an accusation against her that began with extraordinary language, even for those inflamed times:

> In the manner of the Messalinas-Brunhildes, Fredegond and Médecis, whom one called in previous times queens of France, and whose names forever odious will not be effaced from the annals of history, Marie Antoinette, widow of Louis Capet, has been since her time in France, the scourge and the bloodsucker of the French.

The bill of indictment then went on to detail the charges: before the Revolution she had squandered the public monies of France on her "disorderly pleasures" and on secret contributions to the Austrian emperor (her brother); after the Revolution, she was the animating spirit of counter-revolutionary conspiracies at the court. Since the former queen was a woman, it was presumed that she could only achieve her perfidious aims through the agency of men such as the king's brothers and Lafayette. Most threatening, of course, was her influence on the king; she was charged not only with the crime of having had perverse ministers named to office but more significantly and generally with having taught the king how to dissimulate – that is, how to promise one thing in public and plan another in the shadows of the court. Finally, and to my mind most strangely, the bill of indictment specifically claimed that

> the widow Capet, immoral in every way, new Agrippina, is so perverse and so familiar with all crimes that, forgetting her quality of mother and the demarcation prescribed by the laws of nature, she has not stopped short of indulging herself with Louis-Charles Capet, her son, and on the confession of this last, in indecencies whose idea and name make us shudder with horror.[2]

Incest was the final crime, whose very suggestion was cause for horror.

The trial of a queen, especially in a country whose fundamental laws specifically excluded women from ruling, must necessarily be unusual. There was not much in the way of precedent for it – the English, after all, had only tried their king, not his wife – and the relatively long gap between the trial of Louis (in December and January) and that of his queen ten months later seemed even to attenuate the necessary linkage between the two trials. Unlike her husband, Marie Antoinette was not tried by the Convention itself; she was brought before the Revolutionary Criminal Tribunal like all other suspects in Paris, and there her fate was decided by a male jury and nine male judges.[3]

Because queens could never rule in France, except indirectly as regents for under-age sons, they were not imagined as having the two bodies associated with kings. According to the "mystic fiction of the 'King's Two Bodies'" as analyzed by Ernst Kantorowicz, kings in England and France had both a visible, corporeal, mortal body and an invisible, ideal "body politic," which never died. As the French churchman Bossuet explained in a sermon he gave with Louis XIV present in 1662: "You are of the gods, even if you die, your authority never dies. . . . The man dies, it is true, but the king, we say, never dies."[4] It is questionable whether this doctrine still held for French kings by 1793, but it is certain that it never held for French queens. We might then ask why the destruction of the queen's mortal body could have had such interest for the French. What did her decidedly non-mystical body represent? In this chapter, I argue that it represented many things;

Marie Antoinette had, in a manner of speaking, many bodies. These many bodies, hydralike, to use one of the favorite revolutionary metaphors for counter-revolution, were each in turn attacked and destroyed because they represented the threats, conscious and unconscious, that could be posed to the Republic. These were not threats of just the ordinary sort, for the queen represented, not only the ultimate in counter-revolutionary conspiracy, but also the menace of the feminine and the effeminizing to republican notions of manhood and virility.

Most striking is the way in which the obsessive focus on the queen's sexualized body was carried over from the pamphlets and caricatures to the trial itself. In the trial there were frequent references to the "orgies" held at Versailles, which were dated as beginning precisely in 1779 and continuing into 1789. In his closing statement Fouquier-Tinville collapsed sexual and political references in telling fashion when he denounced "the perverse conduct of the former court," Marie Antoinette's "criminal and culpable liaisons" with unfriendly foreign powers, and her "intimacies with a villainous faction."[5] Herman, president of the court, then took up the baton in his summary of the charges against her: he too referred to "her intimate liaisons with infamous ministers, perfidious generals, disloyal representatives of the people." He denounced again the "orgy" at the chateau of Versailles on October 1, 1789, when the queen had presumably encouraged the royal officers present to trample on the revolutionary tricolor cockade. In short, Marie Antoinette had used her sexual body to corrupt the body politic either through "liaisons" or "intimacies" with criminal politicians or through her ability to act sexually upon the king, his ministers, or his soldiers.

In Herman's long denunciation, the queen's body was also held up for scrutiny for signs of interior intentions and motives. On her return from the flight to Varennes, people could observe on her face and her movements "the most marked desire for vengeance." Even when she was incarcerated in the Temple her jailers could "always detect in Antoinette a tone of revolt against the sovereignty of the people."[6] Capture, imprisonment, and the prospect of execution, it was hoped, were finally tearing the veil from the queen's threatening ability to hide her true feelings from the public. Note here, too, the way that Herman clearly juxtaposes the queen and the people as a public force; revelation of the queen's true motives and feelings came not from secrets uncovered in hidden correspondence but from the ability of the people or their representatives to "read" her body.

The attention to the queen's body continued right up to the moment of her execution. At the moment of the announcement of her condemnation to death, she was reported to have kept "a calm and assured countenance," just as she had during the interrogation. On the road to the scaffold, she appeared indifferent to the large gathering of armed forces. "One perceived neither despondency nor pride on her face."[7] More radical newspapers read a different message in her demeanor, but they showed the same attention to her every move. The *Révolutions de Paris* claimed that at the feet of the statue of Liberty (where the guillotine was erected), she demonstrated her usual "character of disimulation and pride up to the last moment". On the way there she had expressed "surprise and indignation" when she realized that she would be taken to the guillotine in a simple cart rather than in a carriage.[8]

The queen's body, then, was of interest, not because of its connection to the sacred and divine, but because it represented the opposite principle – namely, the possible profanation of everything that the nation held sacred. But apparent too in all the concern with the queen's body was the fact that the queen could embody so much. The queen did not have a mystic body in the sense of the king's two bodies, but her body was mystical in the sense of mysteriously symbolic. It could mean so much; it could signify a wide range of threats. Dissimulation was an especially important motif in this regard. The ability to conceal one's true emotions, to act one way in public and another in private, was repeatedly denounced as the chief characteristic of court life and aristocratic manners in general. These relied above all on appearances – that is, on the disciplined and self-conscious use of the body as a mask. The republicans, consequently, valued transparency – the unmediated expression of the heart – above all other personal qualities. Transparency was the perfect fit between public and private; transparency was a body that told no lies and kept no secrets. It was the definition of virtue, and as such it was imagined to be critical to the future of the Republic.[9] Dissimulation, in contrast, threatened to undermine the Republic: it was the chief ingredient in every conspiracy; it lay at the heart of the counter-revolution. Thus, for example, to charge Marie Antoinette with teaching the king how to dissimulate was no minor accusation.

Dissimulation was also described in the eighteenth century as a characteristically feminine quality, not just an aristocratic one. According to both Montesquieu and Rousseau, it was women who taught men how to dissimulate, how to hide their true feelings in order to get what they wanted in the public arena.[10] The salon was the most important site of this teaching, and it was also the one place where society women could enter the public sphere. In a sense, then, women in public (like prostitutes) were synonymous with dissimulation, with the gap between public and private. Virtue could only be restored if women returned to the private sphere.[11] Rousseau had expressed this collection of attitudes best in his *Letter to M. d'Alembert on the Theatre* (1758):

> Meanly devoted to the wills of the sex which we ought to protect and not serve, we have learned to despise it in obeying it, to insult it by our derisive attentions; and every woman at Paris gathers in her apartment a harem of men more womanish than she, who know how to render all sorts of homage to beauty except that of the heart, which is her due.

And, as Rousseau warned ominously about women in the public sphere, "no longer wishing to tolerate separation, unable to make themselves into men, the women make us into women."[12] With her strategic position on the cusp between public and private, Marie Antoinette was emblematic of the much larger problem of the relations between women and the public sphere in the eighteenth century. The sexuality of women, when operating in the public sphere through dissimulation, threatened to effeminize men – that is, literally to transform men's bodies.

Central to the queen's profane and profaning body was the image of her as the bad mother. This might take many, even surprising forms, as in Fouquier-Tinville's charge that she was the calumniator of Paris – described in his closing statement as "this city, mother and conservator of liberty." The queen was the antonym of the nation, depicted by one witness in the trial as the "generous nation that nurtured her as well as her husband and her family."[13] The nation, Paris, and the Revolution were all good mothers; Marie Antoinette was the bad mother. It should be noted, however, that the nation, Paris, and the Revolution were motherly in a very abstract, even non-feminine fashion (in comparison to Marie Antoinette).

The abstractness and non-sexual nature of these political

figures of the mother reinforces what Carole Pateman has telling-
ly described as the characteristic modern Western social contract:

> The story of the original contract is perhaps the greatest tale
> of men's creation of new political life. But this time women
> are already defeated and declared procreatively and politic-
> ally irrelevant. Now the father comes under attack. The
> original contract shows how his monopoly of politically
> creative power is seized and shared equally among men. In
> civil society all men, not just fathers, can generate political
> life and political right. Political creativity belongs not to
> paternity but masculinity.[14]

Thus, *La Nation* had no real feminine qualities; she was not a threatening effeminizing force and hence not incompatible with republicanism. *La Nation* was, in effect, a masculine mother, or a father
capable of giving birth. Marie Antoinette's body stood in the way,
almost literally, of this version of the social contract, since under
the Old Regime she had given birth to potential new sovereigns
herself.[15]

Pateman is unusual among commentators on contract theory
because she takes Freud seriously. As she notes,

> Freud's stories make explicit that power over women and
> not only freedom is at issue before the original agreement is
> made, and he also makes clear that two realms [the civil and
> the private, the political and the sexual] are created through
> the original pact.[16]

She is less successful, however, at explaining the preoccupation
with incest in a case such as Marie Antoinette's.

The charge of incest in the trial was brought by the radical
journalist Jacques-René Hébert, editor of the scabrous *Père Duchesne*, the most determinedly "popular" newspaper of the time.
Hébert appeared at the trial in his capacity as assistant city attorney for Paris, but his paper had been notorious for its continuing
attacks on the queen. Hébert testified that he had been called to
the Temple prison by Simon, the shoemaker who was assigned to
look after Louis's son. Simon had surprised the eight-year-old
masturbating ("indecent pollutions"), and when he questioned
the boy about where he had learned such practices, Louis-Charles
replied that his mother and his aunt (the king's sister) had taught
him. The king's son was asked to repeat his accusations in the

presence of the mayor and city attorney, which he did, claiming that the two women often made him sleep between them. Hébert concluded that

> There is reason to believe that this criminal enjoyment [*jouis-sance* in French, which has several meanings including pleasure, and orgasm] was not at all dictated by pleasure, but rather by the political hope of enervating the physical health of this child, whom they continued to believe would occupy a throne, and on whom they wished, by this maneuver, to assure themselves of the right of ruling afterwards over his morals.

The body of the child showed the effects of this incestuousness; one of his testicles had been injured and had to be bandaged. Since being separated from his mother, Hébert reported, the child's health had become much more robust and vigorous.[17] What better emblem could there be of effeminization than the actual deterioration of the boy's genitals?

As sensational as the charge was, the court did not pursue it much further. When directly confronted with the accusation, the former queen refused to lower herself by responding "to such a charge made against a mother."[18] But there it was in the newspapers, and even the Jacobin Club briefly noted the "shameful scenes between the mother, the aunt, and the son," and denounced "the virus that now runs through [the boy's] veins and which perhaps carries the germ of all sorts of accidents."[19] Since it seems surprising that republican men should be so worried about the degeneration of the royal family, it is not farfetched to conclude that the incest charge had a wider, if largely unconscious, resonance. On the most explicit level, incest was simply another sign of the criminal nature of royalty. As Hébert complained rhetorically to the royalists: "You immolate your brothers, and for what? For an old whore, who has neither faith nor respect for the law, who has made more than a million men die; you are the champions of murder, brigandage, adultery, and incest."[20] Although incest can hardly be termed a major theme in revolutionary discourse, it did appear frequently in the political pornography of both the last decades of the Old Regime and the revolutionary decade itself.[21] Perhaps the most striking example is the pornography of the marquis de Sade, which makes much of incest between fathers and daughters and brothers and sisters.[22]

The official incest charge against the queen has to be set in the context provided by the longer history of pornographic and semi-pornographic pamphlets about the queen's private life. Although the charge itself was based on presumed activities that took place only after the incarceration of the royal family in the Temple prison, it was made more plausible by the scores of pamphlets that had appeared since the earliest days of the Revolution and that had, in fact, had their origins in the political pornography of the Old Regime itself. When the *Révolutions de Paris* exclaimed, "Who could forget the scandalous morals of her private life," or repeated the charges about "her secret orgies with d'Artois [one of the king's brothers], Fersen, Coigny, etc.," the newspaper was simply recalling to readers' minds what they had long imbibed in underground publications about the queen's promiscuity.

Attacks on the queen's morality had begun as early as 1774 (just four years after her arrival in France) with a satirical lampoon about her early morning promenades. Louis XV paid considerable sums in the same year to buy up existing copies in London and Amsterdam of a pamphlet that detailed the sexual impotence of his grandson, the future Louis XVI.[23] Before long, the songs and "little papers" had become frankly obscene, and the first of many long, detailed pamphlets had been published clandestinely. The foremost expert on the subject found 126 pamphlets he could classify in the genre of Marie Antoinette, libertine.[24] Even before the notorious Diamond Necklace Affair of 1785, and continuing long after it, the queen was the focus of an always-proliferating literature of derision preoccupied with her sexual body.[25]

Although fewer than 10 per cent of the anti-Marie Antoinette pamphlets were published before 1789, they often provided the models for later publications.[26] It is difficult to find out much about the publication (the precise dates or location) or authorship of the pre-revolutionary pamphlets, since they were necessarily produced clandestinely. As Robert Darnton has vividly demonstrated, those authors who can be traced were from the French version of Grub Street.[27] Men such as Théveneau de Morande and the count of Paradès worked sometimes for the French crown (as spies), sometimes for rival members of the court, sometimes for foreign printers, and always for themselves. The connection to members of the court is most significant, since it shows the intensity of the interlacing of social networks of communication under the Old Regime. The author of one of the best-known pamphlets, *Portefeuille d'un talon rouge*, made the connection explicit, tracing the circuit from courtiers to their valets, who passed the verses on in the market, where they were picked up by artisans and brought back to the courtiers, who then hypocritically professed surprise.[28] The "popular" images of the queen, then, had their origin in the court, not in the streets.

Politically pornographic pamphlets were often traced to London, Amsterdam, or Germany, where the most notorious of the French Grub Street types made their livings, and the French crown evidently spent large sums having such pamphlets bought up by its agents abroad and destroyed before they could reach France. Indeed, this new industry seems to have become a very lucrative one for those hack writers willing to live abroad, since large sums were paid to secret agents and printers, who·were most likely in collusion with the writers themselves.[29] In 1782 the *Mémoires secrets* described the government's reaction to the recently published *Essais historiques*:

> The dreadful *libelle* against the queen, of which I've spoken
> [in a previous entry], and others of the same genre, have
> determined the government to make an effort on this subject
> and to sacrifice money, which is very distasteful; with this
> help they have gotten to the source and asked for the assist-
> ance of foreign governments. They undertook searches in all
> of the suspect printing shops of Holland and Germany; they
> took away everything that deserved to be, and they have
> even had the printer-booksellers arrested who have taken the
> chance of coming to France to introduce their merchandise;
> they have had them condemned to large fines.[30]

Needless to say, copies still made their way into France; in 1783, 534 copies of *Essais historiques sur la vie de Marie-Antoinette* were officially destroyed at the Bastille prison along with many other offensive productions.[31]

Many of the major accusations against Marie Antoinette were already present in the pre-revolutionary pamphlets. The *Portefeuille d'un talon rouge* (also condemned in 1783) begins in classic eighteenth-century fashion with a preface from the presumed publisher announcing that someone had found a portfolio while crossing the Palais-Royal (the notorious den of prostitution and gambling that was also the residence of the king's cousin, the duke of Orleans, who was assumed to have paid for many of the pamphlets). In it was found a manuscript addressed to Monsieur de la H— of the Académie française. It began, "You are then out of your mind, my dear la H—! You want, they tell me, to write the history of tribades at Versailles." In the text appeared the soon-to-be-standard allegation that Marie Antoinette was amorously involved with the duchesse de Polignac ("her Jules") and Madame Balbi. The comte d'Artois was supposedly the only man who interested her. These charges, as harshly delivered as they were, formed only part of the pamphlet's more general tirade against the court and ministers in general. Speaking of the courtiers, the author exclaimed, "You are an abominable race. You get everything at once from your character as monkeys and as vipers."[32]

The short and witty *Amours de Charlot et de Toinette* took up much the same themes, though in verse, but this time focused exclusively on the queen, the comte d'Artois, and the princesse de Lamballe (who would become the most famous victim of the September Massacres in 1792). Marie Antoinette was depicted as turning to lesbianism because of the impotence of the king. Then she discovers the delights of the king's brother.[33]

The long 1789 edition (146 pages in the augmented French edition) of the *Essai historique sur la vie de Marie-Antoinette* (there had been many variations on the title since its first publication in 1781)[34] already demonstrated the rising tone of personal hostility toward the queen that would characterize revolutionary pornographic pamphlets. In the most detailed of all the anti-Marie Antoinette exposés, it purported to give the queen's own view through the first person: "My death is the object of the desires of an entire people that I oppressed with the greatest barbarism." Marie Antoinette here describes herself as "barbarous queen, adulterous spouse, woman without morals, polluted with crimes and debaucheries," and she details all the charges that had accumulated against her in previous pamphlets. Now her lesbianism is traced back to the Austrian court, and all of the stories of amorous intrigues with princes and great nobles are given substance. Added to the charges is the new one that she herself had poisoned the young heir to the throne (who died in early 1789). Characteristic, too, of many of the later pamphlets will be the curious alternation between frankly pornographic staging – descriptions in the first person of her liaisons, complete with wildly beating hearts and barely stifled sighs of passion – and political moralizing and denunciation put into the mouth of the queen herself. The contrast with the king and his "pure, sincere love, which I so often and so cruelly abused" was striking.[35] The queen may have been representative of the degenerate tendencies of the aristocracy, but she was not yet emblematic of royalty altogether.

With the coming of the Revolution in 1789, the floodgates opened, and the number of pamphlets attacking the queen rapidly rose in number. These took various forms, ranging from songs and fables to presumed biographies (such as the *Essai historique*), confessions, and plays. Sometimes, the writings were pornographic with little explicit political content; the 16-page pamphlet in verse called *Le Godmiché royal* (the royal dildo), for example, told the story of Junon (the queen) and Hébée (presumably either the duchesse de Polignac or the princesse de Lamballe). Junon complained of her inability to obtain satisfaction at home, while pulling a dildo out of her bag ("Happy invention that we owe to the monastery"). Her companion promises her penises of almost unimaginably delicious size.[36] In the much more elaborately pornographic *Fureurs utérines de Marie-Antoinette, femme de Louis XVI* of two years later, colored engravings showed the king impotent and d'Artois and Polignac replacing him.[37]

The Marie Antoinette pamphlets reflect a general tendency in the production of political pornography: the number of titles in this genre rose steadily from 1774 to 1788 and then took off after 1789. The queen was not the only target of hostility; a long series of "private lives" attacked the conduct of courtiers before 1789 and revolutionary politicians from Lafayette to Robespierre afterwards. Aristocrats were shown as impotent, riddled with venereal disease, and given over to debauchery. Homosexuality functioned in a manner similar to impotence in this literature; it showed the decadence of the Old Regime in the person of its priests and aristocrats. Sexual degeneration went hand in hand with political corruption.[38] This proliferation of pornographic pamphlets after 1789 shows that political pornography cannot be viewed simply as a supplement to a political culture that lacked "real" political participation. Once participation increased dramatically, particularly with the explosion of uncensored newspapers and pamphlets, politics did not simply take the high road.[39]

Marie Antoinette was without question the favorite target of such attacks. There were not only more pamphlets about her than about any other single figure, but they were also the most sustained in their viciousness. Henri d'Almeras claimed that the *Essais historiques* alone sold between twenty and thirty thousand copies.[40] The year 1789 does appear to mark a turning-point not only in the number of pamphlets produced but also in their tone. The pre-1789 pamphlets tell dirty stories in secret; after 1789 the rhetoric of the pamphlets begins self-consciously to solicit a wider audience. The public no longer "hears" courtier rumors through the print medium; it now "sees" degeneracy in action. The first-person rendition of the 1789 French edition of *Essai historique* is a good example of this technique.

Obscene engravings with first-person captions worked to the same effect. The engravings that accompanied the long *Vie de Marie-Antoinette d'Autriche, femme de Louis XVI, roi des français; Depuis la perte de son pucelage jusqu'au premier mai 1791*, which was followed by volumes 2 and 3, entitled *Vie privée, libertine, et scandaleuse de Marie-Antoinette d'Autriche, ci-devant reine des français*, are an interesting case in point. They showed Marie Antoinette in amorous embrace with just about everyone imaginable: her first supposed lover, a German officer; the aged Louis XV; Louis XVI impotent; the comte d'Artois; various women; various ménages à trois with two women and a man; the cardinal de Rohan of the Diamond Necklace Affair; Lafayette; Barnave, and so on. The captions are sometimes in the first person (with the princesse de Guéménée: "Dieux! quels transports ah! mon âme s'envole, pour l'exprimer je n'ai plus de parole"), sometimes in the third (with the comte d'Artois: "gémis Louis, ta vigeur inactive, outrage ici ta femme trop lascive"). The effect is the same: a theatricalization of the action so that the reader is made into voyeur and moral judge at the same time. The political effect of the pornography is apparent even in this most obscene of works. In volumes 2 and 3, the pornographic engravings are interspersed with political engravings of aristocratic conspiracy, the assault on the Tuileries palace, and even a curious print showing Louis XVI putting on a red cap of liberty and drinking to the health of the nation in front of the queen and his remaining son and heir.[41]

That the pamphlets succeeded in attracting a public can be seen in the repetition of formulaic expressions in non-pornographic political pamphlets, "popular" newspapers, petitions from "popular societies," and the trial record itself. The *Essai historique* of 1789 already included the soon-to-be-standard comparisons of Marie Antoinette to Catherine de Médecis, Agrippina, and Messalina. These comparisons were expanded at great length in a curious political tract called *Les Crimes des reines de France*, which was written by a woman, Louise de Keralio (though it was published under the name of the publisher, Louis Prudhomme).[42] The "corrected and augmented" edition dated "an II" simply added material on the trial and execution to an already-long version of 1791.[43] The tract is not pornographic; it simply refers to the "turpitudes" committed by the queen as background for its more general political charges. Keralio reviews the history of the queens of France, emphasizing in particular the theme of dissimulation: "The dangerous art of seducing and betraying, perfidious and intoxicating caresses, feigned tears, affected despair, insinuating prayers" (p. 2). These were the weapons of the queens of France (which had been identified as the arms of all women by Rousseau). When the author comes to the wife of Louis Capet, she lists many of the queen's presumed lovers, male and female, but insists upon passing rapidly over the "private crimes" of the queen in favor of consideration of her public ones. Marie Antoinette "was the soul of all the plots, the center of all the intrigues, the foyer of all these horrors" (p. 440). As a "political tarantula," the queen resembled that "impure insect, which, in the darkness, weaves on the right and left fine threads where gnats without experience are caught and of whom she makes her prey" (pp. 445–6). On the next page, the queen is compared to a tigress who, once having tasted blood, can no longer be satisfied. All this to prove what the caption to the frontispiece asserts: "A people is without honor and merits its chains / When it lowers itself beneath the scepter of queens."

The shorter, more occasional political pamphlets picked up the themes of the pornographic literature and used them for straightforward political purposes. A series of pamphlets appeared in 1792, for example, offering lists of political enemies who deserved immediate punishment. They had as their appendices lists of all the people with whom the queen had had "relationships of debauchery." In these pamphlets, the queen was routinely referred to as "mauvaise fille, mauvaise épouse, mauvaise mère, mauvaise reine, monstre en tout" (bad daughter, bad wife, bad mother, bad queen, monster in everything).[44]

292

The movement from sexual misdemeanors to bestial metaphors was characteristic of much "popular" commentary on the queen, especially in her last months. In the *Père Duchesne* Hébert had incorporated the Fredegond and Médecis comparisons by 1791, but still in a relatively innocent context. One of his favorite devices was to portray himself as meeting in person with the queen and trying to talk sense to her.[45] By 1792 the queen had become "Madame Veto," and once the monarchy had been toppled, Hébert made frequent reference to the "ménagerie royale." In prison the former queen was depicted as a she-monkey ("la guenon d'Autriche"), the king as a pig. In one particularly fanciful scene, Père Duchesne presents himself in the queen's cell as the duchesse de Polignac ("cette tribade") thanks to the effect of a magic ring, whereupon the former queen throws herself into her friend's arms and reveals her fervent hopes for the success of the counter-revolution.[46] After her husband had been executed, the tone of hostility escalated, and Marie Antoinette became the she-wolf and the tigress of Austria. At the time of her trial, Hébert suggested that she be chopped up like meat for paté as recompense for all the bloodshed that she had caused.[47]

Local militants picked up the same rhetoric. In a letter to the Convention congratulating it on the execution of the queen, the popular society of Rozoy (Seine-et-Marne department) referred to "this tigress thirsty for the blood of the French . . . this other Messalina whose corrupt heart held the fertile germ of all crimes; may her loathsome memory perish forever." The popular society of Garlin (Basses-Pyrénées department) denounced the "ferocious panther who devoured the French, the female monster whose pores sweated the purest blood of the sans-culottes."[48] Throughout these passages, it is possible to see the horrific transformations of the queen's body; the body that had once been denounced for its debauchery and disorderliness becomes in turn the dangerous beast, the cunning spider, the virtual vampire who sucks the blood of the French.

Explicit in some of the more extreme statements and implicit in many others was a pervasive anxiety about genealogy. For example, the post-1789 pamphlets demonstrated an obsession with determining the true fathers of the king's children (they were often attributed to his brother, the comte d'Artois). In a fascinating twist on this genealogical anxiety, *Père Duchesne* denounced a supposed plot by the queen to raise a young boy who resembled the heir to the throne to take the heir's place.[49] The culminating charge, of course, was incest; in the trial, this was limited to the queen's son, but in the pamphlet literature, the charges of incest included the king's brother, the king's grandfather Louis XV, and her own father, who had taught her "the passion of incest, the dirtiest of pleasures," from which followed "the hatred of the French, the aversion for the duties of spouse and mother, in short, all that reduces humanity to the level of ferocious beasts."[50] Disorderly sexuality was linked to bestialization in the most intimate way.

Promiscuity, incest, poisoning of the heir to the throne, plots to replace the heir with a pliable substitute – all of these charges reflect a fundamental anxiety about queenship as the most extreme form of women invading the public sphere. Where Rousseau had warned that the salon women would turn their "harem of men" into women "more womanish than she," the radical militant Louise de Keralio would warn her readers that "a woman who becomes queen changes sex."[51] The queen, then, was the emblem (and sacrificial victim) of the feared disintegration of gender boundaries that accompanied the Revolution. In his controversial study of ritual violence, René Girard argues that a sacrificial crisis (a crisis in the community that leads to the search for a scapegoat) entails the feared loss of sexual differentiation: "one of the effects of the sacrificial crisis is a certain feminization of the men, accompanied by a masculinization of the women."[52] A scapegoat is chosen in order to reinstitute the community's sense of boundaries. By invoking Girard, I do not mean to suggest that the French Revolution followed his script of sacrificial crisis, or that I subscribe to the nuances of his argument. In fact, the Revolution did not single out a particular scapegoat in the moment of crisis; it was marked instead by a constant search for new victims, as if the community did not have a distinct enough sense of itself to settle upon just one (the king or the queen, for example). Nevertheless, Girard's suggestion that an intense crisis within a community is marked by fears of de-differentiation is very fruitful, for it helps make sense of the peculiar gender charge of the events of the fall of 1793.

The evidence for a feared loss of sexual differentiation in the Revolution is in fact quite extensive. Just two weeks after the execution of the queen (which took place on October 16, 1793), the Convention discussed the participation of women in politics, in particular the women's club called the "Sociéte des républicaines révolutionnaires." The Jacobin deputy Fabre d'Eglantine insisted that "these clubs are not composed of mothers of families, daughters of families, sisters occupied with their younger brothers or sisters, but rather of adventuresses, knights-errant, emancipated women, amazons."[53] The deputy Amar, speaking for the Committee on General Security of the Convention, laid out the official rationale for a separation of women from the public sphere:

> The private functions for which women are destined by their very nature are related to the general order of society; this social order results from the differences between man and woman. Each sex is called to the kind of occupation which is fitting for it. . . . Man is strong, robust, born with great energy, audacity and courage. . . . In general, women are ill suited for elevated thoughts and serious meditations, and if, among ancient peoples, their natural timidity and modesty did not allow them to appear outside their families, then in the French Republic do you want them to be seen coming into the gallery to political assemblies as men do?

To re-establish the "natural order" and prevent the "emancipation" of women from their familial identity, the deputies solemnly outlawed all women's clubs.

In response to a deputation of women wearing red caps that appeared before the Paris city council two weeks later, the well-known radical spokesman (and city official) Chaumette exclaimed:

> It is contrary to all the laws of nature for a woman to want to make herself a man. The Council must recall that some time ago these denatured women, these *viragos*, wandered through the markets with the red cap to sully that badge of liberty. . . . Since when is it permitted to give up one's sex? Since when is it decent to see women abandoning the pious cares of their households, the cribs of their children, to come to public places, to harangues in galleries, at the bar of the senate?

Chaumette then reminded his audience of the recent fate of the "impudent" Olympe de Gouges and the "haughty" Madame

Roland, "who thought herself fit to govern the republic and who rushed to her downfall."[54]

Marie Antoinette was certainly not in alliance with the women of the "Société des républicaines révolutionnaires," with Madame Roland or Olympe de Gouges; they were political enemies. But even political enemies, as Louise de Keralio discovered, shared similar political restrictions if they were women. Keralio herself was accused of being dominated by those same "uterine furies" that beset the queen; by publishing, Keralio too was making herself public. Her detractors put this desire for notoriety down to her ugliness and inability to attract men.[55] As Dorinda Outram has argued, women who wished to participate actively in the French Revolution were caught in a discursive double bind; virtue was a two-edged sword that bisected the sovereign into two different destinies, one male and one female. Male virtue meant participation in the public world of politics; female virtue meant withdrawal into the private world of the family. Even the most prominent female figures of the time had to acquiesce in this division. As Madame Roland recognized, "I knew what role was suitable to my sex and I never abandoned it."[56] Of course, she paid with her life because others did not think that she had so effectively restrained herself from participating in the public sphere.

Read from this perspective on the difference between male and female virtue, the writings and speeches about the queen reveal the fundamental anxieties of republicans about the foundations of their rule. They were not simply concerned to punish a leading counter-revolutionary. They wanted to separate mothers from any public activity, as Carole Pateman argues, and yet give birth by themselves to a new political organism. In order to accomplish this, they had to destroy the Old Regime link between the ruling family and the body politic, between the literal bodies of the rulers and the mystic fiction of royalty. In short, they had to kill the patriarchal father and also the mother.

Strikingly, however, the killing of the father was accompanied by little personal vilification. Hébert's references to the pig, the ogre, or the drunk were relatively isolated; calling the former king a cuckold ("tête de cocu") hardly compared to the insistent denigration of Marie Antoinette.[57] Officials chose not to dwell on the king's execution itself. Newspaper accounts were formal and restrained. On the day of the event, one of the regicide deputies who spoke in the Jacobin Club captured the mood: "Louis Capet has paid his debt; let us speak of it no longer." Most of the visual representations of the execution (medals or engravings) came from outside of France and were meant to serve the cause of counter-revolution.[58] The relative silence about Louis among the revolutionaries reflects the conviction that he represented after all the masculinity of power and sovereignty. The aim was to kill the paternal source of power and yet retain its virility in the republican replacement.

The republican ideal of virtue was profoundly homosocial; it was based on a notion of fraternity between men in which women were relegated to the realm of domesticity. Public virtue required virility, which required in turn the violent rejection of aristocratic degeneracy and any intrusion of the feminine into the public. The many bodies of Marie Antoinette served a kind of triangulating function in this vision of the new world. Through their rejection of her and what she stood for, republican men could reinforce their bonds to one another; she was the negative version of the female icon of republican liberty but nonetheless iconic for the rejection. She was perhaps also an object lesson for other women who might wish to exercise through popular sovereignty the kind of rule that the queen had exercised through royal prerogative. The republican brothers who had overthrown the king and taken upon themselves his mantle did not want their sisters to follow their lead. In this implicit and often unconscious gender drama, the body of Marie Antoinette played a critical, if uncomfortable, role. The bodies of Marie Antoinette could never be sacred by French tradition, but they could certainly be powerful in their own fashion.

NOTES

Source Reprinted from *Eroticism and the Body Politic*, ed. Lynn Hunt (Baltimore: John Hopkins University Press, 1991), pp. 108–30.

1 Robert Darnton, "The High Enlightenment and the Low-Life of Literature," reprinted in *The Literary Underground of the Old Regime* (Cambridge: Harvard University Press, 1982), pp. 1–40, esp. p. 29.
2 I have used the report on the session of 14 October 1793, in the *Moniteur Universel*, 16 October 1793.
3 At least that is how many judges signed the arrest warrant on 14 October 1793 according to the *Moniteur*, 16 October 1793. For the

workings of the Revolutionary Tribunal, see Luc Willette, *Le Tribunal révolutionnaire* (Paris: Denoël, 1981). Since it was not established until March 1793, the tribunal was not in existence at the time of the king's trial.

4 As quoted in Ernst H. Kantorowicz, *The King's Two Bodies: A Study in Mediaeval Political Theology* (Princeton: Princeton University Press, 1957), p. 409, n. 319.

5 *Moniteur*, 27 October 1793, reporting on the trial session of 14 October.

6 *Moniteur*, 27 October 1793.

7 *Ibid.*

8 *Révolutions de Paris*, no. 212 (3 August–28 October 1793).

9 I develop the notion of transparency in a somewhat different context in *Politics, Culture, and Class in the French Revolution* (Berkeley and Los Angeles: University of California Press, 1984), pp. 44–6, 72–4.

10 On the *philosophes'* attitudes toward women, see Paul Hoffmann, *La Femme dans la pensée des lumières* (Paris: Editions Ophrys, 1977), esp. pp. 324–446.

11 I am indebted to the analysis of Joan Landes, *Women and the Public Sphere in the Age of the French Revolution* (Ithaca: Cornell University Press, 1988). Dorinda Outram concludes that the Revolution was committed to anti-feminine rhetoric because it ascribed power in the Old Regime to women. I think that this exaggerates the identification of women with power in the Old Regime, but it nonetheless leads to fruitful reflections about the way in which male revolutionary politicians tried to escape feelings of guilt. See Outram, *"Le Langage mâle de la vertu*: Women and the Discourse of the French Revolution," in *The Social History of Language*, Peter Burke and Roy Porter (eds.), (Cambridge: Cambridge University Press, 1987), pp. 120–35, esp. p. 125.

12 Jean-Jacques Rousseau, *Politics and the Arts: Letter to M. d'Alembert on the Theatre*, Allan Bloom (trans) (Ithaca: Cornell University Press, 1968), pp. 100–1.

13 Quotes from *Moniteur*, 27 October 1793, and 18 October 1793 (the latter the testimony of Roussillon, a barber-surgeon and cannoneer).

14 Carole Pateman, *The Sexual Contract* (Stanford: Stanford University Press, 1988), p. 36.

15 Chantal Thomas argues that the anti-Marie Antoinette pamphlets became especially virulent from the moment of her first pregnancy in 1777 (*La Reine scélérate: Marie-Antoinette dans les pamphlets* [Paris: Editions du Seuil, 1989], p. 40).

16 Pateman, *Sexual Contract*, p. 12.

17 *Moniteur*, 18 October 1793.

18 *Moniteur*, 19 October 1793.

19 *Moniteur*, 20 October 1793.

20 *Père Duchesne*, no. 298 (October 1793).

21 On the last half of the eighteenth century, see Hector Fleischmann, *Les Pamphlets libertins contre Marie-Antoinette* (Paris, 1908 rpt.,

Geneva: Slatkine, 1976), esp. the chapter, "La France galante et libertine à la fin du XVIIIe siécle," pp. 13–36.

22 See, for example, *La Philosophie dans le boudoir*, where Sade offers a defense of incest in the parodic tract "Français, encore un effort si vous voulez être républicains" (Paris: Gallimard, 1976), pp. 229–30.

23 Hector Fleischmann, *Les Pamphlets libertins*, pp. 103–9.

24 Hector Fleischmann, *Marie-Antoinette libertine: Bibliographie critique et analytique des pamphlets politiques, galants, et obscènes contre la reine. Précédé de la réimpression intégrale des quatre libelles rarissimes et d'une histoire des pamphlétaires du règne de Louis XVI* (Paris: Bibliothèque des Curieux, 1911).

25 This essay was written before I had a chance to read the interesting and lively book by Thomas, *La Reine scélérate*. Her account differs from mine in several respects. It is especially strong on the analysis of the anti-Marie-Antoinette pamphlet literature, but has virtually nothing to say about the trial records.

26 Fleischmann gives likely publication dates for the 126 pamphlets that he found in *Marie-Antoinette libertine*, pp. 277ff. These are not all separate pamphlets but include major revised editions. Fleischmann no doubt ignored some pamphlets in existence, but the basic balance of pamphlets is most likely correctly rendered in his bibliography.

27 Darnton, "High Enlightenment and the Low-Life of Literature."

28 *Portefeuille d'un talon rouge, contenant des anecdotes galantes et secrètes de la cour de France* (rpt., Paris: Bibliothèque de Curieux, 1911), p. 22. Based on the edition dated "l'an 178–, De l'Imprimerie du Comte de Paradès." The passage is translated in Robert Darnton, "Reading, Writing, and Publishing," in *Literary Underground*, p. 201. See also *ibid.* p. 248, n. 63.

29 Fleischmann, *Les Pamphlets libertins*, pp. 117–29. See also, Henri d'Almeras, *Marie-Antoinette et les pamphlets royalistes et révolutionnaires: les amoureux de la Reine* (Paris: Librairie Mondiale, 1907), pp. 299–328.

30 As quoted in d'Almeras, *Marie-Antoinette*, pp. 309–10.

31 Fleischmann, *Marie-Antoinette libertine*, p. 64.

32 Quotes from the edition cited in n. 28 above.

33 Sections of the pamphlet are reproduced in d'Almeras, *Marie-Antoinette*, pp. 56–60. According to Maurice Tourneux, this eight-page pamphlet was published in 1779 and it cost 17,400 livres for the crown to have it destroyed. It was reprinted several times after 1789 (*Marie-Antoinette devant l'histoire: Essai bibliographique* (Paris: Leclerc, 1895), p. 42).

34 See d'Almeras, *Marie-Antoinette*, pp. 399–403, for title variations.

35 Quotations from *Essai historique sur la vie de Marie-Antoinette, reine de France et de Navarre, née archiduchesse d'Autriche, le deux novembre 1755: Orné de son portrait, et rédigé sur plusieurs manuscrits de sa main* ("A Versailles, Chez La Montensier [one of her supposed female lovers], Hôtel des Courtisannes," 1789), pp. 4, 8, 19–20. Some have attributed this pamphlet to Brissot, but d'Almeras and Fleischmann both dispute this (d'Almeras, *Marie-Antoinette*, p. 339; Fleischmann,

Marie-Antoinette libertine, pp. 67–70). Fleischmann reports the view that the marquis de Sade wrote the second part of this 1789 edition (p. 68). Earlier in 1789 a shorter, 88-page work titled *Essais historiques sur la vie de Marie-Antoinette d'Autriche, reine de France; pour servir à l'histoire de cette princesse* (London, 1789) struck a much less violent tone. It was not written in the first person and though it discussed the queen's amorous intrigues in detail, it was not particularly pornographic in style. This version was written very much in the vein of attempts to convince the queen of her errors: "Fasse le ciel cependant que ces vérités, si elles sont présentées à cette princesse, puissent la corriger, et la faire briller d'autant de vertus qu'elle l'a fait par ses étourderies" (p. 78).

36 *Le Godmiché royal* (Paris, 1789).

37 The publication page after the title read: "La mère en proscrira la lecture à sa fille. Au Manège. Et dans tous les bordels de Paris, 1791." It is interesting to note that one of the early editions of Sade's *La Philosophie dans le boudoir* includes on its title page the obvious parody: "La mère en prescrira la lecture à sa fille." This was the 1795 London edition. See Pascal Pia, *Les Livres de l'Enfer, du XVIᵉ siècle à nos jours* (Paris: C. Coulet and A. Favre, 1978), 2: 1044.

38 See, for example, *Les Enfans de Sodome à l'Assemblée Nationale* (Paris, 1790), Enfer no. 638, Bibliothèque Nationale. For a general overview emphasizing the contrast between aristocratic degeneracy and republican health, see Antoine de Baecque, "Pamphlets: Libel and Political Mythology," in *Revolution in Print: The Press in France, 1775–1800*, Robert Darnton and Daniel Roche (eds) (Berkeley and Los Angeles: University of California Press, 1989), pp. 165–76.

39 See the remarks by Darnton, esp. p. 33, in "High Enlightenment."

40 He provides no evidence for this assertion, however (d'Almeras, *Marie-Antoinette*, p. 403).

41 Enfer nos. 790–92, Bibliothèque Nationale.

42 The correct attribution was brought to my attention by Carla Hesse. While working on another project, I came across a denunciation that verified Keralio's authorship. The anonymous pamphlet *Les Crimes constitutionnels de France, ou la désolation française, décrétée par l'Assemblée dite Nationale Constituante, aux années 1789, 1790, et 1791. Accepté par l'esclave Louis XVI, le 14 septembre 1791* (Paris: Chez Le Petit et Guillemard, 1792) included the following:

> Dlle de Keralio. Laide, et déjà sur le retour; dès avant la révolution, elle se consolait de la disgrace de ses *cheveux gris* et de l'indifférence des hommes, par la culture paisible des lettres. Ses principes étoient purs alors, et sa conduite ne démentoit point la noble délicatesse de sa famille. Livrée, depuis la révolution aux désordres démagogiques, sans doute aussi dominée par les *fureurs utériées*, elle s'est mariée au nommé Robert, ci-devant avocat, sans talens, sans cause, sans pain, à Givet, et maintenant jacobin-cordelier. Abandonée de sa famille, méprisée des honnêtes gens, elle végète honteusement avec ce misérable, chargé de dettes et

d'opprobres, en travaillant à la page, pour le compte de l'infâme *Prudhomme*, au journal dégoûtant de la révolution de Paris. Les *crimes des reines de France* ont mis le comble à sa honte, ainsi qu'à sa noire méchanceté.

43 The full title of the edition I used is *Les Crimes des reines de France depuis le commencement de la monarchie jusqu'à la mort de Marie-Antoinette; avec les pièces justificatives de son procès* ("Publié par L. Prudhomme, avec Cinq gravures. Nouvelle édition corrigée et augmentée. Paris: au Bureau des Révolutions de Paris, an II").

44 See, for example, *Têtes à prix, suivi de la liste de toutes les personnes avec lesquelles la reine a eu des liaisons de débauches*, 2nd ed. (Paris, 1792), 28 pp., and the nearly identical *Liste civile suivie des noms et qualités de ceux qui la composent, et la punition dûe à leurs crimes . . . et la liste des affidés de la ci-devant reine* (Paris, n.d., but Tourneux dates it 1792).

45 *Père Duchesne*, no. 36.

46 *Père Duchesne*, no. 194.

47 *Père Duchesne*, nos. 296 and 298.

48 As quoted by Fleischmann, *Marie-Antoinette libertine*, p. 76.

49 *Père Duchesne*, no. 36 (1791).

50 *Vie privée, libertine et scandaleuse*, as reprinted in Fleischmann, *Marie-Antoinette libertine*, pp. 173–4. This section concludes with the most extreme of all possible epitaphs: "Ci-gît l'impudique Manon, Qui, dans le ventre de sa mère, Savait si bien placer son c—, Qu'elle f— avec son père."

51 [Keralio] *Les Crimes*, p. vii.

52 Rena Girard, *Violence and the Sacred*, Patrick Gregory (trans.) (Baltimore: Johns Hopkins University Press, 1977), p. 141.

53 *Réimpression de l'Ancien Moniteur*, 18: 290 (session of 8 Brumaire, year II, 29 October 1793).

54 Quotes from Darline Gay Levy, Harriet Branson Applewhite, and Mary Durham Johnson, *Women in Revolutionary Paris, 1789–1795* (Urbana: University of Illinois Press, 1979), pp. 215–16, 219–20.

55 See quotation in n. 42 above.

56 Outram, "*Le Langage mâle de la vertu*," p. 125, quotation from p. 126. See also the chapter on "Women and Revolution," in Landes, *Women and the Public Sphere*, pp. 93–151.

57 *Père Duchesne*, no. 180, for example.

58 Lynn Hunt, "The Sacred and the French Revolution," in *Durkheimian Sociology: Cultural Studies*, Jeffrey C. Alexander (ed.) (Cambridge: Cambridge University Press, 1988), pp. 25–43, quotation from p. 32.

10

IN SEARCH OF COUNTER-REVOLUTIONARY WOMEN

Olwen Hufton

The nationalization of the French Catholic Church was one of the most controversial programs begun by the Constituent Assembly. The French government took control of all churches, transforming priests into civil servants, and ordering them to take loyalty oaths to the new nation. The bold move split the clergy down the middle – those who joined the new "Constitutional Church" became known as "juring" clergy; those who refused are called "non-juring" clergy. After France went to war with Austria in 1792, the non-juring clergy became suspected of treason and counter-revolutionary activity. They were often persecuted by government officials and expelled from their parishes. By the fall of Robespierre and the beginning of Thermidor (July 1794), the Constitutional Church had failed to attract most Frenchmen. The religious situation in France was in disarray. What happened next is the subject of Olwen Hufton's fascinating research: ordinary French women, mostly peasants, took back their church from the revolutionaries.

Peasant women, of course, made up a large sector of the French population, but until recently, their experiences in the French Revolution have been ignored. Olwen Hufton seeks to address that gap, despite the difficulty in finding sources that allow these women to speak for themselves, and the variation of conditions from region to region. For Hufton's peasant women, the French Revolution is not their friend: it is clearly their adversary. The Revolution is a constant bother to them, disrupting their lives in ways that make them resentful of its ideals. The Revolution persecuted the clergy and nearly ruined the Catholic Church in France, something dear to the hearts of these peasant women. The Revolution disrupted the peasant economy, making it difficult for women to sell what few goods they took to market and secure what they needed for their families. The Revolution took away their sons and marched them off to war. Rarely, if ever, did the Revolution bring Hufton's peasant women anything to cheer about.

Like Lynn Hunt, Hufton understands a feminist history to be more than just the history of women per se. Ordinary women may have operated far differently than did male politicians, but they nonetheless had a deep and permanent effect on the outcome of the revolutionary crisis. Here Hufton reveals women at the center of the Revolution by showing how the struggle to control the Catholic Church became a gendered process: women saw themselves (and were seen by Jacobins) as the defenders of the faith, and helped to rescue the Church from its near ruin by the Jacobin regime.

Hufton's women did not take events passively. They organized popular resistance, sabotaged revolutionary efforts where they could, and generally put up a struggle against the encroachment of the new centralized government wherever possible. Most of all, they took their faith into their own hands, regenerating a French Catholic Church that would thrive in the nineteenth century. Clearly, Hufton admires these women. In the end they maintained their own lifestyle as best they could, and while the Revolution may have succumbed to Napoleon's dictatorship, Hufton declares the women's struggle a "victory."

* * *

The Revolution . . . was not an optional experience to be embraced or rejected at will. Historians still search for the village which emerged totally unscathed by events. The bulk of French people were, of course, peasants. They lived in scattered hamlets or nuclear villages. They did not have the opportunity to participate in anything approaching a revolutionary *journée* but as taxpayers and suppliers of cannon fodder, they were called upon to defend the Revolution against its enemies. It was also unlikely that they would escape the excesses of Parisian or city revolutionary zeal. The peasant woman, however, has been somewhat neglected by historians of both sexes. This is unfortunate because, arguably, the response of this woman to the Revolution is critical.

We meet her only fleetingly in the history of the Revolution before 1795. She emerges here and there from as early as 1790–1 as the target of minor urban demonstrations in the market for her refusal to surrender milk, cheese, and eggs for *assignats* (paper money), in demonstrations to try to prevent the sale of common land and the abolition of traditional rights of gleaning and harvesting which were often an important part of the family

303

economy of many peasant households. Above all, from 1791, she moves into the defense of traditional religion and its priesthood. In so doing, this woman is transformed little by little into a counter-revolutionary and in due course becomes part of the counter-revolution with a distinctive role to play.

During the bicentenary, an event which above all celebrated discourse and the use of terms, there was considerable debate on what should be considered counter-revolutionary and what anti-revolutionary. Such fine distinctions were not applied by con-temporaries who used the term counter-revolutionary as they did. aristocrat with a conspicuous generosity and contempt for preci-sion. Even Jacques Roux, the militant of militants, was a counter-revolutionary in the mouths of the Jacobins. The women who are the concern here and were designated counter-revolutionary in the reports of police and government officials were not like the *chouans* those who took to the woods to make war on the Republic or who sought to establish an unmodified ancien régime or even those who in the cause of the White Terror were ready to dis-member the bodies of former Jacobin officials. They were more modest personnages who were prepared to turn their backs on the national line. Women who boycotted the mass of the consti-tutional priest, who in the hard years of 1793–4 organized clan-destine masses, who continued to slap a cross on the forehead of the newborn, who placed a Marian girdle on the stomach of the parturient, and who gathered to say the rosary and taught their children their prayers were all committing counter-revolutionary offenses. These women did not name their children after Marat. They continued to hallow a pantheon of saints in the way they had always done. If their husbands elected to buy favor by honor-ing a local official in the naming of their offspring, they slipped a saint's name on as well. They did not when they breast-fed their children reflect that they were endowing them with sound revo-lutionary principles and a hatred of aristocrats. They resented the *décadi* which destroyed traditional sociability patterns. They buried their relatives secretly at the dead of night. They probably encouraged their sons to defect and they certainly did not send their children to state schools. Unlike revolutionary woman, who was a product of the big cities and the revolutionary *journées* and who had her heyday in 1793 and can be thought about as an architect of the Revolution and as deeply committed to the triumph of popular sovereignty, counter-revolutionary woman evolved slowly. She surfaced in the countryside, in some areas sooner than others, or in the small town which knew it was not a priority in the government's provisioning schemes. She began to win after 1795 though the victory was far from absolute or clear cut. Ultimately, however, she could claim to have made a significant contribution to the reversal of the national record. She nullified all attempts by the Directory to re-establish the rule of law by setting at nought its attempts to tolerate a Catholicism which would pronounce its loyalty to the state and by rendering null its attempts through a state-based civic education to create citizens in a patriotic mould, emancipated from the preconceptions of the past. Against change she posited tradition. She gave practical expression to a dicton existing in many provincial patois: "Les hommes font les lois; les femmes les traditions."[1]

This is the woman in revolution whose specter will haunt the politicians of the nineteenth century and serve to confirm them in their efforts to deny women the vote. Certainly, this woman has significance in the history of the Roman Catholic Church for it is her commitment to her religion which determines in the post-thermidorean period the re-emergence of the Catholic church on very particular terms, which included an express rejection of state attempts to control a priesthood and the form of public worship. Counter-revolutionary woman is therefore of consequence in the ongoing religious and political history of France.

Who was she and how does one find out about her? Richard Cobb was able to re-create the sans-culotte from his utterings and voluble disquisitions in the *sociétés populaire*, in the sections, and in police reports: a revolutionary man emerged clearly from his utterings. Such a direct re-creation of counter-revolutionary woman is impossible. When she speaks it is through the official who recounts her misdeeds and such officials, as Cobb reminded us in his study *The Police and the People*, were not dispassionate or innocent reporters. Cobb pointed out that an official report was written with an eye to impressing one's superiors if the official wanted to advance in state service. Objectivity was a low priority when promotion was the official's desideratum.[2] In short, any text we are proffered from this type of source needs careful scrutiny, not least when an official recounts his dealings with women and is conscious that his comportment may be judged according to different criteria from those used if he were dealing with men.

When officials encountered women and described their flout-ings of the law to their superiors, they might, in order to maintain their own image, proffer a distorted version to preserve their own reputation. For example, the description of a local response to the inauguration of the feast of the Supreme Being which ran: "Quelques femmelettes ont fait des propos inciviques" (Some lit-tle women made uncivic remarks) might refer to several dozens of screaming women telling an official exactly what to do with the new deity. The allegation that in a small village of no more than two hundred inhabitants, an official ceded the keys of the church in 1796 to several hundreds of fanatical women who threw him to the ground and tore his clothes might mean that the weary official was tired of standing his ground against reiterated insults and petitioning but needed to convince his superiors that he had ceded to *force majeure* (majority rule). To cite a mere dozen might reveal him for a coward. Or, he might employ a series of euphem-isms to cloak the truth. We need to have recourse to specific examples. "La religion a semé la division dans les familles" (Religion has sown division in families) might be one way of saying that the men are loyal to the religious policy of the Repub-lic but the women are not. What does one make of the Jacobin official who in the post-Thermidor months found it needful to comment on the loyalty of his colleagues in the following way: "il est bon patriot quoi qu'il envoie sa femme à la messe" (He is an excellent patriot although he *sends* his wife to mass)? Does this mean that the man had to seem to control his family if he was to hold an official position or does it mean that the Jacobin mayor had despaired of finding anyone whose wife did not go to mass to fill an official position?[3]

We also have to account for the evident scorn of officialdom in the heady days of the Jacobin dictatorship for what they inter-preted as women's practises. When, in the year II, it was part of national policy to explain through the national agents *les bienfaits de la Révolution* (the benefits of the Revolution) to those villages and hamlets clearly less than 50 per cent committed to national policies, the rhetoric of persuasion stressed the following: first, that the Revolution represented a victory over political tyranny; second, that it achieved the equality of men; third, that it estab-lished the freedom of the individual; and fourth, that it secured the triumph of reason over "fanatisme." In this discourse, a model *homme/patriot, femme/fidèle aux prêtres* (man/patriot, woman/loyal to priests) was allowed to surface. Officialdom clung to the notion that men would embrace the Revolution and that, in the natural order of things, women would in due course follow their husbands. It wallowed in an anti-feminism which was indubitably latent in all politicians and which fed on the experience of resistance to its policies. It expected men to see the logic of its arguments. Young men must die for its principles; the rest must make personal sacrifices in the shape of money and goods and wage an unremitting war on the partisans of the old order, who were those who could not accept the crystal-clear logic of *civisme* (republican patriotism), who did not respect the maximum, who made *propos inciviques* (impolitic proposals), or who behaved like women and went to church. It was in the course of this discourse that rural France heard perhaps for the first time the words *philosophie* and *raison* and that age-old practices were *superstition, momerie, fanatisme,* that peasants were the dupes of the enemies of the state. The discourse also made abundantly clear that peasants were considered idiots by the central authority but idiots who could be coaxed or bullied into acceptance of the official line, and the biggest idiots of all in their persistent irrationality were peasant women. When dealing with women, officialdom gave vent to its latent anti-feminism in a vocabulary of abuse. Virtually unable to call a woman a woman, it used instead derisive derivatives like *femelles, femelettes, bigotes, bêtes, bêtes de laine, moutons, lentilles, légumineuses, fanatiques*.[4] These are merely a few of the more common nouns which were used in this discourse. The adjectives were still more graphic. Woolly-minded and with an intelligence equivalent to that of a farm animal, the peasant was seen as epitomizing ignorance and stupidity. The general questionnaire sent around in January 1794 to all the districts enquired very closely about local reactions to religious change. The rhetorical vocabulary involved transmits the flavor:

> *Question:* Has the sublime movement of the people against superstition encountered obstacles in its development?[5]
> *Answer:* The sublime movement of the people against superstition has met with very considerable obstacles in its development, [no prizes for saying yes]. We do not believe that these are produced by anything more than ancient prejudices which are always very difficult to overcome when one is dealing with the peasant mind because they are a product of ignorance.[6]

This questionnaire was sent out during the early phases of the dechristianizing campaign; within weeks, the peasant mind in official documents was to be presented not merely as ignorant but also as gendered. There was hope for re-educating the men, as far as officialdom was concerned; women were another matter.

Was the division of men and women in this way by officialdom consonant with the realities? Does available evidence show that officialdom based its analysis on hard evidence or deep-rooted anti-feminism? In other words, did the discourse create the issue? Can one weed out fact from fantasy?[7]

It is very obvious that the notion of irrational woman has a venerable history. It is as old as Greek medical treatises, was reaffirmed in renaissance thought, and persisted into modern times. The Enlightenment which immersed woman in nature and made her the creation of her reproductive organs was not prepared to put her on the same rational footing as men. Yet did the promotion of a contrast between manly commitment and female hostility to religious change, justified by reference to the differential reasoning power of the two, itself create a dichotomy of behavior between the two? In other words, if the hostility of women is assumed in the rhetoric do women seize upon the role allotted to them? Did the origins of what French religious sociologists have called *le dimorphisme sexuel* (the differential attitude to religious practice between the sexes) conspicuous in the nineteenth and twentieth centuries spring from revolutionary discourse?

Michel Vovelle in his recent study *La Révolution contre l'Eglise* (Paris 1989) is prepared to give serious consideration to the notion that officialdom created the model of the superstitious priest who controlled woman in order to further his own ends and that this effort may have created new problems. He stresses that the *représentants en mission* and local patriots, when dealing with communities of a traditionally anticlerical disposition, might use gender difference to make a bid for the minds of men.[8] To reinforce this notion one might add that whenever the overthrow of the Catholic faith was mooted the terms used assumed an explicitly masculine quality. In November 1793, for example, the section of Gravilliers proclaimed to the Convention that it had closed its churches, which had served as lairs for filthy beasts who devoured wealth which should have fed young families and introduced desolation and division into the home. "Leur enceinte à jamais consacré à la vérité, ne retentira plus que de la voix des

Républicains qui instruiront leurs frères, que des mâles accents du patriotisme honorant la raison."[9]

Some specialist studies of dechristianization show that in particular localities – the Seine et Oise provides the most striking instances – women shared with men in iconoclastic orgies. Yet, when they did so, as in Paris, there could often be considerable ambivalence. When, for example, Saint Eustache in the middle of Les Halles was desecrated, two hundred or more women defended the baptismal chapel and their boast at the end of the day was that the altar cloth was still spotless.[10] The presence of sans-culotte women at mass was not uncommon and many expressed unfaltering allegiance to a personage known as *la bonne petite mère* (the good little mother), no less than Mary, the suffering mother of God who also lost her son in a good cause. Such devotion, however, could and did coexist with considerable hatred for particular priests and the higher echelons of the ecclesiastical hierarchy.[11]

In the century preceding the Revolution in most rural parishes a near totality of men and women observed, however perfunctorily, their religious obligations. Those who did not do so rarely accounted for more than 5–6 per cent of the parish and in the extreme west (the Vendée, Brittany, the Cotentin), the east (Alsace, Franche Comté and Lorraine), and Flanders, they were virtually non-existent. In a north to center block (including the Ile de France, the Seine Valley, Champagne and Western Burgundy, the Auvergne and the Limousin) enclaves could be found with a mixed commitment to regular practice and a significant discrepancy *could* (though this was not necessarily the case) exist between the conformity of adult men and women in respect of Lenten confession and Sunday observance. For example, at Mennecy near Gonesse (Seine et Oise) 91 of 198 male householders, 149 of 198 married women, 28 of 66 bachelors over the age of 25, and a totality of widows and spinsters performed their Easter duties. As one moved further south to the Midi, marked contrasts between localities occurred. There were pious mountains and impious garrigues, often *frontières de catholicité* (areas maintaining the faith against the onslaught of Protestantism in an earlier era) and villages of the plains and foothills which could be indifferent to religious demands, some of them perhaps former bastions of heresy which had been forced to express some conformity to Catholicism and which only had a very weak commitment.[12]

The Revolution, however, seems at least in a majority of areas to have accentuated the difference in the commitment of men and women to regular religious practice though we need to make allowances for much local variation and in many cases the difference may only have been one of degree. After 1801 and the formal re-establishment of the Roman Catholic Church in France, it was clear that there was a considerable difference in the degree of preparedness of both communities and individuals to return to regular religious worship. As the curé of Ars acknowledged, the battle for the minds of men – who had after all lacked religious instruction in youth or belonged to the revolutionary armies – was much harder to win. In the context of the Revolution, the phenomenon of female commitment and male rejection became clearly visible though we must acknowledge significant regional variation.

From what point in the Revolution does the phenomenon manifest itself? Is there a point at which one can see women rather than men contesting the dismantling of an institution which had been a conspicuous point of reference in their lives? It had, after all, hallowed the great events of life – birth, marriage, and death – as well as vaunted the virtues of Catholic motherhood.

There is evidence, though it is much more striking in some areas than others, of women demonstrating early hostility to "intruder" priests in 1790–1 (those who replaced the non-jurors as parish clergy). Where the incumbent in 1789 was popular and where he made a personal decision not to accept the oath, then his decision could result in riotous incidents when officialdom read out the notification of legislation insisting that such an oath be taken in front of the parish.[13] At this stage, the principles involved in the oath of loyalty to the constitution probably meant very little to the women of the parish. Some priests held special meetings to explain their decisions to their parishioners. The theological niceties involved when they rejected the oath were then spelled out. Particularly pious spinsters or widows who were often the main support of the parish priest and also deeply involved in philanthropic work circulated anti-oath pamphlets and in some towns, such as Strasbourg, actually organized petitions and processions in protest against the obligatory nature of the oath. Perhaps more often, however, the devotion of rural women was to an individual. The spirit of the congregation at La Madeleine in

Bayeux who yelled out to the priest "jurez ou ne jurez pas, cela ne nous fait rien du tout"[14] may be totally representative. Where the local priest was prepared to take the oath, as initially about half of them did, then friction was clearly postponed. The non-juror who found himself ousted from his presbytery used his firm supports, notably widows and spinsters, to participate in an alternative mass either in the parish church at an unseasonal hour or in a convent chapel. Not only did such activity strip the juror of his congregation but it also ensured that babies were not brought to him for baptism and he was not sought to administer the last rites or burial services. These women did not use the juror's confessional and they did not discourage their sons from assaults on his property. Lacking any influence over village education or control of charitable funds, the constitutional priest became a fervent critic of the behavior of the women of the parish and an active proponent of a harsher line towards non-jurors. It is from this point that we have the first written complaints from juring priests and administrators about fanatical women who were exercising their influence over their husbands or destroying domestic harmony or even leaving their husbands altogether. Very occasionally in these reports, the fear of the quasi-sexual power and attraction of the parish priest over women exercised through the confessional surfaces as it had done under the old regime and would again do *ad nauseam* in the second half of the nineteenth century.[15] Such correspondence embodied commentaries on the inherent female attachment to religion. The juring clergy in their frustration fell back on Eve, declared this time to be influenced through a serpent called the non-juror.

When in the summer of 1792, the non-jurors had to choose between flight or hiding, their parishioners did not necessarily flock back to their parish church to hear the juror. Some sought out a priest in hiding – though how many were able to do so is a matter of considerable speculation. Chanoine Flament identified about 400 refractory priests performing services in the Orne, 300 in the Haute Loire, and 100 or more in the Sarthe throughout the Revolution.[16] Such figures, however, must be impressionistic and how frequently clandestine masses were held cannot even be guessed. Until the autumn of 1793 the juring clergy, their salary well in arrears and their future compromised by the dechristianizing surge emanating from the Paris sections, nonetheless continued to proffer their services.

After the spring of 1794, however, even the availability of a juror's mass was not to be taken for granted. The dechristianizing campaign had silenced the jurors and the marriage of priests and ceremonial burnings of *lettres de prêtrise* (documents bestowing priesthood) had destroyed whatever shred of credibility remained to the church created by the Constituent Assembly. Where a clandestine ceremony occurred, it was held in a private house or barn or illicit chapel and depended upon the complicity or ignorance of local officials and the energy of villagers in carrying out an exercise which could put them in danger of arrest. Such masses were celebrated with least risk in villages distant from prying urban officialdom or were held in a particular household by invitation from the individuals who were hiding the priest. Widows and former members of congregations emerged as those most likely to run the risk of priest-sheltering.[17]

Along with the disappearance of a regular mass went the silencing of the parish bell, which had not only been the most constant reminder of religious obligation but had also symbolized community solidarity and had warned of common dangers. On Fridays or Saturdays, it had been commonly rung to call the faithful to confession. Now such a spiritual exercise was rarely available and the habit of confession was generally lost. Nor was there any priest to administer the last rites or to offer catechetical instruction.

What is also abundantly documented is the attack on the old religion in the name of reason. Dechristianization began in Paris and was exported by officialdom, in some instances with an intensity befitting a witch-hunt, which far exceeded anything sanctioned by the government. Sometimes, initiatives were local and emanated from the *sociétés populaires* (popular clubs). More often, an ambitious local official, anxious to make his reputation as a patriot and buttressed by an enthusiastic *représentant en mission* emanating from Paris, took initiatives. The *armées révolutionnaires* used iconoclasm and signs of rejection of the old religion as a test of revolutionary commitment.

Conscious of the antagonizing effect of the destruction of the traditional faith upon some of the rural communities, the Robespierrist response was to attempt a substitute devotion based on rationality. There followed from June 1794 a series of state cults – Liberty, Reason, the Supreme Being – all of them promoted as the worship of the rational.

It is pertinent at this point to consider the role played by religion in the lives of the rural masses and in particular to examine the attraction of reason as an abstract notion supplanting the belief in the supernatural in a traditional village. Just what, one might reasonably ask, is rational about life? Some are born crippled or blind, some sick; some get good husbands, some end up with a wife-beater; some are fertile and some are barren. Rural society lived with the vagaries of the seasons, with drought, with hailstorms which could devastate a crop in an hour. It knew and was powerless against grain weevils or cattle pest. It still knew periodic visitations of epidemics from smallpox to viral pneumonia which could eliminate young and old. Some women died in childbirth; some found the exercise almost effortless. Viewed in this way, life was not rational but a grisly lottery in which the stakes were especially weighted against the poor.

To cope with ever imminent, if not inevitable, disaster, Europeans had over the centuries addressed a supreme if fitful orchestrator through the intercession of a priest who commanded knowledge of the relevant rites and practices. Christians also believed that the deity could be swayed by penitence and supplication to saints and above all to Mary. Marianism was by the eighteenth century perhaps strongest amongst women. Devotion to a woman who had been elected by this terrible god to bear his son in a stable and who had lost a son under terrible circumstances, who knew human suffering, and who, most of all, was prepared to mediate on behalf of suffering women with a male deity who could be manipulated – like most men – through his mother was an intrinsic part of the cult for women. As the Roman Catholic faith progressively became a fortress faith it was driven back into the home and hence largely into the hands of women. It became a faith based on the rosary with its ten Hail Marys for the one Our Father. The rosary was the perfect expression of a fortress faith. It offered the one means whereby the simple and illiterate, stripped of a priesthood and the familiar rituals of church ceremony, could maintain contact with their deity and could do so collectively. The congregation was replaced by the smaller unit of the family or the work group gathered, perhaps, for a *veillée* (evening get-together for work in a particular house, partly to economize on heat and light and partly for company). In some regions such as the lacemaking areas of the Velay or Lower Normandy, or areas characterized by high seasonal male migration like the

Pyrénées or Savoie, or where male sociability patterns focused on the *cabaret* (tavern), these meetings could be entirely female in composition. The recitation of the rosary, for centuries encouraged by churchmen, now gained new significance as the expression of a corporate faith. Many local officials and even the emmissaries of the Comité de Salut Public, the *représentants en mission*, knew about but were prepared to turn a blind eye to such practices. "Let them have their rosaries," wrote one *représentant* to the Comité de Salut Publique, "they will eventually weary of the ridiculous practice and will give it up." Perhaps such tolerance emanated from the uneasy realization that the wives and mothers of patriots were to be counted amongst the bead-tellers. Or, the exercise, when merely performed by women, was perceived to carry no threat. In short, and this did not pass unacknowledged by authority, the faith feminized. It also Marianized.[18] The rosary was not the only expression of this Marianization. The Mother of God herself appeared in woods and grottoes, tearfully denouncing the work of the Revolution and the assaults on her personage.

Unlike warm and familiar Mary, the official goddesses seemed ice maidens, quite incapable of contributing anything to the business of living or the business of dying. They commanded no hotline to the deity, no proven record in the alleviation of labor pains or the extermination of grain weevils. Frequently personified, if one could be found, by a young girl whose virginity was deemed beyond question, the goddesses were earthbound, a religious travesty, a living testimony to the ridiculousness of a religion based on reason.

The government knew women were not convinced by the changes, just as it was aware that women had most energetically opposed intruder priests and had persistently boycotted the constitutional church. It knew too that there existed rites and practices specific to women which were part of a long process of acculturation. During parturition, for example, a Marian girdle was placed on the mother's heaving stomach to help her in her agony. In Messidor of the year II, an article appeared in the *Moniteur* which included the following statement: "Under a good constitution and a pure sky the parturient mother thinks of the constitution and feels no pain."[19] One wonders how many put this notion to the test. Very clearly, however, the women's world of rituals impenetrable by the merely male caused a disconcerting shudder, or perhaps no more than a transitory sensation of impotence, amongst the politicians.

The central government did try to offer new ceremonies and festivals to fill what it perceived to be a void. These were, however, largely confined to the large towns. Some local authorities were more cognizant of the need to provide an alternative sociability than others. The "Société Populaire de Charolles," for example, on 24 Pluviose an II commented on the dissatisfaction and riotous behavior of women in communes where *les autels de fanatisme* (the altars of fanaticism) had been destroyed. A debate followed which asked the question: why did women behave in this way? Was it because they had a greater taste for mysticism than men? Of course not. What were the realities of Sunday? Old women walked to church and gossiped with other women and shared meals. This last was important for widows. Young girls went along enthusiastically to gape at the boys in a protected environment. On the *décadi*, in contrast, men went to the tavern, which could never be a suitable place for women and consequently they were left grumbling at home. One solution proposed to win over the women was a dance every *décadi* which could be chaperoned by the old. This would provide women with an acceptable alternative social outlet and hence render the old religious practices redundant.[20]

Such debates, however, did not solve the immediate problem of what was often a source of bitter contention between women in the parishes and officialdom, the issue of the closure of the church. The government and local officials, perhaps in default of alternative strategies, chose the immediate tactic of appealing to the men and hence attempting to isolate the women from them. Then, and perhaps more persistently from the mid-nineties, it also tried a policy designed to remold the acculturation of the French citizen.

Yet, in spite of knowing and becoming increasingly aware of women's resentment at the destruction of a conventional religion, in the year III when officialdom called upon men to stand up and be counted through oaths of loyalty and *certificates de civisme*, it made no such demands of women. It held that theirs was the private sphere and it was their husbands' job to exercise control. They were not citizens, that is, those partaking of the political, but citizenesses, owing first allegiance to the responsible citizen in the shape of husband or father. Their relationship to politics placed them at one remove. Let the citizen bring them to obedience.

Some clubs and *sociétés populaires* encouraged men to force their wives into gestures of contempt for the Catholic faith. For such efforts the officials were subsequently to pay dearly. The insistence of the *société populaire* at Arles, for example, that every male householder bring his wife to a ceremony where they could spit in unison upon the host to show that he was a patriot husband in control of his household, may help to explain why these officials were so brutally murdered during the White Terror.[21] Certainly, the attitude of the central government was that male obedience was the priority and that the obedience of irrational woman was of less significance. A woman's acts were in the first instance to be regulated by her husband. This existence at one remove from state control may have opened up some scope for subversive activity: the actions of women were to a degree condoned. This should not, however, be taken too far. Women died on the scaffold for their beliefs, if not as often as did men, and there is nothing, as Olympe de Gouges pointed out, apolitical about the guillotine.

The Terror not only demanded an appraisal of how one felt about the Revolution but also, by a new intrusiveness, applied the letter of revolutionary law with a new determination. It came forward with a new brand of officialdom prepared to push the law in some instances far beyond the intention of the Comité de salut public and this officialdom dominated departmental and local authorities and the *société populaires*. This officialdom defined itself as the agent of reason, the disciple of philosophy. It took upon itself the function of converting the people, if need be through force and confrontation. It is from the pens of this officialdom that our version of counter-revolutionary woman emerges. It is not a neutral source, for this macho culture dreaded loss of face and sought scapegoats for its failures.[22] Nevertheless, it did not invent counter-revolutionary women and though we need to be hypercritical of the evidence, it cannot be ignored.

The examples which will now be used are proffered to re-create the figure of the counter-revolutionary woman from the Haute Loire.[23] We are fortunate to be able to draw on the maps of Michel Vovelle and Timothy Tacket to follow the ripples of the dechristianizing movement. The Haute Loire was not as tranquil as the Aube or the Pas de Calais but nor was it as immediately oppositional as the Vendée, Franche Comté or the Lyonnais. It did not come out in open revolt like its neighbor, the Gévaudan and it worried the government less than did the contiguous Puy de

316

Dôme. It is an area of impenetrable gorges, crags, with mountain streams and inadequate roads. It is not an easy place to penetrate and one might have thought it possible to live out one's life there relatively untroubled by the Revolution. Terror, after all, was without doubt at its most successful on flat land where communications were good and news of insubordination traveled easily.[24] However, the area was to experience a group of ambitious local officials, the home-brewed equivalent of Maximilien de Robespierre, headed by Solon Reynaud, an ex-priest, one time mayor of Le Puy (1789), later in control of the department and Paris deputy, who chose to try to make his reputation in the area. He spoke of himself as the Couthon of the Haute Loire and hence was to confront the practices of the past in a particularly nasty and authoritarian manner. The department boasted the greatest number of guillotined priests in France. Moreover this was a region whose economy suffered particularly in the context of Revolution. It was a lacemaking economy directed and worked by women. These two factors allow us perhaps to paint a counter-revolutionary woman in very vivid oils rather than more delicate pastels. La Ponote and the woman of the Velay may not be totally typical but nor are they totally abnormal. There is no single model, perhaps of counter-revolutionary woman but there are variations on a number of basic themes.

In this area, then, our counter-revolutionary woman was a lacemaker out of work because of the slump in luxury commodities. She lived in a hamlet, rather than a nuclear village. She had received her education at the hands of a *béate* (devout), a local widow or spinster who lived in a house owned by the village in exchange for teaching girls to make lace and to recite the catechism and who in the evening organized work sessions in which lighting and heating were shared. The bell above her door punctuated the phases of the day and in winter when the snow fell and the church was unreachable, the *béate* replaced the priest and read a holy story and organized hymn singing.[25] When the Catholic Church became a schismatic church, she clung to the non-juror and her premises became the locale of the clandestine church. In this way, though with progressive disenchantment both economically and socially, the villages of the Velay weathered the first three years of Revolution. The *status quo*, however, was to be dramatically challenged by the advent in the summer of 1793 of the conventionnel Reynaud who had political ambitions and wished to make his name at a national level. He identified religion as the disintegrant and disaffective factor in the relationship between the state and its citizenry. He took it upon himself, aided by a team of subordinates, to make war on a religion of royalism and women, the latter graphically described by him as *cette vermine malfaisante* (this evil vermin).[26] His attack had a specific gender approach and it produced a specific gender response. His tactics could be thus summarized: first a more overt attack on the juring priesthood backed by the erection of a permanent guillotine at Le Puy; second, an attack on *les signes extérieures du culte* (the outer symbols of the faith), bells, statues, crucifixes worn around the necks of women; third, the institution of the *décadi*, civil marriage and burial and penalties for non-observance. A particular eye was to be kept on women here because they were prone to ignore the *décadi* and he suggested some token arrests. The heaviest punitive action was of course against the priest. Lastly an end was to be put to the *béate* and her activities. She must be forced to take a civil oath in front of the women of the village or small town. This was in fact overstretching the law.

It was in response to this package that counter-revolutionary woman learned her techniques. The first was collective obstinacy – there was no room in this situation for individual heroism because an insurgent individual could be easily picked off whilst the women of an entire village acting together were much less vulnerable. The second technique was to use ridicule of an explicitly sexual or sexist variety. The spirit of such ridicule was in the vein of "imagine grown men taking all this trouble with little us and see how we can embarrass you." The third was to isolate an official recognized as weak or isolated in his devotion to the central line. The fourth was to vote with one's feet on issues where maternal authority mattered. These techniques, presently to be exemplified, were learned during the Terror and perfected under the Directory whose intent was to give the Revolution a second chance and this policy was to necessitate a second, if much emasculated, terror. This terror was in turn undermined by a war of attrition, much of it the work of women.

The first example of action by women is chosen to demonstrate the efficacy of standing one's ground in opposition to a particular issue and seeing how far obstinacy could go. We are in Montpigié, a small town with three sections in Ventôse an III (February 1795) and Albitte, one of the *représentants en mission* boasting the most success as a dechristianizer, has arrived from Le Puy to receive the oath of loyalty from the *béates*. He has decided to make a holiday of the event and announces that the women of each section should gather separately in the Temple of Reason because it is important that the women should see their leader being brought into line:

> We summoned girls and women, female patriots, female aristocrats, the stupid, the *béates* [a play on the words *bêtes* (beasts) and *béates* (devout)] without distinction to assemble in their section. I did not count on the fanatical hotheads presenting themselves. I was overjoyed to see a large assembly of stupid little women.

He took to the tribune and addressed them in terms designed to be understandable to the mentally retarded:

> I outlined the simplicity, the necessity and the importance of the oath they were asked to take: the bloody horrors of fanaticism and the belief of republicans in the existence of a gracious god who can only be worshipped by the practice of virtue and not by an exterior cult, full of theatricality and all for nothing.[27]

He then asked for the handful of *béates* from Montpigié and the surrounding hamlets to take the oath. They stood up and announced themselves prepared to go to the guillotine rather than express loyalty to a pagan regime. Immediately all the other women present got to their feet and cheered resoundingly. These women, Albitte protested, were mothers of families and acting contrary to their husbands' wishes, the latter being absent. Seeing this, he said, he had no option but to dismiss the assembly and try again. The next day he had got a few guards to support him and tried another section of the town. This time, before he had had time to enter the tribune, a *béate* touched him on the arm and said she was ready for the guillotine now. The women of the village came to her support. Albitte's men moved in and rounded up about a hundred although the town did not have a really safe prison and this proved a considerable error. By evening the husbands of the married women facing household chores and coping with their children were demanding the release of their wives. The mayor's refusal to comply led to a gaol rising a few days later with a concerted effort from within and without. The *représentant en mission* released the married women and sent them home. They promptly mobilized the other women of the town. There was then a concentrated attack on the prison which resulted in the liberation of the *béates* and the incarceration of the mayor and the national agent.

It will be immediately apparent that no regime can support this kind of loss of face. At the same time, to move in the National Guard with its relatively heavy weaponry to confront rebellious but unarmed womanhood was not the answer to the problem. There were armed confrontations between guards and women with some loss of life on both sides but the guards were demeaned by such confrontation and not all were convinced of the need for an oath or by the dechristianizing campaign. Moreover, many of the protesting women were mothers or grandmothers who exercised their own kind of authority over the young guard and often used their first names. Authority was safest when it could pick off offenders one by one. Then there was less risk of loss of official dignity.

The most humiliating scenes for authority were without any doubt enacted less during the dechristianizing campaign than when authority sought to promote alternative deities – Reason, Liberty, the Supreme Being, who followed in quick succession in 1794. All of them were major disasters. One of the most graphic incidents occurred at Saint Vincent near Lavoûte sur Loire, former seat of the Polignacs and a place far from committed to the old regime or to the Revolution. The occasion was an instruction from Le Puy to read, on the *décadi*, in the Temple of Reason, a paean to the Supreme Being (June 1794). In the front row sat the local dignitaries, their wives and children. The unlucky celebrant began his patriotic oration when, at a sign from an old woman, the entire female audience rose, turned their backs on the altar of liberty, and raised their skirts to expose their bare buttocks and to express their feelings to the new deity. Confronted by the spectacle of serried rows of naked female backsides, the celebrant was reduced to gibberish. Officialdom departed in unseemly haste with aspersions on its manhood made from all sides. The humiliated celebrant wrote in anger to the department about his impotence before *ces gestes gigantesques et obscènes* (these gross and obscene gestures).[28] News of this incident promoted its replication in the nearby bourgs of Lavoûte and across the hills at Saint Paulhien. *Montrer le cul aux gens* as an expression of female scorn has a long history in France even before Zola enshrined the practice in *Germinal*. It was emphatically a technique of the working classes. The middle-class or refined equivalent was simply to turn one's back or to sit on one's heels.

In two areas women could sabotage official policy and ideology virtually without effort. The control of birth and death were in the hands of women. The first was contained within the home; anyone could slap a cross on an infant brow. More disconcerting because it spilled over into the public domain was the preparation for death and the burial of the defunct.

Most people are attended in their final suffering by women. Hence, in the present context, their exit was in the hands of those likely to summon a clandestine priest or a female ex-religious. The last could not pronounce absolution but she could urge the dying to repentence and reassure his or her relatives that they had fulfilled their spiritual obligations and opened up the gates of paradise. The juring clergy had from 1791 faced a rejection of their services to the dead and humiliating incidents such as the leaving of the corpses of rotting animals in the parish church for burial. Such gestures stripped the jurors of their hold over the populace. A priest who did not have the keys to the kingdom of heaven could not be taken seriously. Yet to obtain a Christian burial from a non-juring priest was progressively difficult after 1793 and so in the Haute Loire groups of women undertook the burial, if need be at the dead of night. There is, of course, good biblical precedent for the laying away of the dead by faithful women. The contests which could emerge over the issue of burial constitute my third illustrative tale.

The incidents occurred in Canton Vert, the revolutionary name for what had been and is now Chaise Dieu.[29] It is found in a series of letters written by the municipal agent in the year vi (1798–99). The letters, however, relate to incidents stretching back over a longer period. The Directory was committed to freedom of worship provided the celebrant took an oath. To take such an oath of loyalty to the Republic or indeed any oath required by the government exposed any priest to rejection by the community. As in this case, the community might attempt to run an alternative church using a clandestine priest or someone who knew the liturgy.

The municipal agent of Canton Vert was also a constitutional priest who had suffered imprisonment for failing to surrender his *lettres de prêtrise*. After the laws of Ventôse an III (February, 1795) he struggled to re-establish parochial worship only to find himself frustrated by the women of the bourg who found an effective leadership in a Sister of Saint Joseph du Puy who ran a counter-church, organized clandestine masses, and served as the agent for a hidden non-juror. Worse, she did all this from a house right opposite the legally acceptable church presided over by the agent-priest.

His letters of protest to the department described body-snatching. He recounted how one Sister of Saint Joseph could gather together at any time about thirty fanatical women (*fanatiques*) to help her but that she assumed the role of director, orchestrating the event. The women would surround the body and when the relatives tried to intervene and insist that it should go to the church where the priest had taken an oath of loyalty, the thirty or more "furies and harridans" would attack the relatives and drive them away by throwing stones. In the particular instance that the agent proceeded to recount in some detail, the relatives were only ten in number and were totally intimidated and retired leaving the disposal of the body to the women. Next day there was an open clash on the issue between the priest and the Sister of Saint Joseph. The slanging match is worth recounting since it was done publicly and the priest/agent was humiliated. He called her a *fanatique, druide, mégère, énergumène* (a fanatic, a druid, a vixen, and a fury). She called him a *secteur de Calvin, philosophe*, a disciple of the devil and its child the Republic.[30] Her insults were lent force by a large crucifix which she was carrying when the altercation occurred and she advanced towards him waving it as if to exorcize the devil. As a *signe extérieure du culte*, the crucifix was quite illegal but it helped her to win the contest game, set, and match and she was cheered on by the onlookers. The curé appealed to the department:

> Rid us of these counter-revolutionary tricksters. . . . The Sister of Saint Joseph du Puy as the chief of the fanatics should be pursued with all possible publicity [*avec éclat*] in order to deter the rest. Have the high priestess removed and overthrow her temple and her altar and place a prohibition on their re-establishment with a penalty for infraction. . . . Frightened by the example made of their abbess, the other women will return to their duty.[31]

Rentrer dans le devoir (return to the fold) was exactly the consummation authority devoutly wished as its woman policy. To get the female population back into the home and obedient to husband and the law was summed up in this simple phrase.

The Thermidoreans, confronted with the problems emanating from dearth and the general weariness of local officialdom after 1795 in face of the penury of funds and the hostility of the rural populaces, were prepared to concede a great deal. The law of Ventôse year III (21 February 1795) granted freedom of worship but precluded communes acquiring as a collectivity a church for community worship. It did not cede the parish church although it left to local authorities the option on offering such a building by auction. However, only individuals were allowed to bid and such individuals were then responsible before the law for what occurred within its walls. Resolutely, all exterior manifestations of religious affiliation were prohibited. There were to be no bells, no processions, no banners, no pilgrimages. If the Christian religion was celebrated within the church or elsewhere, only clergy who had taken a civil oath of loyalty might officiate. In short, and whilst explicitly committing itself to the official cults, the Thermidoreans ceded something but it fell far short of what many communities wanted.

The policies of the Thermidoreans were interpreted at the local level in very different ways. Some who took office in the aftermath of the Terror had overtly "royalist", that is to say anti-Jacobin, tendencies and were prepared to turn a blind eye to what was going on. Others adopted a much harder line.[32] The government's decision to let Catholic worship occur, provided it was contained within the framework outlined above, was doomed to failure because by mid-1795 a religious revival was underway and in many, if not all regions, this revival was female-orchestrated. The west, where religion fuelled civil war, and the east, where exiled clergy could return more easily and assume direction, provide strong exceptions to the more general picture. The pattern of the religious revival and the emotions which fuelled it varied between individuals and social groups, between villages, between town and country, and between one geographical location and another. It depended too upon how local officials were prepared to ignore much of what was happening. In some areas, the anarchy of the period allowed religion to resurface relatively unchecked. For women in large towns and cities, particularly in the Paris provisioning zone which formed a 200-mile radius around the city and included cities like Rouen and Amiens, dearth prompted a desperate search for religious solace. Even in Paris, a police official commented on two queues, one at the baker's and one for mass.[33]

For many urban women, there was more than a touch of guilt for a political past in which they had been very active collaborators, and the return to religion was by way of atonement. No such sense of personal guilt tinged the attitudes of rural women. In their view, what had happened was the fault of others. If the Thermidoreans had hoped that their tolerance would bring peace, they were to be disillusioned.

To reconstruct the devotional patterns of the past, communities needed to take a number of basic steps. These were: the restoration of the church to its primitive usage; the procuring of sacred vessels and the means to summon the faithful to mass; the restitution of Sunday and the rejection of the *décadi* as the day of rest and the one on which an individual could fulfil his or her obligations and participate in a community ceremony. Then, at some stage, the decision had to be made of whom should be asked to officiate at the parish mass but this was seen as secondary to securing the ancient locale for public worship.

Where local officialdom was prepared to hire out the church at auction and where such auctions have been carefully studied, as have those in Normandy by the abbé Sévestre, then women, particularly widows, are seen to have been in the forefront.[34] Even at impious Gonesse where some women had participated in the dechristianizing surge, "the women took control." At Mende, there was a curious contest for the honor of restoring the cathedral as parish church. Two women were rival contenders. One, Rose Bros, wife of a tailor and leader of a bread riot in 1789, proffered 300 livres. Given the penury of her circumstances, it seems unlikely that the money was hers but rather that she was known as a courageous activist and was prepared to take the lead. Another woman, however, made a rival bid. She was Citoyenne Randon, wife of a former district official during the Terror. Her actions raise a string of questions. Was she distancing herself from her husband's past record? Was she seeking to save his skin from the fury of the populace in changing times? Was she anxious to wrench control from a troublemaker believing that she could direct the developing situation better?[35] Did the women (largely, it would appear, widows with some means) generally act on their own behalf or on that of the community as a whole, believing that the work of women would be shrugged off if reported to a timid set of officials? There are occasional instances of husbands denouncing the activities of their wives but others may have been pleased enough to shelter behind their activities. However, what is clear is that in matters of religion in many of the villages and bourgs of provincial France, women dominated the public action. They did not sit obediently at home.

If no auctions were held, then very frequently riots occurred in which the doors of the church were forced and the community simply occupied the building, cleaned it up, and made it available for worship. News of a successful occupation in one community often encouraged surrounding ones to make a similar attempt. The riots had a distinctive form characteristic of female protest movements. The weaponry did not exceed stones and ashes. Women relied on their special status as women to promote their cause. Old and pregnant women were placed in the forefront and the rest, frequently bolstered by women from neighboring parishes, brought up the rear with their aprons full of ashes to throw in the eyes of any opposition.[36] If they succeeded in laying hold of the church, then they might move on to confront the official whom they thought to be guardian of religious vessels, or entire communities might rally to achieve the pealing of the bells. This act was the one encountering the most stubborn opposition from officialdom since a pealing bell pronounced to the outside world that republican law was ignored in the community.[37] It pointed to their failure to control the situation in their parish, and it is the issue of the bells that provokes the most exaggerated accounts of women confronting unwilling officialdom. Often the seizure of the bell, followed by its rebellious peal, was used to symbolize local triumph over official policy and the angelus was tolled up to three times a day. In towns and larger villages, however, particularly those which were accessible, such activities brought out the National Guard and officials forced a more discreet religion upon the people. At Montpellier failure to gain control of the bells meant that those anxious to gather for parish worship had to fall back on the cowbell rung by small boys sent into the streets by their mothers.[38]

Other issues were in their way decisive but took the citadel of

325

republican authority by sap rather than direct confrontation. Amongst such issues was that of Sunday versus the *décadi*, the tenth day of rest decreed by the Jacobins when a republican calendar was inaugurated. Resented at the popular level as an evident reduction of leisure, to rural women, since the event was accompanied by no ritual or extended social contact, the laicized feast seemed a sham. The populace voted on this issue with its feet but the lead was frequently given by women giving their servants Sunday, not the *décadi*, as partial holiday.

Time off for the working man during the early nineties had come to mean drinking and for many men tavern sociability was a more than acceptable alternative to religious ritual. Under the Ancien Régime, this was a choice denied to many since the opening hours of the *cabaret* were limited on Sundays and *fêtes* (holidays). However, the removal of the curé as a check on the tavern-keeper's business led to a burgeoning of tavern sociability. Associated also with local politics as the meeting place of the *société populaire*, the tavern became a more widely used place by men but not one for respectable women.[39]

Frequently Sunday was hallowed by men lounging in the tavern whilst the women went to mass but the very indolence of the men on the sabbath was itself interpreted as an act of protest.[40] Certainly, and this was particularly apparent in the years immediately after the Concordat before the church had mobilized itself anew to make a bid for the allegiance of men, the return to regular religious worship was far more conspicuous than was that of their menfolk.

It was very important that the renascent church should be served by personnel acceptable to the women. Where possible, this meant a non-juror but such a personage could only operate illegally and hence much depended upon the compliance of the local authorities in turning a blind eye to his activities. Where a non-juror could not be found, or where local circumstances were hostile to such illegal activity, women contented themselves with the services of a lay figure who knew the liturgy. Such a person could not offer communion but he satisfied the local need for a ceremony which was an expression of community solidarity. This practice disquieted churchmen and hostile lay authorities alike but it was well within the letter of the law.

The rejection of the juror by women caused the abbé Grégoire extreme bitterness; his efforts to seize the initiative for the constitutional church in re-establishing Catholic worship were frustrated by what he termed *des femmes crapuleuses et séditieuses* (debauched and seditious women).[41]

Perhaps, however, the *messes blanches*, or "blind masses" as they were called, tell us a great deal about what women valorized in religion. They rejoiced in a safe expression of community sociability, the warmth and comfort of a religion with visible rituals, and those *signes extérieurs du culte* (outer symbols of faith) which both jurors and non-jurors were at pains to stress were of least spiritual significance to the Catholic faith. They were relatively indifferent to actual clerics themselves. Although there are instances of loyalty to one individual parish priest sustained throughout the Revolution, an uninterrupted relationship was rare. Driven underground and subjected often to considerable physical suffering in order to keep their identities secret from the authorities, many of the emergent non-juring clergy were in very poor physical shape, and the lack of new recruits increasingly took its toll upon their numbers. This perhaps did not matter if rituals could be replicated. Their absence was then not noted.

The returning clerics wanted penitence. In the immediate context of famine, they got it but progressively after 1798 this spirit faltered. City women and men fell away and though the rural congregations remained large, the peasants did not expect to make financial sacrifices for their deity. The returning clergy claimed that interest in catechism classes and sending for the priest to perform the last rites were lost habits which no one was interested in reacquiring. They feared that they had lost control of the minds of an entire generation which had grown up without formal religious instruction other than that which the family could bestow.

The religious revival of the late 1790s occurred against a background of resolute opposition in the localities to government policies. If women's protest focused on re-establishing a church, that of young men took the form of draft-dodging and desertion. By 1795, volunteers and conscripts no longer deserted in ones or twos but *en masse*, taking with them their weapons and effects. We hear of whole companies of soldiers in full uniform – which became progressively more bedraggled as the days wore on – walking the roads of France. One group crossed a half-dozen departments without being challenged.[42] In order to survive, such gangs robbed the countryside mercilessly. Whilst some returned home, others lived in woods and mountainous areas known to their relatives, who helped to keep them provisioned. We hear most reports of desertion from the departments of the Massif Central, the Alps, and the Pyrénées and of course from the Vendée. There was no longer any emotive appeal to arms in defense of the Republic. The politicians tried to blame the English and "emissaries of royalism." Lacking the repressive forces necessary to round up the young men and fearful of the consequences of making desertion a capital offence lest still more defections occurred, authority lost control of the situation. Occasionally, it tried to stage a show trial as in the round-up of Jehu and his companions in the Haute Loire in 1798. This band, allegedly of several hundred young men, had gained an evil reputation for uncontrolled brigandage. To bring them to justice once captured, the Directory sanctioned a cordon around Le Puy lest a prison break should be attempted. Jehu, however, like Macheath in Gay's opera, won the heart of the prison warder's daughter who managed to get him out of jail, and the forces of authority suffered conspicuous loss of face. Other young men sought to get out of their military commitment by severing the fingers on their right hand so that they could not fire a rifle. In the Tarn the suggestion was made to dress such cowards in women's bonnets and march them round the town on the *décadi*, so that this parade might have the effect of drawing to the revolutionary spectacle "a public utterly indifferent to republican institutions."[43] Cobb and Forrest are insistent that desertion was one of the most effective means the common people had of expressing their hostility to a regime which had repressed and impoverished them and to which they felt no commitment.[44]

For older men, those who did not have to go to war, there was a dangerous form of passive resistance which took the form of not paying taxes, idling in the tavern on a Sunday, and working in flagrant disrespect on the *décadi*. There was, however, in the Midi, a deadlier form of revenge on former terrorist supporters. Deserters played their part in flushing out republican strongholds but there was also a communal violence in which the adult males of a village or small town formed a gang of *égorgeurs* (throat slitters), who did not in fact do what their name suggested but beat up or threatened, insulted and humiliated, the households of men who were identified as former Jacobins, the supporters of Terror. Such violence was not the work of women but the latter could provide the incitement for action and contribute to the atmosphere of hostility by extending threats to the wives and children of those identified with Jacobin government.[45] In part we may be looking at a kind of squaring of the record in societies where the vendetta flourished and without this act of revenge for loved ones lost or families severed by the revolutionary record, normality could not be achieved.

However, such an interpretation must not obscure the violence or the anarchy of this period. The more one familiarizes oneself with the years 1796-1801, the more apparent it becomes that the attempt by women to establish a pattern of religious worship, and an expression of community solidarity which simultaneously hallowed the structure of family life, was the most constructive force one can determine at work in society. It was one which was working in the direction of normalization and a return to a structured lifestyle. Peacefully but purposefully, they sought to re-establish a pattern of life punctuated by a pealing bell and one in which rites of passage – birth, marriage, and death – were respected and hallowed. The state had intruded too far and women entered the public arena to push it back and won. It was one of the most resounding political statements to be made by the populace in the entire history of the Revolution.

NOTES

Source Reprinted in an abridged format from Olwen Hufton, *Women and the Limits of Citizenship in the French Revolution* (Toronto: University of Toronto Press, 1992), pp. 89–130, 168–74.

1 The saying "Men make laws, women customs" was often evoked in the nineteenth century and interpreted as a reason for clerical influence. The clergy themselves had recourse to the saying as a means of urging upon the female laity the extent of their influence: e.g., Donnet, archbishop of Bordeaux, in his *Instruction Pastorale sur l'éducation de famille* (1845), J.P. Migne, *Collection intégrale et universelle des orateurs sacrés*, 99 vols, vol. 81, p. 69

2 R.C. Cobb, *The Police and the People: French Popular Protest, 1789–1820* (Oxford, 1970) pp. 50–2. This entire section of Cobb's work should be obligatory reading for anyone who wants to comment seriously on the meaning of discourse. The official makes even porters and fishwives declaim in the language of *la rhétorique*. The simple phrase "merde à la Convention" can thus be stretched to a twelve-line paragraph. The more words one used and the more paper covered, the

more assiduous the official appeared. Since officials acted as the filters of popular discourse, we cannot ever be sure exactly what the people were saying.

3 Examples taken from the Archives Départementales de la Haute Loire L430, 371, 1206

3 "Females, little women, bigots, animals, woolly beasts, sheep, lentils, vegetables, fanatics." The use of the term *lentilles* was obviously specific to an area like the Haute Loire where they were a staple. Certainly women, in this discourse, were what they ate.

5 This was the official phrase for dechristianization.

6 An example of this questionnaire is found in J. Hardman, *French Revolution Documents* (Oxford 1973), p. 173.

7 If such a notion could be proved, it would lend a particular twist to the legend of the priest supported by women which developed in the nineteenth century. However, the record of women as supporters of the priest during the years 1789–93 probably constitutes the decisive evidence which serves to undermine the idea.

8 M. Vovelle, *La Révolution contre l'Eglise: De la Raison à l'Etre Suprême* (Paris, 1989), pp. 221–6.

9 "These buildings will only contain the voices of republicans instructing their brothers and manly accents of patriotism honouring reason." Section de Gravilliers; cited in Hardman, *Documents*, pp. 369–70. There seems to be little space here for sisters' or women's voices.

10 On the bewildering religious commitment of the sans-culotte's wife, F. Le Brun (ed.), *Histoire des Catholiques en France du XVe siècle jusqu'à nos jours* (Toulouse, 1980).

11 In the early winter of 1794, a so-called sans-culottes paternoster circulated which suggests that women were not the only ones to maintain some allegiance to a deity if not to its priesthood. "Our Father who art in heaven whence you protect the French Republic and the sans-culottes, its most ardent defenders, let your name be hallowed amongst us as it has always been. May thy will to let man live free, equal and happy be done on earth as it is in heaven. Preserve our supply of daily bread threatened by the efforts of Pitt Cobourg and the coalition of tyrants. Forgive us the errors committed by tolerating for so long the tyrants now purged from France. As we forgive the enslaved nations when they intimidate us. Let them not delay too long in casting off their shackles . . . May they be delivered like us from nobles, priests and kings. Amen." Cited by Hardman, *Documents*, p. 367.

12 On these differences before the Revolution, O. Hufton, "The French Church," in W.J. Callahan and D. Higgs (eds) *Church and Society in Catholic Europe of the Eighteenth Century* (Cambridge, 1979), pp. 13–33.

13 The oath of allegiance was not initially envisaged when the first legislation on the civil constitution of clergy which converted the priesthood into salaried officials of the state, reduced the number of bishops, abolished many cathedral canonries, and made all appointments subject to lay election was enacted. It was only perceived as necessary when it became clear that many clerics – at first

about half and subsequently more – were fundamentally opposed to the principles it embodied. Perhaps the most alienating aspect was that of lay election which represented a total breach of the autonomy of the church. In diocesan centres where seminaries existed, the theological implications of the oath were hotly debated and parish priests, who may well have welcomed becoming state salaried employees on a generous stipend, recoiled before the wider implications of state control. They then explained to their flocks the reasons for their rejection of the oath. The clergy hence became the first really explicit oppositional Revolution. T. Tackett, *Religion, Revolution, and Regional Culture in Eighteenth Century France: The Ecclesiastical Oath in 1791* (Princeton, 1986); the particular opposition of women is outlined on pp. 172–7.

14 Archives Départementales Calvados Lv Liasse de Serments Bayeux. "Take it or not, it doesn't bother us."

15 T. Tackett, *Religion, Revolution . . .* p. 175, and *Priest and Parish in Eighteenth Century France* (Princeton, 1977), p. 192

16 Chanoine Pierre Flament, "Recherche sur le ministre clandestin dans le département de l'Orne sous la Révolution," *Bullétin de la Société historique et archéologique de l'Orne* xc (1972), 45–74; E. Gonnet, *Essai sur l'histoire du diocèse du Puy en Velay (1789–1802)* (Paris, 1907), p. 209; Charles Girault, *Le Clergé Sarthois face au serment consitutionel* (Laval, 1959), pp. 31–3.

17 René and Suzanne Pillorget, "Les Messes clandestines en France entre 1793 et 1802," *Université d'Angers centre de Recherches d'Histoire Religieuse et de l'histoire des idées: Histoire de la Messe XVII–XIX siècle* (Angers, 1979), pp. 155–67. This work has a valuable bibliography of local and other published work on this elusive subject.

18 Actes du Comité de Salut Public, i, p. 353 and R. and S. Pilorget, "Les Messes clandestines en France," p. 160

19 *Moniteur*, 19 Messidor an II. I am indebted to Carol Blum for this reference.

20 Cited by M. Vovelle, *La Révolution contre l'Eglise*, p. 224

21 The White Terror was a terrorist movement which broke out after 1795 in the Midi. It was directed against former partisans of the Terror and hence could be called a counter-Terror. Essentially it was a movement designed to wreak revenge for loss of life or unpopular policies and some aspects of it will presently be discussed. On this theme and for many nuances in this movement: C. Lucas, "Themes in Southern Violence after 9 Thermidor", in G. Lewis and C. Lucas (eds) *Beyond the Terror* (Cambridge, 1983), pp. 152–94. The case from Arles appears in M. Vovelle, *Les Métamorphoses de la fête en Provence, 1750–1820* (Paris, 1976), p. 251.

22 The designation "macho" is used deliberately because the rhetoric of officialdom demanded admiration for the rational male who could alone make decisions. The female symbol of Liberty was removed from official correspondence after the end of 1793 and replaced by the symbol of Hercules, manly vigour, because a female symbol suggested weakness. The indelicacy and lack of consideration

demonstrated by both local officials and the *armées révolutionnaires* towards niceties appreciated by women are illustrated in an incident from Saint Germain de Laval in the Mâconnais wherein local Jacobins took a classical nude statue from a local chateau and painted a tricolore on her and stood her in the square having felled a crucifix, proclaiming her the Goddess of Liberty. Days later it began to rain and the paint started to wash off and descended in a purplish red trickle between her legs. The young men, drunken and jesting, proclaimed a miracle of a menstruating goddess. The village women, outraged, seized the statue, carried her several miles to the river, and washed her, purified her, and restored her dignity as a woman. Then they laid her on her side. A day later they broke into a church and reclaimed it for worship. (Archives Départementales Rhône 42 L161; I am grateful to Colin Lucas for this reference.)

23 I have deliberately confined myself to a particular area and drawn analogies in the notes for coherence.

24 Woods and hedges certainly made for better oppositional activity by young men as the history of the Vendée demonstrates. However, during 1796 even the Beauce, which was flat land not far distant from Orléans and even from Paris, was the locus of banditry which the government could not curtail. See R.C. Cobb, *Reactions to the French Revolution* (Oxford, 1792), p. 180.

25 She has been designated *un ministre laïque* by a historian of the nineteenth century. (A. Rives, " 'Des ministres laïques' au XIX siècle", *Revue d'histoire de l'église de France*, 1978: 27–38.

26 More often this term was reserved for the *béates* (Archives Départementales, Conseil Général Le Puy, 10 October 1793).

27 Rapport du 5 Prairial an III, Archives Départementales Haute Loire LB14 (ancien côte), cited in part in Gonnet, *Essai sur l'histoire du diocèse du Puy en Velay*, pp. 245–7.

28 Archives Départementales Haute Loire L376 ancien côte.

29 Archives Départementales Haute Loire L802 ancien côte.

30 This area was a frontier between Catholicism and Protestantism and the Revolution was presented as a Protestant promotion.

31 This case may reflect the reclaiming of a former sister in death.

32 A great deal would seem to have depended upon how secure these local authorities felt as well as their personal predictions. The diocesan histories which are being published by Beauchesne make one aware of very differing levels of tolerance and persecution from area to area.

33 Hufton, "The Reconstruction of a Church, 1796–1801," in *Beyond the Terror*, p. 35.

34 Abbé E. Sévestre, *Les problèmes religieux de la Révolution et l'Empire en Normandie*, p. 1070.

35 Abbé P.J.B. Delon, *La Revolution en Lozère* (Mende, 1922), p. 52. In the riot of 1790, Rose Bros (née Castan) led the attack on the cathedral chapter's grain supply. She led the movement to hire the church, 23, Ventose an II (13 March 1795), Delon, p. 740.

36 M. de Roux, *Histoire de la Révolution à Poitiers et dans la Vienne*

(Lyons 1952), 251, and G. Lefebvre, *Les Paysans du Nord* (Bari, 1959), p. 874.

37 G. Cholvy, *Histoire du diocèse de Montpellier* (Paris, 1976), p. 186, for example, states that in the Lodevois in May 1795, "Les cultes sont librement exercés. Le peuple est appelé aux messes et vèpres par le son de la cloche que l'on met en branle, en outre, trois fois par jour . . ."; in Lefebvre, *Les Paysans du Nord*, p. 874, women occupy bell towers.

38 J. Duval Jouve, *Montpellier pendant la Révolution* (Montpellier 1879), p. 327.

39 "Est-on plus altéré qu'autrefois?" ran a leader article in a Grenoble journal for 1810. The need of the church to extricate men from the tavern on a Sunday became a recurrent preoccupation of the clergy after the Concordat. J. Godel, *La Réconstruction concordataire dans le diocèse de Grenoble après la Révolution (1802–1809)* (Grenoble, 1968), pp. 266–7.

40 On the eve of the Concordat, the mayor of Lain near Auxerre wrote to the prefect: "tout le monde est catholique ici . . . or un bon tiers des habitants ne veulent plus observer le dimanche. On reste au cabaret; on joue aux cartes pendant les messes et vèpres; on fauche, on charroie . . . nos concitoyens ont toujours tenu une conduite tout a fait opposée à tout ce que la loi prescrit. Pendant l'exercise des jours de décadi tout le monde travaillait ce jour là et célébrait religieusement le dimanche. Aujourd'hui que la décadi est supprimée, on ne veut plus reconnaitre le dimanche." Cited by H. Forestier, "Le Culte laïcal," *Annales de Bourgogne*, xxiv (1952), p. 107.

41 D. Woronoff, *La République bourgeoise de Thermidor à Brumaire, 1794–1799* (Paris, 1972), pp. 143–4, gives a short account of Grégoire's efforts and frustrations. Blind masses have recently been interpreted by S. Desan, *Reclaiming the Sacred: Lay Religion and Popular Politics in Revolutionary France* (Ithaca, 1991), as an attempt by women to create new rituals. I would prefer to see them as the resurrection of old rituals, as perfect in all details as possible except for the presence of a priest and, even here, the lay celebrant did not intrude upon the prerogatives of the real priesthood by giving communion.

42 Cobb cites the case of one such group walking from Sarrelouis to Meulan in *Police and the People*, p. 95.

43 Archives Nationales ₣9 316, Desertion, Tarn, Lautrec, 9 Brumaire an VII.

44 Cobb, *Police and the People*, p. 104, and A. Forrest, "Conscription and Crime in Rural France during the Directory and the Consulate," in G. Lewis and C. Lucas (eds), *Beyond the Terror*, p. 92.

45 C. Lucas, "Themes in Southern Violence after 9 Thermidor," in G. Lewis and C. Lucas (eds), *Beyond the Terror*, pp. 152–94.

Part V

NAPOLEON AND THE FRENCH REVOLUTION

[George] Washington is dead. This great man fought
tyranny, established the liberty of his country. His memory
must always be dear to the French people, as well as to all
the people of the free world and especially to the French
soldiers, who, like him and his American troops, fight in the
defense of liberty and equality.

Napoleon Bonaparte

11

NAPOLEON BONAPARTE

François Furet

There are two ways to think about Napoleon, perhaps only two: either he was the great destroyer of the Revolution, who transformed a republican government dedicated to liberty into a ruthless empire entirely devoid of civil liberties, or else he was the great Jacobin consolidator of the Revolution, who constructed a new kind of society both in France and throughout Europe. Clearly, François Furet is closer to the latter camp than the former. For him, Napoleon was inextricably tied to the Revolution: far from renouncing it, that is where Napoleon found his sustenance and his legitimacy. But the Revolution itself was no incubator of freedom. As we saw earlier, for Furet the Revolution harbored in its very essence new forms of dictatorship and political coercion that would make the Ancien Régime seem liberal. If one views the Revolution itself as essentially despotic, it is but a small step to see the whole decade from 1789–99 leading to Bonaparte's rule. This "proletarian king" ruled as much in the name of the French nation as over its people. In that sense, perhaps Furet is correct to think of the empire as the "dictatorship of public opinion."

* * *

The French Revolution had no use for the elderly, and not even Napoleon Bonaparte, its greatest and perhaps its only hero, was an exception to this rule. In contrast to the American Revolution, whose aging leaders, consecrated by the role they had played and respected by all citizens, were transformed into Fathers of the Country, the French Revolution was a theater that used up its heroes and cut them down in their prime, transforming those left alive into survivors and its vanquishers into bourgeois. For a few years, however, it had its Washington in Bonaparte – but a

Washington who was thirty years old. Ten years later he was a king, and a few years after that, a defeated, captive king. Not even he had been able to master the course of events for long. The moment his power became hereditary it cut itself off from its source: he embarked upon a course different from that of the Revolution, and the fortunes of war reasserted their rights. By attempting to root his reign in the law of monarchy, the emperor deprived it of both its magic and its necessity.

In order to understand him, to bring him into clearer focus, we may therefore begin by asking why this Corsican, this Italian, this foreigner – Buonaparte, as the dowagers of the Restoration called him – became so profoundly a part of the history of France. And the answer is that he was chosen by the Revolution, from which he received his strange power not only to embody the new nation (a power that others before him, most notably Mirabeau and Robespierre, had possessed) but also to fulfill its destiny. Of this fate he was so well aware that on Saint Helena he would hark back to these beginnings as to an obsession, not so much in order to turn the origin of his power into a posthumous propaganda weapon (which it nevertheless became) as from a need to remember what was at least explicable in this most extraordinary of lives.

He had been born at the right time, twenty years prior to 1789, but on an out-of-the-way island that had only recently – and unwillingly – become French. Napoleon was the second son of Charles Bonaparte and Laetitia Ramolini, parents of twelve children in all, of whom eight survived, five boys and three girls. They were a Corsican family, a tribe under parental authority and speaking Corsican like everyone else on the island. They came from the marginal "nobility" of Ajaccio, eking out a living from vineyards and olive trees. The family patriarch had the clever idea of throwing in his lot with the French, thus abandoning his friend Paoli and the cause of independence. He thus became one of the beneficiaries of the edicts of 1776, which stipulated that scions of impoverished noblemen were entitled to a free education in the royal military academies. The two eldest boys obtained these scholarships, which enabled them to look forward to a career similar to that of so many of their compatriots since that time: from rural township between sea and scrub to a lifetime of public service on the continent. Napoleon studied at Brienne (1779–84), where he received a good education, although Stendhal later deplored its governmental character: "Had he been educated in a school independent of the government, he might have studied Hume and Montesquieu: he might have understood the strength that public opinion bestows upon government" (*Life of Napoleon*, Chapter l). Perhaps. But at Brienne's military school he learned to speak French – though without ever entirely losing his Italian accent; he also studied history, with which he filled his solitary days, and mathematics, for which he demonstrated a gift. In 1784 he was admitted to the Ecole Militaire, and in 1785 he graduated forty-second in a class of fifty-eight and was assigned as a sublieutenant of artillery to the regiment of La Fère. Ségur and Taine attribute the following judgment to his history teacher: "Corsican in character and nationality, this young man will go far if circumstances permit."

The "circumstances" of his youth and his first posts were the final flickers of the Ancien Régime. Napoleon remained a stranger to the life and passions of the age; education's effects are often delayed. "Corsican in character," he was typically moody, somewhat rough around the edges, and lacking in worldly experience. And "Corsican in nationality," he took the island to be the framework of his world, and he would join the cause of Paoli, which his father had abandoned. His garrison duty was interrupted by lengthy stays in Corsica. He had yet to make his rendezvous with France, and even after the Revolution it was a long time coming. Nothing linked him to the losing side in 1789, but neither was there any sign of anything more than modest enthusiasm for the victors. He continued to spend the better part of his time in Corsica. As late as the spring of 1792, if his Brienne classmate Bourrienne is to be believed, he was contemptuous of Louis XVI for not having ordered his troops to fire on the rioters of 20 June. This is one of the rare glimpses we have of him between 1789 and 1793. When, somewhat later, the cannon roared at Valmy, Napoleon was once again awaiting the boat that would take him back to Corsica. Paradoxically, it was the victory of Paoli's insurrection in April 1793 that would break this powerful tie to his native island. The Bonaparte tribe, marked down as pro-French, was banished. Headed by a handsome widow flanked by pretty daughters and ambitious sons, the family disembarked with all their belongings at Marseilles.

Napoleon was *already* twenty-four. (In three years people would say, "He's only twenty-seven!") He was a captain of artillery but still had done nothing. His encounter with the new France, like everything else in his life, came about by chance, but at a time – the summer of 1793 – when the true partisans of the Revolution, those willing to burn their bridges behind them, were being singled out from their more tepid comrades. It was then that Napoleon became not only a Montagnard but a Robespierrist. In August he authored a broadside against the Federalists, who had brought civil war to the south. An unoriginal text, it consists of a discussion among a soldier, a man from Nîmes, a merchant from Marseilles, and a manufacturer from Montpellier concerning the Federalist uprising in Marseilles, for which the soldier pleads the cause of "public safety." Despite the work's lack of originality, it is an important document because it marks the moment at which the Corsican artillery captain joined the history of the Revolution and thereby – carrying a Jacobin passport – entered the history of France.

What in those terrible months did this young officer find so much to his liking? Probably that which accorded with his temperament and tastes: the government's energy, worthy of the ancients; its unlimited authority; and also the fact that careers were open to talents, that military men were honored if they were victorious, and that a young officer might hope for equal treatment in a profession still encumbered by particles and prejudices. By serving the Montagnard dictatorship, which in Marseilles wore the visage of a Corsican compatriot, Saliceti, Napoleon served both his predilections and his interests. When, following his advice, Toulon was recaptured from the English on 17 December, he was promoted to brigadier-general; in February 1794, he became commander of artillery in the army in Italy in the offensive against the Austrians.

When the Thermidorians sidelined him temporarily and even imprisoned him for several weeks, they confirmed his reputation as a Robespierrist general. Yet in spite of appearances Thermidor carried the Revolution forward, and in the following year it provided him with an opportunity for a spectacular comeback on the occasion of 13 Vendémiaire (5 October) 1795. If Toulon was the first phase of his marriage with revolutionary France, this was the second. It was Barras who put Napoleon back in the saddle – Barras, that staunch defender of the Republic, who ordered its troops to fire on the young *muscadins* leading the insurgency against the Convention. There was also a more civilized aspect to

Barras' patronage: Bonaparte became a minor figure in Paris's newly reconstituted high society.

That society was an amalgam of the revolutionary *nomenklatura* with the monied élite; the former had survived long enough to celebrate the return of the latter. A modern alliance between power and finance supplanted the Robespierrist utopia of a virtuous republic. The time had come to mix business with pleasure and over it all presided Barras, former viscount and ex-Terrorist now ensconced in a court worthy of the late Roman Empire. In this environment the young general cut a peculiar figure: emaciated, taciturn, his youthful face devoured by his huge eyes, he had a full head of hair that hung down to his shoulders like "the ears of a dog." His marriage to Josephine tells us a great deal about what drew him to this society. The story can be recounted as a farce: in marrying a half-impoverished denizen of the demimonde whom Barras had placed in his bed, Bonaparte believed he was marrying a wealthy aristocratic heiress. Yet it can also be told in colors less lurid but no less true: the burning passion he felt for Josephine, fanned by all that the name Beauharnais evoked, was the product not so much of vulgar *arrivisme* as of all the childhood humiliations that his union with her erased. The minor noble from Corsica was critical of the bourgeoisie, to which he would never belong, yet he shared its deepest collective sentiment, its love-hate relationship with the aristocracy: that peculiarly French passion for equality, the unwitting legacy of the Ancien Régime, which can be temporarily assuaged only by acquiring recognized, guaranteed superiority over one's neighbor and "equal." Later, Stendhal, like Napoleon, would refer to this passion as "vanity." In marrying a Beauharnais, little Bonaparte became a naturalized citizen of France.

His vanity, however, was sustained by an imagination that was anything but bourgeois, or at any rate more than just bourgeois – although the words that he spoke to his brother at Notre Dame on the day of his anointment – "Joseph! If only our father could see us now!" – might well have been those of a character in Balzac. Yet the success that so amazed the man who earned it was not a question of money or power. It can be compared only to the empire of Charlemagne or the triumph of Caesar. The Bonaparte of 1796 had inherited from his many predecessors – Mirabeau, Lafayette, Brissot, Danton, Robespierre, and so many others – the ambition of governing the Revolution. But from the outset, the dreamy, clever Mediterranean had one advantage over the rest: he came from the outside at a time when the political program of the Revolution was exhausted, and he could impose upon it an agenda of his own choosing. Like the others he was a champion of equality, but to the nation's glory he lent the powerful luster of his personal genius.

Within the space of a few months, between spring and autumn, he would emerge from Italy as the arbiter of France's political future. Italy had been in his dreams since the campaign of 1794. To some extent it was his country, it spoke his language, and it offered the ideal arena in which to join his two fatherlands in victory. His plan had been ready for a long time: to drive a wedge between the Piedmontese and the Austrians by means of a quick offensive, thus obliging the monarchy of Turin to agree to peace or even to enter an alliance with the French, after which victory he would drive the Austrians out of Lombardy. The first phase of the plan was executed in two weeks, but the second ran into difficulty, for when Bonaparte took Milan in the middle of May the Austrian army was still intact and would continue to cause trouble until November. But the French commander had given an impressive demonstration of his tactical prowess, which relied on rapid troop movements and co-ordinated attacks, and he did not wait for others to sing his praises. No one had more fully grasped the fact that the reign of the well-born had ended and that of public opinion begun. In his victory communiqués Napoleon revealed a real genius for publicity.

He was not yet king of France, but as of May he became king of poor, defeated, plundered, ransomed Italy, which he made over as though it were his by patrimonial right. He lived in the Montebello palace in Milan, more like a sovereign than a general of the Republic, surrounded by a court, protected by strict etiquette, and already ensconced in omnipotence. Josephine, false as ever, accompanied by one of her lovers, joined him. Napoleon's brothers and sisters had preceded her, trading on his victories and avid for honors and profits, liberally helping themselves to whatever they could get. This Balzacian side of his life as a parvenu was destined to continue unabated. Napoleon tolerated and even encouraged these sordid activities, provided they originated with him. These indulgences were the perquisites of glory, prizes to be given to those who served him. But already distinguished from his most famous generals by their acquiescence in his superiority, conferring as an equal with the Directory, on which he imposed his views thanks to his power over public opinion, and receiving republican France's most eminent thinkers and scientists, he belonged to another world. He had conceived an idea of what his life could be, of what he was now sure it would be: "Fate will not resist my will," as he would later put it, in what might be a definition of modern happiness.

Of the things he said at Montebello, already recorded by numerous attentive witnesses, the most interesting is this confidence:

> What I have done up to now is still nothing. I am only at the beginning of my career. Do you think that I have triumphed in Italy only to make the reputations of the lawyers of the Directory, the Carnots and Barrases? And do you suppose that it was in order to establish a republic? What an idea! A republic of thirty million people! With our customs and our vices! Is such a thing possible? It is a chimera of which the French have become enamored, but it, too, will pass, like so many other things. They need their glory, the satisfactions of vanity. But they understand nothing of liberty.

This declaration is far more than an avowal of ambition, which by this point was evident anyway. We hear echoes of what Napoleon had learned from the literature of the day about the impossibility of a republic in a large country, a judgment reinforced by a pessimistic assessment of Thermidorian society, whose citizens exhibited the opposite of republican virtues. Slaves to self-interest and pleasure, their great passion was "vanity": individual vanity, which demanded "perks," the petty gradations of status and prestige upon which egalitarian societies thrive; and collective vanity, jealously protective of the glory of the nation and the grandeur of the new France. Let the government satisfy these passions and it would not have to worry about liberty any more than the French people did. Formulated at a very early date, this philosophy of power enabled the commander-in-chief of the army of Italy to shape his plans to flatter the nation's passion – a simple, almost simplistic, yet masterly strategy, a formula for revolutionary dictatorship based not on virtue but on self-interest.

A lengthy peregrination in Egypt still stood between Bonaparte and power, but he bided his time brilliantly in anticipation of what was to come. Even before this undertaking, in 1797, on 18 Fructidor, the army of Italy had saved the Directory, but its commander-in-chief had wisely delegated Augerau for the purpose, thereby managing both to avoid working for a discredited government and to keep clear of the renewal of terror that followed the *coup d'état*. Young as he was, he exhibited all the caution of a wizened politician, aged by his participation in the battles of the Revolution. The subsequent Egyptian expedition was an exercise in image-building. Ill-conceived but executed with great panache, this useless foray served no purpose but to magnify Napoleon's glory. The man who abandoned his army in almost clandestine fashion on 22 August 1799, added the Pyramids to his list of victories. When he reached Fréjus on 9 October, time had in effect worked in his favor. He was acclaimed by the public, and even the politicians offered him the reins of power – on their own terms, to be sure, but without the means to enforce those terms. Paris theaters interrupted performances to announce his arrival. On 27 October municipal officials in Pontarlier informed the directors that "the news of Bonaparte's arrival so electrified republicans that a number of them shed tears."

Napoleon's landing at Fréjus threw all Paris's plans into turmoil by introducing a joker into the deck, a joker that Sieyés had not anticipated: the popularity of a hero. From the moment he returned Bonaparte had the upper hand over his associates, for in a crowd of notables he was "the people." Well-conceived but executed in panic, 18 Brumaire enjoyed the nation's blessing before the fact.

Now began the happiest period of Napoleon's life: his marriage to the Revolution. The Republic persisted, with the general holding the supreme office of first consul, in accordance with the public's wish. Stendhal, who had come to Paris as an adolescent from his native Grenoble in November 1799, learned of the *coup d'état* at Nemours on the day after it took place: "We heard the news in the evening. I understood little of what it meant, and I was delighted that young General Bonaparte had made himself king of France" (*La vie de Henry Brulard*, Chapter 35). Revolutionary France was indeed under the spell of the new sovereign, who was its son and had saved it from the danger of a restoration: anything royal about him came from his being the hero of the Republic. France had finally found the republican monarchy toward which it had been groping since 1789.

The "citizen consul" at age thirty was physically at his most prepossesing, less sallow than the general of the Italian campaign but not yet the plump emperor to come. He lived amid the clamor of his fame and the fever of governmental work, the two passions of his daily life, and even devoted a little of his time to recreation and amusement: this was the heyday of Malmaison, as recounted by Junot's wife, the future duchesse d'Abrantès. Bonaparte as yet had no court and lived among his aides-de-camp and generals, above them but not cut off from them. Josephine had at last understood that she had accidentally picked the winning number, and the two of them, in the very uniqueness of their fate, exemplify the uncertainties of life in the new society. Insignificant bystanders during the Revolution, the courtesan from the islands and the little soldier from Corsica ultimately came to embody landlord France. The public, having chosen its leader, discovered that in style and habit he exhibited all the requisite attributes of republican simplicity and civilian government. The first consul partook of none of the foolish customs of the Bourbons: he ate quickly, always wore the same clothes and old hats, and wasted no time in court ceremonies. He worked and made decisions.

Such, at any rate, was the public image that he so cleverly created, and at the time it was also the truth. Consul Napoleon combined the qualities of a republican hero and bourgeois monarch with tendencies in his personality that were already despotic and uncontrollable. He himself had a clear understanding of the conditions that had brought him to power and of the civilian nature of his dictatorship.

> I govern not as a general but because the nation believes that I have the civilian qualities necessary to govern. If it did not have this opinion, the government could not stand. I knew full well what I was doing when, as general of the army, I accepted the position of member of the Institute. I was sure of being understood by even the lowliest drummer. Nothing about present conditions can be deduced from centuries of barbarism. We are thirty million people united by enlightenment, property, and commerce. Three or four hundred thousand troops are nothing compared with that mass.

(May 1802, to the Council of State)

Enlightenment, property, commerce: a definition of the nation that might have been put forward by Necker, Sieyes, or Benjamin

Constant, who had learned it from the philosophers – except that none of the three had been in a position to deal with the instability and civil conflict likely to result from the application of that definition. Napoleon saw himself as the heir and symbol of this tradition, its long-sought champion, and there was a whole bourgeois side of him that was well suited to this role: he believed in the sanctity of property, the idea of marriage and the family, women in the home, order in the streets, and careers open to talent. To all this prosaic legacy of 1789 he lent his flamboyant genius, while at the same time subjecting it to a kind of Corsican exaggeration, injecting the new France with a dose of the patriarchal spirit. In doing so he responded in two ways to the wishes of the nation. With an epic revolution barely behind them, the French were not ready for a less brilliant leader. But tired of the revolutionary agenda and jealously guarding what they had acquired, they wanted guarantees for the safety of property and the preservation of law and order. At once revolutionary and conservative, a rural and petit-bourgeois nation awaited Bonaparte's Civil Code. It spontaneously supported the program he set forth in 1800 to the Council of State:

> We have finished the romance of the Revolution. Now we must begin its history, looking only for what is real and possible in the application of principles and not what is speculative and hypothetical. To pursue a different course today would be to philosophize, not to govern.

A dictatorship of public opinion intended to consolidate the Revolution, the Consulate was thus also, in Bonaparte's mind, the "beginning" of its history. The revolutionary "romance" had been written by the intellectuals who had led it before him and who had explored its "speculative" side. Napoleon surely had in mind Robespierre and his Republic of Virtue, but he was probably also thinking of other leaders as well, from the Constituent Assembly to the Institute – Sieyés, for example, his temporary ally in Brumaire and the champion of the "perfect Constitution." To begin the real history of the Revolution was to treat in terms of practical reason problems with which his predecessors had dealt as metaphysicians, and to establish a modern state on a foundation of experience and realism. This was the other side of the Consulate, which Bonaparte used to modify the model of despotism to suit the new post-revolutionary society. As early as 1790, Mirabeau, in his secret correspondence with the king, had attempted to convince poor Louis XVI of the wisdom of such a course: why, he wrote in substance, do you balk at accepting the new state of things? Instead of mourning the loss of aristocratic society, with its nobility, parlements, and privileged corps that constantly hindered your authority, take advantage of its demise to root the monarchy in the new society by becoming the head of the nation.

While the king of the Ancien Régime had not heeded or even heard this advice, the new sovereign possessed all the qualities required to put it into practice. He was by temperament a thousand times more authoritarian than the former king, and he governed a society that had become more than ever a society of equal individuals, relatively defenseless against the power of the state. In contrast to 1790, moreover, the revolutionary tide had by this time been ebbing for several years, and as it waned it became possible to see that the idea of absolute power remained intact, as potent as ever, the monarchy's legacy to the new democracy. The sovereignty of the people had replaced the sovereignty of the monarch, but sovereignty itself remained unlimited in extent and indivisible by its very nature. The consular monarchy thus incorporated three elements that combined to make it more powerful than any previous monarchy. First, it reigned over isolated individuals, deprived of the right to assemble but guaranteed equality. Second, it derived its authority from the people and was thus rid of that divine scrutiny that had served as a brake on the power of the king. And third, it unwittingly derived part of its power from the absolutist tradition – unwittingly, because France remained profoundly convinced that it had broken all ties with the past, of which the war, the émigrés, and the brothers of Louis XVI were all reminders. But the first consul understood, for on several occasions he said that his power derived in part from the history of France and the habits of the nation.

Such was the foundation upon which Napoleon was to erect his most enduring achievement, the modern French state. The Civil Code and much of the work of legal unification and new legislation were already underway before he came to power and could have been finished without him in much the same fashion. But the new structure of government bore his stamp. He drew liberally on tradition: on Cartesian rationalism as applied to politics, on enlightened despotism, on the body of laws born of the interminable conflicts between the state and the corporations

347

FRANÇOIS FURET

under the Ancien Régime, and on established customs and attitudes. But he also left his mark, at once Corsican and military, on the new system, in its tendency to value order and authority above all human needs and in its very structure, so well adapted to his principal passion: undivided rule.

The administration, Napoleon believed, is the nervous system of government. It should run by itself, a well-regulated organ whose function is to convey the will of the center to the extremities:

> I have made all my ministries so easy that they can be staffed by anyone possessing the necessary loyalty, zeal, energy, and industriousness.... The prefectures were admirably well organized and yielded excellent results. Forty million people were spurred to do the same thing at the same time, and with the aid of these local centers of activity, the extremities moved as quickly as the heart itself.
> (Council of State, 1806, Molé)

Thus centralization not only permitted the unified and ubiquitous application of rational power, it also allowed the state to rely on agents whose only qualities were "industriousness" and "loyalty." Every prefect became a "miniature emperor" in his own département, but the prefect's power had nothing to do with his merit or personality; he was merely the representative of the central government.

Although Bonaparte on occasion liked to raise the "public safety" argument, that the dictatorship and the suppression of local liberties were due to the war, it is difficult to take him at his word, so much do his designs bear the unmistakable imprint of his education and character. The strong point of the system was also its weak point: himself. To make the government work he employed all the resources of his charismatic yet realistic genius. He was capable of mastering numerous subjects in a short time, pleased by the variety of experience offered by the work of government, aware of the value of detail and knowledge of the terrain, and excited by the possibility of controlling everything by knowing all, as on the battlefield. According to Chateaubriand, he

> was involved in everything. His mind was never at rest. His ideas were in perpetual motion. Impetuous by nature, he proceeded not in a steady, straightforward fashion but by

fits and starts. He threw himself upon the world and shook it.

(*Mémoires d'outre-tombe*, Chapter 24, p. 6)

But this very energy carried with it the seeds of its own corruption, and implicit in the ambition to exert absolute authority was the possibility of a degradation of authority into tyranny. And such corruption, such degradation were quickly evident in the first consul. No one carried out his orders with sufficient haste; no one ever obeyed fully enough. In a country where fawning was a national pastime, flattery wreaked havoc on a character that constantly elicited it, and was soon intoxicated by it. Thus the famous charming smile was joined by an impatience with contradiction, a dark and violent energy, outbursts of anger, and a crudeness of insult for which Bonaparte soon became noted. Following a very French dialectic, the same man who apotheosized the abstract sovereignty of the state was also the man who weakened that sovereignty by acting as though it were embodied solely in himself. Napoleon was the Louis XIV of the democratic state.

Yet his possessive passion never blinded him to the point where he confused public with private. Temperament aside, his extraordinary ascent by itself would account for his tendency to regard all that he acquired, including the Republic, as his patrimony. Nevertheless, he remained first and foremost the heir of the Revolution, since the administrative state that he created in opposition to local powers was established upon the universality of law. Though in later years he resorted increasingly to arbitrary actions and established a nobility that owed its titles to the state, the source of his power over the nation remained the fact that he was the chosen embodiment of popular sovereignty, its instrument for making and enforcing laws that were to be the same for all. In this sense he was the ultimate incarnation of that crisis of political representation that was the essence of the Revolution. And he resolved that crisis by becoming the people's sole representative; he diluted the effects of universal suffrage by filtering it through restricted electoral lists, and he dominated the legislature by fragmenting the responsibilities of the assemblies. Yet he – and the administration that was nothing but an extension of him – remained the symbols of a new state, based on the consent of its equal citizens and embodying the general interest.

It was this public image that the people approved, and their approval enabled Napoleon to restore order and reconcile a nation divided by the Revolution. Ex-Constituents, ex-Girondins, ex-Terrorists, and of course ex-Thermidorians worked in his administration and served as his state councillors, magistrates, prefects, and military commissars, and in thousands upon thousands of other government employments. Even émigrés returned, many to the same two careers in which their ancestors had distinguished themselves, careers now expanded and democratized yet somehow more brilliant than ever: the government and the army. No one needed to teach them how to be courtiers. The Consulate was a cornucopia of patronage, and Bonaparte played on a national scale one of the king's great roles at court: handing out rewards, honors, and jobs. He had more to distribute than any king had ever had, because he was the founder of the modern state. He therefore had not only to flatter the "vanity" of the nation but also to supply the needs of a vast administration and an immense army. More than any king in history he banked on the national passion for "position." This democratic transformation of noble values was the Corsican aristocrat's final secret. In a way it restored to the nation the aristocratic legacy that the Revolution had attempted to abolish and thus brought the reinforcement of the past to the hero of modern politics.

One last achievement seems to have rooted his work in the age: he bound the Church to his success. The Concordat of 1801 bears the mark of his genius: an intelligent use of a position of strength tempered by a revival of tradition and a bourgeois philosophy of religion. To a Catholic Church violently deprived of its history and its possessions by the Revolution he restored not its property, now in the hands of new lords, but its unity and status, in exchange for even more strict submission to the civil authorities than in the days of the kings. The Church he dealt with was of course no longer the powerful corporation it had been under the Ancien Régime, with its myriad ties to aristocratic society. Napoleon could therefore afford to restore its position without restoring its former power, in fact using it as a kind of buttress to his own power. This strategy his old friends from the Institute failed to understand, for they remained as staunchly anti-clerical as in the halcyon days of the Directory, and they reproached Napoleon for the Concordat. But he was a man for naked political calculation, unencumbered by futile passions inherited from the Revolution. Nevertheless, his thoughts on religion were shaped in part by a very French bourgeois wisdom that owed more to Voltaire than to Machiavelli and that would continue to shape conservative policy throughout the nineteenth century: "Deprive the people of their faith and you will be left with nothing but highway robbers" (Council of State, 1805, Marquiset).

Such was Bonaparte, first consul, son and king of the Revolution, product of an event that the French cherished as part of their national heritage and therefore wished to enjoy in peace. A self-made dictator, he enthroned equality at his side. The best way to understand the chemistry that wedded him to the French people is to look at the years that followed 18 Brumaire. When he was able to offer the nation a triumphant peace with Europe, as he did at Amiens (1802), his triumph over public opinion seemed complete and unshakable.

Yet the man who gave France the Civil Code was also the most improbable of bourgeois rulers. If it was not as a general that he governed France, it was indeed as a general that he conquered public opinion. His dictatorship, born of the war, managed to control the war for only a few months.

So the great question is, "Could the dictatorship have endured?" So deeply was it rooted and so easily had it taken hold that it is tempting to answer "yes." What is more, the only French regimes since 1789 not to be overthrown from within have been the First and Second Empires. But the fact that the First Empire was born with the resumption of war in 1803 and collapsed slightly more than ten years later in military defeat is likely to suggest to the historian that what actually happened was in fact inevitable, and that the fate of Napoleon was linked to an interminable war that one day he was bound to lose.

Again we must give the Revolution its due. For the war was yet another legacy of the Revolution and of its conflict with Europe, which began in 1792–3 and to which a complex of interests, hopes, and passions became attached over the ensuing decade. The revolutionary spirit was rekindled with the volunteers of Year I and the *levée en masse*. Within the army, discipline had been maintained ever since by the heroic defenders of the threatened Republic: neither 9 Thermidor nor 18 Brumaire seriously disturbed this republican institution, and if the army intervened on 18 Fructidor it was to save the Republic from royalist machinations. It was never seriously threatened by any of the major cleavages on the domestic front. The army and the future were one: it was the training ground for future leaders and the reward of talent. But it was more than that: it was an army created in the image of the new nation, the sans-culotte having matured to become the soldier.

The army, as old as the Revolution itself, became the bearer of French messianism as popular passions waned at home. After 9 Thermidor, after Vendémiaire, Year III, the syndicate of regicides that governed the Republic was all the more dependent on the war because it had disarmed the faubourgs of Paris; the only way to wrest the Terror from the control of the sans-culottes was to keep up the war with royalist Europe. There can be no doubt that the French public received the news of the peace of Amiens with joy. But this welcome was the result of a misunderstanding. The public interpreted first Lunéville and then Amiens as signs of triumph implying that Europe and England at last recognized the "great nation" and its universal mission. But this was not the case.

In December – the treaty of Amiens had been signed in March – at the news that the comte d'Artois, "wearing an order of a monarchy that England no longer recognizes," had reviewed a regiment, Bonaparte asked Talleyrand to represent to London

> that our dignity, and we daresay the honor of the British government, demands that the princes be expelled from England, or that, if they are to be shown hospitality, they not be suffered to wear any order of a monarchy that England no longer recognizes; that to permit them to do so is a continual insult to the French people; [and] that the time of tranquillity has arrived in Europe.

But this "tranquillity" was so poorly established that as soon as the war resumed it was England that hired assassins to act on behalf of the Bourbons against the usurper in Paris. On the morning of the duc d'Enghien's execution, Napoleon therefore declared: "I shall never agree to peace with England until she agrees to return the Bourbons as Louis XIV returned the Stuarts, because their presence in England will always be dangerous for France." On that 21 March 1804, the consul joined the regicide camp in spectacular fashion. What he expressed in dynastic terms – at bottom speaking the same language as those who wished to kill him – was merely another way of stating the popular conviction that there would never be peace between the Republic and the kings of Europe.

Nevertheless, the interminable war against the Ancien Régime, the war that carried him to the imperial throne (1804), also transformed his republican principate into a personal reign, inextricably bound up with his character and destiny. With the coronation of 1804, when his domination of the Revolution turned into a monarchy, it plainly ceased to be a matter of means and ends. When Napoleon became a hereditary monarch, he reached the height of his independence from revolutionary France, but never was he more dependent upon what can only be called his star. The great question was what he would do now that the revolutionary torrent that had brought him to the throne had subsided. His domestic policies daily revealed with increasing clarity the corruption of his domineering character by the exercise of absolute power, by his mania to control everything and make every decision, by his overestimation of his luck and his strength, and by his development of a police state of which Louis XIV could never even have dreamed. Yet the French, prisoners of his glory even more than of his police, had no alternative political future to offer: the Bourbons would bring back the nobles, and the Republic would bring back either Terror or disorder. The fate of the Empire would be decided outside its borders, which is to say, by the mystery of its intentions and the fortunes of war.

What did he want, this imposing and accidental heir to a unique moment in the fortunes of the nation? It is easier to say what he had, which at least explains his vast superiority over each of his adversaries taken individually. He was the master of a centralized and efficient modern state and able to mobilize all its resources to maximum advantage. He was the leader of an egalitarian society that recruited government officials and military officers from every stratum. In other words, he had no technological secrets – those belonged to England – but a social secret: an eighteenth-century nation and army liberated by the convulsion of revolution and rationalized by his enlightened despotism. Even more important, however, was another secret: his genius for action and what can only be called, for want of a better word, his star: for if the Revolution could never clearly define its war aims – Danton had his, and Carnot his, and Sieyès his – neither could he. He had studied war, he had experienced it, he was born of it, and it never ceased to shape his life. Condemned never to be compelled to make peace or even to lose an important battle, he continued to up the ante with each new round. In this respect, Bonaparte as Charlemagne was the same man as Bonaparte the consul, a man obsessed with his own unique adventure. Though his army became increasingly a professional army, though he married a daughter of the Hapsburgs, though he dreamed of a universal empire, he remained the plaything of chance. The moment he surrendered his sword in 1814, his son and heir vanished from the world stage along with himself. Ultimately only his administrative reorganization of France was solid, or, what comes to the same thing, necessary. This internal structure was his bourgeois achievement. The rest of his life was an incomparable improvisation, which remade the face of Europe but ultimately left France with the same borders it had in 1789.

Yet his final adventure, the most insane of his life, showed that even the Empire, a regime without tradition and dependent solely on battlefield victory, could be restored, just as the monarchy had been the year before. The Hundred Days were extraordinary theater: no sooner had the legitimate king regained his throne than the imperial usurper was restored in turn, as though a few triumphant years could outweigh the possession of the throne by one family for centuries. The truth is that the triumphant march in March 1815 from Gulf Juan to the Tuileries resurrected not so much Napoleon as the Little Corporal, not so much the Empire as the Revolution. It crystallized a popular sentiment that combined Jacobin egalitarianism and the glory of the tricolor with a tinge of revolutionary souvenirs and national nostalgia, a formula that was destined to enjoy a long career in nineteenth-century French politics. The Emperor's final appearance on the world stage cost France dearly; but in this hopeless venture, soon to end at Waterloo, Napoleon rediscovered a little of his youthful popularity along with something of the spirit of the army of Italy. Ultimately the English, by locking him up at the other end of the world, provided him with a final, tailor-made cell in which the cause of liberty could share his misfortune; the ultras, the *chambre introuvable*, and the White Terror would do the rest. When, from Saint Helena, he dictated his "Memorial" to his loyal supporters, the defeated Napoleon once again became the soldier of the triumphant Revolution. Thus he erected his own monument in the nation's collective memory, and there the nation would indeed worship him.

To this encounter between a man and a people, so brief yet so difficult to forget – its memory would endure for nearly a century – there was no more penetrating witness than Chateaubriand, and on Bonaparte's tomb there is no better epitaph than his, composed in the inglorious days of the Orleanist monarchy:

> Daily experience makes plain that the French are instinctively attracted to power. They have no use for liberty; equality is their only idol. But there are secret ties between equality and despotism. On these two counts Napoleon drew his strength from the heart of the French, a people militarily inclined toward force but democratically enamored of leveling. Risen to the throne, he seated the people there beside him. A proletarian king, he humiliated kings and nobles in his antechambers. He leveled ranks not by lowering but by raising them. Lowering would have been more pleasing to plebeian envy, but lifting was more flattering to its pride. French vanity also swelled at the superiority that Bonaparte gave us over the rest of Europe. Another source of Napoleon's popularity was the affliction of his last days. After his death, the more people learned of his sufferings on Saint Helena, the more they softened toward him. They forgot his tyranny and remembered that first he defeated our enemies, and then having drawn them into France he defended us against them. We imagine that he could save us today from the shame into which we have fallen: his renown was brought back to us by his misfortune; his glory has benefited from his misery.

Source Reprinted from *A Critical Dictionary of the French Revolution*, ed. François Furet and Mona Ozouf, trans. Arthur Goldhammer (Cambridge, MA: Harvard University Press, 1989), pp. 273–86.

INDEX

Ado, Anatoly 239, 245
Almeras, Henri d' 291
Alsace 36, 256–7
American Revolution 25, 34, 96, 107, 337
Ancien Régime: aristocracy in 25; characteristics of 28–9; consumer society in 174; destruction of 38; divisions within 53–4; élite in 52–4; feudalism in 30–1; individualism in 82; nobility in 51; political democracy in 172–3; political pornography in 279–80, 286–9; privilege in 47–50, 60; revisionist view of 160–1; social distinctions in 47; Third Estate ideology and 175; trading in 47–8, 51; venal office in 169–72; and "zero point" in history 80
Annales historique de la révolution française 3
Annales school 161
aristocracy: in Capuchin Society 216; loss of privilege of 155; in National Assembly 219–20; political pornography about 290; and rise of bourgeoisie 26–8; role of, in *Ancien Régime* 25; Sieyes on 149
Aulard, Alphonse 2, 215

Baker, Keith 7–8, 145–7, 161, 169
balance of powers 100–5, 108
banalités 30
Barbotin, Emmanuel 206
Barère, Bertrand de 109–10, 117, 178, 260

Barnave, Antoine-Pierre-Joseph-Marie 28, 119
Barras, Paul-François-Nicolas, vicomte de 340–1
Bastille 114, 158
Baudeau, Nicolas 104–5
Beauregard, Jean-Baptiste Grellet de 198
Bien, David 166–7, 175
bills of rights 94, 96–8
Blanc, Louis 75
Blum, Jerome 262–3
Boisgelin, archbishop 209
Bolshevik Revolution 71, 77
Bonaparte, Josephine 341–2, 345
Bonaparte, Napoleon: ambitions of 343; arrival in France 344; biography of 338–40; bourgeois values of 346; and Catholic Church 350–1; character of 349, 353; as consular monarch 89–90, 347, 353; dictatorship of 351; epitaph 355; expedition in Egypt of 343–4; final adventure of 354; Leon Trotsky and 78; marriage to Josephine 341; and modern French state 347–8, 350; public image of 344–5; as Robespierrist 340; as soldier of French Revolution 38–9; tactical skills of 342; importance of war to 352–4; as George Washington 337–8
Boncerf, Pierre-François 243
Bouche, Charles-François 116–17
Boulainvillers, comte de 25
bourgeoisie: alliance with popular masses of 29, 31–2; as beneficiaries of French

356